F

THE
SMALL BUSINESS
HANDBOOK

A Comprehensive Guide to Starting and Running Your Own Business

THIRD EDITION

IRVING BURSTINER

A FIRESIDE BOOK
Published by Simon & Schuster

With love to Razel;
our children, Harry, Alan, and Roseanne;
our grandchildren, Joseph, Brian, and David;
and
in loving memory of Ronald and Stuart

F

FIRESIDE
Rockefeller Center
1230 Avenue of the Americas
New York, NY 10020

FIRESIDE and colophon are registered trademarks
of Simon & Schuster Inc.

Designed by Irving Perkins Associates

Manufactured in the United States of America

1   3   5   7   9   10   8   6   4   2

Library of Congress Cataloging-in-Publication Data

Burstiner, Irving.
The small business handbook : a comprehensive guide to starting and running
your own business / Irving Burstiner.—3rd ed.
p.   cm.
"A Fireside book."
Includes bibliographical references.
1. Small business—Management—Handbooks, manuals, etc.   2. Small
business—Handbooks, manuals, etc.   I. Title.
HD62.7.B84   1997
658.02′2—dc21   97-20330
CIP

ISBN 0-684-83022-1

CONTENTS

III: MANAGING THE BUSINESS ORGANIZATION

IV: PRODUCTION MANAGEMENT

V: MARKETING BASICS

VI: FINANCIAL MANAGEMENT OF THE SMALL FIRM

VII: IMPROVING THE NEW BUSINESS OPERATION

VIII: THE FUTURE OF YOUR BUSINESS

FOREWORD

Relinquishing the security of a job to launch one's own business venture is both an American tradition and part of the great American dream. Every year, more than half a million new enterprises are started up. Unfortunately, a nearly equal number annually close up shop.

The most often quoted reason for business failure is *managerial ineptitude*. Obviously, some education and experience are fundamental but even with a fair amount of each, most people who start businesses need help. Few are expert in even a single functional area, such as finance, production, purchasing, or sales. Fewer still understand the details of legal requirements, tax regulations, financial and risk management, and other specialized facets of business administration.

Still, interest in owning a business grows each year. Attendance at small business shows and conventions is way up; colleges and universities show their awareness of increasing public interest by offering courses in entrepreneurship; and the federal government frequently sponsors small business institutes.

Most assuredly, small business *is* American business. Nearly nine out of every ten manufacturing companies, wholesale establishments, retail stores, and service operations are small enterprises—small in annual sales volume, in number of employees, and in scope of operations. Yet the small business sector is where the vast majority of new jobs are created.

PREFACE

The Small Business Handbook is an informative, comprehensive, and balanced guide to effective small business management. Written in clear, nontechnical language, it is packed with facts and techniques needed to: (1) make the initial decision to start your own business; (2) plan, organize, arrange financing for, locate staff, and finally launch the new enterprise; (3) ensure its viability; and (4) sustain both profitability and growth over the long term.

Thoroughly revised and updated, the third edition of the *Handbook* also presents these four new chapters:

Chapter 13, Advertising; chapter 14, Personal Selling; chapter 15, Sales Promotion; and chapter 18, Computerizing Your Business Operation.

Although the Handbook has been targeted primarily at the general public, colleges may find it suitable for the basic course in entrepreneurship or as recommended reading for several of the offerings in their management and marketing curricula. It should also be of interest to continuing education departments as well as to small business institutes.

This edition contains twenty-six chapters and is organized into eight sections:

Part I aims to help you make two important decisions: (1) whether or not to start a business of your own; and (2) what type of business to go into, if you do decide to proceed. First you'll learn about the advantages and disadvantages of both choices, the kinds of risks new entrepreneurs can expect to face, and what you'll need to make a success of your enterprise. Useful facts about four major sectors of our economy are then presented: manufacturing, wholesaling, retailing, and the service sector.

Part II deals with the principal "start-up" questions often asked by aspiring entrepreneurs. It begins by stressing the importance of knowing—and targeting—your customer and offers basic insights into buyer psychology. Next, the various routes by which you can enter the business community will be reviewed, along with the pros and cons of operating your business as a sole proprietorship, partnership, or corporation. You will be shown how to estimate your financial requirements and introduced to sources of capital, balance sheets, and income (profit-and-loss) statements. You'll also learn how to prepare your business plan. Finally, you will be given valuable insights into the areas of location choice and layout planning.

A thorough grounding in organization management is offered in part III. The four management functions—planning, organizing, directing, and controlling—are explained, and the importance of maintaining open lines of communication within the company is emphasized. A detailed overview of the "human resources" area then follows, along with worthwhile information about personnel management, leadership dynamics, employee motivation, and the decision-making process.

In part IV, the manufacturing function is explored. Following a discussion of production processes and methods, you will be introduced to the different kinds of departments found in the typical plant. Useful descriptions are provided of such significant activities as production planning, operations management, inventory control, and materials management.

Part V is actually a nine-chapter "minicourse" in the fundamentals of marketing. Each chapter is devoted to a single major marketing area. In the product/services area, you will learn about the product life-cycle concept and its marketing implications, the new product development process (and creative thinking techniques), packaging, branding, and the marketing of services. Following this, you will be introduced to the approaches that companies use to set prices and to a variety of pricing policies and promotional pricing techniques. Over the following four chapters, you will delve into promotion's role in the marketing mix. You will discover how companies arrive at their promotion budgets and how well-planned public relations programs and publicity can help bolster company image. An overview of the advertising function follows, along with a survey of the advantages and disadvantages of the various advertising media and helpful information about writing advertising messages. Next, you will enter the profitable and exciting area of personal selling and learn how to start and manage a sales force. You will then be introduced to the many sales promotion tools of today's marketers and to the use of displays to attract buyers.

You will become aware of the roles that agents and wholesalers play in the marketing channels and acquainted with the major modes of transportation. You will gain insights into warehousing operations. An informative introduction to marketing research methods follows; this includes discussions about the collection of both secondary and primary data and a detailed treatment of a valuable and easy-to-use research tool. Part V concludes with a chapter that centers on the usefulness of a personal computer in running your business.

Important aspects of financial management for the small business manager are outlined in part VI. Following a brief review of the basic accounting statements, the usefulness and methods of ratio analysis are explained. You will be shown how to avoid cash-flow problems, prepare budgets, manage expenses, handle credit sales, and keep records. An entire chapter is devoted to risk reduction; this includes a thorough discussion of your business's insurance needs and suggestions as to the measures you can take to help reduce both internal and external theft. The following chapter reviews those aspects of the legal environment with which an entrepreneur should be familiar. A detailed discussion of the entire taxation area is then provided, along with valuable, up-to-date information. (Note: Sample federal income-tax returns are included at the back of the book, in appendix B.)

Part VII makes a unique contribution not found in other books on small business management. It consists of four chapters, each of which offers helpful suggestions for improving results in four different types of business, once that enterprise has been successfully launched. Manufacturing, wholesaling, retailing, and services businesses are covered.

The final section of the book, part VIII, focuses on the future of your new business. Outlined here are approaches to growth and continuity, mergers and acquisitions, and management succession.

—Irving Burstiner

MAKING THE DECISION

WHAT IT TAKES TO SUCCEED IN YOUR OWN BUSINESS

EVER THINK ABOUT going into business for yourself?

Even if you haven't yet explored the thought, you probably will at some point in your life. Most people do.

Each year well over half a million Americans try their hand at businesses of their own. Increase that figure tenfold, and you'll probably still be far short of the number of people who *think* about going into business but who put it off to the indeterminate future. To some it represents the kind of freedom and challenge they cannot hope to find working for others—and much more money than they could ever earn in a job. Others are completely turned off by the thought, preferring the security of a steady position.

In this first chapter you'll be led into exploring the advantages and disadvantages of working for other people and for yourself. You'll learn a few of the reasons why some people go into business—and the kinds of risks they face. And—most important of all if you follow the instructions carefully—you'll find out if *you* have what it takes to make a go of it.

SHOULD YOU GO INTO BUSINESS?

The decision to try your hand at business should never be approached lightly. This is a major decision. Once you've committed yourself, you can be certain that the road ahead will be long, winding, tumultuous on occasion, and blocked by obstacles. If the business fails—and it *could*—it may not only wreak havoc with your personal savings (and perhaps other assets as well), it may also deal a blow to your ego. Indeed, business owners who are compelled to declare bankruptcy often show severe signs of psychological strain. The question that floors many people after declaring bankruptcy is, "Where do I go from here?"

No, I am not planning to discourage you from trying your own business. Rather, I am attempting to paint a realistic picture and foster caution on your part, because as many as one-half of all enterprises started up each year are nowhere to be found five or six years later.

If your notion of a satisfying career involves being situated in an agreeable environment, working five days a week at your assigned tasks while accepting little responsibility, leaving your job promptly after eight hours, and then forgetting all about your firm until the next working day, then don't think about venturing into a business of your own. On the other hand, if you are lucky enough to possess a higher-than-average level of self-confidence; if you can think positively about (and are not turned off by) the prospect of hard work, long hours, and onerous responsibility; if each new problem challenges you to tackle it with everything at your command, then owning your own business might be the proper route to chart.

The balance of this chapter may help you make up your mind one way or the other.

WHAT'S GOOD ABOUT WORKING FOR OTHERS?

Holding a job isn't the worst thing in the world. Working for someone else offers lots of advantages; some of the more significant ones for you to think about follow:

- Most likely, as an employee, you work regular hours and no more than eight each day. Your evenings and weekends remain free to enjoy family, friends, hobbies, and other leisure activities.
- You have occasional holidays off with pay, paid vacations after a while, and maybe some medical benefits, too.
- You have security, in the form of a regular income that you can count on, for your rent, utility bills, groceries, clothing, transportation, and all the other expenses that characterize modern living.
- Your personal savings remain relatively untouched—at least, they won't be risked on an enterprise of your own.
- You can expect to receive occasional pay increases as the years roll by.
- You may be blessed with special bonuses or profit sharing.
- The chances are fairly good that your efforts will be recognized, leading to one or more promotions.

- Even though you may be saddled with more and more responsibilities as the years pass, the business will always remain someone else's. You'll be able to spend evenings and weekends with a relatively clear head.
- You may find that your job provides adequately for the personal needs most people want filled, such as status and a sense of belonging, pride in your work, and the like.

WHAT'S NOT SO GOOD ABOUT WORKING FOR OTHERS?

Only a few disadvantages of working for others need to be mentioned. For one, you're subject to the vagaries of the economy. Should conditions deteriorate, your company may decide to lay off some employees (including you, perhaps), close down, or make a major move to another part of the country. Also, since you're working for others, you're subject to their whims and pleasures. For example, you may discover that your supervisor is totally illogical, unfair, and highly emotional; he or she could make working conditions rather unpleasant. Or, you may find yourself unexpectedly replaced by a brother, friend, or cousin of the owner, despite the fact that you have put in quite a few years on your job.

There's really no such thing as job security, no matter what you may believe. (Even civil service positions with tenure are no longer totally secure.) As you must know, your only security is *you*. Even though you may move up over the years into the higher echelons of management, you may ultimately be replaced if your firm is acquired by another company. Should you be replaced (and many hundreds of thousands of people have been), you might find it difficult to secure another comparable position. Or, your company might decide to downsize.

Finally, while you may rise to a position where you enjoy a fine salary, your job, like most, will have a "cap" or ceiling on it. Your earnings are therefore limited.

WHY SOME PEOPLE BECOME ENTREPRENEURS

Consider this partial list of reasons, presented in no particular order, as to why people go into business:

- A strong desire to be independent, my own master, not taking orders from others and relying on my own talents
- The chance to work at something I enjoy, instead of settling for second- or third-best because of a desire for security in the form of a steady income
- The feeling that I would like to operate at my own pace

- A yearning for recognition and prestige
- A powerful drive to accumulate wealth—and the opportunity to earn far more than I ever could working for others
- The discovery of an opportunity that others have overlooked or ignored
- The challenge of pitting my resources and skills against the environment

Of the many more reasons for going into business, some are thoroughly logical, others emotional, and most probably a combination of the two.

BE SURE TO WEIGH THE DRAWBACKS

While there are indeed many benefits to starting one's own business, disadvantages such as the following need to be kept in mind:

- You can forget about the eight-hour day, as well as carefree evenings and weekends—at least for the first few months (or perhaps years) of business operation. You'll put in long, irregular hours and take your business home with you religiously.
- You may lose your capital investment and, perhaps, other people's money as well.
- You probably won't be able to count on a regular income—or any income, for that matter—at the beginning. Indeed, it may take years before you attain the same salary level you enjoyed on the job.
- You'll carry a tremendous weight of responsibility on your shoulders. You'll have to make all the decisions (unless you share them with a partner—who presents another problem completely). You'll be embroiled in all phases of your business.
- Along these lines, you may find yourself having to perform chores that you dislike or actually abhor.
- By no means can you be "boss-free." Your customers—and your suppliers—will, in effect, become your new bosses (in the sense that you'll have to accede to their wishes and commands).
- Like it or not, your business will tend to consume just about all your time and all your energies. You'll have little time to spare for family, friends, or fun (except for the fun of running your own business!).

THE KINDS OF RISKS YOU FACE

Each new business venture represents a considerable gamble involving time, effort, and money on the part of the gambler. Moreover, the odds of surviving for the first few years may be no greater than fifty-fifty.

To quote from Dun & Bradstreet's *Business Failure Record*:

> Every year thousands of firms are started, many either fail or discontinue, and others transfer ownership or control. Each business day, over 35,000 changes are made to the Dun & Bradstreet database of over 10.1 million businesses at our National Business Information Center. New names are added and closed businesses are deleted, name styles altered, and financial information revised. This is all evidence of the dynamic change and turnover constantly taking place in the business population.*

In table 1-1, more than 71,000 businesses that failed in 1994 are analyzed by both the type of business and the age of the firm. The results are cross-tabulated. As Dun & Bradstreet wisely cautions with regard to this analysis:

> Business failures do not represent total businesses closings, which consist of both business failures and business discontinuances. As defined in Dun & Bradstreet's statistics, business failures consist of businesses involved in court proceedings or voluntary actions involving losses to creditors. In contrast, businesses that discontinue operations for reasons such as loss of capital, inadequate profits, ill health, retirement, etc., are not recorded as failures by Dun & Bradstreet if creditors are paid in full. Although they represent only a percentage of total closings, failures have the most severe impact upon the economy.**

Note that across the various businesses covered in the analysis, some 39.8 percent of the failures were companies that had been in operation for five or fewer years.

BUSINESS MORTALITY

Regardless of your mode of entry into the business arena—through purchasing an existing company, signing up for a franchise, or launching a brand-new enterprise—the gambling aspect is not your only concern. Any new business represents a contest—a struggle over the long term, replete with an unending series of challenges to your knowledge and skills. Some might look at these challenges as a steady stream of

---

* The Dun & Bradstreet Corporation, *Business Failure Record: 1993 Final/1994 Preliminary* (Wilton, Conn.: The Dun & Bradstreet Corporation, 1995), 19. Used with permission.
** Ibid.

TABLE 1-1. AGES OF 71,520 BUSINESSES THAT FAILED IN 1994.*

Age of Business	All Types Combined**	Manufac- turing	Wholesale Trade	Retail Trade	Services
1 year or less	7.0%	6.2%	6.1%	8.7%	8.7%
2 years	8.5	8.7	8.8	11.3	8.0
3 years	8.8	9.5	9.0	9.7	9.3
4 years	7.9	8.0	9.1	8.9	8.1
5 years	7.4	7.6	7.9	7.9	7.0
Total 5 years or less	39.8%	39.9%	41.0%	46.4%	41.1%
6 to 10 years	27.2	27.0	26.1	25.4	27.3
Over 10 years	33.1	33.1	32.9	28.2	31.6
Total	100.0%	100.0%	100.0%	100.0%	100.0%

Source: Economic Analysis Department, The Dun & Bradstreet Corporation, *Business Failure Record: 1993 Final/1994 Preliminary* (Wilton, Conn.: The Dun & Bradstreet Corporation, 1995), 19. Used with permission.

* These are preliminary statistics for 1994.

** Other categories included in total, although not shown, are: agriculture, forestry, and fishing; mining; construction; transportation and public utilities; and finance, insurance, and real estate.

small, gambling situations that must be resolved—the outcomes of which, when totaled up, will result in a business success or demise.

Yes, businesses fail. Indeed, many knowledgeable advisers ascribe such failures, in the main, to initial errors in judgment. Among these are selecting the wrong business location; offering the wrong product or product line; deciding to proceed with insufficient capital; ignoring the need for doing one's homework (projections and the like); or even choosing the wrong type of business to go into in the first place.

As we probe behind these initial errors, we find several other major factors, such as a lack of experience in the particular field of endeavor or sheer incompetence in business management.

WHAT YOU NEED TO MAKE IT

Before rushing into a business of your own, you owe it to yourself to increase your chances for success by:

1. Preparing for the challenge by obtaining a good education, preferably one that includes some business courses
2. Accumulating months, or even a year or more, of experience in the field you seek to enter
3. Securing a managerial post in that field in order to gain as much exposure as possible to the many facets of business administration: sales, purchasing, production, inventory control, financial management, and so forth
4. Keeping up with change and innovation in the industry by reading business and trade publications, and through personal contacts

Only four ingredients are truly essential to a new business success:

- A qualified entrepreneur
- A potential business opportunity
- A solid and detailed plan
- Sufficient capital

Upon further reflection, we should add a fifth element to that list: *luck*.

Of course, the biggest single factor in this recipe for success is the entrepreneur. This man or woman needs business experience plus knowledge and skills. In addition to such obvious traits as drive, willingness to take chances, and persistence, the following personal qualities appear to characterize most individuals who make a go of their own businesses:

energy	imagination
good health	self-control
inquisitiveness	good sense of
confidence	timing
boldness	independence
empathy	self-discipline
innovativeness	consideration
sense of ethics	of others
tact	good judgment
adaptability	sociability

Moreover, the successful entrepreneur:

- Is willing to work hard
- Gets along well with others
- Has good communication skills
- Knows how to organize
- Takes pride in what he or she does
- Maintains good interpersonal relations
- Is a self-starter
- Welcomes responsibility
- Is willing and able to make decisions

You have checked over these characteristics and decided that they describe you very well. You're ready, willing, and eager to go into business. Now you need to discover a bona fide business opportunity and then develop a comprehensive business plan.

The balance of part I of this book, along with the four chapters that comprise part II, will help you do just that.

WHAT ABOUT MONEY?

Yes, launching a business takes money. The days of starting out on a shoestring are long gone, although thousands of people still attempt this feat every year.

You'll need two kinds of capital: *initial capital* to set up the business properly and *working capital* to keep it going until the business begins to pay off. Of course, the amount of money you'll need depends on the kind of business you select. There will be rent to pay, a deposit plus one or more month's rent in advance, utility deposits and monthly bills to meet, and equipment to buy. You'll also need funds for incidentals (legal fees, permits, and insurance premiums) and, of course, initial inventory to begin operations.

You'll learn more about capital—and about where to find it—in chapter 5 (How to Estimate Your Financial Needs).

THINK BEFORE YOU LEAP—TRY SELF-ANALYSIS

Before committing yourself to the extraordinary investment of time, energy, and money that starting a business requires, wouldn't it make sense to engage in some personal soul-searching? You ought to pause and think about the following questions:

- What am I looking for? What do I want out of life?
- Are my aspirations realistic? Attainable?

- Am I prepared to struggle and make sacrifices?
- Am I a self-starter?
- Am I in good health?
- Am I blessed with plain, old-fashioned common sense?
- Can I usually control my emotions?
- Do I have self-discipline?
- Do I have good managerial skills?
- Do I have enough experience in this field?
- Am I more of a doer than a dreamer?

The entrepreneur *is* the business—its originator, its motivating force, its energy. Do you have what it takes to make a success of your own business? Review your pluses and your minuses, your strengths and your weaknesses. In toto, are you a suitable match for this challenge? A few hours of introspection—with a pencil for recording your own self-portrait—should be enough to make this decision.

As a cautionary note, bear in mind that some individuals have difficulty seeing themselves in a realistic light. Many have overly inflated egos and believe they can do anything, even things that are definitely beyond their reach and capabilities. Such confidence is admirable when deserved; it becomes a powerful weapon in the struggle for success. On the other hand, when unreasonably egotistical people fail, they quickly blame others (competitors, luck or fate, or even their spouses or relatives).

The majority of people, however, can see themselves pretty much as they really are if they: (a) make the effort, and (b) proceed on an intellectual and unemotional basis. To help you along, in appendix A we offer two aids designed to facilitate your self-analysis. These are exhibit A–1 (Do You Have What It Takes?) and exhibit A–2 (The Creativity/Leadership Self-Rating Chart).

A FRIEND IN NEED: THE SMALL BUSINESS ADMINISTRATION

The U.S. Small Business Administration (SBA) is a federal agency that renders valuable services to small enterprises—and to those interested in small business—in nearly ninety branch offices in major cities around the country. (See exhibit 1–1.) The SBA provides an array of services: financial assistance, management aid, technical advice, help in securing government business, procurement advisement, and so forth. In the management assistance area, for example, the SBA arranges for:

EXHIBIT 1–1. FIELD OFFICES OF THE U.S. SMALL BUSINESS ADMINISTRATION

Albany, N.Y.	Fairbanks, Alaska	Oklahoma City, Okla.
Albuquerque, N. Mex.	Fargo, N. Dak.	Omaha, Nebr.
Anchorage, Alaska	Harlingen, Tex.	Philadelphia, Pa.
Atlanta, Ga.	Harrisburg, Pa.	Phoenix, Ariz.
Augusta, Maine	Hartford, Conn.	Pittsburgh, Pa.
Baltimore, Md.	Hato Rey, P.R.	Portland, Oreg.
Birmingham, Ala.	Helena, Mont.	Providence, R.I.
Boise, Idaho	Honolulu, Hawaii	Richmond, Va.
Boston, Mass.	Houston, Tex.	Rochester, N.Y.
Buffalo, N.Y.	Indianapolis, Ind.	Sacramento, Calif.
Casper, Wyo.	Jackson, Miss.	St. Louis, Mo.
Charleston, W. Va.	Jacksonville, Fla.	San Antonio, Tex.
Charlotte, N.C.	Kansas City, Mo.	San Diego, Calif.
Chicago, Ill.	King of Prussia, Pa.	San Francisco, Calif.
Cincinnati, Ohio	Las Vegas, Nev.	Santa Ana, Calif.
Clarksburg, W. Va.	Little Rock, Ark.	Seattle, Wash.
Cleveland, Ohio	Lubbock, Tex.	Sioux Falls, S. Dak.
Columbia, S.C.	Madison, Wis.	Spokane, Wash.
Columbus, Ohio	Marquette, Mich.	Springfield, Ill.
Concord, N.H.	Marshall, Tex.	Syracuse, N.Y.
Corpus Christi, Tex.	Memphis, Tenn.	Tampa, Fla.
Dallas, Tex.	Milwaukee, Wis.	Tucson, Ariz.
Denver, Colo.	Minneapolis, Minn.	Ventura, Calif.
Des Moines, Iowa	Montpelier, Vt.	Washington, D.C.
Detroit, Mich.	Nashville, Tenn.	West Palm Beach, Fla.
Eau Claire, Wis.	Newark, N.J.	Wichita, Kans.
Elmira, N.Y.	New Orleans, La.	Wilkes-Barre, Pa.
El Paso, Tex.	New York, N.Y.	Wilmington, Del.

For addresses and telephone numbers of the field offices, look under "United States Government" in the appropriate telephone directories.

Source: Minority Business Development Agency, *Franchise Opportunities Handbook* (Washington, D.C.: U.S. Department of Commerce, June 1991), xvi–xviii.

- Conferences dealing with topics of interest to small business
- Business management courses cosponsored with educational institutions
- Information and counseling
- Small business clinics
- Many printed aids, leaflets, and pamphlets

Moreover, the SBA works closely with the Service Corps of Retired Executives (SCORE). This organization provides consulting services to small businesses free of charge.

Financial assistance may be made available in the form of loans, mostly in cooperation with banks. These include various types of special-purpose loans, such as those for disadvantaged individuals (Economic Opportunity Loans), for handicapped persons, and for businesses hit by disaster.

Small Business Investment Corporations (SBICs), licensed by the SBA, also make funds available and offer management assistance to small enterprises. These came into being following the enactment, in 1958, of the Small Business Investment Act. Minority Small Business Investment Corporations (MESBICs) provide the same services to minority group members.

For Further Information

Bygrave, William D. *The Portable MBA in Entrepreneurship.* New York: Wiley, 1994.

Carland, Jim, and JoAnn Carland. *Small Business Management: Tools for Success.* Belmont, Calif.: Wadsworth, 1990.

Davidson, Jeffrey P. *Avoiding the Pitfalls of Starting Your Own Business.* New York: Sure Sellers, 1990.

Eyler, David R. *Starting and Operating Your Home-Based Business.* New York: Wiley, 1989.

Feingold, Norman, and Leonard Perlman. *Making It on Your Own: What to Know Before You Start Your Own Business.* Sarasota, Fla.: Acropolis, 1991.

Gallagher, Richard R. *Your Small Business Made Simple.* New York: Doubleday, 1989.

Hodgetts, Richard M., and Donald F. Kuratko. *Effective Small Business Management.* 4th ed. Orlando, Fla.: Dryden, 1992.

Kuriloff, Arthur H. *Starting and Managing the Small Business.* 3rd ed. New York: McGraw-Hill, 1992.

Rye, David E. *The Vest Pocket Entrepreneur: Everything You Need to Start and Run Your Own Business.* Englewood Cliffs, N.J.: Prentice-Hall, 1995.

Shefsky, Lloyd E. *Entrepreneurs Are Made, Not Born.* New York: McGraw-Hill, 1994.

Steinhoff, Daniel, and John F. Burgess. *Small Business Management Fundamentals.* 6th ed. New York: McGraw-Hill, 1993.

Walthall, Wylie A., and Michael J. Wirth. *Getting into Business: An Introduction to Business.* 5th ed. New York: Harper & Row, 1988.

2

HOW TO CHOOSE THE RIGHT BUSINESS FOR *YOU*

IF YOU'VE READ the introductory material in chapter 1 thoroughly and have concluded from your self-analysis that you have what it takes to succeed in your own business, the logical next step is to think about the type of business that suits your needs better than any other.

To help you make up your mind, you should know something about the business world in general, the various types of businesses available to the new entrepreneur, and the general characteristics shared by each.

Ultimately, your choice will be influenced by a variety of factors, a few of which are listed below:

- The size of your pocketbook (how much capital you can invest)
- The potential payoff *(return on investment)*
- The nature of the work activities involved
- Your past work experiences
- The objectives you set
- Your attitudes and opinions
- Your personality
- Your knowledge and skills

THE WORLD OF SMALL BUSINESS IN AMERICA

Ours is a vigorous economy. Living standards here are among the highest in the world. In recent decades there has been infringement into the private sector by all levels of government. However, private control of business and industry is assured by custom and by statute.

Ours is a capitalist society where business is open to everyone who has what it takes—including courage.

Today there are approximately 19 million firms in operation in the United States. According to the U.S. Small Business Administration, nine out of every ten would most likely be considered small businesses—at least for business loan eligibility.

Most small enterprises reflect the following characteristics:

- Independently owned and operated
- Localized scope of operations
- Not dominant in its field
- Relatively small size in the particular industry
- Comparatively limited initial investment of capital

The vast majority of today's giant corporations were once small businesses. In fact, the entire aviation industry began in a small garage run by two brothers who earned their livelihood repairing bicycles. You never know—today's tiny home business or part-time hobby might become tomorrow's successful large corporation!

The law favors small business. Monopolies, unfair methods of competition, and restraint of free trade are illegal in the United States. In 1953, the Small Business Administration was created to "encourage, assist and protect the interests of small businesses."

According to the federal government's *Standard Industrial Classification System,* the country's business structure is divided into a number of categories. Among these categories are:

agriculture	wholesale trade
mining	retail trade
construction	finance, insurance, and
manufacturing	real estate services
transportation	

EXPLORING THE MAJOR BUSINESS ARENAS

Chances are your new venture will fall into one of the following areas: (1) manufacturing, (2) wholesaling, (3) retailing, or (4) services. Of the four, retailing is the area most favored by new entrepreneurs (possibly because it's easy to enter the field and because it's the one kind of business most familiar to consumers). On the other hand, services has been the fastest growing area in recent years.

MANUFACTURING

Manufacturers are makers or producers—individuals and companies that produce goods by hand or by machine. Several different types of manufacturing processes are found in the economy: the conversion of raw materials into finished products; the assembling of parts into wholes; the fabrication of machinery and equipment; and so on.

More often than not, the new manufacturing enterprise calls for a heavy initial investment in a plant and machinery, needs a number of specialized employees, and requires large purchases of raw or semiprocessed materials and supplies. Depending on what you manufacture, your customers may be the public at large (or special segments of the consumer population), wholesalers, retailers, industry itself, commerce, the agricultural sector, or government agencies at any level.

Among the manufacturing enterprises favored by small operators are printing establishments, machine shops, sportswear and other apparel plants, and bakeries. Figure 2–1 lists some of the more common types of manufacturing businesses in the United States, along with the approximate number of establishments in each category in 1987.

Of far more interest at this point, however, are the financial percentages furnished in table 2–1 for some selected manufacturing types. All figures are expressed as percentages of net sales. For example, the first entry (SIC Number 2064—Candy and other confectionery products) indicates a 61.4 percent cost of sales. The term *gross profit* (or *gross margin*) refers to what is left over after the cost of sales is subtracted from the net sales figure. Hence, the gross profit in this case is 38.6 percent.

Note that gross profit percentages for these different types of manufacturing enterprises run from as low as 36.9 percent (miscellaneous plastic products, wood kitchen cabinets) to as high as 49.1 percent (coating, engraving, and allied services). The range of operating profit before taxes for this group runs from 3.2 percent (jewelry and precious metals) to 6.8 percent (miscellaneous fabricated metal products).

WHOLESALING

Wholesalers act as intermediaries between manufacturers and retailers—if their business is consumer products—or between manufacturers and industry, commerce, professionals, and other buyers if they are marketing industrial goods.

FIGURE 2–1. MANUFACTURING IN AMERICA: TEN MOST POPULAR TYPES AND APPROXIMATE NUMBER OF ESTABLISHMENTS, 1987

Printing and publishing	61,774
Industrial machinery and equipment	52,135
Fabricated metal products	36,105
Apparel and other textile products	22,872
Food and kindred products	20,624
Furniture, home furnishings	16,500
Stone, clay, and glass products	16,166
Electronics and other electric equipment	15,964
Rubber and miscellaneous plastic products	14,515
Chemicals and allied products	12,109

Source: U.S. Department of Commerce, Bureau of the Census, *Statistical Abstract of the United States, 1995,* 115th ed. (Washington, D.C.: U.S. Government Printing Office, September 1995), 749–53.

TABLE 2–1. FINANCIAL DATA FOR SELECTED MANUFACTURING BUSINESSES*

SIC Number	Type of Business	Cost of Sales	Gross Profit	Operating Expenses	Operating Profit
2064	Candy and other confectionery products	61.4%	38.6%	34.9%	3.7%
3471, 79	Coating, engraving, and allied services	50.9	49.1	43.0	6.1
2759	Commercial printing, letterpress and screen	53.3	46.7	42.0	4.7
3671, 72, 74–79	Electronic components and accessories	60.0	40.0	36.7	3.3
3499	Miscellaneous fabricated metal products	54.2	45.8	39.0	6.8
3911	Jewelry and precious metals	62.0	38.0	34.8	3.2
3599	Machine shops—jobbing and repair	59.7	40.3	34.4	5.9
3089	Miscellaneous plastic products	63.1	36.9	33.4	3.6
3993	Signs and advertising specialties	51.9	48.1	42.3	5.7
3949	Sporting and athletic goods	56.9	43.1	37.9	5.2
2434	Wood kitchen cabinets	63.1	36.9	32.0	5.0

Source: Robert Morris Associates, *Annual Statement Studies, 1995* (Philadelphia: Robert Morris Associates, 1995). Copyright © 1995 by Robert Morris Associates. Used with permission. (See "Note Regarding Interpretation of Statement Studies Figures" at end of table 2–6 on page 26.)

* Based on statement studies of firms with fiscal year-ends April 1, 1994 through March 31, 1995. All statistics are expressed in terms of percentages of annual sales volume. (*Note:* Only data for firms with from $0 to $500,000 in assets have been shown since this would be characteristic of the beginning business.)

There are about 500,000 wholesale establishments in the United States. More than two-thirds of these firms are merchant wholesalers; the balance are of several types, including manufacturers' sales branches and offices, merchandise agents and brokers, and others. Most merchant wholesalers buy large quantities of goods, store them in their warehouses, then break them down into smaller amounts to sell to their customers. Consequently, the typical wholesale firm needs: (1) a warehouse, (2) a large investment in inventory, and (3) a sales staff. In addition, an efficient inventory control system is mandatory.

More information about wholesalers can be found in chapter 16. In the meantime, more common types and the approximate number of organizations in each classification are shown in figure 2–2.

Budding entrepreneurs who enter the wholesale trade seem to be attracted to such major lines of goods as office supplies, ceramics, hardware, chemical cleaning compounds and janitorial supplies, plants and flowers, beauty salon supplies, confectionery, stationery, and wall coverings.

Table 2–2 contains significant financial data for selected types of wholesale enterprises. The table reveals that pretax operating profit figures run from a low of 0.6 percent of sales (electrical supplies and apparatus) to a high of 4.5 percent (men's and boys' clothing). Note, too, that the wholesaling of fresh fruits and vegetables resulted in a loss of 1.0 percent of sales.

RETAILING

Like wholesalers, retailers are intermediaries in the marketing channels that forward goods from the nation's producers through to the final consumer. Retailers attempt to satisfy consumer needs and wants by selling them merchandise and/or services.

Retailing is a vital sector of the economy that employs well over 20 million people. Since 1980, total annual sales in this sector have more than doubled, reaching $2.2 trillion in 1994.*

Of all categories of business, retailing is the type most familiar to consumers. There are approximately 1.9 million retail establishments across the land. For the most part, these are *store* retailers.

Store retailers are shopkeepers—merchants who buy goods from wholesalers or manufacturers for resale to the public. For the new small store operation, you need: a good location, suitable space, fixtures, displays, and an initial stock of merchandise to sell. Depending on the size of the business, your initial investment can either be as low as a few thousand dollars or considerably more than $100,000.

Some common types of retail establishments are indicated in table 2–3, along with estimates of their average per-unit yearly sales. Eating places (restaurants, fast-food drive-ins) lead the pack by far, with grocery stores and gasoline service stations running far behind.

Table 2–4 contains financial information for some of the types of retailing that appeal to small-scale operators. For this group, the spread of operating profit percentages of sales runs from 0.2 percent (variety stores) to 7.9 percent (musical instruments and supplies).

---

* U.S. Department of Commerce, Bureau of the Census, *Statistical Abstract of the United States, 1995,* 115th ed. (Washington, D.C.: U.S. Government Printing Office, September 1995), 782.

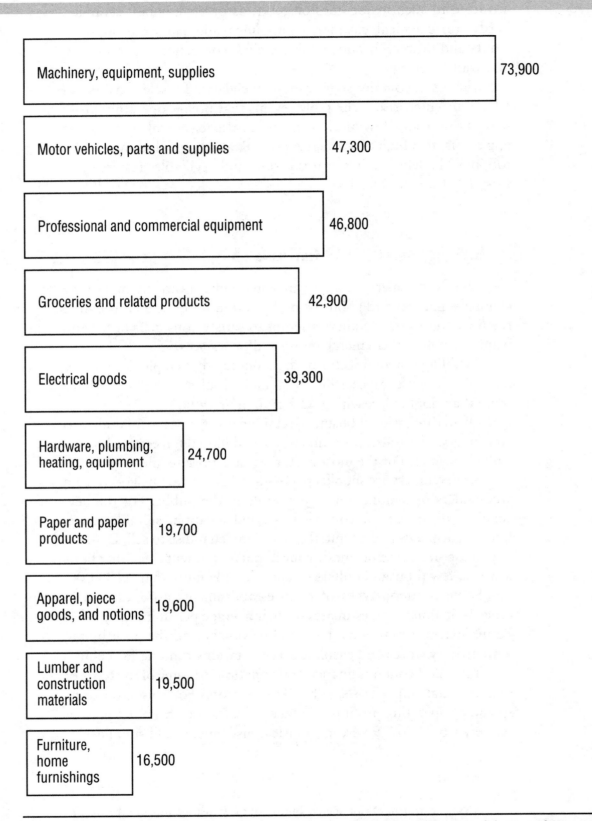

Source: U.S. Department of Commerce, Bureau of the Census, *Statistical Abstract of the United States, 1995,* 115th ed. (Washington, D.C.: U.S. Government Printing Office, September 1995), 790.

TABLE 2–2. FINANCIAL DATA FOR SELECTED WHOLESALING BUSINESSES*

SIC Number	Type of Business	Cost of Sales	Gross Profit	Operating Expenses	Operating Profit
5169	Chemicals and allied products	65.3%	34.7%	31.4%	3.4%
5063	Electrical supplies and apparatus	70.7	29.3	28.7	0.6
5193	Flowers, nursery stock, and florists' supplies	59.1	40.9	36.6	4.3
5148	Fresh fruits and vegetables	80.7	19.3	20.3	−1.0
5021	Furniture	69.7	30.3	29.1	1.1
5141	General groceries	69.2	30.8	27.9	2.9
5199	General merchandise	61.4	38.6	35.7	2.8
5072, 5198	Hardware and paints	69.0	31.0	28.1	2.9
5087	Janitorial supplies	63.4	36.6	33.9	2.6
5094	Jewelry	63.2	36.8	33.5	3.3
5136	Men's and boys' clothing	69.5	30.5	26.0	4.5
5044	Office equipment	58.1	41.9	38.6	3.3
5112	Stationery and office supplies	63.3	36.7	34.1	2.6
5091	Sporting and recreational goods and supplies	65.2	34.8	33.0	1.8

Source: Robert Morris Associates, *Annual Statement Studies, 1995* (Philadelphia: Robert Morris Associates, 1995). Copyright 1995 by Robert Morris Associates. Used with permission. (See "Note Regarding Interpretation of Statement Studies Figures" at end of table 2–6 on page 26.)

*Based on statement studies of firms with fiscal year-ends April 1, 1994 through March 31, 1995. All statistics are expressed in terms of percentages of annual sales volume. (*Note:* Only data for firms with from $0 to $500,000 in assets have been shown since this would be characteristic of the beginning business.)

TABLE 2–3. STORE RETAILING IN AMERICA: SELECTED TYPES, 1992

Kind of Business	Approximate Number of Establishments	Estimated Average Annual Sales/Unit*
Eating places	474,000	$3,961,000
Grocery stores	186,000	1,925,500
Gasoline service stations	120,000	1,141,250
Gift, novelty, and souvenir shops	104,000	115,700
Drinking places	84,000	147,700
Women's clothing stores	65,000	489,700
Home furnishings stores	64,000	330,200
Auto- and home-supply stores	63,000	473,300
Florists	55,000	117,000
Jewelry stores	55,000	277,400

TABLE 2–3. (continued)

Kind of Business	Approximate Number of Establishments	Estimated Average Annual Sales/Unit*
Sporting-goods stores, bicycle shops	55,000	283,900
Building materials and supply stores	51,000	1,477,600
Drug stores and proprietary stores	51,000	1,525,300
Furniture stores	48,000	650,300
Shoe stores	42,000	431,500
Liquor stores	40,000	542,450
Family clothing stores	33,000	1,006,700
Retail bakeries	31,000	184,900
Radio, TV, and electronic stores	28,000	724,100
Book stores	23,000	362,130
Men's and boys' clothing stores	19,000	536,700

Source: U.S. Department of Commerce, Bureau of the Census, *Statistical Abstract of the United States, 1995,* 115th ed. (Washington, D.C.: U.S. Government Printing Office, September 1995), 781.

* These estimates were derived by dividing the total sales volume for each category by the number of establishments recorded. (*Note:* The sale of large chain-store units are included as well as those of smaller independent retailers.)

TABLE 2–4. FINANCIAL DATA FOR SELECTED RETAIL BUSINESSES*

SIC Number	Type of Business	Cost of Sales	Gross Profit	Operating Expenses	Operating Profit
5942	Books	62.1%	37.9%	33.2%	4.6%
5734	Computers and software	64.0	36.0	33.1	2.8
5992	Cut flowers and growing plants	49.6	50.4	47.4	3.1
5912	Drugs	71.2	28.8	26.0	2.8
5399	Dry goods and general merchandise	57.2	42.8	38.4	4.3
5651	Family clothing	59.4	40.6	37.2	3.4
5713	Floor coverings	65.5	34.5	31.8	2.7
5712	Furniture	59.4	40.6	37.6	3.0
5541	Gasoline service stations	76.8	23.2	21.0	2.2
5411	Groceries and meats	76.0	24.0	22.0	2.0
5251	Hardware	65.3	34.7	32.1	2.6
5945	Hobbies, toys, and games	60.8	39.2	36.4	2.8
5722	Household appliances	67.5	32.5	29.3	3.2
5944	Jewelry	53.2	46.8	40.2	6.6

TABLE 2–4. (continued)

SIC Number	Type of Business	Cost of Sales	Gross Profit	Operating Expenses	Operating Profit
5921	Liquor	77.5	22.5	21.0	1.5
5947, 48	Luggage and gifts	56.4	43.6	38.9	4.7
5611	Men's and boys' clothing	57.4	42.6	39.4	3.2
5736	Musical instruments and supplies	56.3	43.7	35.8	7.9
5812	Restaurants	43.0	57.0	52.4	4.6
5661	Shoes	60.9	39.1	35.2	3.9
5943	Stationery and office supplies	64.8	35.2	31.8	3.4
5331	Variety stores	58.4	41.6	41.4	0.2
5621	Women's ready-to-wear	60.5	39.5	37.8	1.6

Source: Robert Morris Associates, *Annual Statement Studies, 1995* (Philadelphia: Robert Morris Associates, 1995). Copyright 1995 by Robert Morris Associates. Used with permission. (See "Note Regarding Interpretation of Statement Studies Figures" at end of table 2–6 on page 26.)

* Based on statement studies of firms with fiscal year-ends April 1, 1994 through March 31, 1995. All statistics are expressed in terms of percentages of annual sales volume. (*Note:* Only data for firms with from $0 to $500,000 in assets have been shown since this would be characteristic of the beginning business.)

Nonstore Retailers There are other types of retailers who do not depend on store premises to transact business. Three major types of *nonstore retailers* are the direct selling company, mail-order house, and vending-machine operator. Many other kinds of operations exist; examples include flea marketers and street vendors.

Direct-selling companies sell directly to consumers through sales representatives. Some of these firms depend on door-to-door *canvassing* for contacting prospective buyers. Others rely on *party-plan selling,* arranging at-home or in-office "parties" where sales presentations are made to small groups of neighbors and friends or coworkers.

Vending-machine operators install coin-actuated machines in locations where considerable numbers of people may be expected to pass by: in bus stations, large stores, movie theaters, and so forth. In addition to candy, beverages, snack foods, and cigarettes, they offer the public a wide variety of other merchandise.

Mail-order houses promote merchandise of every conceivable description through catalogs, brochures, and other types of direct-mail pieces. They distribute these to lists of shoppers or in response to media advertising (including advertising on both regular and cable television).

SERVICE BUSINESSES

In recent years the service sector has reflected the sharpest growth of all segments of American private enterprise. In 1991, service industries contributed nearly $1.1 trillion to our economy. This represented more than a tenfold increase over the $104 billion in national income posted by such businesses back in 1970.* Today, more than thirty million people are employed in this sector.

Perhaps the most plausible reason for the popularity of service businesses is that there is no need either to carry substantial merchandise inventory for resale—as is the case in retailing or wholesaling—or to make a heavy investment in machinery and other capital goods, as in manufacturing. Often, little more is required than purchasing several relatively inexpensive pieces of equipment, printing business cards, and placing a few advertisements. Indeed, your own home, garage, or apartment can serve as the place of business until the enterprise grows too big.

Here are just a few of the types of service businesses that can be launched with little money and some talent/training/knowledge/skill:

lawn care	tutoring
home typing	equipment rental
sewing	upholstering
carpet cleaning	interior decorating
bookkeeping	seminars
consulting	delivery service
flower decorating	appliance repair
party planning	newsletter publishing
monogramming	bicycle repair
painting	baby sitting
apparel design	dance instruction
translation bureau	résumé preparation
automotive repair	travel agency

Many of today's successful service companies had their beginnings in part-time avocations, hobbies, or home businesses before growing large enough to require expanded premises. No doubt the same will be true for tomorrow's successes. Because of certain inher-

---

* U.S. Department of Commerce, Bureau of the Census, *Statistical Abstract of the United States, 1994,* 114th ed. (Washington, D.C.: U.S. Government Printing Office, 1994), 783.

ent characteristics of services that distinguish them from products (such as their intangibility), the marketing of services can be more intricate than product marketing.

Table 2–5 lists a number of service industries along with representative types in each category. Financial operating data for a number of different types of service businesses are presented in table 2–6.

Note that the format in table 2–6 differs somewhat from that seen in the earlier tables; for example, there are no columns that show the cost of sales or the gross margin. Among the types of service enterprises listed, pretax profit runs from a low of 2.1 percent of sales (bowling centers) to a high of 11.6 percent (accounting, auditing, and bookkeeping).

TABLE 2–5. SELECTED SERVICE INDUSTRIES, BY CATEGORIES (1987)

Business Classification	Approximate Number of Establishments	Representative Types
Business services	2,056,200	Advertising, data processing services, cleaning and maintenance services
Personal services	1,320,900	Laundries, dry cleaners, photographic studios, beauty and barber shops
Health services	1,005,500	Doctors' and dentists' offices, nursing home facilities, hospitals, laboratories
Management and public relations services	735,800	(Not broken down)
Amusement and recreation services	691,700	Motion-picture production and distribution services, theaters, bands, entertainers
Automotive repair, services, and parking	454,300	Automotive-repair shops, car rental and leasing, parking lots
Legal services	326,900	(Not broken down)
Accounting, auditing, and bookkeeping services	325,500	(Not broken down)
Miscellaneous repair services	269,800	Electrical repair shops, reupholstery and furniture repair shops

Source: U.S. Department of Commerce, Bureau of the Census, *Statistical Abstract of the United States, 1995,* 115th ed. (Washington, D.C.: U.S. Government Printing Office, September 1995), 795.

OPPORTUNITIES IN FRANCHISING

Many people regard franchising as something comparatively new on the American scene, but it has been around since the turn of the century. In the early 1900s, the new automobile manufacturers began to license dealers, and gas stations opened up across the country.

By the 1950s, many of today's better-known franchisors had begun a rapid expansion of their outlets. There are now more than a

TABLE 2–6. FINANCIAL DATA FOR SELECTED SERVICE BUSINESSES*

SIC Number	Type of Business	Operating Expenses	All Other Expenses	Profit Before Taxes
8721	Accounting, auditing, and bookkeeping	86.9%	1.5%	11.6%
7538	Auto repair—general	94.8	1.2	4.0
7933	Bowling centers	95.5	2.4	2.1
7542	Car washes	87.8	6.2	6.0
7371	Computer programming	94.2	1.1	4.7
7361	Employment agencies	94.4	0.3	5.3
7231, 41	Hair stylists	94.4	1.2	4.4
7211, 16	Laundries and dry cleaners	93.0	3.0	4.0
7515	Leasing—passenger cars	91.7	2.5	5.8
7011	Motels, hotels, and tourist courts	87.5	3.9	8.6
7832	Motion-picture theaters, except drive-ins	92.3	0.2	7.6
7221, 7335	Photographic studios, including commercial photography	93.7	1.4	4.9
6531	Real-estate agents and brokers	82.3	7.4	10.4
4724	Travel agencies	97.0	0.3	2.6
4212	Trucking, local—without storage	93.3	1.0	5.7
7841	Videotape rentals	90.3	1.8	7.9

Source: Robert Morris Associates, *Annual Statement Studies, 1995* (Philadelphia: Robert Morris Associates, 1995). Copyright 1995 by Robert Morris Associates. Used with permission. (See "Note Regarding Interpretation of Statement Studies Figures" at end of this table.)

* Based on statement studies of firms with fiscal year-ends April 1, 1994 through March 31, 1995. All statistics are expressed in terms of percentages of annual sales volume. (*Note:* Only data for firms with from $0 to $500,000 in assets have been shown since this would be characteristic of the beginning business.)

Note Regarding Interpretation of Statement Studies Figures

RMA cautions that the Studies be regarded only as a general guideline and not as an absolute industry norm. This is due to limited samples within categories, the categorization of companies by their primary Standard Industrial Classification (SIC) number only, and different methods of operations by companies within the same industry. For these reasons, RMA recommends that the figures be used only as general guidelines in addition to other methods of financial analysis.

half million franchised enterprises in the United States. Nearly nine out of every ten are retail businesses; annually, these generate nearly one third of all retail sales.

The franchise concept is simple to grasp: You (the *franchisee*) sign a contract with a successful franchising company (the *franchisor*) that spells out the terms and conditions under which you are permitted to operate your business—a unit of a large chain. The contract is a license to operate under the parent corporation's trade name, and in accordance with their policies and marketing procedures.

The more popular franchises are fried chicken, hamburger, pizza, and other fast-food outlets; motels and hotels; ice cream stores; doughnut-and-coffee places; employment agencies; and convenience stores. Such names as Stuckeys, Kentucky Fried Chicken, Burger King, Bonanza, Dunkin' Donuts, International House of Pancakes, H&R Block, and Holiday Inn come readily to mind.

The advantages and disadvantages of selecting the franchise mode are presented in chapter 4, along with a list of some well-known franchisors, their home offices, and number of franchisees.

FOR FURTHER INFORMATION

Burstiner, Irving. *Basic Retailing*. 2d ed. Homewood, Ill.: Irwin, 1991.

———. *How to Start and Run Your Own Retail Business*. New York: Carol Press, 1994.

———. *Start and Run Your Own Profitable Service Business*. Englewood Cliffs, N.J.: Prentice-Hall, 1993.

Cunningham, William H. et al. *Business in a Changing World*. 3rd ed. Cincinnati: South-Western, 1993.

Dunne, Patrick, Robert Lusch, and Myron Gable. *Retailing*. 2d ed. Cincinnati: South-Western, 1995.

Hall, Daryl Allen. *1101 Businesses You Can Start from Home*. rev. ed. New York: Wiley, 1995.

Kuriloff, Arthur H. et al. *How to Start Your Own Business and Succeed*. 2d ed. New York: McGraw-Hill, 1992.

Longenecker, Justin G., Carlos W. Moore, and Bill Petty. *Small Business Management: An Entrepreneurial Emphasis*. 9th ed. Cincinnati: South-Western, 1994.

Lusch, Robert F., Patrick Dunne, and Randall Gebhardt. *Retail Marketing*. 2d ed. Cincinnati: South-Western, 1993.

Pickle, Hal B., and Royce L. Abrahamson. *Small Business Management*. 5th ed. New York: Wiley, 1990.

Straub, Joseph T., and Raymond F. Attner. *Introduction to Business*. 5th ed. Cincinnati: South-Western, 1994.

STARTING-UP
ISSUES

3

CUSTOMER TARGETING: HOW TO OPTIMIZE YOUR CHANCES FOR SUCCESS

Let's assume you have finally selected the kind of business that you want to go into. Maybe you'll be fortunate enough to find a top-notch location, clever enough to manufacture or purchase a terrific line of merchandise, shrewd enough to price your goods so they're profitable yet marketable, and smart enough to institute tight financial controls. Yet unless you build a steady and loyal clientele, you'll find yourself going out of business in a very short time!

Customers are the people who make or break a business.

WHAT CUSTOMERS ARE LIKE

Most of us readily link the term *customers* with the final consumers in this country, like you and me. There are, however, many thousands of firms that do not sell directly to the 265 million-plus consumers that make up our total population. These companies sell just about everything—raw materials, semi-processed goods, and finished products—to industry, commerce, schools and universities, banks and hospitals, government agencies, and countless other types of establishments and institutions. They sell *industrial* goods and services: items and materials that are generally consumed by companies or organizations as they conduct their day-to-day business. These products differ from *consumer* goods and services, which are sold to the final consumer either directly or through marketing channels (agents, wholesalers, retailers).

Marketing practitioners distinguish between *consumer marketing* and *industrial marketing*, on the basis of the kind of customer (or prospective buyer) being targeted. For the purpose of gaining more insight into these two vast and distinct market areas, we might more appropriately classify them as the *consumer* and *organizational* markets.

Sharp differences characterize these two markets (see exhibit 3–1).

Today's professional industrial marketers think in terms of specific submarkets, rather than the total marketplace. They face a twofold task: (1) to select groups of customers (organizations) with similar needs, wants, purchasing power, and the authority to buy what is for sale; and (2) to develop the appropriate mix of products, prices, promotion, and distribution to reach those customers and sell the product effectively. (See chapter 10.)

Much the same approach applies to the far broader consumer marketplace. Ways must be explored to select and target groups of those consumers who seem to be excellent prospects for one's products or services; then one needs to learn all one can about those individuals in order to prepare the proper "concoction" (products, prices, promotion, distribution) for wooing and winning them.

EXHIBIT 3–1. CONTRASTING CONSUMER AND ORGANIZATIONAL MARKETS

1. While the American consumer market consists of more than 265 million individuals, the "customers" that comprise the organizational market number far fewer than one-tenth that amount. At most, they total no more than 16 to 18 million.
2. Those who buy for the organizational market are generally trained purchasing agents for the organizations they represent. On the other hand, most consumers lack training in the finer, more technical aspects of buying for personal and family needs. Moreover, the consumer's buying motives are more confused, often tinged with emotional overtones, and less rational than the motives for purchasing industrial goods and services.
3. While the consumer usually buys often and in small amounts, larger and less frequent purchases are characteristic of the organizational market.
4. Targeting the general consumer market can be a complex, time-consuming, even frustrating task because of this market's sheer magnitude. By comparison, although selling to organizational users is by no means a simple task, help is available from various government reference works, trade associations, and other sources. Consequently, companies that sell industrial goods and services can get assistance in customer targeting in such areas as company size, product usage, and so forth.

CUSTOMER TARGETING HELPS YOU SUCCEED

Aiming at the entire consumer population isn't much different from firing a shotgun indiscriminately into a flock of geese in flight. Here and there, a single pellet might find its mark—but what a waste of good ammunition!

This kind of umbrella targeting is aptly termed the *shotgun* approach (as opposed to the *rifle* approach) and is completely out of the question for the smaller enterprise. Small business has neither the promotional budget, the production capacity, nor the staff to conduct business in this manner.

Of course, no one firm should expect to be able to fulfill the needs of all buyers. Nevertheless, some companies subscribe to a policy of *mass marketing*—a strategy whereby the same basic marketing "package" is offered to large numbers of customers of diverse types. Another recognized name for this approach is *undifferentiated marketing*—so designated because the marketing company makes no attempt to differentiate among specific groups of customers at which to aim its promotional efforts.

Among the many examples of products that have been successfully mass marketed to the American consumer are white bread, butter, and sugar; car radiator antifreeze; metropolitan daily newspapers; and room air fresheners.

Nowadays, the majority of American firms favor a different strategy. They first identify and then take careful aim at one or more viable market segments—groups of prospects who share similar needs, wants, preferences, and other characteristics. This approach, known as *market segmentation,* makes more sense. It enables marketers to tailor their presentations directly to one or more specific customer groups, thus "rifling in" on the target or targets. The information they gather about these "submarkets" is of value in planning every facet of the marketing process, from product development and pricing to the creation of copy and artwork for advertisements and the strengthening of sales presentations.

SEGMENTING CONSUMER MARKETS

Modern marketers usually segment the consumer population in one or more of the following ways:

- Geographically
- Demographically

- Psychographically
- By benefits sought
- By the rate of product/service usage

GEOGRAPHIC SEGMENTATION

The oldest and most readily understood of all approaches to differentiating among consumer markets is *geographic segmentation*—targeting people to market to on the basis of where they live. For example, clothing worn in California, Florida, and Louisiana is more informal and lighter in weight than the apparel popular in colder climates—a fact of considerable importance to the apparel industry.

Geography also plays an important role when it comes to marketing swimming pools, ski equipment, insect sprays, and many seasonal items. For a good many other products and services, consumption patterns often differ considerably from one section of the country to the next. Thus, knowledge of local needs and preferences may be essential to business success.

DEMOGRAPHIC SEGMENTATION

Demography is the most popular of all avenues to segmenting the vast consumer market. In *demographic segmentation,* a total group is analyzed by studying statistical variables such as age, sex, income level, occupation, nationality, educational level, race, and religion.

People who fall into one classification may have quite different purchasing patterns from those in another category. For example, young married couples without children are typically more likely to furnish their apartments or homes with appliances, furniture, and other durable goods than adults at any other stage of the family life cycle. Consequently, manufacturers and distributors of durable products may deliberately tailor their promotional efforts specifically to this lucrative market, rather than try to sell to other consumer groups. A cosmetics manufacturer will design one product or product line for the young woman and target another product or line at the older woman. A menswear retailer might seek to cater primarily to big men by carrying only the larger sizes in clothing and accessories.

PSYCHOGRAPHIC SEGMENTATION

Marketers who employ *psychographic segmentation* group consumers according to their attitudes, interests, lifestyles, or other personality attributes. There is merit to this approach, especially when it is used in combination with the more established demographic techniques. For example, all women are logical targets for cosmetic products. Yet when women are categorized according to lifestyle, the manufacturer (or retailer) must offer products and advertising with very specific appeal in order to be successful.

Likewise, classifying consumers according to different stages of the family life cycle (a demographic technique) leads to more effective results if they are also cross-categorized according to their interests and attitudes.

Remember, too, that consumers often select products—and retail stores as well—with "personalities" that correspond to their own self-images.

BENEFIT SEGMENTATION

Still another method of differentiating among sizable groups of consumers is *benefit segmentation:* sectioning off groups of people according to the kinds of benefits they seek from a product or service.

In a classic study conducted during the 1960s, this technique was successfully applied to the American toothpaste market.* The researchers were able to identify several distinct and large groups of toothpaste users, including people who buy the product primarily because they want a clean, fresh taste in their mouths in the morning; those who use the product mostly for appearance's sake (they want white teeth); and those who seek to prevent cavities.

As a result of the findings, toothpaste manufacturers were thereafter able to tailor their products and brands, pricing approaches, and promotional efforts to specific segments of the consumer population. Subsequently, too, other types of manufacturers began to rely on information acquired from benefit segmentation studies.

Today's car manufacturers, for instance, know that many prospective buyers are primarily looking for economy of operation while others are more interested in ample interior space and a feeling of luxury. Still other consumers are simply seeking a dependable vehicle that will take them where they want to go. Each of these segments, of course, calls for a distinct product/marketing approach.

USAGE-RATE SEGMENTATION

In *usage-rate segmentation,* the total consumer population is first divided according to users and nonusers of the product or service.

---

* Russell I. Haley, "Benefit Segmentation: A Decision-Oriented Research Tool," *Journal of Marketing* 32 (July 1968), 30–35.

Then the user population is broken down further into *heavy, medium,* and *light* users according to quantities consumed. Finally, the characteristics of these user subgroups are studied and compared in order to uncover significant differences among them. Such differences are then used to give direction to the development of specific marketing mixes designed to reach and sell to those subgroups.

Usage segmentation can be an exceptionally valuable tool. In some product categories, the heavy users account for as much as 30, 40, and even 50 percent or more of the total sales.

CONSUMER PSYCHOLOGY

Depending upon the market(s) you are trying to reach, your customers may be consumers or they may be organizations. In the first part of this section we touch briefly on the shopping and purchasing behavior of consumers. After that we consider some aspects of the industrial sphere, including how organizations buy and how to market to them.

CONSUMER PURCHASING BEHAVIOR

The social sciences (particularly psychology) have furnished the basics for marketing researchers to investigate why people select certain products and services as opposed to others, and why they prefer to shop at certain stores. These investigators have probed motives, perceptions, individual needs and wants (both innate and learned), attitudes, how people learn and remember or forget, and many other facets of the human personality and psyche. All of these factors appear to affect purchasing behavior.

Marketing theorists have also devised intricate models of the purchasing process itself to aid the businessperson's understanding of the complexities of consumer behavior. Moreover, they have borrowed from studies in sociology and social psychology to demonstrate how social class, culture, subcultures, family influences, and reference groups—indeed, the entire social environment—affect the consumer's shopping behavior.

These studies are certainly fascinating. They are also valuable. The information yielded by a single textbook on consumer behavior can provide you with dozens of tips that you can readily use in your business. Unfortunately, there isn't room in this book for even the more salient details of buyer psychology. Several of the works listed at the end of this chapter contain invaluable information for successful consumer targeting.

Certainly a cardinal requirement for success in business is to *know your customer.*

POSITIONING

In the marketing of consumer goods and services, one of the more interesting management strategies these days is that of *positioning.* To gain an edge over its competitors, a manufacturing company may study and "map" the perceptions of consumers with regard to its product(s) (or brand) *in relation to those of its major competitors.* It will strive to determine its unique niche in the total marketplace and then target for sales one or more specific consumer segments to which its offerings are likely to appeal.

Packaging, branding, advertising, sales promotion, and other aspects of the promotional mix are then used to reinforce this position vis-à-vis competitive products or brands.

Marketing practitioners sometimes refer to this approach as product positioning, even though it can be applied just as well to positioning a company itself and selecting specific groups to market to.

INDUSTRIAL MARKETING: SELLING ORGANIZATIONS

In actuality, the organizational market comprises several distinct, and relatively large, submarkets. The principal submarkets here are the producer, reseller, and government markets.

The Producer Market This area of the economy encompasses not only manufacturers of every conceivable type of goods but also organizations engaged in other "productive" industries, such as agriculture, cattle raising, mining, and fishing. Also included are many types of service-producing companies: utilities (electric, gas, water); commercial banks, savings and loans associations, brokerage houses, and other organizations that offer financial services; public and private hospitals and schools; hotels and other places of lodging; computer service firms and telephone companies; theaters, racetracks, baseball and football stadiums; bowling alleys and other recreational facilities; employment agencies; and legal and consulting services.

These organizations must arrange to purchase (or rent) the kinds of goods and services they require for running their businesses. They buy raw materials, semifinished products, and components (parts). These goods may run the gamut from a complete manufacturing facility or the installation of heavy machinery to an astounding variety of accessory items, equipment, and supplies. Typically, the organization must also provide for a number of services, such as insurance, transportation, and advertising.

The Reseller Market Resellers are organizations and individuals who buy goods and/or services regularly and then resell them at higher prices to others, thereby earning a profit. Because of the part they play in the economy's marketing channels, the reseller is also known by the more familiar term *distributor.* Indeed, businesspeople often apply the label *distributive trades* to this segment of the organizational market. Included in the category are the 500,000 or so organizations and individuals engaged in wholesaling activities and some 2 million retailers. Although most of the latter are "store" retailers, others operate without the aid of store premises. Among the more important groups of "nonstore" retailers are direct-selling organizations, vending-machine operators, and mail-order houses.

Of course, reseller purchases are not entirely limited to the goods and services they acquire for resale. These organizations must also buy *industrially,* that is, they must purchase products for their own use. Wholesale and retail establishments alike have need of facilities in which to run their machines or to display and sell their merchandise. They require different kinds of equipment and various supplies, office furniture, small tools and replacement parts, trucks, cleaning and maintenance services, and stationery.

The Government Market In sheer volume, the government market represents the largest segment of the vast organizational market. It includes all agencies, sections, divisions, departments, committees, and other governmental units at all three levels—federal, state, and local (county, town, village). As you no doubt realize, between its annual expenditures for both civilian aspects and the military, our federal government accounts for far more than one-half of all governmental consumption each year in the United States.

At the state and local level, the government market includes many types of groups: state troopers and local police departments; city councils and public hospitals; state universities and community colleges; public school districts; motor vehicle agencies; and departments of health, housing, and welfare.

Collectively, the government market seeks to purchase goods and services of all kinds. In addition to the complex requirements of the military branches (as well as local police and fire protection)—aircraft, ships, tanks, guns, munitions, firefighting equipment—these customers also require work premises; office furniture, equipment, and supplies; motor vehicles, gasoline, and oil; janitorial services; and many other types of goods and services.

SEGMENTING THE INDUSTRIAL MARKET

As is the case in the marketing of consumer goods and services, market segmentation techniques are also profitably employed in the industrial marketing sector.

Although such familiar approaches as geographical, benefit, and usage-rate segmentation are used, other techniques are seen more often. These include segmentation by end user, by type of company (SIC code), and by size of customer organization (large, average, and small accounts). Combinations of two or three approaches are also quite popular.

WHAT CONSUMERISM MEANS TO YOU

The present consumerism climate in America is not a new phenomenon. The twentieth century witnessed two earlier consumer movements. The first began just before the turn of the century, culminating (in 1906) in two major proconsumer legislative acts: the Pure Food and Drug Act and the Meat Inspection Act. The second movement originated in the Great Depression. In 1938, the FDA (Food and Drug Administration) was substantially strengthened by the passage of the Food, Drug, and Cosmetic Act.

The current movement, spurred during the early 1960s, seems to have resulted from many influences: a more affluent consumer, a higher level of educational attainment, a more relaxed work ethic, emphasis on self-assertiveness and other changing values, the unethical practices of some business firms, misleading advertising and promotion, inferior products, and poor service.

Among the more important pieces of federal legislation evolving out of the present movement are the Fair Packaging and Labeling Act (1966), the Consumer Credit Protection Act (1968), the Child Protection and Toy Safety Act (1969), the Consumer Product Safety Act (1972), and the Fair Debt Collection Practices Act (1977).

In addition to various consumer associations and cooperatives and the Better Business Bureau, the welfare of the American public is monitored by government consumer protection agencies that have been established in metropolitan areas and in county seats.

This consumer protection trend means that small business owners need to obtain detailed information regarding pertinent consumer legislation at all levels (federal, state, and local). They also need to understand how such laws affect their own particular type of business. Today's enlightened customer tolerates no mishandling, mislabeling, misrepresentation, or misunderstanding. As a business owner, you'll need to be fair and aboveboard in your dealings with the public if you want to retain your clientele.

ETHICAL AND SOCIAL RESPONSIBILITIES OF THE BUSINESS OWNER

Business today is more than profits and growth—it has a greater obligation to the public good than ever before. The callous disregard for the human element that characterized the first few decades of this century no longer exists. Instead there is an increasing struggle to maintain the quality of modern life as a counterpoint to humankind's harmful behavior. The new ethos pursues higher and nobler objectives, rather than merely aiming at earning profits at any cost.

The small business owner of today must be aware of the needs of the physical environment. Our lakes, streams, and rivers are contaminated with industrial waste. The atmosphere is polluted with harmful levels of sulphur and carbon compounds from our nation's factories and from the millions of vehicles operating daily on our highways. Year after year, our fields and groves are battered—sprayed with pesticides and dusted with chemicals. Poultry, cattle, and other livestock are raised on chemical fatteners. Our giant industrial machine has nearly exhausted many natural resources; shortages are becoming more common. Our ears are assaulted by the din of city traffic, roaring machinery, and thundering aircraft overhead.

In recent decades the federal government has enacted many laws to protect our population from these ravages. Among them are the Clean Air Act of 1963 (and subsequent amendments), the Solid Waste Disposal Act and the Water Quality Act (both enacted in 1965), the Noise Control Act (1972), the Pesticide Control Act (1972), and the Resource Conservation and Recovery Act (1976).

As a small business owner, you'll need to be concerned with the social environment, too. Today's corporation is responsible not only to its shareholders and customers but to other groups as well: employees, suppliers, residents of the community where the business is located, and even society at large. Inherent in the concept of a democratic society is the belief that those who are more affluent are responsible for the less able and less fortunate: hence, the Social Security system, antidiscrimination laws, programs for training the hardcore unemployed, and the welfare system. Clearly, the rate of unemployment in the country is disturbingly high. Moreover, it is not expected to drop in the next few years. More than 30 million Americans are living today at or below the poverty level.

Small wonder, then, that the public now expects private enterprise, which has taken liberally from the environment and its resources, to return some portion of its profits to the society that nurtured it. At the very least, modern business managers need to bear in mind at all times the social implications of the decisions they may make.

FOR FURTHER INFORMATION

Assael, Henry. *Consumer Behavior and Marketing Action.* 5th ed. Cincinnati: South-Western, 1995.

Bonoma, Thomas V., and Benson P. Shapiro. *Segmenting the Industrial Market.* Lexington, Mass.: D. C. Heath, 1983.

Davidson, Jeffrey P. *Marketing to Home-Based Businesses.* Homewood, Ill.: Business One Irwin, 1991.

Emerick, Tracy, and Bernie Goldberg. *Business-to-Business Direct Marketing.* 2d ed. New York: AMACOM, 1988.

Engel, James F. et al. *Consumer Behavior.* 7th ed. Ft. Worth, Tex.: Dryden, 1993.

Hunt, Michael, and Thomas Speh. *Industrial Marketing Management.* 2d ed. New York: Dryden Press, 1985.

Mowen, John C. *Consumer Behavior.* 3rd ed. New York: Macmillan, 1992.

Peter, J. Paul, and Jerry C. Olson. *Consumer Behavior and Marketing Strategy.* 3rd ed. Homewood, Ill.: Irwin, 1993.

Schiffman, Leon G., and Leslie Lazar Kanuk. *Consumer Behavior.* 5th ed. Englewood Cliffs, N.J.: Prentice-Hall, 1994.

Walters, C. Glenn, and Blaise J. Bergiel. *Consumer Behavior: A Decision-Making Approach.* Cincinnati: South-Western, 1989.

Wilkie, William L. *Consumer Behavior.* 3rd ed. New York: Wiley, 1994.

4

HOW TO JOIN THE BUSINESS COMMUNITY

ONCE UPON A time, the aspiring entrepreneur had only two alternatives: either to start up a brand-new business from scratch or to purchase a thriving operation from someone else. (Some lucky people, of course, have a successful enterprise deeded over to them by a parent or wealthy relative!) Both alternatives represented a gamble. Obviously, the new business risked more than one already tested—provided that the ongoing business was not already on its way out.

Today, people are luckier. A third way to enter the business community has become popular over the last few decades. Now you can go the franchise route. Moreover, a responsible, well-established company behind you improves your chances of succeeding.

Read the statistics on new ventures. They're grim. Many enterprises fail within the first few years of operation. A good franchised outlet, however, has an excellent chance to succeed. According to some reports, nine out of ten franchises are successful.

This chapter is designed to help you avoid becoming another grim statistic. You'll find details on these alternate routes to business. Each has its attractive features and its drawbacks. The differences among them include the amount of investment capital required, the chances of survival, and the profits you can expect.

LAUNCHING THE NEW ENTERPRISE

Most people who try their hand at business select the riskiest approach—they start a brand-new business. For many, the motivating factor behind this decision is probably a lack of sufficient capital to purchase an already existing business or a franchise. Other people may want to test their capabilities and ingenuity to the fullest. Still others may desire the challenge of creating their own future, stone by stone. Some people choose to start a new business because they see a timely opportunity for a new product or service, with no competition.

Whatever the reason for the choice, one thing is certain: This route is by far the most perilous of the three in the long run.

THE POSITIVES

Nevertheless, if you choose this route, you'll find all options wide open. You'll have total and unrestricted freedom of choice in your decision making—the pleasure of choosing when, where, and how you set up shop. You won't be bound to a specific location or facility. You won't be limited to what products or services to manufacture or sell. Nor will you be tied to any particular suppliers, employees, or customers. All policies and procedures will be up to you—they'll be yours alone to establish.

THE NEGATIVES

There is another side to the coin. Here are some troublesome aspects to think about. You might choose the wrong business to go into in the first place. You might err in your choice of product(s) to manufacture or sell. Or you might select a poor location for your new enterprise. Further, a new business takes time to get rolling. Weeks—maybe months—may pass before sales reach a high enough level to allow you to draw a small salary. (Compare this to the purchase of a business. Here you also purchase instant sales and instant wages the day you take it over.)

If you need additional funds, you'll probably find it more difficult to borrow money for a brand-new enterprise than for an existing business or a franchise unit.

A new business generally starts off with *zero* customers and *zero* suppliers. Unless you have had prior experience with sources of supply in the same field, you'll have to search out and cultivate a string of suppliers for your new business. This task occupies a lot of your time and energy in the beginning. Also, other than a few friends and relatives who may buy from you, you'll have to take the initiative to build up, over time, a satisfied and loyal clientele.

With little or nothing charted for you, you should expect to make a good many mistakes along the way. A new business is strictly a "learning-by-doing" experience. You'll have to live with, and hopefully learn from, your errors. This may prove costly—in time, money, and perhaps emotions. You should definitely seek the assistance of professionals whenever possible.

Certainly, it is foolhardy to contemplate setting up a new business without being thoroughly convinced that your business will be special and useful to the network of free enterprise. This means that you must direct your proposed business toward fulfilling unmet needs of specific customer groups.

You need a detailed analysis of possible markets for your particular product(s) and/or service(s). You need to assess the strengths and weaknesses of competitors and study industry trends. You must pay attention to many other facets of business planning: the type and location of the facility, the amount of financial backing, and machinery and equipment needed.

TAKING ON A FRANCHISE

The franchising concept was introduced in chapter 2, in the section on Opportunities in Franchising. Now, let's explore the advantages and disadvantages of this form of business operation.

ADVANTAGES OF THE FRANCHISE FORM

A franchise offers you the opportunity to jump aboard the bandwagon and become part of a tried-and-true success story. This is certainly the least risky of the three avenues to business ownership. Reputedly, nearly 90 percent of all high-quality franchises are profitable. You ride with the popularity of the brand name: It is known by hundreds of thousands—if not millions—of people.

When you sign with a reputable franchisor, you purchase a complete package designed to help you succeed. You receive professional assistance in most phases of the business: location hunting, construction of the facility, the proper equipment to use, inventory control system, bookkeeping methods, and promotion approaches.

Moreover, the franchising organization has a vital stake in keeping your new branch alive and growing. Consequently, they will continue to give you assistance in such important areas as merchandising, advertising, sales promotion, and even finance. They will literally teach you the business. Most franchisors insist on an initial period of intensive training and continue to render management help through supervision.

Table 4–1 offers information regarding a number of popular franchisors.

THE DISADVANTAGES

The financial aspects of a franchise unit merit careful consideration. Depending on the operation, start-up costs can range from as little as several thousand dollars to $100,000, $200,000, and much more. These figures include not only the initial franchise fee but also the entire cost of constructing and equipping the facility. (Some of these expenses may be spread out over a period of years under a financing arrangement.) In addition, you'll probably be required to pay the franchisor a set percentage of your sales for the duration of your franchise.

If you plan to take on a franchise, you'll need a fundamental change in perspective. You'll have to relinquish some of your independence. You might end up feeling more like a worker or junior partner than a boss.

The products you sell—as well as the methods that you follow—will be selected for you by the franchisor. You'll have little say in these areas, and as a result your business may be adversely affected. As a retail franchisee, for example, you may be required to carry one or more items that do not move at all in your particular neighborhood. You might have to sell your merchandise at prices that are either too high or too low for your area.

Furthermore, the franchise is a license granted to you by the franchising company, and if you want to close up shop someday, you cannot simply sell your business to a third party without involving the franchisor.

The contract generally contains an "escape clause" that favors the franchisor. For instance, if your sales do not meet the expectations spelled out in the agreement, the franchisor may exercise the option not to renew the contract. In this case, you would be forced to remove all identification, signs, products, and materials that denote your connection with the parent company and begin operating on your own if you choose. Usually, there is a "buy-back" clause as well. This gives the franchisor the right to repurchase your franchise at will; this clause could be a serious drawback if you are doing extremely well in the location.

LOOK BEFORE YOU LEAP INTO FRANCHISING

Because the franchising field can be lucrative, it attracts not only hundreds of responsible, well-managed companies but also some less respectable firms. These fly-by-night companies are more concerned with making a quick buck than with sustaining growth over a long period. Therefore, you need to proceed with caution and thoroughly

TABLE 4–1. SELECTED FRANCHISE COMPANIES

Franchisor (and Home Offices)	Number of Franchised Units	Type of Business
AAMCO Transmissions 1 Presidential Boulevard Bala Cynwyd, PA 19004	635	Transmission services
Barbizon School of Modeling 1900 Glades Road, #300 Boca Raton, FL 33431	65	School of modeling and related creative arts
Ben Franklin Crafts 500 E. North Avenue Carol Stream, IL 60188	929	Crafts and variety stores
Budget Rent A Car 4225 Naperville Road Lisle, IL 60532	2,772	Car- and truck-rental agencies
Century 21 Real Estate 2601 S.E. Main Street Century Centre Irvine, CA 92713	6,000	Real estate brokerage
Days Inn of America 339 Jefferson Road Parsippany, NJ 07054	1,450	Guest-lodging facilities
Deck the Walls 16825 Northchase Drive, #910 Houston, TX 77060	196	Art and custom-framing stores
Godfather's Pizza 9140 W. Dodge Road, #300 Omaha, NE 68114	376	Pizza restaurants
Great Clips 3800 W. 80th Street, #400 Minnesota, MN 55431	368	Hair salons
Holiday Inn 3 Ravinia Drive, #200 Atlanta, GA 30346	1,608	Hotels and motels
Insty-Prints 1010 S. Seventh Street, #450 Minneapolis, MN 55415	277	Printing centers
Jazzercise 2808 Roosevelt Street Carlsbad, CA 92008	5,200	Dance fitness program

TABLE 4–1. (continued)

Franchisor (and Home Offices)	Number of Franchised Units	Type of Business
Kampgrounds of America/KOA 550 N. 31st TW III P.O. Box 30558 Billings, MT 59114	543	Campgrounds for recreational vehicles
Lawn Doctor Inc. 142 Highway 34 Box 512 Matawan, NJ 07747	292	Automated lawn services
Long John Silver's Restaurants P.O. Box 11988 101 Jerico Drive Lexington, KY 40579	470	Seafood restaurants
Meineke Discount Muffler Shops, Inc. 128 S. Tryon Street, #900 Charlotte, NC 28202	917	Muffler and other automotive-repair shops
Merry Maids 11117 Mill Valley Road Omaha, NE 68154	700	Maid service
Snelling Personnel Services 12801 N. Central Expressway, #700 Dallas, TX 75243	259	Temporary and permanent personnel service agency
Subway 325 Bic Drive Milford, CT 06460	8,191	Subway sandwich shops
Wendy's International P.O. Box 256 Dublin, OH 43017	2,644	Quick-service hamburger restaurants
Western Sizzlin P.O. Box 291509 Nashville, TN 37229	315	Family steak houses
White Hen Pantry, Inc. 660 Industrial Drive Elmhurst, IL 60126	344	Convenience food stores
Winchell's Donuts 1800 E. 16th Street Santa Ana, CA 92701	75	Shops selling coffee, doughnuts, and other bakery products

Source: Minority Business Development Agency, U.S. Department of Commerce, *Franchise Opportunities Handbook* (Washington, D.C.: U.S. Government Printing Office, October 1994).

investigate any franchise offer that comes your way. Be sure to ask for a prospectus and read it carefully.

At the very least, you should resist any pressure exerted by sales representatives who try to sell you a franchise unit. The rosy pictures they paint for you should be taken with more than a few grains of salt. Even when representing a reliable firm, a salesperson tends to present an overly optimistic assessment of the sales and profit potential of the franchise.

Before you sign anything, consult your accountant, your banker, the local Chamber of Commerce, Dun & Bradstreet, and the trade organization(s) in your field for unbiased information about the company. Make it your business to visit several of the outlets currently operating under contract to the franchisor and ask their operators how satisfied they are with the situation. Find out whatever additional facts you can. Of course, shy away from those units selected for you by the sales representative.

BUYING AN ESTABLISHED BUSINESS

ADVANTAGES

You avoid much of the tedious planning and downright hard work required to set up a new business when you buy an established enterprise. There is no need to search for a desirable location or to construct a facility and lay out the premises. (You can, of course, make changes later on.)

Since the previous owner(s) may have dealt with a number of suppliers before you entered the picture, chances are excellent that you'll spend little time initially developing your own sources of supply. With an ongoing business you also acquire experienced employees. They'll help you over the hurdles during the transition period. Likewise, you're rewarded with a bank of customers you can draw on immediately.

This kind of business is often purchased at a good price because the owner wants to sell quickly for some compelling reason (poor health, retirement, or the like). He or she may even be willing to assist you in the financing. In cases like this, an owner may be satisfied with a partial payment and take notes for the balance; these notes stretch out your obligation for years.

Finally, since the business has had a history, internal records are available to guide you.

DISADVANTAGES

You may have serious problems with one or two aspects of the business, and you may have to make changes before you move in. You may have to relocate or enlarge the premises. You may have to do extensive repairs or redecoration. The layout may be in dire need of improvement.

Some of the inventory may be unusable, or you may have too many of some items and too few of others. Merchandise may be imperfect, damaged, or outdated. Machinery and equipment may need to be repaired or replaced. Consider your new employees, suppliers, and customers. In the past, relations between these people and the former owner(s) may not have been good. The "good will" you've bought may prove to be "bad will" that will detract from your immediate success. You might inherit several below-par employees whom you'll have to replace in time. If these employees are unionized, this will pose another problem.

WHAT TO LOOK INTO BEFORE BUYING

No matter how attractive the deal seems to you or how eager you are to get started, make up your mind to approach buying a business unemotionally and with caution. Thoroughly check out the following:

- The firm's location and premises
- Its past history and estimated future potential
- Its assets and liabilities

Location and Premises Visit the location and the surrounding neighborhood. Talk with the manager of the local bank and with other business owners in the area. Interview neighborhood residents and shoppers. Survey the businesses of competitors in the area. Try to ascertain whether the area is growing, maintaining its status quo, or deteriorating. (See chapter 6 for more help in evaluating a location.)

Bring in a consultant with experience in the particular kind of business to examine the premises thoroughly. Examine everything closely and make detailed notes. Be sure to check the interior and exterior; lighting, heating, and plumbing; elevators and staircases; stairwells and basements; shipping and receiving docks.

Make certain the facility has ample room not only to conduct the business activities that you find necessary but also to expand within— or adjacent to—the facility.

Past History and Future Potential Ask your accountant and your lawyer for help in piecing together a picture of the firm's past. You'll discover problem areas you would be dealing with if you decided to buy, as well as trends for projecting into the company's future. Bear this in mind: Most businesses for sale are not of "dream quality." There's almost always a need for improvement.

Examine company records. In addition to copies of past tax returns and other vital financial reports (annual balance sheets, operating statements), you'll find important information for future decision making in records of sales figures, production records, inventory counts, personnel files—even the shipping and receiving room logs. If you properly analyze sales, production, and financial data, you'll possess helpful ratios that can be compared over a succession of years. (See chapter 19.)

Survey the market potential for your firm's products and services as compared to those of your competitors. Analyze the demographic characteristics of present customers, along with their needs and wants. Also survey other market segments from which you could draw additional customers in the future. A worthwhile exercise here is to translate such details into projected dollars-and-cents sales figures, at least for the first two or three years after your takeover.

Assets and Liabilities *Assets* include not only the cash and securities owned by the company you plan to acquire but also all property, including machinery and equipment, inventories, accounts receivable, and contracts. By extension, it might also include personnel! Exercise caution with the firm's assets. This is the primary area to which any buyer of an existing business must address his or her attention. The major concern here is the *condition* of the assets. *Liabilities* include short- and long-term loans, unpaid taxes, mortgages, accounts payable (moneys owed to suppliers), and other business obligations. These terms are explained more fully in the next chapter.

HOW TO SET THE PRICE

Determining the proper price to pay for a business is a difficult problem. The seller usually tries to get more money for the business than it is worth—and the buyer tries to get it for as little as possible. Somewhere between the two extremes lies a price that is fair to both parties and that is finally agreed upon.

The two common approaches to solving this dilemma are (1) the *total-the-assets* technique and (2) the *return-through-profits* method.

Total-the-Assets Technique This method is the more frequently used, though not, in fact, the more advantageous of the two to the buyer. As the name indicates, it calls for a complete audit of the enterprise, usually best conducted by independent auditors. They should appraise the real and other property owned by the firm—including inventories, equipment, and machinery—check into all liabilities, and subtract the liabilities from the assets owned. You'll then have an estimate of the company's *net worth*.

Return-through-Profits Method The logic behind this approach is as follows: Buying an established business represents a considerable capital investment; you therefore have every right to expect a solid return on your investment. Considering the complexity of investing in an enterprise—including the need for your personal involvement and dedication for years to come (as well as the risk of failure)—your rate of return should certainly exceed by far those rates currently available to investors at banks and in corporate or government bonds.

There are desirable alternatives to buying a going business, which require nothing more than plunking down capital. Government bonds, about the safest of all investments, may bring you 6 percent or more on your money. The return from a long-term savings certificate (federally insured) may pay you as much or more. The total yield from quality corporate bonds may run several points higher. It would be illogical to invest in an existing business for a return comparable to these other kinds of investments. So, an ideal target to shoot for would be something in the neighborhood of 18 to 25 percent—taking a few percentage points less *only* if you have to!

As an illustration, assume that you've discovered an attractive business for sale, and the asking price is $150,000. If you placed that sum of money in a long-term certificate or similar investment, you would receive interest totaling somewhere between $9,000 and $10,000 annually. These earnings do not require your working hard to protect your money—or leaving your current employment! Suppose, however, that an analysis of the business's operations reveals that its net profit each year would probably be in the $30,000 range. This return would indicate that you could pay back to yourself the cost of your investment within five years. Simply by dividing $30,000 by $150,000, you could calculate an effective *return on investment* (R.O.I.) of 20 percent.

When it comes to setting a fair price for a going business, then, you can use the following rough rule of thumb: Multiply the average yearly profit by four (for an R.O.I. of 25 percent) or by five (for a 20 percent R.O.I.).

There's one additional factor to include in determining how much you ought to pay for the business. If you invest your capital in bonds or certificates, you'll be able to keep your current job. Once you purchase a business, you'll most likely leave your job and give up the salary you've been earning. The price you eventually pay for a business should take this earnings factor into consideration. Make sure your proposed operations budget covers your current salary (even if you do not choose to draw a salary in the beginning) and the desired annual profit as well.

The present owner(s) may be willing to accept a down payment—perhaps $30,000—and take notes for the rest. This arrangement makes it easier for you to buy. Your investment is then only one-fifth of what you originally thought. Don't be tempted to think that an annual profit of only $6,000 is needed to make this a sound investment (because it *seems* as if you'd be earning 20 percent on your money). The fallacy here is that you need to generate enough additional profit each year to cover the notes as they mature.

For additional suggestions, see exhibit 4–1.

EXHIBIT 4–1. SOME ADDITIONAL THOUGHTS BEFORE YOU BUY

- Never enter into any major transaction such as the purchase of a business without the full knowledge, cooperation, and assistance of both your attorney and your accountant. Your attorney must check on many details including ownership titles; occupancy leases, as well as leases on equipment, machinery, and vehicles; contracts with contractors, services, and employees; zoning restrictions and local permits; compliance with the bulk sales act; and so on. Your accountant must delve into all financial aspects of operations, assist you in preparing pro forma statements, and point out deficiencies and weaknesses.
- Do not neglect to obtain from the former owner an agreement to the effect that he or she will not seek to compete with you, for example, by opening a similar business in the area.
- Be sure to call in an independent appraiser to determine the value of any property. Don't rely on book inventories; insist on a physical count by you or your representative side by side with the owner.
- It's a good idea to investigate all personnel records to ascertain the caliber of the employees and the size of the current payroll. Check union contracts, employee contracts, and benefits to be paid. Assess the general state of employee morale.
- Lastly, check into the owner's real reason for selling. A declaration that he or she is ready to retire, wants to move to Arizona for reasons of health, or wants to be near the children may be the truth. On the other hand, such reasons may serve as a "cover" for a poor profit picture, increasing competition, anticipated changes in the neighborhood, or legal problems that threaten the life of the enterprise.

Source: Compiled by the author.

WHICH LEGAL FORM TO CHOOSE?

Early in the game you need to decide on the *legal form of ownership* for your business: the sole proprietorship, the partnership, or the corporation. Each form has drawbacks as well as advantages. Consider carefully the pros and cons of each. The key is to select the one that will best meet your specific needs.

This is the customary procedure followed by many people who launch an enterprise:

- Start out as a sole proprietor if you have enough funds for the required investment and if you have enough self-confidence.
- Select the partnership form if you don't have the funds or the confidence, or if the expected workload will be too much for one person to handle.
- Form a corporation if you are planning to expand. (This need not be done at the outset; a corporation can be formed after the business has demonstrated its viability.)

THE SOLE PROPRIETORSHIP

The sole proprietorship is the simplest of the three legal forms of ownership and the form in which the majority of new businesses start off. You can't beat this form for its simplicity of organization, which is structured around your every wish and command (right or wrong!).

WHAT'S GOOD ABOUT A PROPRIETORSHIP

The sole proprietorship is the easiest and quickest form to initiate. At least three quarters of the 13 million businesses in the United States are in this category. If you believe in the old "safety in numbers" approach and know that so many choose this particular route, how can you go wrong? Barring the need for special licenses or permits, all you have to do to get a business off the ground is to start working at it.

There are no set-up costs involved, as long as you plan on doing business under your own name. You might decide (as many people do) that you prefer to operate under a *trade name* instead. In that case you have to file the details with the local authorities at the offices of the town/city/county clerk. The form used for this purpose is available at business stationery stores. It's called a Certificate of Conducting Business Under an Assumed Name (see exhibit 4–2). The fee for filing is minimal—a few dollars at most. In some states you must first publish your intent to conduct business under a fictitious name in a local newspaper before filing your certificate.

EXHIBIT 4–2. CERTIFICATE OF CONDUCTING BUSINESS UNDER AN ASSUMED NAME

Blumbergs Law Products

X 201—Certificate of Conducting Business under an Assumed Name
For Individual, 11-88

JULIUS BLUMBERG, INC.,
PUBLISHER, NYC 10013

Business Certificate

I HEREBY CERTIFY *that I am conducting or transacting business under the name or designation*

of

at

City or Town of   *County of*   *State of New York.*

My full name is*
and I reside at

I FURTHER CERTIFY *that I am the successor in interest to*

the person or persons heretofore using such name or names to carry on or conduct or transact business.

IN WITNESS WHEREOF, *I have this*   *day of*   *19*   *, made*
and signed this certificate.

....

* Print or type name.
* If under 21 years of age, state "I am..................years of age".

STATE OF NEW YORK
COUNTY OF   } ss.:

On this   *day of*   *19*   *, before me personally appeared*

to me known and known to me to be the individual *described in and who executed the foregoing*
certificate, and *he* *thereupon* *duly acknowledged to me that* *he* *executed the same.*

....

Source: Forms may be purchased from Julius Blumberg, Inc., New York, NY 10013, or any of its dealers.
Reproduction prohibited.

EXHIBIT 4–2. (continued)

INDEX No. _____

Certificate

of

CONDUCTING BUSINESS UNDER

THE NAME OF

You also save on legal fees with a proprietorship; no special contracts or agreements need to be drawn up as is the case with a partnership or corporation.

A sole proprietorship offers you the greatest psychological rewards because you can run the business as you see fit. There are no bosses to issue orders to you, supervise your comings and goings, challenge your decisions, or take you to task for errors. This means that you must pit all your resources—mental, physical, and emotional, as well as financial—against the challenging business environment. It's somewhat like playing football without teammates: You not only get to carry the ball, but if you make it through the goalposts, you also get to keep all the profits—after taxes, of course!

If you run your operation honorably (and keep accurate records), no one will interfere with how you conduct your business. Furthermore, you will avoid unnecessary pressure from the Better Business Bureau, consumer groups, the Internal Revenue Service, or any other government agency. Of the three legal forms, this is the one that gets the least attention from the federal bureaucracy. (The corporate form receives the most.)

Tax-wise, you and your sole proprietorship are treated as inseparable companions. This identity can be helpful to you. Typically, the new venture ends up its first six months (and often longer) in the red. This initial lack of success can be disheartening, especially if you left a good-paying job for your new venture. If your enterprise incurs a loss for the year, you're entitled to deduct those lost dollars on your tax return against any other income you may have earned that year. Moreover, this holds true for succeeding years.

Finally, terminating your proprietorship is also simple. To close down the operation, all you need to do is liquidate your assets, pay off your debts, lock the door, and walk away from it all. (Of course, it's much better all around to simply sell it—providing that it's a successful business.)

Now for the Minuses . . .

Perhaps the most serious drawback to the sole proprietorship is the problem of unlimited personal liability. Legally, you and the business are one and the same. All the liabilities of the enterprise are therefore yours.

Of course, no one expects to fail when he or she first starts up a venture. Despite all your preparation and planning (let alone your financial commitment!), however, you must have a healthy outlook and plan for the possibility of failure. Indeed, some business advisers claim that it's more probable than possible! If your business fails and the business assets you are able to muster aren't sufficient to cover your obligations, your creditors can move in and take away your home, your automobile, your bank accounts, and any other personal assets you hold until the debts are fully satisfied. (The types of items that can be taken from you depend on different state bankruptcy rules and regulations and on different civil procedure laws.) Consequently, if your personal holdings are considerable, you might be better off opting for the corporate mode.

As a one-person operation, your business is limited by your own skills and capabilities. Under the right circumstances, you can hire additional talent—specialists who can provide the expertise you lack. However, it is generally wise to avoid hiring high-priced experts until your business has expanded enough to absorb this additional cost, and then only if the enterprise is certain to prosper.

The success of your business will be in jeopardy if you become seriously ill or disabled through accidental injury. You can and should anticipate this possibility and take steps early in the game to prevent it. You ought to train one or two key people to shoulder the responsibility at the helm, in the event that you're incapacitated for any substantial period of time.

Furthermore, because the business *is* the proprietor, you'll probably find it difficult to attract more capital into your enterprise for growth or expansion. Understandably, banks and other financial sources might be reluctant to advance funds to you. After all, the debt would have to be paid back over time by a single, fragile human being. What if something were to happen that rendered you incapable of managing the business?

This point leads us to the last consideration: If you die while owning the business, your sole proprietorship automatically terminates.

THE PARTNERSHIP

You may consider forming a partnership if you can't personally generate enough capital to make your new business a success, if the workload is too heavy for you alone, or if you simply need moral support and are afraid of going it alone.

The partnership consists of two or more persons, or *principals,* who have contracted to set up a business. In many respects, this form of ownership does not differ much from the sole proprietorship, except that you can count on one or more associates to help you share the responsibilities, the work, the problem solving, and the decision making. Of course, you must expect to share the profits as well.

This sharing aspect is based on the assumption that two or more *ordinary,* or *general,* partners are involved in the business. Another type of partner is the *limited* partner; this kind of arrangement, which is recognized in most states, permits a quasi-corporate entity to exist. In this situation, one or more individuals make an investment in the business and are given part ownership in return. However, they cannot participate in the operation of the business; the enterprise is run by the general partner(s). Limited partners earn their share of company profits but avoid the danger of being held personally liable for business debts.

Two clarion notes of caution should be trumpeted at this point. First, take care that your emotions don't interfere with sound logic and common sense, such as being too eager to go into business with family or friends, or with anyone who happens to come up with the money; a clear head at this early stage can save you lots of grief later. Second, avoid the all-too-common temptation to back up your partnership with nothing more than a verbal understanding and an amicable handshake. For the sake of good business practice and for your own peace of mind thereafter, you should draw up a partnership agreement with the help of your attorney (see exhibit 4–3). This legal instrument not only spells out the duties and responsibilities of the partners but also should include a "buy-sell" clause to forestall future headaches.

As a concluding comment, don't go into a partnership, if at all possible, unless you hold 51 percent of the ownership.

ADVANTAGES OF THE PARTNERSHIP FORM

Like the sole proprietorship, a partnership is relatively easy and inexpensive to establish. You'll probably want to operate under an assumed name, requiring you to file a Certificate of Conducting Business as Partners (see exhibit 4–4). Having the partnership contract prepared is an additional cost.

Naturally, you can count on more initial capital than if you go it alone; the pooled investments of two or more individuals are involved. You also have more leverage when seeking trade credit, loans, or additional equity capital in the future simply because several people are involved.

Rarely does one person possess all the skills and experience required to make a new enterprise a success. If you aren't that rare individual, taking on a partner or two can provide the missing elements. A broader array of talent can be brought to bear on your business operations. (Of course, you must be astute enough to select partners whose skills complement yours and who make up for your shortcomings.)

Finally, the partnership form is relatively free of governmental

EXHIBIT 4–3. PARTNERSHIP AGREEMENT

M107—Partnership agreement 1-96   ©1995 JULIUS BLUMBERG, INC., PUBLISHER NYC 10013

Partnership Agreement

THIS PARTNERSHIP AGREEMENT dated   entered into by

(include full name and address of each Partner)

The parties named above ("the Partners") agree to become partners and form a partnership under the trade name of

for the following purpose:

and to occupy the following premises:

The partnership is to commence on   and to continue

and to that end and purpose the Partners contribute the following property

Source: Forms may be purchased from Julius Blumberg, Inc., New York, NY 10013, or any of its dealers. Reproduction prohibited.

EXHIBIT 4-3. (CONTINUED)

to be used and employed in common between them for the support and management of the business, to their mutual benefit and advantage. It is agreed by the Partners that at all times during the continuance of their partnership, they and each of them will give their attendance, and their best endeavors, and, to the utmost of their skill and power, exert themselves for their joint interest, profit, benefit and advantage, and truly employ, buy, sell, service and merchandise with their joint reserves and any increase thereof, for the business purposes stated above. AND ALSO, that they shall at all times during the partnership, bear, pay and discharge among them, all rents and other expenses that may be required for the support and management of the business as follows:

and that all gains, profit and increase that shall come, grow or arise from or by means of their business shall be divided among them, as follows:

and all loss that result from their business shall be borne and paid between them, as follows:

AND it is agreed by and between the Partners, that at all times during the continuance of their partnership, there shall be kept just and true books of account of all money received, paid, laid out and expended for the business, as also all goods, wares, commodities and merchandise bought or sold, by reason or on account of the business, and all other matters and things whatsoever belonging in any way to the business and the management thereof; which books shall be used in common among the Partners, so that any of the Partners may have access to the books without any interruption or hindrance by the others. AND ALSO, the Partners, shall, on the following schedule

or more often if necessary, make, yield and render, each to the other, a true and just inventory and account of all profits and increases, made, and of all losses sustained; and also all payments, receipts, disbursements and all other things received, disbursed, acted, done, or suffered in this partnership and business; and the same account so made, shall clear, adjust, pay and deliver, each to the other their just share of the profits made.

AND the Partners hereby mutually covenant and agree that during the continuance of the partnership,   of them shall endorse any note, or otherwise become surety for any person or persons whomsoever, nor will sell, assign, transfer, mortgage or otherwise dispose of the business of the partnership, nor each of their share, title and interest therein without the written consent of the Partners. And at the termination of their partnership the Partners shall make a true, just and final account of all things relating to their business, including all stock which shall remain either in money, goods, wares, fixtures, debts or otherwise, which shall be divided among the Partners as follows:

EXHIBIT 4–3. (continued)

after the payment of the partnership liabilities; and should the Partners be unable to ascertain the value of any of the assets belonging to the partnership at the termination of the partnership, the assets shall then be sold, either at private or public sale to be agreed upon by the Partners, and a division of the proceeds of such sale shall be made as provided above.

IT IS FURTHER AGREED that during the continuance of the partnership, all notes, drafts or money received for and in behalf of the partnership by the Partners shall be deposited in a bank to be agreed upon by the Partners and the moneys credited to the partnership shall only be withdrawn by check signed by

who shall also receive such notes, drafts or moneys or other orders for payment of moneys of the partnership for the purpose of making deposits.

IT IS FURTHER AGREED that during the continuance of the partnership, the Partners shall mutually agree in writing upon payment to be made to any of the Partners for services to be rendered, and said payment shall be charged as an item of expense of the partnership business, or, if otherwise agreed upon in writing, may be charged against their personal interest in the business.

IN THE EVENT of the death of a Partner, the surviving Partner(s) shall, within a period of
make and give to the legal representative of the deceased Partner, a true, just and final account of all things relating to the partnership business, and within a period of   in all things truly adjust the same with the legal representative of the deceased Partner. The surviving Partner(s) shall have the right to purchase the interest of the deceased Partner from the legal representative, upon a true and proper valuation of the interest of the deceased Partner; and until the purchase of such interest by the surviving Partner(s), or a division as herein agreed upon, the legal representative of the deceased Partner shall, during the reasonable business hours, have access to the books of the partnership, to examine them personally or with the aid of others and to make copies of any portion without interruption or hindrance, and the legal representative of a deceased Partner shall have equal and joint control of the partnership with the surviving Partner or Partners.

EXHIBIT 4–3. (CONTINUED)

This instrument may not be changed orally.

In Witness Whereof, the Partners have hereunto set their hands and seals the day and year first above mentioned

In presence of:

_____

_____

_____

_____

_____

_____

STATE OF

COUNTY OF
} ss.:

On   before me personally came

to me known, and known to me to be the individual(s) described in, and who executed the foregoing instrument, and acknowledged to me that   he   executed the same.

_____

and

Partnership Agreement

Dated:

EXHIBIT 4–4. CERTIFICATE OF CONDUCTING BUSINESS AS PARTNERS

Blumbergs Law Products X 74—Certificate of Conducting Business as Partners
Individual - Corporation. 12-88

© 1973 BY JULIUS BLUMBERG, INC.,
PUBLISHER, NYC 10013

Business Certificate for Partners

The undersigned do hereby certify that they are conducting or transacting business as members of a partnership under the name or designation of

at

in the County of   *, State of New York, and do further certify that the full names of all the persons conducting or transacting such partnership including the full names of all the partners with the residence address of each such person, and the age of any who may be infants, are as follows:*

NAME *Specify which are infants and state ages.*   **RESIDENCE**

....

....

....

....

....

....

WE DO FURTHER CERTIFY *that we are the successors in interest to*

the person or persons heretofore using such name or names to carry on or conduct or transact business.

In Witness Whereof, *We have this*   *day of*   *19*   *made and signed this certificate.*

....

....

....

....

....

....

State of New York, County of   **ss.:**   INDIVIDUAL ACKNOWLEDGMENT

On this   *day of*   *19*   *, before me personally appeared*

to me known and known to me to be the individual described in, and who executed the foregoing certificate, and he thereupon duly acknowledged to me that he executed the same.

Source: Forms may be purchased from Julius Blumberg, Inc., New York, NY 10013, or any of its dealers. Reproduction prohibited.

EXHIBIT 4–4. (continued)

State of New York, County of   ss.:   CORPORATE ACKNOWLEDGMENT

On this   day of   19   , before me personally appeared

to me known, who being by me duly sworn, did depose and say, that   he resides in

that   he is the   of

the corporation described in and which executed the foregoing certificate; that   he knows the seal of said corporation; that the seal affixed to said certificate is such corporate seal; that it was so affixed by order of the Board of   of said corporation, and that   he signed h   name thereto by like order.

INDEX No.

Certificate of Partners

CONDUCTING BUSINESS UNDER
THE NAME OF

State of New York, County of   ss.:   INDIVIDUAL ACKNOWLEDGMENT

On this   day of   19   , before me personally appeared

to me known and known to me to be the individual   described in, and who executed the foregoing certificate, and   he   thereupon   duly acknowledged to me that   he   executed the same.

red tape. Little is required in the way of paperwork (as is the case with a corporation). Each year, however, you must complete an information return, Form 1065, U.S. Partnership Return of Income (see appendix B).

DRAWBACKS TO THE PARTNERSHIP FORM

If you elect this form of ownership, be prepared to relinquish a good deal of your freedom. You have to work along with one or more cobosses; you must share the authority and the responsibilities. The need to cooperate can provide a continuing assault on your entrepreneurial spirit. No longer can you enjoy the thrill and the challenge of running the entire show.

There can also be formidable adjustment problems. Disagreements with partners can develop not only over important business problems but also over such insignificant trivia as who will open up (or close) on Wednesdays or Saturdays, when to take vacations (and for how long), who will run the machines, do the buying, supervise the office staff, and so forth. It's difficult enough at times for spouses to get along with each other. Imagine the tensions inherent in a situation where two or more individuals, often unrelated, must act, work, plan, and operate in tandem for years and years! It's wise to make certain that your new partner(s) are as highly motivated and cooperative as you are and that your personalities do not clash. Be especially wary of close friends and relatives. Your affection, loyalty, or friendship can easily blind you to their deficiencies and lead you to make allowances for their mistakes.

In any event, you and the other(s) have to learn to work together if your business is to be successful. If you do become unhappy with the situation, only three courses are open to you: (1) sell out your share of the business to the other(s); (2) buy out your partner(s); or (3) stay put and learn to live with it.

Be aware that any business decisions or actions taken by your partner(s) legally bind you as well under the general rules of agency, which spell out the duties and financial liability of partners, even in a case where you knew nothing about the move. This obligation is something to think about: It applies to any contracts that may be signed as well as to other acts.

Again, as with the sole proprietorship, you will run the considerable risk of incurring personal liability. As a general partner, your personal assets (as well as those of other general partners) are subject to seizure for the payment of business debts.

Finally, this form of ownership is also subject to the frailties of human nature. The death of any one partner, unless provided for in the partnership contract, automatically terminates the partnership.

THE CORPORATION

The third major legal form of business ownership is the corporation. To set up a corporation, one or more individuals apply for a charter within the state where they want to transact business and where the principal office of the business is located. (*Note:* The number of persons involved depends on state regulations. Most states require only one director in order to create a corporate entity.) Application is accomplished by preparing a Certificate of Incorporation in detail (names and addresses of both the proposed corporation and of the incorporators, purpose and type of business activities contemplated, and amount of stock authorized), filing the certificate with the secretary of state, and paying the required fee. (See exhibit 4–5.)

While it isn't absolutely necessary, I strongly recommend that your attorney handle all the details. Corporation law is complicated; a lawyer will save you needless headaches in the future. At the very least, the attorney may widen the horizons of your business by broadening the purposes of your activities listed in the application. State law limits the activities of your corporation to those spelled out in the charter. Moreover, your attorney can help you prepare a Preincorporation Agreement with the other principals.

WHY INCORPORATE?

Of the three legal forms, this is the only one with a built-in capacity for permanence in that the death of one or more of its founders or stockholders does not affect the business's legal status. Corporations are recognized as legal entities in and of themselves. They exist apart from their stockholders, who can come and go.

Consequently, you avoid the problem of unlimited liability that characterizes the other two forms of ownership. Your liability is limited to the amount of your investment. Your personal holdings do not come up for grabs if the corporation becomes insolvent and its assets are insufficient to satisfy the creditors. This fact alone explains the attraction of the corporate form for many who start their own businesses.

Banks and other lenders are generally more willing to advance loans to a corporation that has been operating successfully for some time or to a new corporation with sufficient equity and promise than

EXHIBIT 4–5. CERTIFICATE OF INCORPORATION

A 234—Certificate of Incorporation
Business Corporation Law §402: 1-89

© 1975 BY JULIUS BLUMBERG, INC.
PUBLISHER, NYC 10013

Certificate of Incorporation of

under Section 402 of the Business Corporation Law

IT IS HEREBY CERTIFIED THAT:

(1) The name of the proposed corporation is

(2) The purpose or purposes for which this corporation is formed, are as follows, to wit:
To engage in any lawful act or activity for which corporations may be organized under the Business Corporation Law. The corporation is not formed to engage in any act or activity requiring the consent or approval of any state official, department, board, agency or other body.*

The corporation, in furtherance of its corporate purposes above set forth, shall have all of the powers enumerated in Section 202 of the Business Corporation Law, subject to any limitations provided in the Business Corporation Law or any other statute of the State of New York.

*If specific consent or approval is required delete this paragraph, insert specific purposes and obtain consent or approval prior to filing.

Source: Forms may be purchased from Julius Blumberg, Inc., New York, NY 10013, or any of its dealers. Reproduction prohibited.

EXHIBIT 4–5. (continued)

(3) The office of the corporation is to be located in the County of
State of New York.

(4) The aggregate number of shares which the corporation shall have the authority to issue is

EXHIBIT 4-5. (continued)

(5) The Secretary of State is designated as agent of the corporation upon whom process against it may be served. The post office address to which the Secretary of State shall mail a copy of any process against the corporation served upon him is

(6) A director of the corporation shall not be liable to the corporation or its shareholders for damages for any breach of duty in such capacity except for

   (i) liability if a judgment or other final adjudication adverse to a director establishes that his or her acts or omissions were in bad faith or involved intentional misconduct or a knowing violation of law or that the director personally gained in fact a financial profit or other advantage to which he or she was not legally entitled or that the director's acts violated BCL § 719, or

   (ii) liability for any act or omission prior to the adoption of this provision.

The undersigned incorporator, or each of them if there are more than one, is of the age of eighteen years or over.

IN WITNESS WHEREOF, this certificate has been subscribed on _____ 19___ by the undersigned who affirm(s) that the statements made herein are true under the penalties of perjury.

....	....
Type name of incorporator	Signature
....	
Address	
....	....
Type name of incorporator	Signature
....	
Address	
....	....
Type name of incorporator	Signature
....	
Address	

EXHIBIT 4–5. (continued)

Certificate of Incorporation

of

under Section 402 of the Business Corporation Law

Filed By:

Office and Post Office Address

to an individual or partnership. (The lender sometimes insists on collateral or requires personal signatures from stockholders as a precautionary measure.) Individuals with money to invest might purchase some of the new corporation's stock.

You aren't locked into the corporation forever. If you someday decide you want to embark on an entirely different enterprise, relocate, or retire, all you have to do is sell your stock in the company. Ownership of stock is readily transferred.

As a final point, there can be certain advantages to the corporate form in the area of fringe benefits, such as pension and stock plans, and insurance.

DISADVANTAGES OF INCORPORATION

A major limitation to the corporate form is the problem of *double taxation*. Corporate profits are taxed once per se since a corporation is a distinct taxable entity. Then they are taxed again as income, when distributed to the stockholders. Although you serve as corporation president and chairman of the board, you're legally an employee of the business. Hence, you are liable for income tax not only on your salary but also on your share of the distributed profits. The total tax bite can be substantial. Unfortunately, any losses sustained by a corporation are not available to stockholders as deductions from other earned income!

It takes time and effort as well as money to set up a corporation. Your costs can run from as little as several hundred dollars to well over a thousand dollars.

Corporations are closely regulated by the state in which they are franchised. In your home state, yours is known as a *domestic corporation*. *Foreign corporation* is the term applied to your firm when you operate in another state. In reality, you're not supposed to conduct business in a second or third state without making formal application to the respective secretaries of state for permission to conduct operations there. (Generally, this regulation comes up in matters of a corporation's right to sue for nonpayments, etc.) A company doing business in another state isn't stopped merely because of failure to file.

A corporation is also required to promulgate bylaws, hold stockholders' meetings, and keep records. (Most states use preprinted forms that alleviate much of the initial preparations.) Of all three forms of ownership, the corporation comes under the most scrutiny by the federal government.

THE S CORPORATION

Given certain specific qualifications and requirements, a corporation may choose to adopt the *S corporation* form. An outstanding advantage of this legal form (formerly known as a *subchapter S corporation*) is that both income and losses are usually taxed to the individual shareholders, rather than to the corporation itself. This can be especially important in the first year of operation, when new companies frequently lose money. Any loss suffered can be applied against other personal income, such as that from an earlier job. This will reduce the amount of income tax levied. In this respect, the firm is taxed more like a proprietorship or partnership, yet the unlimited personal liability problem common to those two legal forms is avoided.

A corporation can elect to be an S corporation if:

- It "qualifies" (see below)
- All shareholders give their consent to the firm's choice of S corporation status
- It has a permitted tax year
- It files Form 2553 (Election by a Small Business Corporation)

Some of the requirements needed to "qualify": The company must be a domestic corporation; there should be only one class of stock; and the shareholders should number no more than thirty-five.

YOUR NEED FOR PROFESSIONAL ASSISTANCE

If you're like most other entrepreneurs, you're undoubtedly highly motivated and convinced that you'll be able to manage all aspects of your new business masterfully and by yourself. You also plan to run your affairs in a professional, open, and aboveboard manner. You want to treat both your customers and suppliers well, conform to all legal requirements and restrictions, maintain accurate records, and pay your taxes on time.

Despite your high level of self-confidence, however, you must realize that the complexities of today's business environment call for reliance on the assistance of specialists. At the very least you will need an accountant, a banker, an insurance agent or broker, possibly one or two business consultants, and, of course, an attorney. The accountant can help you set up your books according to approved accounting procedures. This will enable you to make vital merchandising and other decisions in the future. Your accountant can also help you keep tabs on your business growth, point out minor problems before they become serious, and complete your tax returns.

Your banker can furnish you with information about the kind of business you are considering and about the community where it will be situated. Furthermore, he or she will be happy to recommend other professionals if you need them, assist your operation with loans and lines of credit, and advise you generally on economic trends.

Your insurance representative takes care of your special business needs for protection against fire and other perils.

Consultants are usually tapped for a variety of one-shot problems: designing a plant or store layout, appraising a going business in which you are interested, making a feasibility study for a new location or for electronic data processing (EDP) equipment under consideration, setting up an initial advertising campaign, and so on.

If at all feasible, it's worth your while to engage an attorney for your business on a retainer basis. Your lawyer's services are valuable at the very beginning, in assisting you with all the legal aspects of starting an enterprise: setting up the legal form of the business, negotiating leases and contracts, securing the necessary licenses and permits, and preparing partnership or stockholder agreements. Subsequently, your attorney will see to it that you become thoroughly familiar with the details of pertinent legislative acts and local ordinances. These run the gamut from the minimum wage and labor laws, through health and safety regulations, to tax responsibilities. You'll probably call on your attorney later on for assistance in a variety of situations too numerous to mention.

FOR FURTHER INFORMATION

Coltman, Michael M. *Buying and Selling a Small Business.* 2d ed. Bellingham, Wash.: Self-Counsel Press, 1988.

Cooke, Robert A. *How to Start Your Own (Subchapter) "S" Corporation.* New York: Wiley, 1995.

Diamond, Michael R. and Julie L. Williams. *How to Incorporate: A Handbook for Entrepreneurs and Professionals.* 3rd ed. New York: Wiley, 1996.

Foster, Dennis L. *The Complete Franchise Book.* Rochlin, Calif.: Prima Publishing, 1988.

Lauer, Mark T. *Buying and Selling a Business.* Deerfield Beach, Fla.: Garrett, 1995.

O'Hara, Patrick D. *SBA Loans.* 2d ed. New York: Wiley, 1994.

Rust, Herbert. *Owning Your Own Franchise.* Englewood Cliffs, N.J.: Prentice-Hall, 1991.

Snowden, Richard W. *The Complete Guide to Buying a Business.* New York: AMACOM, 1994.

5

HOW TO ESTIMATE YOUR FINANCIAL NEEDS

EACH YEAR A surprisingly high percentage of new ventures are launched with insufficient funding behind them. Initial undercapitalization is a major cause of early business failure. Even when an enterprise manages to last for three or four years before going under, its demise is often directly traceable to poor financial planning at the beginning.

Unfortunately, there are individuals who scrape together whatever money they can, perhaps in their eagerness to get started, and go in with an amazingly slim financial commitment. Somehow, they don't realize that they need more than just a month's rent in advance, a few fixtures, and a minimum inventory. At the very least, some reserves are required to cover personal needs and family responsibilities until the profits start to trickle in.

Of course, we've all heard anecdotes about this or that entrepreneur who in no time at all was able to pyramid an insignificant investment of $300 or $500 to a moderate-sized, going business. Though such stories may contain a few elements of truth, the odds are probably a thousand to one (if not higher) *against* your being so fortunate!

Lots of careful thinking and sound planning must characterize your own approach to business, if you want to succeed. Your capital requirements should be diligently formulated well in advance of taking the plunge.

HOW MUCH CAPITAL DO YOU NEED?

It appears to be fashionable in financial circles to separate the term *capital* into a number of classifications. Terms such as *initial, operating, working,* and *reserve* are often attached to the word *capital.* Of course, all of these are variations on the same theme: Enough money must be available to see the business (and yourself) off to a good start.

You need *initial capital* to cover all your start-up costs: legal fees, deposits with public utility companies, licenses and permits, machinery and fixtures, advances for the rental of premises, and franchise fees (if required). Included here are funds set aside for your opening promotion; this money is sometimes referred to as *promotional capital.*

You need *operating* (or *working*) *capital* to purchase raw materials or merchandise for resale and supplies, to pay your employees, and to liquidate obligations—in short, to keep on operating until profits begin to show up.

Finally, you'll need *reserve capital* not only for unexpected contingencies but also to be able to eat three meals a day, buy clothing, pay your monthly rent bill or mortgage, and cover medical expenses.

How to Determine Your Requirements

Now that you know you need three kinds of capital, you must pin down the approximate sales volume you expect your business to attain during its first year. This *sales target* guides you in calculating your overall capital requirements. It should be as accurate as you can make it: neither an optimistic nor a pessimistic estimate, but a fair appraisal of just how much you believe your sales will total.

Using this figure as a base—with the aid of obtainable trade information such as average markups in your kind of business, space productivity, and other ratios—you should be able to deduce other important details. These include the kinds (and values) of assets required to reach that level of sales, the size of the facility needed, and approximate overhead costs.

As an illustration of this general approach, assume you're planning to open a small gift shop. First you tap the services of your trade association and, perhaps, other sources such as Robert Morris Associates (Philadelphia) or Dun & Bradstreet (New York City).

Let's assume you discover that the average gift shop of the size you intend to open generally operates on a gross margin (sales, less cost of goods sold) of about 46 percent of sales. Operating expenses amount to another 41 percent of sales. When you think about it, these two little facts alone provide substantial direction for your planning. Say you've set a first year's sales figure of $350,000. From these percentages, you can then calculate that your operating expenses (for rent, utilities, labor, insurance, advertising, and other costs) should total around $143,500. You should also realize a gross margin of about $161,000 on some $189,000 worth of merchandise (at cost) to be sold. Subtracting the $143,500 figure from this gross, you'd expect to come out with about $17,500 in profit before taxes.

By the same token, you may learn from available tables that the customary rate of inventory turnover in gift shops is about 2.4 times annually. By dividing your cost-of-merchandise figure of $189,000 by 2.4 turns of stock, you can then conclude that you'll need to keep on hand an average inventory of approximately $78,750. The basic formula to use for this kind of calculation is:

$$\text{Stockturn (at cost)} = \frac{\text{Sales at Cost}}{\text{Average stock at cost}}$$

From trade sources you can also gain information as to the dollar sales per square foot of selling space typical of gift shops. This information will help you to decide how many square feet you need in your own store to do the kind of sales volume you project. By checking with other retailers, local representatives, and your bank, you'll also be able to ascertain how much is required for deposits against utility bills and about how much you can expect to be billed each month for utilities, insurance, and other operating expenses.

Take a few minutes now to look over the form in exhibit 5–1; it's designed to help you estimate the amount of capital you'll need to start your business. As you can see, it's self-explanatory.

EXHIBIT 5–1. A WORKSHEET FOR ESTIMATING YOUR FINANCIAL NEEDS

WORKSHEET NO. 2

ESTIMATED MONTHLY EXPENSES			
Item	Your estimate of monthly expenses based on sales of $ _____ per year	Your estimate of how much cash you need to start your business (See column 3.)	What to put in column 2 (These figures are typical for one kind of business. You will have to decide how many months to allow for in your business.)
	Column 1	Column 2	Column 3
Salary of owner-manager	$	$	2 times column 1
All other salaries and wages			3 times column 1
Rent			3 times column 1
Advertising			3 times column 1
Delivery expense			3 times column 1
Supplies			3 times column 1
Telephone and telegraph			3 times column 1
Other utilities			3 times column 1
Insurance			Payment required by insurance company
Taxes, including Social Security			4 times column 1
Interest			3 times column 1
Maintenance			3 times column 1
Legal and other professional fees			3 times column 1
Miscellaneous			3 times column 1
STARTING COSTS YOU ONLY HAVE TO PAY ONCE			Leave column 2 blank
Fixtures and equipment			Fill in worksheet 3 on page 12 and put the total here
Decorating and remodeling			Talk it over with a contractor
Installation of fixtures and equipment			Talk to suppliers from whom you buy these
Starting inventory			Suppliers will probably help you estimate this
Deposits with public utilities			Find out from utilities companies
Legal and other professional fees			Lawyer, accountant, and so on
Licenses and permits			Find out from city offices what you have to have
Advertising and promotion for opening			Estimate what you'll use
Accounts receivable			What you need to buy more stock until credit customers pay
Cash			For unexpected expenses or losses, special purchases, etc.
Other			Make a separate list and enter total
TOTAL ESTIMATED CASH YOU NEED TO START WITH		$	Add up all the numbers in column 2

Source: "Checklist for Going into Business," Management Aid No. 2.016 (Washington, D.C.: Small Business Administration, 1975), 6–7.

WHERE TO FIND THE MONEY YOU WILL NEED

After you've devoted many hours to planning your new enterprise, and after you've worked and reworked your figures and pared them to the bone, you finally decide you need a minimum of five, ten, or perhaps twenty thousand dollars to assure your business success. Your next hurdle is to locate the required capital.

Many sources of capital are available—and most have strings attached. Perhaps the best type for you to use, if only because it's the least expensive in the long run, is your own personal resources.

USE YOUR OWN FUNDS, IF POSSIBLE

Knowledgeable business consultants recommend that at least one-half, if not more, of your business investment should come from your own reserves. Consequently, it makes sense for you to work at a job for a year or two while you try to accumulate some savings.

Understandably, you'll be somewhat reluctant to gamble your own hard-earned capital. Few individuals escape a confrontation with this dilemma: Why not play with other people's money, instead of with your own?

Face it. Neither individuals nor firms are likely to advance moneys to anyone without expecting some sort of gain on the loans they make. They desire a return on their investment either in the form of "equity" (part ownership) in your business or the payment of an attractive rate of interest. Incidentally, you'll also find that banks and other lenders are unwilling to lend you money unless you're prepared to risk your own funds as well.

You need not invest all your savings, nor do you have to relinquish any part of your business. There are ways to borrow additional funds on favorable terms. A loan on your savings bank passbook, for example, can bring you supplementary capital at low cost. While the bank may charge you 8 or 9 percent, the funds you maintain on deposit in your account continue to earn interest. This interest offsets much of your cost and results in your paying a differential interest rate of only 5 or 6 percent.

If you own your own home or other real property, there's also the possibility of taking out a mortgage or refinancing an existing mortgage. The mortgage rates available at the time of the loan or refinancing must be balanced against your rate of return.

Another possibility is a life insurance policy that has accumulated cash value over the years. Loans on such policies generally bear a relatively low rate of interest.

TAPPING THE RESOURCES OF FAMILY AND FRIENDS

A popular source of additional investment capital is your family. Needless to say, in most families it seems to be relatively easy (no pun intended!) to locate family members who might be willing to lend a relatively small sum of money to the entrepreneur. Good friends might also be eager to help out. Even acquaintances can be sold on investing in a new corporation, if you can persuade them to have faith in you and your ideas.

You have to decide for yourself whether this avenue is for you. It could be sticky. There are some things you ought to think about: How will your relationships with these individuals be affected if your business does *not* succeed? How will you be able to pay them back?

If you decide to borrow from family or friends, you should work out in advance some method of paying them back over time, possibly in installments. Be prepared: They'll have difficulty restraining themselves from getting involved in the operation of your business. You need to be firm from the beginning, to avoid psychological wear and tear on yourself.

BANK LOANS

Banks lend money to launch a new business only occasionally—and only when you've accompanied your application with an attractive and comprehensive business plan. More often than not, a commercial bank is more interested in offering funds for operating capital to a business with some history of successful operations behind it. The bank's primary usefulness is for short-term loans for the leasing of equipment, the purchasing of real estate, and the buying of additional stocks of goods for resale.

Finally, many individuals are able to secure personal loans of five thousand dollars or more on their signatures alone if they have a preferred credit rating from repaying past loans on time. It helps if you can show personal assets on your loan application in the form of bank accounts, stocks, and bonds.

FINANCE COMPANIES

Business executives can often borrow short-term funds from commercial finance companies by offering inventories, receivables, and similar holdings as collateral. Many personal finance companies are more than willing to extend loans to persons in whom they have confidence. However, the high interest rates these firms generally charge should rule out this source for the alert entrepreneur.

VENTURE CAPITALISTS

You may be able to locate private individuals, small investment groups, and companies in the business of investing in small enterprise. These *venture capitalists* are eager to put their excess financial resources to work. They seldom become involved with a new undertaking, however, unless they're convinced by a well-developed proposal that the new business will indeed be a winner. Yet these people can be of value to you *after* your new firm has demonstrated viability and vigor for several years and is in need of additional moneys for further growth or expansion. Venture capitalists are usually not interested in granting loans outright. They prefer to put additional capital into a growing business in exchange for part of the ownership. In short, they look to make capital gains.

SMALL BUSINESS INVESTMENT CORPORATIONS (SBICs)

These private companies were authorized by an act of Congress back in the 1950s. SBICs are licensed to provide financial services to small businesses in the form of equity/venture financing for modernization and expansion. Especially interested in purchasing stock in the promising small corporation, the SBIC usually seeks to become involved in actual business operations by providing management direction.

The federal government encourages private enterprise by members of minority groups. Minority Enterprise Small Business Investment Corporations (MESBICs) are licensed to provide the identical kind of aid to small enterprises owned by minority-group members.

ISSUING STOCK

If you've organized your new firm into a corporation, your charter specifies the amount of shares the corporation is authorized to issue. You may be able to raise equity funds by selling some shares to others, making them shareholders and thereby endowing them with part ownership of your business.

Stocks may be either *preferred* or *common* shares. Preferred shares include certain privileges for the shareholder—for example, if the business fails, the shareholder is guaranteed a proportionate share of the remaining assets. Usually, though, only holders of common stock enjoy voting rights in the company.

SUPPLIERS' CREDIT

Business makes abundant use of *trade,* or *supplier's, credit,* a practice of special significance to retailers and wholesalers. For example, if you own a store, your suppliers generally extend credit to you, albeit after some favorable experience. This means they ship goods and supplies to your business, bill you, and give you time to pay the invoice (usually thirty days). This is tantamount to financing of a short-term nature.

Along the same lines, where fixtures, machinery, and other equipment are concerned, suppliers are often more than happy to extend long-term credit. After making a down payment, you pay them back the balance of the debt on an installment basis. Some may even lease the equipment to you instead of insisting on an outright sale.

THE BALANCE SHEET

Every business must balance its books properly at the close of its business year, for tax purposes if for nothing else. The culmination of this activity is the issuance of a major accounting statement—the *balance sheet.*

This summarizes the status of the business at that point in time—its assets, liabilities, and net worth. The balance sheet is useful, too, for purposes of control, management direction, and decision making. By interpreting this statement, management is able to glean insights that are of value in planning. For example, the *current ratio* (one of the so-called *liquidity ratios*) is calculated by dividing the business's current assets by its current liabilities in order to assess the firm's ability to pay off its debts promptly. As a general rule, this ratio should be at least two to one. (An expanded treatment of the topic of ratio analysis will be found in chapter 19.)

The sample balance sheet in exhibit 5–2 shows that the current ratio for the small manufacturing company is well in excess of the acceptable figure. A brief explanation of the major items on the balance sheet follows:

- *Assets*   Cash, property, and other items owned by the company
- *Current assets*   Cash and property temporarily in your firm's possession that can be quickly liquidated
- *Cash*   In addition to currency and coin, this includes checks and money orders
- *Accounts receivable*   A collective term for moneys owed the firm on credit
- *Fixed assets*   Tangible property of a long-term or permanent nature

EXHIBIT 5–2. A SAMPLE BALANCE SHEET

ADG-Tenafly Manufacturing Company
Balance Sheet
December 31, 1996

Assets

CURRENT ASSETS		
Cash on hand	$500	
Cash in bank	28,850	
Accounts receivable, less allowance for bad debts	47,730	
Merchandise inventory	52,600	
Total current assets		**$129,680**
FIXED ASSETS		
Land	$21,440	
Building, less depreciation	143,310	
Equipment, less depreciation	58,640	
Furniture and fixtures, less depreciation	21,800	
Total fixed assets		**$245,190**
Total Assets		**$374,870**

Source: Compiled by the author.

- *Liabilities*   The debts your business must pay back
- *Current liabilities*   Debts that must be met within the year, such as your *accounts payable* (moneys owed out to suppliers), short-term loans, and accrued taxes
- *Accounts payable*   Money you owe to creditors
- *Accrued payroll taxes*   Payroll taxes you have accumulated but not yet sent in to the government
- *Long-term liabilities*   Debts of a long-term nature (over one year)
- *Capital*   Also referred to as *owner's equity* or *net worth,* this is the excess of your assets over your liabilities. It is equivalent to what you originally invested in the business plus subsequent additions or subtractions

In the case of a corporation, the outstanding capital stock (at its original issue price) is listed here, as well as any accumulated profit.

EXHIBIT 5–2. (continued)

ADG-Tenafly Manufacturing Company
Balance Sheet
December 31, 1996

Liabilities

CURRENT LIABILITIES

Accounts payable	$16,800	
Notes payable within one year	6,000	
Accrued payroll taxes	4,260	
Total current liabilities		**$27,060**

LONG-TERM LIABILITIES

Note payable, due 1998	$12,000	
Note payable, due 1999	18,000	
Note payable, due 2000	18,000	
Total long-term liabilities		48,000

Capital (Net Worth)

Capital, December 31, 1996	$299,810
Total Liabilities and Capital	**$374,870**

THE PROFIT-AND-LOSS STATEMENT

Also called an *income statement* or *operating statement,* the profit-and-loss statement (or *P&L*) is another major accounting device. Prepared at least once a year, it depicts the results of business operation for the period covered. An abbreviated statement for a small retail shop is shown in exhibit 5–3.

A major element of the profit-and-loss statement is the *bottom-line* figure—the one that reveals how much net profit the company earned during the particular period or, perhaps, the magnitude of the loss it may have suffered.

EXHIBIT 5–3. A SAMPLE P&L

The Two Sisters' Dress Shoppe
Profit-and-Loss Statement
October 1996

Gross Sales for October	$35,450	
Less returns and allowances	980	
Net sales		$34,470
Cost of Goods		
Merchandise inventory, October 1	16,415	
Purchases during month	9,080	
Freight charges	165	
Total merchandise handled	25,660	
Less inventory, October 31	8,470	
Cost of goods sold		17,190
Gross profit (margin)		$17,280
Operating Expenses		
Salaries	6,825	
Utilities	680	
Rent	2,300	
Stationery and printing	225	
Insurance	390	
Advertising and promotion	865	
Telephone	270	
Travel and entertainment	255	
Dues and subscriptions	110	
Bad debts	290	
Depreciation	1,835	
Total operating expenses		$14,045
Operating profit		3,235
Other Income		
Dividends	120	
Interest on bank account	70	
Total other income		190
Total income before taxes		3,425
Less provision for income taxes		1,370
Net Income (or Loss)		$2,055

Source: Compiled by the author.

The major parts of a P&L are readily seen in the following skeletal outline:

Gross sales
− Returns and allowances
Net sales
− Cost of goods
Gross profit (or gross margin)
− Operating expenses
Operating profit
+ Other income
Total income before taxes
− Provision for income taxes
Net income (or loss)

Management that allows a full year to go by without seeing a P&L shows signs of shortsightedness. Any attempts to correct an unfavorable picture are negated once months have rolled past. Smart business owners insist on having income statements prepared by their accountant or bookkeeping staff on at least a quarterly basis or, even better, monthly. That way, they can keep current with what is happening and take immediate steps to rectify any problems. Moreover, they can take advantage of opportunities that crop up unexpectedly.

PREPARE YOUR STATEMENTS IN ADVANCE

One of the healthiest steps you can take before starting up your business is to work out, well ahead of time, both an estimated balance sheet and an estimated profit-and-loss statement for at least your first year of operation. Indeed, smart planners will prepare these pro forma statements for the first two or three years following the start-up.

This suggestion is not made simply to offer you an exercise in thinking things through. It should provide you with foresight: You'll be able to determine what is likely to happen, be prepared for it, and rule out the unexpected.

MAKING YOUR BUSINESS PLAN

At this point, it may prove worthwhile to list once more those ingredients mentioned in chapter 1 as being essential to the success of a new business. As you may recall, they are

- A qualified entrepreneur
- A potential business opportunity
- A solid and detailed plan
- Sufficient capital
- Luck

That third item—a solid and detailed plan—is not always perceived by many people as being an absolute requirement. It is often pointed out that many of today's successful companies were initially started without much in the way of real, solid planning.

While this may be true in some instances, logic tells us that careful and thorough planning cannot hurt our chances. It can only make things better.

Indeed, the U.S. Small Business Administration suggests that a detailed business plan:

- Offers a path to follow (shows you how to achieve your goals)
- May help in securing loans
- Can provide useful information for suppliers, personnel, and others
- Can help you develop your management capabilities*

Exhibit 5–4 contains a useful outline for your business plan. Note that the outline is intended only as a planning aid. It's not designed for the sole purpose of attracting venture capital.

EXHIBIT 5–4. AN OUTLINE FOR YOUR BUSINESS PLAN

A. *An Overview of the Business:*
  1. Name of firm
  2. Nature of the business
  3. Major business objectives
  4. Legal form of business
  5. Desired image
B. *The Physical Plant:*
  1. Description of location (area, neighborhood, site)
  2. Transportation facilities
  3. Parking facilities
  4. The building (description, condition, façade, renovation/remodeling required)

---

* Management Assistance Support Services Section, U.S. Small Business Administration, "Business Plan for Retailers," *Management Aid No. 2.020.* (Washington, D.C.: U.S. Small Business Administration, April 1981 reprint), 2.

EXHIBIT 5–4. (continued)

5. Licenses and permits required
6. Terms of lease and other occupancy details
7. Arrangements to be made with utilities
8. Machinery required
9. Equipment needed
10. Fixturization
11. Interior layout
12. Interior design
13. Supplies required

C. *The Financial Plan:*

1. Initial investment required
2. Additional financing to be sought, along with likely sources
3. Projected sales figures
4. Pro forma balance sheets (2 to 3 years)
5. Pro forma income statements (2 to 3 years)
6. Cash flow projections
7. Needed insurance program
8. Internal risk-reduction measures to be taken
9. Bookkeeping method
10. Expected taxation liabilities and responsibilities

D. *The Marketing Plan:*

1. Targeted customer groups: their characteristics, size of market segments
2. Analysis of the competition
3. Product mix
4. Services mix
5. Pricing policies (price ranges, price lines, promotional pricing approaches)
6. Discount policies
7. Markdown (and markup) policies
8. Budget for promotion
9. First year's promotion calendar
10. Advertising plans: media selection, schedules, use of cooperative advertising
11. Personal selling efforts and sales training programs
12. Sales promotion tools to be used
13. Plans for window and interior displays (if a retail store)
14. Distribution methods and channels
15. Needed marketing research
16. Credit extension and supervision of program

E. *The Personnel Plan:*

1. Organizational chart for the business
2. Key personnel—names, job titles, educational background, experience, and skills
3. Written job specifications for all positions

EXHIBIT 5–4. (continued)

        4. Openings still to be filled

        5. Personnel sources to draw on

        6. Details of employee compensation, including fringe benefits

        7. Plans for employee training

  F. *The Inventory Plan:*

        1. Initial inventory required (amount, depth and width, quality level)

        2. Methods for inventory management, planning, and control

        3. Expected rates of inventory turnover

        4. Buying: names and addresses of suppliers

        5. Buying: terms and delivery policies

Source: Compiled by the author.

FOR FURTHER INFORMATION

Alarid, William. *Money Sources for Small Business.* Santa Monica, Calif.: Puma, 1991.

Bandler, James. *How to Use Financial Statements: A Guide to Understanding the Numbers.* Burr Ridge, Ill.: Irwin, 1994.

Brooks, Julie K., and Barry A. Stevens. *How to Write a Successful Business Plan.* New York: AMACOM, 1987.

Cohen, William A. *Model Business Plans for Product Businesses.* New York: Wiley, 1995.

———. *Model Business Plans for Service Businesses.* New York: Wiley, 1995.

Coltman, Michael M. *Buying and Selling a Small Business.* 2d ed. Bellingham, Wash.: Self-Counsel Press, 1990.

Ernst & Young. *The Ernst & Young Business Plan Guide.* 2d ed. New York: Wiley, 1993.

Hayes, Rick Stephan. *Business Loans: A Guide to Money Sources and How to Approach Them.* rev. ed. New York: Wiley, 1989.

Lister, Kate, and Tom Harnish. *Finding Money: The Small Business Guide to Financing.* New York: Wiley, 1995.

Livingstone, John Leslie. *The Portable MBA in Finance and Accounting.* New York: Wiley, 1995.

McLaughlin, Thomas A. *Streetsmart Financial Basics for Nonprofit Managers.* New York: Wiley, 1995.

Miller, Barry E., and Donald E. Miller. *How to Interpret Financial Statements for Better Business Decisions.* New York: AMACOM, 1990.

O'Hara, Patrick D. *SBA Loans: A Step-by-Step Guide.* 2d ed. New York: Wiley, 1994.

Pinson, Linda, and Jerry Jinnett. *Anatomy of a Business Plan.* 2d ed. Chicago: Enterprise-Dearborn, 1993.

Plewa, Franklin, and George T. Friedlob. *Understanding Income Statements.* New York: Wiley, 1995.

Seglin, Jeffrey L. *Financing Your Small Business.* New York: McGraw-Hill, 1990.

Spiro, Herbert T. *Finance for the Non-Financial Manager.* 4th ed. New York: Wiley, 1996.

Tabet, Joseph, and Jeffrey Slater. *Financial Essentials for Small Business Success.* Dover, N.H.: Upstart Publishing, 1994.

Touchie, Rodger. *Preparing a Successful Business Plan: A Practical Guide for Small Business.* Bellingham, Wash.: Self-Counsel Press, 1989.

6

FINDING THE RIGHT LOCATION

SELECTING THE PLACE to set up your operation is one of the most important decisions you have to make. More often than not, the seeds of business success or demise are sown along with the choice of location.

It's sad but true that many location decisions are based on personal preferences or whim, instead of on an objective, orderly approach. Often, an entrepreneur chooses to set up shop close to home purely for the sake of convenience, discovers a promising-looking empty store along a busy thoroughfare, or rides past a vacant building that strikes him or her as ideal for a new plant.

This person is relying more on intuition than on logic. Underlying this approach to decision making are emotional, or nonrational, factors. Strangely, too, the typical new business owner often neglects, among other things, to seek out pertinent helpful materials on location finding that are readily available from the Small Business Administration, the Government Printing Office, or the local branch of the public library.

If you plan to gamble your life's savings in launching a new enterprise, as so many do, you would do well to seize the reins and proceed in a coldly logical, businesslike fashion.

HOW TO ANALYZE YOUR REQUIREMENTS

Obviously, the right choice of location for a retail store can easily mean the difference between success and failure. Many types of retail shops depend almost entirely on passersby for their sales. Your selection of a side street location or a deteriorating neighborhood could indeed prove to be a costly mistake.

Less evident is the importance of the proper site for a service business, wholesale operation, or factory. Yet, even here, you should be concerned about several essential characteristics. Both manufacturing plants and wholesaling establishments, for instance, must have access to good transportation facilities, for bringing in raw materials or finished goods, and for distributing their products. Similarly, these enterprises must often be able to count on a healthy "labor pool" in the area from which to draw machine operators, office workers, supervisory personnel, and technicians.

Yes, the requirements for different types of businesses may vary considerably. There are, however, some common areas to take into account when choosing a location, regardless of the kind of business you are setting up. In addition to such general considerations as the character of the community, the local environment, and your personal preferences, take pains to study the following:

- Accessibility to transportation
- Availability of labor
- Closeness to the company's markets
- Cost factors, such as land, construction, materials, and labor
- Local ordinances and regulations
- Quality of local services (police and fire protection)
- Residency factors (climate, quality of schools, places of worship, recreational facilities)
- Sewers, water supply, power, and other utilities
- Space for future expansion
- Tax structure

DETERMINING FACILITY NEEDS

Our nation's manufacturing companies purchase raw materials, semiprocessed goods, and/or components. In their factories, they utilize these elements in the fabrication of other products designed for both consumer and nonconsumer markets.

Obviously, then, there may be several other location requirements for the manufacturing facility (in addition to many of the factors listed at the end of the preceding section). For example, the new factory may need to be erected on a sizable parcel of land. Because of the high cost of space in most American cities, many of today's plants are situated in more rural areas, where land costs are relatively low. Preferably, too, the plant should be convenient to necessary distribution facilities—a major highway, if truck transport is commonly used, or a railroad spur, if outgoing goods are destined for distribution by train. Still another requirement may be the ready availability of sufficient local labor, since the company may need to employ a considerable number of workers.

The typical wholesaling company has need of ample warehouse facilities to store the large quantities of goods it must purchase all during the year for eventual resale to industrial accounts and/or retail firms. Like the manufacturing plant, the wholesale operation requires bays and docks for handling incoming and outgoing shipments as well as ready access to one or more of the major transportation modes. Still another similarity between today's warehouse and the modern factory is that both types of buildings are often found in rural or suburban areas where the cost of land is not too high. More often than not, the modern warehouse facility occupies a flat, one-story building rather than the older, multistory type commonly seen in the downtown sections of many cities. Within these single-level structures, forklifts and other equipment can move pallets and skids of merchandise about rather easily.

As mentioned above, with a retail store operation, a good location is often the primary requisite for success. Retailers need to open stores where the traffic that passes by is brisk. They look for a "trading area" that is extensive, carefully investigate the demographic and other characteristics of consumers in the area, check into their competitors' strengths and weaknesses, and seek ample parking facilities. (These and other location criteria for retail operations are treated in greater detail in the next section.)

As to the service sector, it's evident that in many different types of service enterprises, the business premises often play a significant role. An obvious illustration can be found in the lodging industry. Certainly, the hotel, motel, or inn that aspires to more than modest success has need of a location that is convenient to traffic, along with an attractive entrance, building, and appropriate furniture and decor.

In much the same way, theaters, beauty salons, dry cleaning establishments, dance studios, and the like require locations that are convenient to large numbers of consumers, and premises that will contribute toward building continued patronage.

THE RETAIL LOCATION

The majority of new businesses spawned each year are retail stores. These outlets are particularly vulnerable to failure due to the wrong location. Consequently, the subject of store location is treated here in more detail.

Success in a retail store depends to a large extent on the quantity and the quality of the traffic passing by. Most often this is pedestrian traffic, though in some cases, the number of passing automobiles and available parking facilities can be of vital significance. In addition to the need for sufficient space for the display and sale of merchandise and for work room and storage, consider these factors:

- The extent of the store's "trading area"
- The demographics of the population in the area (see "Demographic Segmentation" in chapter 3)
- The nature of the competition
- The compatibility of neighboring stores
- Parking facilities
- The availability of public transportation
- The volume of traffic (pedestrian and vehicular)
- The store building itself
- The storefront

In cities, you also need to weigh the benefits of a corner location against those of a spot within a block and determine whether you have selected the "right" side of the street.

THE TRADING AREA

If you plan to open a retail shop, become familiar with both the *trading area* concept and the various types of locations that are available to you. The trading area is the area surrounding a particular store (or group of stores) from which it draws most of its shoppers. For the average, small "in-city" shop that sells convenience goods and impulse items, the trading area may only extend for a few blocks in one or two directions and for even less in the other directions. The trading area can be far larger for a high-image specialty goods store that caters to an elite clientele. Discount houses, department stores, and the larger planned shopping centers may pull shoppers from many miles away.

TYPES OF RETAIL LOCATIONS

Let's consider the different kinds of shopping areas that make up the retail structure of a typical city. We may arbitrarily assign the various types into two categories: the older, in-city (and largely unplanned) retail areas and the newer, planned shopping centers. Those in the first category consist of the central business district (CBD), secondary business districts, neighborhood shopping streets, and a few other types.

The Central Business District This is the "downtown" or "center-city" section where a large number of stores are concentrated. Traditionally, the CBD is a bustling area with office buildings, banks, theaters, restaurants, and many types of retail stores. Sizable window frontage and floor space characterize these outlets. The main branches of department stores and large units of the major chains are usually found here, along with shops offering specialty merchandise and shopping goods (for which consumers are willing to expend time and effort in comparison shopping) as well as convenience items. Although the "downtown" sales picture has become bleaker over the years as the population mix in many cities has shifted to a less economically advantaged clientele, many locations in the central business district still enjoy brisk sales. Rents, however, have increased at a prodigious rate. This fact, along with the deteriorating "quality of life" in many of these sections, has lead many business owners to react negatively toward CBD locations.

Here and there across the country, though, we have seen some successful instances of revitalized downtown areas. Some notable examples are Hawthorne Plaza in Los Angeles, Faneuil Hall Marketplace in Boston, and Canal Place in New Orleans.

Secondary Business Districts   Found along the major arteries leading out of downtown districts, secondary business districts often present a more attractive situation than CBDs. Most cities have several of these sections; major metropolitan areas may have many more. Rents here, too, are comparatively high, but area residents favor these shopping areas because they can buy just about anything in this concentration of stores. Traffic can be quite heavy, especially during the afternoons and on Saturdays. As a retailer, don't be put off by a high rent—all too often low monthly rent means low monthly sales.

Neighborhood Shopping Streets   In most cities, there are a good number of areas where brisk retail sales are registered. Dependent for the most part on the density of residents in the vicinity, neighborhood shopping streets may extend from one or two city blocks in length to as many as eight or more. The typical shopping area presents a well-balanced assortment of store types: small branches of chain-store operations (supermarkets, variety stores, fast-food outlets); a liberal sprinkling of specialty stores; and a much larger number of shops that sell convenience merchandise. Here you find bakeries, hardware stores, dry cleaners, meat and fish stores, bars and luncheonettes, pharmacies, and shoe stores. Rents in the section are usually moderate. Business failures are relatively rare, and empty stores are quickly grabbed up.

Clusters and Freestanding Stores   Woven throughout the residential areas of large cities are numerous small clusters of shops. Generally, the stores are located on or near the corner of a single city block. You may also find an occasional freestanding retail outlet with its own parking facility. More often than not, this type of store is positioned at a major intersection or along a highway.

Planned Shopping Centers Often situated on the outskirts of cities and in the suburbs are the relatively new retail developments—the so-called *planned shopping centers*. Three distinct types of these store groupings can be seen: the neighborhood, community, and regional shopping centers.

Neighborhood Centers The smallest of the three types is the *neighborhood shopping center*. It usually consists of a row of stores, which complement each other. For this reason, it's also known as a *strip center* (or *strip mall*), even though many of them have been erected in the shape of an L or a U. Frequently, its main attraction (or *anchor store*) is a supermarket or large drugstore. Parking space is available for a limited number of automobiles. When situated in areas that are still being built up, neighborhood center locations can be attractive for many types of retail businesses. Their drawing power generally extends for a few miles around.

Community Shopping Centers The trading area of the *community shopping center* is much larger. There may be twenty or thirty stores in the center and parking for hundreds of cars. Often, the cornerstone retailer is a junior department or discount store of the KMart or Wal-Mart type.

Regional Centers Today's typical *regional shopping center* is a huge, one-stop shopping complex thirty to fifty or more acres in size. It contains department store branches, restaurants, banks, theaters, chain-store units, and independent retailers. Here, consumers are able to shop in a leisurely fashion for merchandise and services of just about every conceivable kind—from impulse products and convenience items to shopping goods and specialty merchandise. This type of center draws shoppers from villages and towns as far as an hour away by car. Often, its parking facilities can handle a thousand or more vehicles.

These locations have their good and bad points. If you rent a store in a shopping center, you're assured of some customers, especially in the evenings and on Saturdays. The majority of shoppers are, of course, attracted by the department store(s). Many, however, like to stroll through the rows of other stores in the mall. Consumers enjoy the frequent shows, demonstrations, exhibits, and other public relations gestures put on by the shopping center association. The general atmosphere, the security, maintenance, and group sales promotions are all typically well managed. However, as a tenant, you're limited in your display and promotion approaches. Many centers, for example, don't permit a retailer to display a banner on the surface of the store window. You might be compelled to keep your store open in accordance with the shopping center's hours, even on days—or at times—when you do very little business and can't really afford to keep on help. You'll also be required to join the mall association and pay your proportion of the dues.

If you're considering a shopping-center location, you should visit a number of centers and talk to various store owners. Discuss the pros and cons with real-estate people before deciding on this type of location. Keep in mind, too, that the location *within* the shopping center can be especially important to the success of a retail store.

A PLAN FOR CHOOSING YOUR LOCATION

This section presents an organized, step-by-step procedure designed to widen your horizons and help you make your location decision. The plan presumes you'll conduct your location hunt at a leisurely pace. Above all, avoid the temptation to rush into business. Adopt a leisurely, investigative stance!

Here are the recommended steps:

1. Convince yourself that you should not limit your choice of location to any one area before taking this entire list into consideration.
2. Remind yourself that there are fifty states to choose from. (Trying your hand—and luck—in a foreign country might be more complicated than you would care to attempt at this stage of the game.)
3. Draw on your personal storehouse of information: What have friends, relatives, and coworkers told you about other places? What have you learned about the states from your own travels or through reading?
4. Narrow your thoughts down to two or three states where you would like to live and, specifically, where you feel an excellent opportunity exists for the type of business you have in mind.
5. Read everything you can about these states. Write away for information about the climate, the local economy, the per capita income, the characteristics of the population, and the industry. Try to narrow down your preferences to one state.
6. Next, survey the one state you have targeted for half a dozen areas that seem attractive. Preferably, these should be growing areas and places where the quality of life seems to jibe with your own values.

    For help at this point, you can contact the state development agency and city planning commissions, chambers of commerce, utility companies, and local banks. The latest

Census of Business also provides details about the types of businesses in those areas.

7. Now the difficult work begins. You'll need to carefully select criteria by which you can evaluate the various locations and make your final decision. Judging each location by this list enables you to rank them in order from "most promising" to "least promising" for your new enterprise.

   Read once more through the location factors treated in the first few pages of this chapter. Choose the criteria most appropriate for your particular business. Jot them down on a sheet of paper. You may be able to add one or two of your own that have not been listed. For example, you may decide that an important consideration for you is the quality of life in the particular community (in light of your personality, personal goals, and leisure-time preferences). Add the phrase *quality of life* to your list.

8. Prepare a chart like the one shown in exhibit 6–1 to rate or score the locations you're considering.

9. Use a simple rating scale: for example, a scale of 1 to 5, with 1 signifying a rating of "poor," as follows:

   1 Poor
   2 Fair
   3 Good
   4 Very good
   5 Excellent

   Take care to work out the rationale behind your ratings so you understand the numbers you use. For instance, in rating "Trading-area size," you would assign a 1 to a location with a limited trade area of one or two blocks around while an extensive area might earn a 4 or 5 rating. Where competition might interfere substantially with your business in a particular location, assign a score of 1; where competition is weak or nonexistent, give a rating of 5.

10. Now rate each of the possible locations, A, B, C, and so on, working on one criterion at a time. After all criteria have been considered, total up the columns. Obviously, the location with the highest score would be the one to select. Or, so it would seem. However, there is one more step to consider.

11. In any set of criteria, some are always more important than others to you. As an example, if you're contemplating opening a retail shop, the volume of pedestrian traffic that passes by is likely to be of great importance to your business success.

EXHIBIT 6–1. LOCATION RATING SHEET FOR A MANUFACTURING PLANT

			Alternative Locations:			
Criteria	A	B	C	D	E	F
Accessibility to transportation						
Availability of labor						
Proximity to company's markets						
Competition						
Cost factors						
Demographics of community						
Parking facilities						
Quality of life for me						
Quality of local services						
Trading-area size						

Source: Compiled by the author.

The demographics of the neighborhood (population mix, income characteristics) might be much more significant than many of the other criteria on your list. If so, some of the criteria ought to be *weighted* in order to take their relative importance into account.

To accomplish this, you would assign a weight factor of 2 or 3 to one or more of the criteria (depending on their value to you) and then multiply your earlier ratings by 2 or 3 across the various locations you're considering. According to the criteria you have selected and the assigned weightings you have given them, location D in exhibit 6–2 should be your first choice, locations E and C your second and third choices.

But you're still not ready to make your final decision. Once you have ranked the six locations, you then need to consider several other aspects, such as the comparative rents you'll have to pay for the three top locations, the availability of suitable living quarters for yourself in those areas, and local living costs. In other words, any one of the three might be a good choice; now you must narrow it down to the one location best suited to your needs.

EXHIBIT 6–2. WEIGHTED RATING SHEET FOR RETAIL LOCATIONS

Criteria	Weights	Alternative Locations					
		A	B	C	D	E	F
Competition	2	6	6	6	10	8	4
Demographics of community	3	6	3	9	12	3	9
Parking facilities	1	2	5	3	4	3	1
Quality of life for me	3	12	3	9	12	15	6
Space for future expansion	1	1	3	4	4	3	2
Trading-area size	1	3	3	1	2	4	3
Volume of traffic	3	9	3	9	12	6	12
Total Scores:		39	26	41	56	42	37

Source: Compiled by the author.

BUILD, RENT, OR BUY?

Having set your sights on the best location for your proposed business, you'll now face still another major decision area: Should you build, rent, or buy the facilities you need?

Here are just a few of the possibilities:

- There may not be a location readily available. In this case, you might consider buying out someone else's business.
- Premises—a building or a store—may indeed be available, either for rent or for sale. There's a good chance, however, that the premises may not be suitable for your purposes. A substantial and costly remodeling job might be necessary.
- If you're thinking about building, you may discover nothing more than a vacant lot (or small piece of land) obtainable in the area. This situation might require you to have suitable premises erected on the spot. Furthermore, time and cost factors must be weighed carefully.

TO BUILD OR NOT TO BUILD?

The ideal solution is to construct premises of the exact dimensions, type, architectural style, and materials that meet your every need, down to the most minute specification, with an exacting eye to the future and eventual expansion.

Among the advantages to this approach are a considerable depreciation allowance to help you curtail your tax liability each succeeding year; the benefit of being able to secure a mortgage on your property when you need to improve your cash position; and the delight of anticipating a probable, sizable capital gain when you finally dispose of the building, years later.

Of course, the big negative here is that you'll need to invest a significant chunk of capital at the very beginning. This is the time when you can least afford such an investment. There are also some real problem areas in constructing your own place of business. Experts and specialists must be consulted and closely involved every step along the way.

WHY NOT RENT?

Renting your business premises is comparatively easy on your firm's bank account. Other than the necessity of putting down a security deposit and paying one or two months' rent in advance, your capital remains relatively untapped. Moreover, with the help of your attorney and a cooperative landlord, you might arrange a favorable lease. As long as you continue to pay your rent regularly and live within the terms of your agreement, you'll have few problems and you'll avoid unnecessary headaches. Your landlord worries about paying insurance premiums; meeting property tax liabilities; and repairing, heating, or air conditioning the premises.

Yet, the fact that you remain a tenant does leave you vulnerable to some extent. When your lease expires, your landlord may opt for a sharp rise in your rent (unless you anticipated this situation in the wording of the original lease). You may even discover that you've lost the location to some other bidder, even though you may have built up the location over years of persistent effort.

SHOULD YOU BUY?

On the other hand, if you decide to purchase the property, some of the disadvantages of renting will be eliminated. You need not worry about losing the location or about an unexpected rent increase. You will have to take into account increases in real estate taxes as time goes by. Rising labor and maintenance costs can also put a dent in profits.

Although buying your premises necessitates a large initial investment, you can reap tax benefits through depreciation. And—as with building your own place—you can always mortgage the premises when you need cash or sell them for a healthy profit.

YOUR PREMISES—GENERAL CONSIDERATIONS

The style, construction, and overall external appearance of your business building are vital factors in the formulation, over time, of your "company image." A modern, well-maintained building has a far more favorable impact on customers, suppliers, and the general public than a seedy-looking façade.

Entrances and exits should be clearly indicated and kept free of litter. Walkways should be kept clean and in excellent repair. Lawns, hedges, and shrubbery must be kept neatly trimmed and healthy looking. If at all possible, steps should be avoided. Though they may be needed because of different levels between buildings and sidewalks, steps present a psychological barrier to many people. Naturally, an attractive place of business is important to the retail enterprise because it relies heavily on passersby.

THE INTERIOR

Visualize the inside of your premises as a well-lined box or series of boxes. Walls, ceilings, and floors need to be covered by paint or other materials.

Walls serve two functions: that of lending some support to the building itself and, more important, that of dividing the inside area into separate compartments for specific business activities, such as the offices and selling floor. Consequently, their thickness and composition are determined by both structural and acoustic factors. Any columns or pillars necessary to the building structure must remain intact; walls must be built around them, or else they must be incorporated into the walls.

With regard to ceilings, an attentive eye is needed for considerations like good acoustics, space requirements, and proper lighting. Low ceilings convey the impression of tight, confining quarters, which in turn can psychologically hamper employee productivity. On the other hand, high ceilings create an open, roomy environment.

Selecting proper lighting for the premises calls for the advice of a specialist. There are basically two types of lighting: fluorescent and incandescent. Both have advantages and disadvantages. Fluorescent lighting provides a high level of light intensity, does not generate much of a heat load in a room, and is relatively inexpensive in its consumption of electricity. Yet, colors often appear different under such lighting—a fact of considerable significance in a women's dress shop, for instance. Incandescent lighting, like the bulbs you burn in your table lamps at home, reveals warm, lifelike tones in clothing and other merchandise or when used to highlight special displays.

As to the flooring, consider its load-bearing capability (as in the case of a factory containing heavy machinery), its wearability, its resistance to chemicals, and nonskid surfaces to avoid accidents. Sometimes, leaving the floor totally uncovered may be more prudent. Or painting might be the solution, with a stone or cement floor in a plant or with a well-made wooden floor in a retail shop. Floor coverings range from linoleums and carpeting of many qualities and shades to an abundant variety of tiles and other materials.

SOME NOTES ON LAYOUT

In addition to the more obvious construction features mentioned above, premises planning must include staircases and stairwells, aisles, elevators, and conveyors, all of which facilitate the flow of people, supplies, and merchandise. Moreover, attention must be paid to plumbing, air conditioning, heating, and sanitary facilities as well.

The critical factor in setting up a business operation is the understanding that different activities must be performed under one roof. With regard to the proper layout of your premises, this means that internal layout is largely dictated by the functions to be performed. The natural temptation is to fulfill only your immediate requirements because space always seems to be at a premium. Forgo that temptation. Even at this early stage, good business administration looks to the future—and to growth. For this reason you should consider hiring, at the outset, the services of an architect experienced in your particular field of business.

FACTORIES AND WAREHOUSES

Most manufacturing plants and warehouses have certain activities in common. Special areas are usually needed for receiving incoming deliveries of materials (or merchandise) and supplies, for storage or stockkeeping, for performing office-type activities, and for shipping out goods. A factory must also incorporate space for production machinery and equipment, an area for cleaning materials and tools (a maintenance shop), and perhaps temperature-controlled rooms for certain types of materials or goods.

In the ideal factory or wholesaler's warehouse, activities are arranged in as straight a line as possible in order to minimize the flow of materials throughout. The receiving department should be at one end of the building, where the raw materials/finished products are brought in. Here, one or more bays are needed for trucks to draw up and unload. There should also be an unloading platform and a checking area where incoming deliveries can be checked off against their bills of lading. At the building's other end, one would expect to find the shipping department where, again, bays and loading platforms are required. In between the two ends, space should be allocated to the warehoused stock (and to machinery in the case of a factory), with special areas sectioned off for office work, machine shop, loading and handling equipment, and other necessary goods and activities.

An alternate layout might be the common U shape, where both shipping and receiving departments are located at the same end of the building. This setup enables the company to avail itself of a single (or double) bay and dock. In this type of layout, stocks and supplies are stored down the center of the U.

In the final analysis, the internal layout of a manufacturing plant depends heavily on the production flow pattern used: whether the firm employs job, batch, or mass production methods. The type of production approach determines how the machinery should be arranged.

RETAIL STORES

In the case of the retail store, layout becomes even more important because of its direct impact on sales. Again, function largely determines the internal arrangement and contents. At the same time, you should also strive to project not only a particular "store image" but also a "merchandising environment" that will contribute effectively to sales. Proper interior design and decor can be used to create the desired setting. Thus, we may find plush carpeting, rich wall colors, and expensive chandeliers in a high-quality shoe store—or a charming Oriental decor in a Japanese restaurant.

The larger portion of the premises is usually devoted to selling activities, with additional space for workrooms and storage. Among the more important considerations here are an ample entrance, aisles that comfortably permit customer traffic (and store merchandise) to flow freely, store fixtures and displays located for maximum shopper exposure, good lighting, and an attractive decor.

The entrance should open into an unobstructed view of the

selling area. Interior design often encompasses the *grid layout,* where in-store traffic is compelled to follow a prearranged path (often, one that calls for making right-angle turns) as shoppers pass more deeply into the store. This type of setup can be readily seen in a typical supermarket, self-service drugstore, or variety store. An example of the grid layout can be seen in exhibit 6–3.

Many retailers prefer this layout approach because it maximizes shopper exposure to many different products carried by the store.

Another possibility is the *free-form layout.* Here, no attempt is made to direct the flow of traffic. Shoppers can proceed in any direction. They are also able to pause easily in front of any one display for leisurely examination. Aesthetically, this type of layout is also more pleasing to consumers. Department boundaries are usually curved or irregular in shape, rather than straight, as is the case with the grid layout. (See exhibit 6–4.)

Some stores, of course, combine the basic elements of both approaches to layout.

EXHIBIT 6–3. A GRID LAYOUT

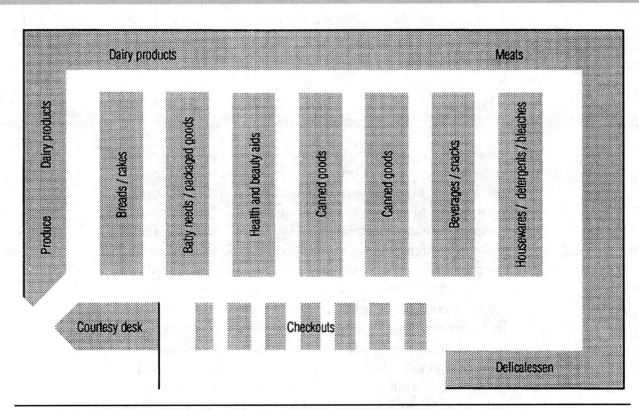

Source: Irving Burstiner, *Basic Retailing,* 2d ed. (Homewood, Ill.: Irwin, 1991), 301.

EXHIBIT 6–4. A FREE-FORM LAYOUT

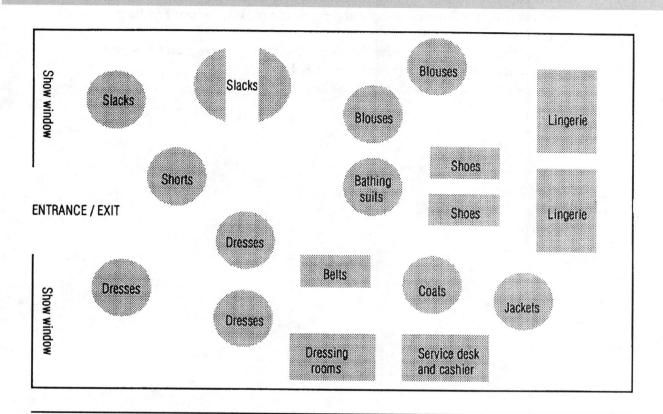

Source: Irving Burstiner, *Basic Retailing,* 2d ed. (Homewood, Ill.: Irwin, 1991), 303.

FOR FURTHER INFORMATION

Baarr, Vilma, and Charles E. Broudy. *Time-Saver Details for Retail Planning and Design.* New York: McGraw-Hill, 1994.

Burstiner, Irving. *Basic Retailing.* 2d ed. Homewood, Ill.: Irwin, 1991.

———. *How to Start and Run Your Own Retail Business.* New York: Citadel Press, 1994.

Fitch, Rodney. *Retail Design.* New York: Watson-Guptill, 1991.

Francis, Richard L., and John A. White. *Facility Layout and Location: An Analytical Approach.* 2d ed. Englewood Cliffs, N.J.: Prentice-Hall, 1991.

Ghosh, Avajit, and Sara L. McLafferty. *Location Strategies for Retail and Service Firms.* Lexington, Mass.: Lexington Books, 1987.

Green, William R. *The Retail Store: Design and Construction.* 2d ed. New York: Van Nostrand Reinhold, 1991.

Israel, Lawrence J. *Store Planning-Design: History, Theory, Process.* New York: Wiley, 1994.

Jones, Ken, and Jim Simons. *The Retail Environment.* Routledge, New York: Routledge, 1991.

Moffats, Donald W. *Plant Monitoring and Inspecting Handbook.* Englewood Cliffs, N.J.: Prentice-Hall, 1996.

Novak, Adolph. *Store Planning and Design.* Tampa, Fla.: Lebhar Friedman, 1977.

Sule, Dileep R. *Manufacturing Facilities: Location, Planning, and Design.* Boston, Mass.: PWS Publications, 1994.

Tompkins, James A., and John A. White. *Facilities Planning.* New York: Wiley, 1984.

MANAGING THE BUSINESS ORGANIZATION

7

BUSINESS ADMINISTRATION: AN INTRODUCTION

A VITAL COMPONENT of human rationality, which distinguishes humankind from the beast, is the faculty for making order out of chaos. People must organize innumerable pieces of knowledge into usable wholes in order to function effectively in their environment. Organizing involves arranging, classifying, and systematizing, as well as thinking and planning. These processes are characteristic of individuals and of groups. Every organization or institution reflects these processes because they are established and administered by human beings. Moreover, since people are so incredibly diverse, we find that their groupings and institutions reflect countless variations in both form and substance.

THIS BUSINESS OF BUSINESS

On a purely philosophical plane, it would seem that all living things are motivated by two basic goals: the programmed will to maintain their existence (to continue to live, to protect, to defend, and when necessary, to repair themselves) and the instinct to grow, to perpetuate their kind.

Plants, animals, the tiniest of microscopic organisms, and humans as well all possess these two essential motivations. Furthermore, all human groups display these same drives, whether they be families or social groups, religious denominations or political associations, small villages or sprawling nations.

A new business is just such a grouping, engaged in a purposeful activity and endowed with a spirit and vitality that stem from those built-in goals. It's a curious mixture of people, things, and activities. It's ideally so ordered, so arranged and woven into an intricate network, so purposeful and coordinated, that it's able to strive toward those two overriding objectives like a single, though complex, organism. Operating like a complicated piece of machinery, your new firm will be a system of individual pieces, parts, cogs, and wheels all working together toward a common endeavor: to continue its existence and to grow.

Every business is also a society in miniature with its own body of rules and regulations, its ways and customs. As in society at large, its "citizens" play out their assigned roles. A business is also a stratified—that is, a grouped and subgrouped—society that designates expected behavior for each person according to status, class, and other criteria.

To demonstrate this, think about the traditional department store organization with its hundreds of employees distributed throughout a hierarchy of power and authority. Top management includes the board of directors, its chairperson, and the corporation's president. Next is the operating management, generally a committee of assorted vice presidents heading up specialized functions of store operations, merchandising, personnel management, and others. Then there are various levels of middle and lower management including the merchandise managers, floor and department managers, buyers, salesclerks, and cashiers.

Within this society in miniature, there are two kinds of people: the leaders, who use their power and authority, skills and techniques to influence the others; and the rest, the larger number of helpers who collectively push the organization toward its objectives.

Yes, the structure and organization of your company will be integrated into a total master plan that you design to accomplish your goals. This network places people into niches, and each niche becomes a vital link in the overall effective operation of this dynamic system.

THE MEANING OF ADMINISTRATION

To administer any activity (or, for that matter, any business or institution) is to run it, to direct it, or, more simply, to manage it. From giant multinational corporations to tiny, one-person operations, *every* enterprise needs an astute administrator to direct and integrate all the components—the people, the equipment, the practices and techniques applied in daily functioning, the financial aspects, and so forth.

The words *administrator, executive, leader,* and *manager* all connote similar basic work.

With relation to your business, *you* are the administrator, the directing force. To administer your business successfully, you'll find that you must be continually exercising one or more of the four managerial functions: *planning, organizing, directing,* and *controlling.*

Over the next few pages, all four functions are discussed in some detail.

PLANNING

Effective management necessarily begins with planning, which in turn implies goal-setting. Planning is the most important function of all in establishing and maintaining a business. Planning is hard work, no doubt about it. It involves thinking, and thinking is always hard work. In essence, planning is problem solving and decision making: speculating on the future (both near and far), setting objectives (long- and short-term), considering alternatives, and making choices. Planning calls for sufficient flexibility for coping with the unexpected, setting timetables, fixing priorities, and deciding methods to be used and the people who will be involved. As administrator you must analyze the existing situation, formulate targets, and apply both logic and creativity to all the details in between.

Owners of small-scale enterprises are typically so busy running their operations that they often shunt planning to the sidelines. Yet, its importance cannot be overemphasized! As the owner of a small business, you *must* plan for it even more intensively than the head of a large corporation because you don't have the large financial resources to cover a serious mistake. Poor planning can put you out of business.

A list of preliminary planning activities for small-business managers appears in exhibit 7–1.

TYPES OF PLANS

Long-term and *master* plans are set up by top management to give overall direction to company efforts. Strategic in nature, long-term plans are needed to cope with an ever-changing environment. *Operational* plans design day-to-day work details. *Single-use* plans are formulated for specific situations. *Standing* plans, on the other hand, are set up for repeated use over a longer period of time.

Company policies are examples of standing plans. They serve as guidelines for management and employees, imparting a solidarity and dependability to company operations. These policies exist in all areas of a well-administered business: in production, pricing, distribution, personnel, and finance. To illustrate, consider these few examples of production policies:

- We shall manufacture only those products that enjoy a brisk sales volume (that is, over 10,000 units a month).
- We intend to add to the product line up to three new items each year.
- We shall produce only items requiring raw materials that can be purchased domestically (or from several different sources).

Budgets are plans that have been translated into dollars-and-cents projections and that are the culmination of a great deal of careful analysis. In effect, they're both guides to follow and targets to shoot for. Materials budgets, sales budgets, labor budgets, and budgets for capital expenditures—all become standards for management action. Good budgeting is needed to direct internal activity and to assign responsibility.

For more information about planning, see exhibit 7–2.

SOME COMMENTS ON FORECASTING

Planning is disciplined thinking, which is based on the present and oriented to the future. Plans begin with an analysis of the way things are and with a forecast of the way things will (or should) be. Of course, predicting future events based on an extrapolation of current—and incomplete—information can never be entirely accurate.

Begin any major forecasting effort with a full consideration of the general state of the economy. Then move down to the next level

EXHIBIT 7–1. AN INTRODUCTION TO PLANNING FOR THE SMALL-BUSINESS MANAGER

1. Explore diligently your firm's "mission," or raison d'être, and clarify the purposes for which you have established it.
2. After careful discussion of these purposes, formulate your overall, long-term company goals.
3. Examine these goals one by one, and then make a list of specific objectives to be accomplished over, say, the next five years.
4. Designate specific goals for each subdivision within your firm (such as marketing, production, finance, and personnel).
5. Decide on policies for each department, making sure they conform to those objectives.
6. Finally, outline strategies for reaching the objectives, using the available company resources.

Source: Compiled by the author.

and appraise conditions within the industry of which your firm is a member. After that, evaluate the state of the company itself.

Among the variables affecting your forecast are such uncontrollable factors as the Gross National Product (present and future), employment and unemployment levels, productivity indexes, population trends, and government policies. When you make predictions, watch the various business indicators and project accordingly: stock prices, corporate profits, wholesale price levels, and others.

You should not only use such indexes and study trends but also gather opinions and interpretations from other people. You must also exercise personal judgment; for example, when you make projections for next year's sales, you should not only use the available statistics but also evaluate the capabilities of your sales force and sales manager.

EXHIBIT 7–2. A STEP-BY-STEP APPROACH TO PLANNING

Using the outline offered below, plan for two or three separate events; this exercise will help you internalize the method rapidly. Practice, after all, makes perfect! It's helpful to plan for something concrete the first time around, such as a major promotion for the spring.

1. Assess the present state of affairs, external (the economy, your competition) as well as internal.
2. Set the target date for the activation of the plan.
3. Make a forecast of the future state of affairs (at the target date and thereafter, for the duration of the plan-to-be).
4. List specific objectives that are both reasonable and attainable.
5. Develop methods for reaching the objectives.
6. Work out the details by using the "Five Ws" (who, what, where, when, why, and how). Determine your resources and structure your plan with a time schedule.
7. Commit the details to paper.
8. Set up a control system to monitor the plan's operation and make adjustments for deviations from planned outcomes.
9. As the plan unfolds, make the necessary changes to compensate for such deviations.

Source: Compiled by the author.

ORGANIZING YOUR ORGANIZATION

As your business grows, you'll discover that along with increasing volume come additional duties and responsibilities. Eventually, you'll reach the point where you have to seek assistance so you can allocate your energies and time more beneficially to your business.

At that point, the seeds of your new organization have sprouted. Now you must pay heed to management principles like *specialization* and the *division of work*.

As each new employee is hired, he or she must be placed in an appropriate niche and assigned a specific set of duties. As the business administrator, your task is to define those niches and then locate the right people to fill them. Essentially, you must match people with jobs.

Figure 7–1, for example, describes some of the activities that need to be performed in a small retail business in its preorganization or one-person-operation stage. According to this chart, the owner must allocate time to three activity areas: buying, selling, and controlling finances. In addition, however, each work cluster or category involves a number of specific tasks. Buying merchandise for resale, for example, would include seeking out and visiting sources of supply, viewing potential items to carry in the store, negotiating prices and terms, and arranging for delivery.

FIGURE 7–1. Organization Chart for a One-Person Retail Business

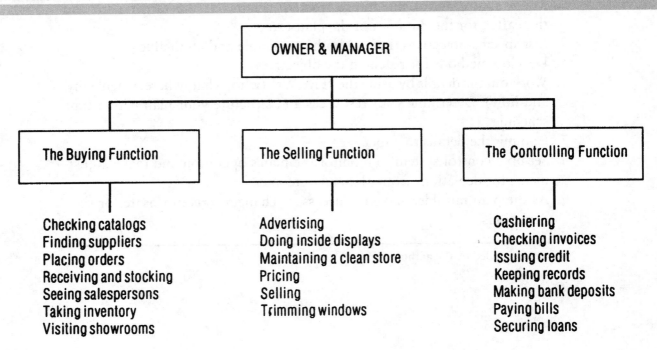

At first, all these necessary functions are performed by one individual. Then, as sales increase, there's more work to be done. When the first employee, or helper, is hired, business owners are inclined to delegate very few tasks. They won't permit the newcomer to do the buying, for example, simply because experience is needed before a person can do the purchasing job well. Moreover, buying the right goods at the right prices is a major factor in the firm's profit picture, and an owner is understandably reluctant to relinquish control over this vital area.

For similar reasons, the entrepreneur usually resists turning over any of the major financial aspects of the business to the new employee. So, in most cases the employee in the typical small store is assigned to the selling function, thus affording the proprietor more time to do a better job at both purchasing and controlling finances.

The chart in figure 7–2 depicts the work responsibilities of a small retail company with four employees. A breakdown of the functions that may be seen in a growing manufacturing enterprise is shown in figure 7–3.

FIGURE 7–2. ORGANIZATION CHART FOR A SMALL, GROWING RETAIL FIRM

Owner can now devote more time to the buying and control functions. In addition, he or she must now oversee all the employees. The owner begins to rely more heavily upon the first employee to train and supervise the others.

FIGURE 7–3. ORGANIZATION CHART FOR A SMALL, GROWING MANUFACTURING COMPANY

Over time, a company's management is increasingly challenged by the task of coordinating the activities of daily operations. Each business depends on the people within who, interlocked and strategically deployed in some structural arrangement, perform all the functions necessary for the total system to accomplish its objectives. This framework or structure called *organization* represents, in actuality, the overall strategic design for operating the business. A positive, forward-looking structure, it is a unified plan of action.

SOME BASICS FROM ORGANIZATION THEORY

Organization is not and cannot be an exact science; theories of organization cannot specify wholly "right" answers. Nevertheless, the small business manager ought to be familiar with the dimensions that are most frequently discussed by organizational theorists. Some examples are conflict between individual and organizational goals, departmentalization, line and staff positions, flat versus tall organizations, and unity of command.

Employee Goals Can Be at Odds with Company Goals You should recognize at the outset that people working in your organization are there primarily to satisfy their own needs. Perhaps they want security and income or the feeling that they have a place within a group; or they need to be recognized as somebody important. Although they'll work willingly toward your firm's objectives, this will happen only if their personal aims remain attainable through employment with you. Their goals and yours are not identical; at times, differences between individual and group goals will result in conflict. For the sake of internal harmony, you must concentrate on reconciling any differences that arise.

The Need for Departmentalization As anyone in business knows, a wealth of activities needs to be performed by your employees. Handling these myriad tasks is made easier by classifying the many work details into departments. Departments are segments of the business whose work functions are interrelated and can be grouped together under the supervision of a single specialist. In addition to the sales, production, and bookkeeping departments, other departments commonly seen in business include purchasing, shipping, receiving, payroll, and advertising.

Line and Staff Personnel Most organizations have been arranged according to the *line-and-staff* concept. Line people both give and receive orders along the chain of command from the head of the company down to the lowest-level worker. People in staff positions, on the other hand, are outside this chain of command. They are present to aid and support the line personnel. Examples of these staffers include administrative assistants, legal advisers, personnel department employees, and other supportive service workers. These people possess a much more limited kind of authority. Within their own specialized areas of responsibility, of course, they direct their own department personnel.

Should Your Organization Be Flat or Tall? As a business grows, the organizational structure shows layers of authority: top, middle, and lower (supervisory) management. Communication barriers tend to form between the layers. People at the top of the hierarchy tend to have little contact with people at the bottom. In the traditional "tall" structure, people become relatively confined within their own specialized positions, and dissatisfaction begins to emerge from persons in middle and lower positions. Broadly interpreted, their feeling is that they're not really making a significant contribution to the business. This attitude spreads or deepens, and more and more decisions tend to be made at the top and filtered down to the bottom levels.

Furthermore, management positions multiply. The organization gradually becomes laden with many chiefs and high salaries. A kind of rigidity sets in that mitigates against creative problem solving and results in an overabundance of red tape.

In the "flat" type of organization, on the other hand, there are only one or two levels of management. The supervisory leadership exercised by the executives is of a more personal nature, with more face-to-face contact. People in lower management niches take on more responsibility for their efforts and make more decisions. The fact that these individuals are closer to the action than higher management and are permitted to make decisions on the spot makes for increased initiative and higher morale.

One Boss or More? The *unity of command* principle is one policy that should seldom be violated. Most workers would agree that no employee, indeed no executive, should have to answer to more than one superior. Having more than one supervisor can cause confusion as, for example, when an employee working within a partnership arrangement is given two opposing directives by the partners.

How Many Subordinates Can You Handle? The principle here is referred to as *span of management* (or *span of control*). The average manager finds it relatively easy to oversee one to several workers on the job: to watch over them, train them, direct them, and guide them. As the number of subordinates increases, it becomes more and more difficult for the supervisor to devote enough attention to each person.

How many people a supervisor can oversee depends on several factors: the supervisor's capabilities; the abilities and characteristics of the subordinates; and the nature of the work being performed. The greater the span of management (that is, the number of individuals under one superior), the fewer the number of supervisors and departments necessary. A narrow span, however, enables supervisors to work more closely with their people.

The average small business owner can often manage up to six or eight subordinates before things become too unwieldy.

Decentralization As a business grows, the mass of work details increases. Yet it's hard for the entrepreneurial personality to delegate, let go of the responsibilities so far handled alone, and assign them to people he or she fears are less capable and less motivated!

Some managers keep a firm grasp on everything. They maintain home offices where power, authority, and tight supervisory controls are centralized. Others decentralize to the point where a capable group, to a large degree autonomous, manages each major division of the business. This concept of decentralization—organizing a firm around self-governing "profit centers" banded together in a loosely controlled federation—maximizes individual initiative, ensures localized decision making, and facilitates the pinpointing of responsibility.

DIRECTING

After you've prepared the plan and organized the necessary components (personnel, finances, methods and procedures, and materials), you're ready to put the plan into action and direct it. Directing really tests the mettle of the operating executive. This is the "hands-on" point. Until now the administrative activity has been mostly in the mind of the planner(s). Now you're involved in a one-to-one "contact sport." The people in your organization must be motivated, persuaded, led, coordinated, and encouraged. Involved here are concepts like teamwork, supervision, and productivity. For the most part, these concepts constitute the subject matter of chapter 8, so little more needs to be said about them at this point.

CONTROLLING

An analysis of the controlling function would seem to indicate the need for measuring results all along the way while the plan is unfolding, as well as the necessity for making adjustments where and when needed. Logically, the control function cannot be separated from the planning function; they are interdependent, much like the two sides of the same coin.

Controlling is a process that includes analysis, setting standards, monitoring, securing feedback, and taking corrective action. (See figure 7–4.)

1. *Analysis* Study and compare, for quantity and quality, the output of people and machines, the products made, the systems employed, and so forth. Examine everything with a careful eye to standards and decision making.
2. *Setting Standards* As a result of analysis, establish acceptable standards of performance in all areas. In turn, these standards become control valves, quantitative and qualitative measurements for future performance, guidelines for projecting cost, time, and sales.

FIGURE 7–4. CONTROLLING: THE PROCESS

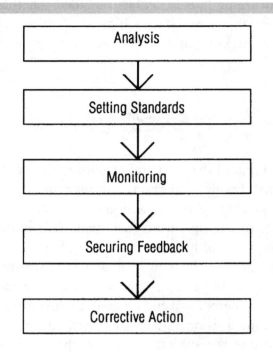

3. *Monitoring*   You need regular inspection and performance checks to note exceptions to the standards you've set and possible reasons for the deviations.
4. *Securing Feedback*   A foolproof system for reporting deviations from standards must be established so that the proper people are notified regularly and promptly.
5. *Corrective Action*   Finally, all exceptions to the established standards must be acted on. Adjustments need to be made promptly so that contingent outcomes are brought back on target.

All areas of a business must be subject to this control function. You might think quite readily of inventory control, order processing, quality control, and production control. Yet controls are just as necessary in the personnel area (for example, in performance evaluation), in the financial end of things (where ratios can be used to investigate a variety of problems), and in the long-term planning of projects.

Control is, in essence, self-discipline.

THE ROLE OF COMMUNICATION

Businesses run on communication. Prospective customers are located, contacted, and persuaded to buy products and services through communication. Similarly, employees are found, hired, trained, and directed; departments are managed; machines are manned and operated. Communication is the oil that lubricates the various gears and cogs in the free-enterprise system.

Let's examine the process of communication in business. There are a number of components involved. Indeed, communication in business appears to be a closed system with all parts interacting in synergistic fashion. The major elements may be seen in figure 7–5, which simplifies a company's external communications with its customers.

Some essential parts of the communication system are:

- *Source:* the sender or originator of the messages
- *Messages:* information emitted by the source and directed to the receivers
- *Media:* the various carriers or transmitters of the messages (such as radio, newspapers, billboards)
- *Receivers:* those for whom the messages are intended
- *Feedback:* customer reactions, demographic information, and other facts returned by or drawn back from customers to assist management in its decision making

FIGURE 7–5. EXTERNAL COMMUNICATIONS DIAGRAM

Improvements within any of these areas—for example, in the quality of messages sent or the refinement or elaboration of the feedback process—affect the productivity of the entire communication system.

Applied to a firm's internal organization, the communications picture looks something like the diagram in figure 7–6. Messages (orders and instructions) are passed down from the top to lower levels, through verbal and written communications. Feedback moves upward, completing the system. Of course, the effectiveness of this internal system also depends on unimpeded horizontal communication on each individual level.

Unfortunately, poor communication is commonly observed within organizations, perhaps due to the pressures of day-to-day details, which often make communicating on a one-to-one, face-to-face basis nearly impossible.

As a business owner, you should make certain that all messages to employees are couched in terms that can be clearly understood and that convey your (or your supervisors') exact meaning. To accomplish this, learn to look at things from the employees' point of view and become familiar with their vocabulary. Moreover, good listening skills constitute an important asset in communication; half-hearted listening interferes considerably with effective management. Encourage your employees to listen, too. Make sure they understand your instructions and encourage them to ask questions.

As a final point, train all your supervisory personnel to be effective communicators, too.

FIGURE 7–6. INTERNAL COMMUNICATIONS DIAGRAM

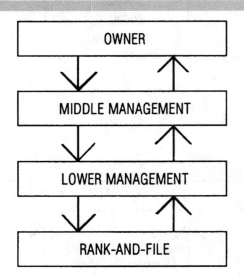

FOR FURTHER INFORMATION

Adelstein, Michael E., and W. Keats Sparrow. *Business Communications*. 2d ed. San Diego, Calif.: Harcourt Brace Jovanovich, 1983.

Aldag, Ramon J., and Timothy M. Stearns. *Management*. 2d ed. Cincinnati: South-Western, 1991.

Catt, Stephen E., and Donald S. Miller. *Supervision: Working with People*. 2d ed. Homewood, Ill.: Irwin, 1991.

Cohen, Allan R. *The Portable MBA in Management*. New York: Wiley, 1993.

DuBrin, Andrew J., and R. Duane Ireland. *Management and Organization*. 2d ed. Cincinnati: South-Western, 1993.

Harcourt, Jules, and A. C. "Buddy" Krizan. *Business Communication*. 2d ed. Cincinnati: South-Western, 1991.

Hodgetts, Richard M., and Donald F. Kuratko. *Management*. 3rd ed. San Diego, Calif.: Harcourt Brace Jovanovich, 1991.

Holton, Bill, and Cher Holton. *The Manager's Short Course*. New York: Wiley, 1992.

Schmidt, Wallace V., and Greg H. Gardner. *Business and Professional Communication*. Cincinnati: South-Western, 1995.

Stoner, James, and R. Edward Freeman. *Management*. 5th ed. Englewood Cliffs, N.J.: Prentice-Hall, 1991.

8

THE MANAGEMENT OF HUMAN RESOURCES

IN THE BEGINNING, the prudent entrepreneur operates alone, perhaps with the assistance of one or two family members. New business owners are usually apprehensive about adding employees, realizing that to do so would add substantially to the overhead costs that they are trying so hard to hold down. Indeed, when the situation finally does demand additional help, often the entrepreneur's immediate reaction is to hire part-timers.

Employees are, of course, a major resource of a firm. Hiring the right people—and training them well—can often mean the difference between scratching out the barest of livelihoods and steady business growth.

Incidentally, personnel problems do not discriminate between small and big business. You find them in all businesses, regardless of size. Usually, new entrepreneurs have had little prior experience with any personnel activities. Staffing, for example, is often done on the combined bases of personal judgment and intuition. New business owners have also probably had little exposure to good supervisory practices unless, by chance, they were fortunate enough to have worked under an excellent supervisor in some past position. Most likely, they're totally unfamiliar with such things as personnel record-keeping, labor legislation, and union relations (from an employer's point of view). Figure 8–1 offers a basic overview of the modern personnel function.

FIGURE 8–1. ACTIVITIES IN THE PERSONNEL-ADMINISTRATION AREA

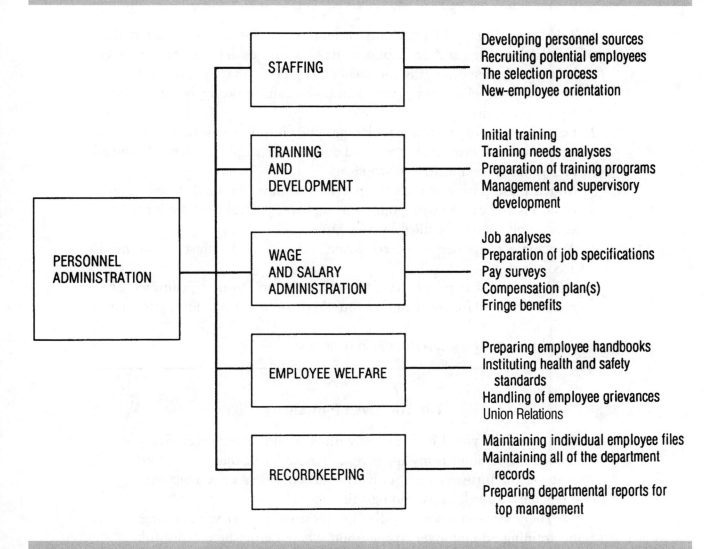

HUMAN RESOURCES PLANNING FOR THE SMALL COMPANY

Like any other phase of your business, the human resources dimension requires your top management skills. You need to set goals, plan, and organize. At the heart of your personnel planning will lie considerations such as how to allocate your human resources to maximum advantage and how to control total labor costs.

When the firm is new and small, there's little immediate need for long-range thinking about personnel. Add people slowly, at least for the first year or so of operation. Thereafter, as soon as you can, you should devise a system for human-resources planning (HRP). (See exhibit 8–1.)

EXHIBIT 8–1. IMPLEMENTING A HUMAN-RESOURCES PLANNING PROGRAM

1. Take an inventory of your current employees. Set down on paper their present job titles and descriptions. Review and assess past performance, listing both their strengths and weaknesses. (This analysis can help you to identify those who show promise and who can, someday, be promoted to higher positions.)
2. Determine the organizational changes your business will require over the next few years. Project the types and numbers of people you'll need to fill all niches in the organizational structure.
3. Match these positions with the people you have on hand. Decide which positions you can fill with your own employees (when the time is ripe) and which will have to be filled by new hires.
4. Anticipate some degree of employee turnover and adjust future needs accordingly.
5. Bear in mind that people have to be "phased in" to new positions. They must be trained for some time before they can be expected to perform at a satisfactory level.
6. At all times, keep a careful watch over costs.

THE TURNOVER PROBLEM

One fact of life you'll have to live with is employee turnover. Every business has it. Some firms lose people at a faster rate than others, but whatever the turnover rate, it always hurts to lose a good employee (financially, as well as psychologically).

There are initial costs involved in locating, interviewing, hiring, and training an employee to the point where he or she reaches full potential. Then, there are intermediate costs of doing without that person until a replacement is found. Still more expenses are incurred in acquiring the replacement.

People leave their jobs for a variety of reasons. Some leave unexpectedly and for unavoidable reasons: ill health, death, marriage, relocation, and deliberate terminations for due cause. Some losses are avoidable. They may be caused by poor supervisory practices on the part of owners or middle managers, by internal friction and personality clashes, or by management's failure to provide proper incentives or opportunities to move up the ladder.

When any employee leaves, an exit interview should be conducted and the results recorded. A review of the findings will be useful to management in taking corrective action to reduce the turnover rate. This step becomes more valuable as the company grows.

SETTING PERSONNEL POLICIES

Few small enterprises can afford even a fledgling personnel department during the first few years of business operation. Nevertheless, a large mass of personnel forms and data generally accumulates rather rapidly from the very beginning. To hold problems to a minimum, specific personnel policies should be established as early as possible. These become useful guides in all areas: recruitment and selection, compensation plan and employee benefits, training, and promotions and terminations. All attendant systems and paperwork should be carefully designed and personnel files set up to hold application forms, testing and medical records, evaluation forms, changes in status, and so forth.

One practical activity that can help in setting policy is the preparation of job descriptions for all positions in your firm. Analyze each position in detail and then set down on paper the specific job title, the duties and responsibilities assigned, the relationships with other segments of the business, and any other relevant details. (This information will help you write up job specifications for every opening that comes up.) In addition to the information already mentioned, add the special qualifications needed by the jobholder, such as the levels of education and experience required, familiarity with special equipment, minimum physical requirements (if these are pertinent), and so on.

A sample job description can be seen in exhibit 8–2.

THE STAFFING PROCESS

Broadly interpreted, the staffing process includes any activities pertinent to the recruitment and selection of employees. Pinning down details and correct procedures in advance prevents errors later on that can cause trouble and expense.

PERSONNEL SOURCES

You need to explore and develop the potential of a variety of sources for future employees. Here's a listing of the more common avenues for you to pursue:

- Advertising through classified and display advertisements in newspapers, radio advertising

EXHIBIT 8–2.   A SAMPLE JOB DESCRIPTION

JOB TITLE:	SERVICE AND SAFETY SUPERVISOR		
DIVISION:	Plastics	D.O.T. CODE:	889.133–010
DEPARTMENT:	Manufacturing	EEO-1 AAP CATEGORIES:	1/2
SOURCE(S):	John Doe	WAGE CATEGORY:	Exempt
JOB ANALYST:	John Smith	VERIFIED BY:	Bill Johnson
DATA ANALYZED:	5/26/83	DATE VERIFIED:	6/5/83

JOB SUMMARY

The SERVICE AND SAFETY SUPERVISOR works under the direction of the IMPREGNATING & LAMINATING MANAGER: **schedules** labor pool employees; **supervises** work of gardeners, cleaners, waste disposal and plant security personnel; **coordinates** plant safety programs; **maintains** daily records on personnel, equipment, and scrap.

JOB DUTIES AND RESPONSIBILITIES

1. **Schedules** labor pool employees to provide relief personnel for all manufacturing departments: **prepares** assignment schedules and **assigns** individuals to departments based on routine as well as special needs in order to maintain adequate labor levels throughout the plant; **notifies** Industrial Relations Department weekly about vacation and layoff status of labor pool employees, contractual disputes, and other employment-related developments.

2. **Supervises** the work of gardeners, cleaners, waste disposal and plant security personnel; **plans** yard, clean-up, and security activities based on weekly determination of needs; **assigns** tasks and responsibilities to employees on a daily basis; **monitors** progress or status of assigned tasks; **disciplines** employees as necessary in accordance with labor contracts.

3. **Coordinates** plant safety programs: **teaches** basic first-aid procedures to security, supervisory, and lead personnel in order to maintain adequate coverage of medical emergencies; **trains** employees in fire fighting and hazardous materials handling procedures; **verifies** plant compliance with new or changing OSHA regulations; **represents** division during company-wide safety programs and meetings.

4. **Maintains** daily records on personnel, equipment, and scrap; **reports** amount of waste and scrap to cost accounting department; **updates** personnel records as necessary; **reviews** maintenance checklists for towmotors.

5. **Performs** other miscellaneous duties as assigned.

JOB REQUIREMENTS

1. Ability to apply basic principles and techniques of supervision.
   a) Knowledge of principles and techniques of supervision.

EXHIBIT 8–2. (continued)

   b) Ability to plan and organize the activities of others.
   c) Ability to get ideas accepted and to guide a group or individual to accomplish a task.
   d) Ability to modify leadership style and management approach to reach a goal.
2. Ability to express ideas clearly both in written and oral communications.
3. Knowledge of recent Red Cross first-aid procedures.
4. Knowledge of OSHA regulations as they affect plant operations.
5. Knowledge of labor pool jobs, company policies, and labor contracts.

MINIMUM QUALIFICATIONS

Twelve years of general education or equivalent, one year supervisory experience, and first-aid instructor's certification.

OR

Substitute 45 hours classroom supervisory training for supervisory experience.

JOB SPECIFICATIONS

1. KNOWLEDGE: Knowledge of supervisory principles/techniques; knowledge of first-aid procedures sufficient to teach others; familiarity with federal safety regulations.
2. Mental Application: Applies effective principles of supervision to direct and motivate employees.
3. Accountability: Directly supervises the work of up to 25 laborers and security personnel; responsible for insuring proper towmotor maintenance.

Source: "Job Descriptions Made Easy," Mark A. Jones, copyright 1984. Reprinted with permission of *Personal Journal,* Costa Mesa, CA. All rights reserved.

- Advertising through posted announcements, window signs, and other "point-of-need" methods
- Recommendations (referrals) from others: friends, employees, and acquaintances
- Schools and universities: vocational, academic, technical, business
- Employment agencies: public, private
- Agencies that provide temporary help
- People who just drop by or write in for positions
- Unions

THE SELECTION OF PERSONNEL

Among the tools available to help you decide who to hire and who to reject are the employment application, the employment interview, the reference check, tests, and the probationary or tryout period for new employees.

The Employment Application Ask prospective employees to complete an employment application. Standard application forms are available at your local business stationery store; they accommodate the applicant's name, address, telephone number, a history of prior work experiences, educational preparation, health and financial information, and personal data. Or, you can devise your own form by thinking through the kinds of information you need.

Generally, you can save both time and expense by using a preliminary *short-form,* or *screening,* application. This is a modified version of the larger application form, often a small, four-by-five-inch printed slip with room for only a few pertinent details: the applicant's name and address and the mandatory job specifications you've outlined in advance for a particular position. Assume, for instance, that you've run a classified ad in the local paper announcing a single opening at your place, and the ad draws twenty to twenty-five applicants. You can have them complete the shorter form quite easily since it only requires several minutes to fill out. You can then make a quick decision as to who does or does not have the qualifications you seek. This way you rapidly narrow down the crowd to just a few persons who can remain for interviews. If one of the requirements is, for example, two years of previous experience in a similar position, it's simple to accomplish this preselection quickly.

Short-form applications can also serve as a resource list for you; that is, a source of future employees if openings develop for which these individuals are more suited.

The Employment Interview An interview is usually the next step. The employment interview is one of the major tools in the processing of job applicants. Essentially, it has two aims: (1) to elicit information to supplement the facts submitted on the application form; and (2) to gain useful insights into the appearance, behavior, and personality of the prospective employee.

Because it's comparatively easy for an interviewer to be overly influenced by an outstanding characteristic of an applicant, it's wise to develop and use an interview rating form that touches on all important areas. This will help you objectify your assessment of an individual. Of course, the more you interview people—and the more you read about how to interview, in books on human resources administration—the better you'll be at it!

Interviews can be patterned and directive. This means you plan out your approach in advance—that is, the kinds of questions you intend to ask, the order in which you'll ask them, what in particular you'll be looking for, and so forth. Interviews can also be nondirective: Here, the basic approach is to refrain from doing much talking and to encourage the interviewee to speak at length.

Reference Checks   As a general rule, you should make it your business to check personally all references offered by job applicants. A simple form letter and questionnaire can be devised to cover the major points in which you are interested. Or you can contact former employers and other references by telephone. This method is often preferable, not only for quicker results but also because many people are reluctant to put negative comments down in writing. At times, telephone checking is useful in that any hesitancy about the person in question can be discerned quite readily and probed diplomatically during the conversation.

Tests   On the whole, most smaller companies do not test job applicants except when a position requires special skills. Measures of typing speed and accuracy (or stenographic skill), arithmetic and spelling tests for clerical employees, tests of manual dexterity for certain occupations, and demonstrations of ability to run specialized equipment (such as lathes) all come under this classification.

Some firms make use of a variety of paper-and-pencil tests to aid in their selection processes. These range from intelligence tests and general knowledge measures to personality batteries and tests of selling ability. These tests are expensive to use and are generally not recommended until a business has grown to a substantial size. Their most valuable contribution is probably in screening out applicants with personality defects or below-average intelligence.

However, many managements shy away from testing because of anxiety over conforming to the intent of equal employment opportunity laws. Tests used must be demonstrably both valid and reliable.

Medical Examinations   These can, of course, be helpful, especially where a position requires frequent physical effort. In some localities, such examinations are mandated by law. (Food handlers, for example, must be licensed.) However, when paid for by the employer, these tests can be quite expensive, especially if the number of employees is considerable.

Orientation   The first few days on the job are crucial to the newly hired person. This is when favorable or unfavorable work-related attitudes are formed and when the employee is either turned on or off. Of course, when you assign an individual to his or her section, you must make sure the person receives some initial instruction—namely, about the company itself, the particular department, and the nature of the work. In addition, it is helpful to appoint an experienced member of the department to coach the new employee.

In this same context, a well-prepared employee handbook can be extremely valuable. The Sample Table of Contents in exhibit 8–3 presents a range of topics that you could include in your firm's handbook.

Probationary Period Actually, the final phase of the selection process (once an individual has been assigned to a post) should be a probationary or tryout period of a few weeks or months. This trial period is a valuable step; it will ensure that you haven't made an erroneous decision. During this time, the new worker should be observed and frequently rated. It's far more difficult to discharge a below-average performer after many months have elapsed, especially if your company has been unionized.

TRAINING

The training function is a vital, ongoing activity that requires your attention as the owner of a small business. Employees need and want training not only to perform their jobs satisfactorily but also as preparation for eventual promotion. Indeed, you owe it to yourself even more than to your employees to make sure they are well trained. Proper training alleviates a good many unnecessary headaches.

Here are a few of the advantages that can result when people are well trained:

- Better employee morale
- Increased sales
- Less waste
- Lower turnover rate
- Increased productivity
- Reduced operational costs
- Speedier employee development

Often, a new employee receives adequate initial training but is thereafter expected to "go it alone." In a healthy business operation, training should be continuous. No clerical worker, salesperson, machine operator, or bookkeeper ever attains 100 percent efficiency or output at his or her job; there's always room for improvement. Moreover, every worker should have the opportunity to move up the ladder; this implies training for a new and higher position. Frankly, there's a substantial difference between satisfactory performance and performance that is outstanding. We're not necessarily talking here about a 5 or 10 percent difference; in some cases, productivity can be doubled or even tripled. As a case in point, there are always a few star performers in any sizable sales force who far outstrip the others in the production of sales.

EXHIBIT 8–3. A SAMPLE TABLE OF CONTENTS FOR AN EMPLOYEE HANDBOOK

EMPLOYEE HANDBOOK

SAMPLE TABLE OF CONTENTS

EXHIBIT 8–3. (continued)

Employee Purchases
Company Cafeteria
Monthly Magazine
Annual Outing
Bowling League
Baseball Team

8. INDEX *or* TABLE OF CONTENTS

Reproduced from "Pointers on Preparing an Employee Handbook," *Management Aid No. 197* (Washington, D.C.: Small Business Administration, 1975), 3.

In a small new enterprise, most training occurs on the job; that is, the immediate supervisor is held responsible for training the worker. But as a business grows, the need for more thorough and professional training becomes evident. It's never too early to begin making plans for better training in the future, if only to fill additional niches as they open up in the organizational hierarchy. This is preferable to hiring supervisors and managers from the outside, usually at a higher cost.

A careful *needs analysis* of your organization and all the people in it should be the first step in coordinating your training efforts.

TRAINING METHODS AND TECHNIQUES

A wide variety of training methods and techniques are available for your purposes. Among the more frequently used approaches are lectures, small group discussions, seminars, conferences, case analyses, programmed instruction, committee work, and role-playing. Of course, the most commonly found method is on-the-job training; variations of this approach include apprenticeships and internships.

For employees pegged for eventual promotion to management levels, there are still other useful techniques: job rotation, in-basket methods (exercises to help one learn how to set priorities among various tasks), special project assignments, management games, sensitivity training, and outside training (at local universities or by trade associations).

WAGE AND SALARY ADMINISTRATION

Wage and salary administration is another significant segment within the human resources management sphere. This area involves setting up and then overseeing the operation of a comprehensive compensation plan to cover all of your employees.

An employee's pay depends, of course, on the levels of education and experience, the skills, and the knowledge needed to do the job. In a large organization, all positions are generally grouped according to different types and levels of work and then arranged in a hierarchy according to levels of authority and responsibility. The jobs are then compared to similar positions in the particular industry. Pay scales are then set at the average prevailing rates for those positions. In a new small business, however, the prevalent approach is simply to "meet the competition" (which, if you think about it, is much the same thing).

As we know, people do expect to earn more over time. Every worker wants an occasional raise. It's therefore a good idea to establish a fixed compensation range for each and every position in the company—that is, a *minimum,* or *starting rate,* and a *maximum* (or *cap*). It is also helpful to initiate a personnel evaluation program whereby all employees are reviewed periodically and pay increases are contingent on satisfactory performance.

COMPENSATING EMPLOYEES

To pay your employees, you can choose from the three basic compensation plans commonly seen in industry: the regular (or "straight") salary approach, the commission-only plan, and the combination plan.

Regular Salary Plan   This is by far the most popular compensation approach. Under this plan, you pay the employee a stated amount each and every week (or on some other regular basis). Most employees like this kind of arrangement because they appreciate the sense of security derived from a steady income to pay for their food, rent, and other bills.

Management, too, usually prefers the regular salary plan because of its simplicity and because it enables them to know their labor costs in advance and budget accordingly. On the negative side, paying a steady salary does little to encourage above-average effort. When a person's salary remains the same regardless of the amount of work performed (or sales produced), there obviously exists little incentive to try harder. (Of course, if an employee is *too* far under par, the possibility of losing the job does provide some motivation to work at an acceptable level!)

Commission-Only Plan Some companies follow the philosophy that their salespeople should be paid only if they deliver sales. Under the commission-only plan, the employee receives a specified percentage of the sales dollars he or she brings in. The rate of commission paid is dependent on (among other things) the type of industry and the nature of the selling job required.

The major advantage of the commission-only approach is that it provides a substantially high level of motivation for many sales employees. While sales costs tend to fluctuate with economic conditions and with productivity, paying more dollars in commission can only mean that the firm is earning higher profits simultaneously. Expressed as a percentage of the sales volume, this cost remains a constant.

Top sales producers seem to like this method. Indeed, many of them do not want to work on any other basis. Of course, there are drawbacks to be considered as well. When earnings depend entirely on sales productivity, people on a commission-only basis sometimes tend to sell more aggressively, possibly generating unfavorable customer reactions. Under this plan, too, a company may find it more difficult to get its sales representatives to perform other necessary, nonselling activities.

A variation of the commission-only approach is the *guaranteed-draw-against-commission* approach. Under this compensation method, the firm is willing to advance several hundreds of dollars each week to a salesperson as an advance against future commissions in order to meet daily expenses.

Combination Plans These plans are designed to incorporate the more desirable features (from management's point of view) of both the regular salary and the commission-only approaches, in an attempt to have the best of both worlds. Although there are a number of variations, the most common is the *salary-plus-commission* method: The company furnishes a basic, steady salary each week that is designed to meet the employee's needs, and then a small percentage of actual sales is earned as a commission. Often, this latter amount is paid monthly. This combination approach guarantees the salesperson some funds for paying current expenses and provides some type of override that will induce the employee to try harder.

FRINGE BENEFITS

All the "extras" that firms have added to the basic compensation of their employees over the years amount to a sizable cost factor today. For the average company, these financial "fringe benefits," which are now expected by employees, can add another 30 percent or more to wages and salaries. (Note that we're not discussing those costs required by law, such as the firm's contribution to the Social Security system.) Small firms are cautioned against adopting these fringe benefits too quickly and too freely. Some are almost mandatory if an organization is to compete effectively for personnel against other firms in the industry. Other fringe benefits, while perhaps desirable, should be postponed until the company is in a strong, healthy position.

Some of these benefits are listed below, in no particular order:

vacation with pay	health insurance
paid holidays	retirement plan
pay for jury duty	awards and prizes
emergency loans	recreational activities
life insurance	medical examinations
severance pay	profit sharing
employee lunchroom	accident insurance
performance bonuses	use of company car
uniforms	tuition reimbursement
employee discounts	social events

FEDERAL LABOR LEGISLATION

Since the mid-1930s, a number of important federal laws have been enacted on behalf of employees. As a result, business owners need to make certain that all facets of personnel administration within their organizations conform to existing regulations.

A list of the more important federal acts appears in table 8–1.

TABLE 8–1. FEDERAL LABOR LEGISLATION

Year	Title	Major Thrust
1935	The National Labor Relations Act (also called the Wagner Act)	Designed to counter unfair practices on the part of employers (in the Depression years) and to reduce industrial unrest, this law gives employees the right to organize and to engage in collective-bargaining. It also established the National Labor Relations Board.
1938	The Fair Labor Standards Act (once known as the Federal Wages and Hours Law)	This act established federal regulation of wages and hours, a minimum wage, provision for overtime pay, and constraints on child labor. A notable exemption here is administrative and executive personnel.
1947	The Labor-Management Relations Act (also known as the Taft-Hartley Act)	This law banned the closed shop and created the Federal Mediation and Conciliation Service.
1963	The Equal Pay Act	This act established the premise of equal pay for men and women who do the same work. It prohibits discrimination against employees on the basis of sex.
1964	The Civil Rights Act	This piece of legislation created the Equal Employment Opportunity Commission. Along with subsequent amendments, it prohibits discrimination against employees on the basis of race, religion, sex, or national origin in hiring practices, compensation levels, or advancement opportunities.
1967	The Age Discrimination in Employment Act	Similar to the Civil Rights Act in its intent, this law bars discrimination against persons between the ages of forty and sixty-five on the basis of age in businesses engaged in interstate commerce. (A subsequent amendment raised the top age to seventy.)

TABLE 8–1. (continued)

Year	Title	Major Thrust
1970	The Occupational Safety and Health Act (OSHA)	This act seeks to assure safe working conditions for employees. Businesses must comply with safety and health standards and keep accurate records pertinent to this area. They are also subject to inspections designed to monitor compliance with the provisions of this act.
1972	The Equal Employment Opportunity Act	An amendment to the Civil Rights Act of 1964, this legislation extended its provisions to include employees of local and state governments, educational institutions (both public and private), and others.
1973	The Vocational Rehabilitation Act	Along with subsequent amendments, this act outlawed employment discrimination against handicapped persons who are able to fulfill their work responsibilities.
1974	The Employee Retirement Income Security Act (ERISA)	Designed to protect the retirement income rights of employees, this act assures vesting rights and specifies the proper funding of retirement plans.
1978	The Mandatory Retirement Act	This legislation eliminated the practice of requiring a worker's retirement at age sixty-five.
1983	The Job Training Partnership Act	This law replaced the earlier CETA (Comprehensive Education and Training Act) of 1978 and provides grants to individual states for the training of unemployed and economically disadvantaged persons.
1991	The Americans with Disabilities Act	Bars discrimination because of disability in all aspects of employment.

Source: Compiled by the author.

MANAGING UNION RELATIONS

Like it or not, unions are a fact of life—a fact that you may need to face, sooner or later.

It's true that small-business owners typically look askance on the unionization situation. Indeed, many entrepreneurs are suspicious of and resent employees who seek union affiliation, feeling that these people are ingrates and even disloyal, at the very least.

This kind of attitude can probably be traced to the belief that any unionization initiative will encroach on an owner's absolute control over a business. This does appear to pose a threat. A visit by the union local's business agent carries with it the weight of an organization far more powerful than the one the entrepreneur administers. Moreover, small business owners are at a total disadvantage in that they usually have little knowledge of unions and management-union relations.

You need to understand, however, that employees have the legal right to organize. Furthermore, if this does take place, you do *not* lose control of your business. The right approach for you to adopt is that both company management and union will work together to help your business grow.

Estimates have placed the number of union members today (excluding agricultural workers) at about one fifth of the nation's labor force. Most locals are affiliated with either a national or international labor organization. The majority of these are tied into (and backed by) the giant AFL-CIO. So, the power is certainly there!

A small-scale enterprise may be able to continue operating for some time before attracting the attention of a union. It helps, too, if you pay your employees decently and treat them well. When a union representative does finally make a call, however, he or she will want to talk with your employees about representing them in labor negotiations. At that time, any resistance on your part can lead to unpleasant action. Imagine the effects of a line of people parading to and fro in front of your building entrance and chanting, "Pass them by! Pass them by!" Imagine them carrying posters that read, in bold black letters, "Do Not Patronize! This Is a Nonunion Shop!"

COLLECTIVE BARGAINING

A healthy attitude to maintain toward union endeavors is one of understanding and tolerance. Unions do have a place in our economy. Workers (as well as employers) do have the right to organize. Consequently, there can be no logical reason for any hostility on your part. In today's climate, management-union relations can be open and aboveboard, businesslike and even friendly, and mature. Bear in mind that the union has almost as much at stake in the continued prosperity and growth of your business as you do.

What happens eventually is that the local representing your employees will want to negotiate a labor contract with you. The process by which the contract is agreed upon is called *collective bargaining.*

Activities during contract negotiations resemble the kind of dickering and bargaining that take place when a firm or an individual attempts to sell an expensive property to a shrewd buyer. Each of the two sides approaches the bargaining table well prepared. Each has a clear idea as to what it's prepared to offer and what it's looking for. Each has plotted its strategy and its tactics in advance.

A period of give and take almost always characterizes the pre-agreement phase. The completed contract spells out all the agreed-upon details: the new wage agreement; paid holidays; a listing of the conditions under which the union members will be expected to work; the procedure for handling employee grievances; a no-strike pledge; and the length of time the contract will be in effect. Today, most contracts also include an *escalator clause* that guarantees a wage increase when the cost-of-living index goes up by a specified percentage.

THE DYNAMICS OF LEADERSHIP

You can't be a leader unless you have someone to lead. This is self-evident. Equally true is the corollary: Where there's a leader, there are followers (at least one). Consequently, your business leadership skills won't truly flourish until you've hired your first employee.

Social psychologists tell us that leadership is a process involving certain types of interpersonal behavior. Acts of leadership exert influence upon other people. Verbs usually associated with leadership—*guiding, instructing, motivating, encouraging*—imply a sense of purpose, of movement, of action.

Studies of work groups in action suggest that much of the behavior of leaders falls into one of two categories:

- The behavior is oriented toward completing the work group's assigned tasks.
- The behavior shows consideration for and support of the members of the group.

The first type of behavior is practical, getting a job done; the second is more personal, involving the care and nurturing of human needs. Put together, these two dimensions define the job of the manager: *The manager works with people and with things to get the job done.*

LEADER CHARACTERISTICS

Many of us are guilty of holding stereotypical notions about leaders. We tend to believe that a good leader is one who commands respect; who electrifies the atmosphere when entering a room; who is, without a doubt, aggressive, domineering, manipulating; a skilled communicator, and an extrovert. Our concepts even go beyond personality to physical attributes; we think that a good leader is usually taller and heavier (and more attractive) than the rest of us.

Oddly enough, some of the greatest leaders in world history, and many capable managers of major corporations, have been quiet, unassuming, introspective, short, and thin people. In fact, leaders can be just like you and me—or anyone else. Management experts have often theorized about the kinds of personal traits necessary for effective performance in the role of leader. Studies have compared the qualities evinced by top executives to those demonstrated by unsuccessful leaders in order to uncover the characteristics that differentiate the two. Yes, several distinguishing attributes keep showing up— but bear in mind that leadership has three dimensions: the leader, those who are led, and the individual situation. Consequently, whether you rate high or low in these attributes does not necessarily make you a good (or bad) leader.

Perhaps you'll find it helpful to review the following list of personal traits, which can be valuable in dealing with others:

adaptability	openmindedness
alertness	optimism
communication skills	patience
confidence	persuasive powers
creativity	poise
curiosity	resourcefulness
dependability	sensitivity to others

drive	supportiveness
enthusiasm	teaching ability
evaluation skills	tolerance
flexibility	warmth
human relations skills	willingness to listen
maturity	willingness to take chances

Inasmuch as leadership activity also has a task-oriented, impersonal dimension, certain additional skills and abilities need to be developed. Among these are:

- The ability to establish priorities
- A capacity for giving credit when due
- Skill at planning and scheduling
- Proficiency in problem-solving
- A willingness to delegate responsibility to others

LEADERSHIP STYLES

Leadership involves interaction. It's a way of behaving—of persuading and inducing, of guiding and motivating. A totally rounded leadership style calls for a mastery of certain skill areas, the creation of the right climate within which the work group can function properly, and the direction and control of group activities.

Leadership style is often a reflection of personality. However, a single, consistent type of behavior may not always be applicable or desirable. What works well with one person (or group) may not necessarily work at all with the next. Individuals as well as groups are extremely varied. Consequently, effective leadership requires an eclectic approach, taking into account the three-way match among leader, group members, and the situation at hand. Most people tend to rely on the style that yields the best results.

The Autocratic Leader   At one end of the leadership continuum is the authoritarian type who tends to rule with absolute power, commanding obedience through domination, intimidation, and threats. This person insists on complete compliance with orders, yields no authority to anyone else, and makes decisions alone. Usually, this "boss" type of leader is production-oriented in thinking (that is, people exist for the sake of performing the required work).

Undoubtedly, autocratic leadership behavior can occasionally be of value as when coping with impending peril or in emergencies. Nevertheless, an autocratically run group will eventually show evidence of some undesirable types of behavior, such as demonstrations of aggression and internal conflict within the group. This kind of employee behavior probably stems from unresolved, ongoing frustrations and from the stifling of individual creativity.

The Democratic Leader   The democratic leader obviously possesses a broader view of the leadership role. He or she understands that workers are needed to help get the job done and accepts the fact that they are people, not machines. Moreover, this person realizes that people have separate and distinct personalities, needs, wants, and drives that must be met if they are to function well. This leader's overall attitude centers on ways to create a climate wherein all do their best to meet both group and company objectives. A democratic-type supervisor knows that the most successful approach is to develop employees over time to the point where they can function ably on their own. Consequently, this person exhibits an openness, remains accessible, and is eager to communicate freely with others. This wise leader keeps employees informed about ongoing conditions and about any impending changes that may affect them. Decisions are arrived at with the group's input. For the most part, the carrot-and-stick principle is dropped out of respect for the individuals; they are encouraged to exercise self-direction and make decisions on their own.

More than any other leadership stance, this type of administration produces workers who are motivated self-starters. As a result of continued democratic leadership, cooperative endeavor is encouraged and productivity should edge upward.

The Laissez-faire Leader   Still a third type of executive, far less often encountered in the business sector than either the autocrat or democrat, is the laissez-faire leader. In truth, managers of this type do not display the kinds of behavior we would customarily expect from business leaders. They practice what is more or less tantamount to a hands-off policy with regard to their subordinates. Typically, they completely abstain from such leadership acts as guiding, directing, training, or even extending encouragement to the members of their groups. Their basic philosophy, which they often confuse with a democratic approach to leadership, can be summed up in the phrase, "I'll let my subordinates take care of things."

UNDERSTANDING YOUR EMPLOYEES

People are complex. This statement, of course, doesn't surprise you at all! Yet, it's so important to bear in mind in your relationships with your employees. Each individual is multifaceted: among his or her many sides are the intellectual, the physical, the emotional; and the economic, social, political, and moral as well. So it's not surprising that people's behavior can be as complex and as difficult to interpret as people are themselves.

Over the next few pages, we offer a few facts derived from basic psychology and social psychology (the psychology of people in groups), which can help you in your role as leader. But first, let's review three basic points:

1. *People hold values.* Values are concepts we come to accept over the years as we interact with others and with our environment.
2. *People form attitudes.* Attitudes serve as vehicles for organizing knowledge, for adjusting to the world around us, for shielding us from confusion and pain, and for orienting us toward things that are pleasurable.
3. *People develop response traits.* We have habitual ways of responding to and dealing with others.

Personality is an amalgam of values, attitudes, and interpersonal response traits.

You might prepare yourself by reading a basic psychology textbook, which will give you many insights into what makes people tick. In turn, this could lead to an increased capability on your part to motivate and direct your employees.

WHAT MOTIVATES PEOPLE

Motives are the energizing forces that drive all of us and are behind most behavior. Many of our actions result from the interplay of several motives. Some motives are largely rational; this means that they are based on logic. For example, you probably avoid speeding in your automobile because (1) it might involve you in an accident that could endanger your life or your vehicle; and (2) you might receive a speeding ticket. These two motives are clearly logical.

On the other hand, many motives are of an emotional (or nonrational) nature. Consider the urge to place a ten-dollar bet on a particular horse in the third race at the track. Logically, your chances of winning are far less than fifty-fifty, yet you have a feeling you might win.

The line of demarcation between rational and emotional motives is rather hazy. You might avoid speeding because of an emotional motive: *fear* of being ticketed or of having an accident. Similarly, there could be a rational motive for the gambling situation; for example, if you needed considerably more money for a vital purpose than you had in your pocket at the time.

Furthermore, what motivates one person does not necessarily budge the next. The same motive can lead to varied behaviors in different people. The same behavior in different people can result from different motives.

All of us are driven by many motives: economic motives, safety motives, social motives, and so forth. Some of our motives derive from inborn drives like hunger, thirst, sleep, and sex. The majority of our motives, however, are learned—those that we develop as we interact with our environment.

LEVELS OF HUMAN NEEDS

One way to better understand the subject of human needs and wants is to review a notable theory proposed many years ago by the eminent psychologist Abraham Maslow.* He maintained that people are animals who are continually wanting and that human needs can be arranged on different levels according to their "potency" for influencing behavior. He postulated that all of us are constantly struggling upward to attain higher levels on this "pyramid of needs" until we reach its pinnacle. From time to time, most people are restrained from proceeding up the hierarchy or may be knocked down to lower levels by outside conditions (or, perhaps, by inner forces).

Needs at the lowest level—and therefore the most powerful of all—are the ones Maslow describes as the *physiological,* or *bodily, needs.* These include hunger, thirst, and sex. Once these needs have been largely satisfied, the human being will want still more and will move up to the next level of the pyramid, to the *safety needs.* On this level, people think of their safety: of gaining shelter from the elements and protection from accidents and other threats to well-being. If a person can provide for these needs, other wants soon develop; these Maslow termed the *love and belongingness needs.*

At this point, the individual needs love and affection and actively seeks friends, a mate, and groups for affiliation. When this level has been successfully attained, people still want (naturally!) more, and they move up to the *esteem needs.* Here, the individual wants to be respected by others, to be noticed and acclaimed, to build a reputation. By this time, the person has almost everything: income, a sense of security, family, and friends and is acquiring a reputation and the respect of others. Yet he or she still feels an inadequacy, a sense of

---

* Adapted from: A. H. Maslow, "A Theory of Human Motivation," *Psychological Review* 50 (1943), 370–96 (in the public domain). See also Abraham H. Maslow, *Motivation and Personality,* 2d ed. (New York: Harper & Row, 1970).

missing out on something, a feeling that there's still something more needed.

To the fifth—and highest—level of the pyramid of needs, Maslow affixed the name *self-actualization*. He explained this as the highest level of aspiration: to become in actuality that which an individual was designed to be. Only then was the person truly "matured." This is the supreme goal that all of us are climbing toward, all our lives.

INTERPRETING MASLOW'S THEORY IN PRACTICE

Translating Maslow's concepts into modern personnel thinking, you can expect your employees to seek such things as the following:

- *Level 1 (Physiological Needs):* a decent salary—enough to keep the wolf from the door, to keep the refrigerator well stocked, and to maintain a comfortable dwelling place.
- *Level 2 (Safety Needs):* job security and safe working conditions. This need may lead to seeking life-insurance coverage for spouse and children.
- *Level 3 (Love and Belongingness Needs):* the feeling of being part of an organization and having a place in the group; acceptance by coworkers and employer; a friendly environment.
- *Level 4 (Esteem Needs):* ego satisfaction, recognition (an occasional pat on the back), authority, and status within the group; the belief that the person's work is both responsible and respected.
- *Level 5 (Need for Self-Actualization):* a chance for growth and the opportunity to demonstrate initiative; encouragement for the individual to participate and contribute to the fullest.

SUPERVISING YOUR EMPLOYEES: SOME SUGGESTIONS

It's only natural for your employees to regard you as their mentor, guide, leader, and counselor. If you set high standards for yourself as well as for them, if you continually demonstrate good human relations and treat your employees as people—and not like pawns—your skills as a supervisor will be above average. To increase your leadership skills, follow the "dos" and "don'ts" suggested in exhibit 8–4.

EXHIBIT 8–4. SOME "DOS" AND "DON'TS" FOR MANAGERS

Do:	*Don't:*
Be consistent	Be argumentative
Be fair	Be autocratic
Be honest	Be overly demanding
Build enthusiasm among your employees	Be unreasonable
Encourage them to ask questions	Conceal the truth
Encourage them to make their own decisions	Discourage initiative
Instill confidence in them	Discourage new ideas
Keep an open door	Do your thinking for your employees
Listen attentively to what they have to say	Fail to clarify your instructions
Recognize individual differences	Play favorites
Set a personal example for them	Reprimand an employee in front of others
Show consideration for the feelings of others	Think small

Source: Compiled by the author.

EMPLOYEE CHARACTERISTICS

What should you be looking for in your employees? Here's a representative list of characteristics that are valuable in an employee:

- A good level of productivity
- Consistency
- Honesty
- Loyalty
- No rocking the boat
- Pleasant personality
- Promptness
- Proper behavior on the job
- Regular attendance
- Respect for authority

SOME OTHER THOUGHTS ON MOTIVATION

As a potential small business owner, you may be able to glean some worthwhile insights from several other well-known management concepts.

Theories X and Y   Nearly four decades ago, management theorist Douglas McGregor investigated the attitudes of supervisors toward their employees.* His studies led him to conclude that most

---

* Douglas McGregor, *The Human Side of Enterprise* (New York: McGraw-Hill, 1960), 31–44, 47–48. Reproduced with permission of the McGraw-Hill Companies.

supervisors could be classified as belonging to one of two camps. Those who subscribe to what McGregor termed the *Theory X* approach are convinced that the average person doesn't like to work, has little if any ambition, and tries to avoid responsibility. Consequently, these supervisors feel that they need to watch workers closely and depend on the strategic application of both rewards and punishment in order to obtain satisfactory performance.

Other supervisors follow a different philosophy, the more positive *Theory Y* approach. They believe employees consider work to be as natural as play and rest, and that once committed to specific objectives, they will not only put out effort willingly but will also seek responsibility.

Theory Z Over the 1970s and 1980s, much favorable publicity appeared in the press with regard to Japanese management techniques. One popular book outlined the more salient attributes of the Japanese approach, dubbing the overall concept *Theory Z*—an obvious reference to McGregor's assessment of supervisory types.* Substantial delegation of responsibility, trust in each individual, and decision by group consensus are characteristically seen in Japanese companies. Of course, some of their attributes (such as lifetime employment) cannot be incorporated easily into our own economy. Still, owners of small businesses might well profit by modifying and applying other attributes to their own enterprises; for example, the participative approach to decision making and a genuine concern for one's employees.**

Job Motivators and Hygiene Factors In the 1960s, management theorist Frederick Herzberg researched the workplace to uncover those factors that appeared to exert some influence on the job satisfaction of employees or on worker motivation.† He found two distinct sets of such factors: *motivators* (or *satisfiers*) and *hygiene factors* (*dissatisfiers*). Herzberg maintained that motivators appeal to higher-level human needs and therefore not only motivate employees but can also increase the level of job satisfaction. Examples include recognition, responsibility, advancement, growth, and the work itself. On the other hand, some factors in the workplace that

---

* William Ouchi, *Theory Z* (Reading, Mass.: Addison-Wesley, 1981).

** Matthew C. Sonfield, "Can Japanese Management Techniques Be Applied to American Small Business?" *Journal of Small Business Management* 22 (July 1984), 18–23.

† Frederick Herzberg, *Work and the Nature of Man* (New York: Thomas Y. Crowell, 1966), 71–91. See also: Frederick Herzberg, "One More Time: How Do You Motivate Employees?" *Harvard Business Review* 46 (January–February 1968), 53–62.

cater to people's lower needs (hygiene factors) apparently do little to encourage worker motivation. However, they can, of course, contribute to employee dissatisfaction. Salary, working conditions, company policies, and relations with one's supervisor are hygiene factors.

Obviously, then, small business owners might do well to review Herzberg's findings. More highly motivated and satisfied employees might be developed through effective management policies that lead to (among other results):

- Top-quality working conditions
- Catering to the worker's need for security
- Delegating more responsibility
- Encouraging group goal setting and decision making
- Flexible scheduling
- Job enhancement and/or redesign
- Offering a promotional ladder with the company
- Recognizing and rewarding the exceptional contribution

DECISION MAKING

In business, most management decisions are made by intuition. Intuitive decision making stems partially from a lack of familiarity with problem-solving techniques and partially from the realization that extensive resources—time, energy, and funds—should only be diverted to the most serious and complex problems. Happily, these major problems don't occur very often. When they do (for example, when one is contemplating major relocation of a factory or designing a new system), the owner is often better off relying on the assistance of an experienced consultant.

Luckily, most problems in business repeat themselves, so once a satisfactory solution has been worked out (or accidentally hit upon), the entrepreneur knows how to solve the problem the next time it pops up. Only the new, infrequent, unique problems present a strong challenge.

Decision making is but one step in the problem-solving process. It's the last step, in which you choose the one alternative that seems best. When you're confronted with any problem that merits your time and energy, try applying the steps outlined in exhibit 8–5.

Of course, many more sophisticated techniques are currently in vogue for solving business problems. For the most part, these approaches are used by the larger companies and not by the small firm. There are methods that take into account chance or probability, those that use mathematics and statistics, those that require computer programming, and so on. You may have read or heard about some of the following techniques: game theory, decision theory, queuing theory, decision matrices, simulation, and linear programming. All of these methods (and others, too) lie well outside the scope of this book. If, at a later date, you become interested in learning more about them, a number of good books are available on the topic of decision making in business and industry.

EXHIBIT 8–5. STEPS IN THE PROBLEM-SOLVING PROCESS

1. *Diagnose the problem.* On a sheet of paper, write down a clear statement of the problem's "essence"; this will help you keep the pinpointed problem clearly in mind as you begin to work toward its solution. Many problems are quite complex; often, you need to go further and break down the original problem statement into its major parts. Each part should then be summarized and written down as a "subproblem" statement. Another useful trick is to draw a simple diagram of the problem situation, making certain you put in all the elements involved.
2. *Gather information.* Hunt for pertinent information to help you solve the problem. (Facts are not only available from internal records, external sources of data, and primary research; they are also readily obtained from people.)
3. *Generate alternative solutions.* Develop a number of alternative solutions to the problem. (Creative thinking can help here. See chapter 12 for approaches to use in generating ideas.)
4. *Evaluate the alternatives.* Rate the alternatives according to each of several criteria: for example, cost, time, judged effectiveness or payoff, effect on you, and so on. Use a simple numerical rating scale, such as 0 = Poor, 1 = Fair, 2 = Good, 3 = Very Good, and 4 = Excellent. If some criteria are more important to you than others, then accord more weight to those in your analysis.
5. *Select the best alternative(s).* At this juncture, you make your decision.
6. *Translate your decision into action.*

Source: Compiled by the author.

FOR FURTHER INFORMATION

Beach, Dale S. *Personnel: The Management of People at Work.* 6th rev. ed. New York: Macmillan, 1994.

Bounds, Gregory M., Gregory H. Dobbins, and Oscar S. Fowler. *Management: A Total Quality Perspective.* Cincinnati: South-Western, 1995.

Carr, Clay. *The New Manager's Survival Guide*. 2d ed. New York: Wiley, 1995.

Catt, Stephen E., and Donald S. Miller. *Supervision: Working with People*. 2d ed. Homewood, Ill.: Irwin, 1991.

DuBrin, Andrew J., and R. Duane Ireland. *Management and Organization*. 2d ed. Cincinnati: South-Western, 1993.

Fuller, George. *The Manager's Portable Answer Book*. Englewood Cliffs, N.J.: Prentice-Hall, 1996.

Hilgert, Raymond. *Supervision: Concepts and Practices of Management*. 6th ed. Cincinnati: South-Western, 1995.

Longenecker, Justin G., Carlos W. Moore, and Bill Petty. *Small Business Management: An Entrepreneurial Emphasis*. 9th ed. Cincinnati: South-Western, 1994.

Mosley, Donald C., Leon C. Megginson, and Paul H. Pietri, Jr. *Supervisory Management: The Art of Empowering and Developing People*. 3rd ed. Cincinnati: South-Western, 1993.

Plunkett, Warren R., and Raymond F. Attner. *Introduction to Management*. 5th ed. Cincinnati: South-Western, 1994.

Schuster, John, Jill Carpenter, and Patricia Kane. *The Power of Open-Book Management*. New York: Wiley, 1996.

Stoner, James, and R. Edward Freeman. *Management*. 5th ed. Englewood Cliffs, N.J.: Prentice-Hall, 1991.

IV

PRODUCTION MANAGEMENT

PRODUCTION: PROCESSES AND OPERATIONS MANAGEMENT

Here's a sampling of small businesses, all of which have one thing in common:

- Baking breads and cakes
- Manufacturing cleaning compounds
- Glass-cutting for windows
- Dressmaking
- Assembling pocket radios
- Printing circulars and business cards
- Handcrafting beaded flowers
- Molding plastic toys
- Building houses
- Tool and die making
- Coating metals

The common thread that binds together these different types of enterprises is *production*. Production is an activity that converts materials into useful forms. A great deal of activity must take place in order to produce useful things. Management must plan, organize, direct operations, and control the overall situation. The materials involved may be raw materials, semiprocessed or semifinished goods, or even finished products. Machinery and equipment, methods, and processes are the basic elements of production.

Traditionally, there are four types of manufacturing processes:

- *Analysis* The breaking down of raw materials, such as crude petroleum, into their components.
- *Extraction* The removal of substances from other materials, as in the extraction of copper from ore.

- *Fabrication* Changing the form of materials in some way such as by pressing, weaving, or cutting. Examples include the manufacture of clothing, shoes, metal bolts, and so forth.
- *Synthesis* Combining materials to form new products, as in the manufacture of glassware, metal products, or synthetic fibers. Another kind of synthesis is *assembly,* whereby various fabricated parts are placed together to form a new product (as in the manufacture of automobiles).

Among small businesses, synthesis and fabrication are by far the most common types of manufacturing.

PRODUCTION PROCESSES

Production can be either continuous or intermittent. In *continuous production,* materials are brought uninterruptedly to the machines, the equipment runs smoothly for long periods of time, and standard products roll off the machines to be stored in the warehouse as reserves against future orders. This process is often called *flow production.* Good illustrations of factories in continuous production are television assembly plants and automobile plants. Of course, a completely automated factory is ideal for this type of production.

Intermittent production is often referred to as *job* or *job lot production* (and where less intermittent, *batch production*). This kind is typical of most small manufacturing enterprises. Machinery (or hand labor) "runs" are characteristically short—*interrupted*—as opposed to continuous. The materials flow varies; that is, frequent changes in setting up, dismantling, or changing the equipment are necessary. The products turned out are usually custom-made items. A printing shop is an excellent example of intermittent production.

PRODUCTION METHODS

Before the advent of factories, early manufacturing processes combined manual skills with small hand tools to produce useful objects. Although handcrafted items are still with us, production today is more machine-oriented than ever, and this tendency toward automation becomes more pronounced with each passing decade. Today, we have machines that

stamp	melt	carry	pour
heat	lift	roll	mix
sift	cut	weld	mill
chop	affix	blow	press
sort	turn	shape	depress

Nowadays, there are machines designed to duplicate nearly every imaginable function formerly performed by hand. Moreover, the use of robots to assist production has been increasing steadily.

A factory, though, is more than its machinery. The typical plant could be compared to a large, activity-choked arena. To run this arena profitably, all the major resources of the firm must be drawn together in a logical, businesslike way: management, capital, human resources, machinery, materials, and methods. Brief comments regarding several of these resources follow.

Management One or more layers of management are needed to set objectives and then to formulate plans in line with those objectives; to marshal and organize all the other resources in order to accomplish those objectives; to direct operations; and to control all the elements of this giant jigsaw puzzle.

Human Resources A human resources support system is required to operate not only the machinery but all production activities. In any factory there are many specialized functions to manage. This leads to the principle of *specialization of labor* and to the setting up of an organizational structure designed to accomplish the various jobs. Consequently, both semiskilled and skilled workers may be needed as well as a variety of functional departments, such as purchasing, receiving, production, stockkeeping, and quality control.

Machinery This includes power equipment and tools (both those that are permanently positioned and those that are portable), hand tools and equipment, and auxiliary equipment such as dies, gauges, jigs, and fixtures. In addition to running the machines, important activities here include purchasing, maintaining, and replacing equipment.

Methods Because of the intricate nature of the production process, methods and systems used in factory settings are many and varied. Some examples include methods for production planning and production control, setting detailed procedures, fixing standards, and designing layouts.

FUNCTIONAL DEPARTMENTS WITHIN THE PLANT

In addition to the primary production function, there are a number of other major functions that must be performed in a factory. These include purchasing, receiving, shipping, quality control, research and development (R&D), maintenance, and stockkeeping. In the smallest manufacturing firms, of course, such functions are shared among the owners and a few employees. As the firm grows larger, specialists are eventually sought to manage those areas, and departmental divisions soon follow.

PURCHASING

In plant operations, the *purchasing* function has to do with the procurement of all raw materials, components, machinery, equipment, supplies, and necessary services. Eventually, this area comes under the direction of a purchasing agent. Responsibilities assigned to this department include cultivating sources of supply for all items to be purchased; placing purchase orders (after securing quotations and working out prices and terms); following up on goods ordered; comparing invoice after receipt of goods with purchase order; and approving and forwarding invoices to the accounts payable department. The purchasing agent maintains a close liaison with the receiving department and is kept abreast of stock levels of all materials and supplies. (The agent must keep a perpetual running inventory if there is no stockkeeping department.)

RECEIVING

All purchases of raw materials, semiprocessed goods, equipment, and supplies come into the plant through the receiving department. Activities generally in the receiving category are described as follows:

1. Receiving onto the unloading platform all incoming materials, goods, and supplies, including returns from customers
2. Checking all incoming merchandise for quantity, price, and quality against both the packing slip and the accompanying bill of lading; further, checking each delivery against a copy of the original purchase order issued from the plant
3. Routing and transporting all materials to the proper department or assigned area(s) of the warehouse

4. Keeping records of various types, ranging from the receiving register (*log*) where all pertinent details of each shipment are recorded, to the invoices submitted to the purchasing department for payment.

SHIPPING

The shipping department is similar to the receiving department except that it lies at the other end (figuratively if not literally) of plant activities.

As with the receiving department, the importance of maintaining tight internal control along with the necessary paperwork cannot be overemphasized. Some of the major activities that take place in the shipping department are:

- Order processing
- Order picking
- Order assembly
- Order checking
- Special packing (where required)
- Routing shipments
- Scheduling shipments
- Following up on damage claims

QUALITY CONTROL

This area of specialization is an essential phase of good factory management. The quality-control function ensures that established standards are observed and that what is produced by the plant indeed conforms to customer (and company) specifications.

In the small production facility, this function is often vested in a single individual who may also have other duties. However, where the products or the manufacturing processes are more complicated, a small department may be needed to inspect products and maintain effective control. An efficient factory operation regularly checks not only its output but also all incoming merchandise (whether raw materials, semifinished components, or finished goods such as supplies).

Generally speaking, quality control involves sampling products from time to time, running tests, using measuring devices, and even statistical methods. The goal is to detect inferior or substandard products early in the game and then take steps to correct these deviations from the norm.

RESEARCH AND DEVELOPMENT

A separate and distinct R&D facility is characteristic only of large corporations. Rarely does a small manufacturer have an individual, let alone a section or department, dedicated to researching and developing new products, methods, machinery, and the like. Even among the larger firms, the research and development function is most often found within companies that are committed to industry leadership and a policy of "being first in their field."

Consequently, this R&D function isn't at all organized in a small manufacturing company but is spread among the various people who comprise the firm. Results, therefore, emerge only occasionally and in a serendipitous fashion rather than from deliberate, planned effort. In the typical small firm, development comes about largely through trial and error.

MAINTENANCE

Usually a well-organized factory is quickly placed under the capable administration of a skilled plant engineer. This is a logical step, because the breakdown or interruption of a machine, a boiler, a transformer, or any other important piece of equipment can rapidly bring activities to a virtual standstill. Plant engineers must frequently have at their disposal other specialists, such as electricians, machinists, plumbers, and carpenters.

The maintenance shop or section is responsible for keeping all machinery and equipment in top-notch operating condition, constructing new facilities when needed within the plant, moving machines from one location to another, assembling newly purchased equipment, and so forth. It's extremely important to schedule any major maintenance efforts so as to avoid interfering in any way with the flow of production. Likewise, good plant maintenance is *preventive* in the sense that all equipment is inspected on a regular, scheduled basis to avoid a slowdown or stoppage.

STOCKKEEPING

Materials supply is of paramount importance in the efficient operation of every stage of the manufacturing cycle. Raw materials must be readily available for scheduled production runs. Semifinished and fabricated components need to be in place when called for. Finished products have to be warehoused as ready stocks until drawn against the customer orders.

Overseeing substantial quantities of materials is a major, ongoing effort within the plant. In actuality, stockkeeping is the part of the overall inventory control system that deals with specifics like organizing and maintaining the storage area, placing and moving about the stored goods, protecting the materials, issuing merchandise from the storage area, and doing the necessary paperwork.

MANUFACTURING: INVENTORY AND MATERIALS

We may define *production management* as the planning, organizing, directing, and controlling of the production function. Among the primary areas of concern for the production manager are estimates of product demand, production layout, labor requirements, use of machinery and equipment, inspection and control systems, materials management, maintenance of product quality, inventory control, and plant maintenance.

PRODUCTION PLANNING AND OPERATIONS MANAGEMENT

It is useful to regard the production process as a closed system that consists of three significant dimensions: (1) inputs, (2) operations, and (3) outputs. Items one and three require only a brief note of explanation. The second calls for a somewhat more detailed discussion.

INPUTS AND OUTPUTS

Into this production system, we enter our *primary* inputs—the raw materials and/or semiprocessed goods and components (parts) we may need to manufacture our products. In addition, we must also avail ourselves of additional resources, which we may regard as inputs required for the system to operate. These include labor, capital, machinery, equipment, and supplies.

The outputs are, of course, the products we manufacture in our plant.

Much of the activity within any manufacturing facility lies within the operations area. Operations may be defined as the processing, or conversion, of inputs.

FUNCTIONS IN OPERATIONS MANAGEMENT

As you recall from earlier in this chapter, a bill of materials for each product is worked up during the product description phase. This bill is a written list of all materials needed to manufacture the particular item. It is at this point that operations management takes over. During the next phase (product description), management charts the production process, selects the machines to be used, determines sequences to be followed and labor needs, and outlines setup instructions. Plans are made for the following processing stages: routing, loading, scheduling, dispatching, and follow-up. (See figure 9–1.) Here's what these terms mean:

Routing   This is initiated once the bill of materials for the product has been prepared and the process description completed. Each individual operation as a component of the total product is planned; a sequence of steps is indicated; time and labor are apportioned to the various steps in the progression; and work stations, machines, and departments are spelled out. Route sheets and flow charts are used.

Loading   This function involves computing the amount of time required for each operation and adding that to work already planned for each machine or work station. This results in a *machine load chart* (traditionally, a bar chart).

Scheduling   This production phase deals with the timing of production in order to meet deadlines and delivery requirements. It involves determining when each operation is to be performed, starting and completion times, and so forth. The operation and flow processes charts, the machine load chart, and the network Program Evaluation and Review Technique (PERT) chart are the principal charts used for scheduling.

Dispatching   This involves the authorization of operations in the shop through work orders (instructions).

Follow-up   Also called *reporting*, this function is normally the bailiwick of the dispatcher, whose job it is to supply information about work in progress. The reporting of delays and other problems can lead to rapid corrective action.

FIGURE 9–1. PROCESSING STAGES

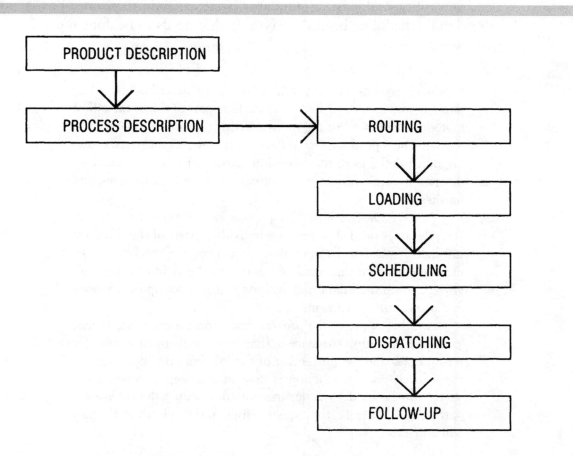

PRODUCTION SCHEDULING

The Small Business Administration maintains the following:

> Some small manufacturers take production schedules for granted because bottlenecks are few and far between. Minor problems are easily ironed out, and orders are delivered to customers on time.
>
> Other small manufacturers are not as fortunate. Scheduling in their plants is complicated by the nature of the process, the complexity of the products, and frequent changes in quantity requirements.*

The SBA also suggests that the small-plant production scheduler should be familiar with these important factors before lining up

---

* John B. Kline, "Pointers on Scheduling Production," *Management Aid No. 207.* (Washington: Small Business Administration, June 1977 reprint), 2.

production: production layout; factory workload; factory capability and versatility; and existing standards, systems, and procedures. Before actual scheduling begins, everything that needs to be done must be spelled out:

Product Description. The product description describes individual parts as well as the finished product. One part of this is the bill of materials. It lists all of the items needed to produce a part, or in total, the final product. Prints and drawings depict the parts, showing much detail as to their physical characteristics. Specifications describe in detail the allowable tolerances in dimensions, sizes, and finishes.

Process Description. The process description is concerned with the steps needed to produce individual parts of the complete product. It will list the operations sequences, the machines to be used, the amount and kind of labor, and the estimated time involved. Additional data may include machine set-up instructions and inspection instructions.

Another phase of the process description is the *route sheets*. These are operation sequence outline forms with an allowance for set-up times and for movement of the job from one operation to the next. If your production is divided into departments, route sheets can be used by a department to schedule the time for a particular job, to monitor a series of jobs, and to tell where the part will go next.[*]

MAINTAINING PRODUCT QUALITY

The small manufacturer who struggles to build a profitable business should realize that success over the long term can be assured only by emphasizing product quality (for the price, of course). To maintain the proper quality levels in all goods produced at the plant, serious and continuous attention needs to be paid to the following product aspects:

- Performance
- Features
- Reliability
- Conformance
- Durability

[*] Ibid., 4.

- Serviceability
- Aesthetics
- Perceived Quality*

At the same time, for the operation to remain profitable, production management needs to balance product quality with effective cost control.

Production operations can be refined to bring about product improvement as well as to reduce manufacturing costs. One worthwhile approach is to encourage the formation and participation of one or more *quality circles* within the company. Not only do these groups facilitate plant operations, but the results of their efforts can be better product quality as well as greater output. Other likely benefits are increased job satisfaction and higher employee morale.

Other methods the manufacturing firm can use to build a healthy organization, reduce expenses, ensure continued product quality, and improve decision making in general are to adopt a participative management stance, create an internal task team to wrestle with company difficulties, and institute a value analysis program.

INVENTORY MANAGEMENT AND CONTROL

There should be little difficulty in understanding the significance of the inventory control concept in the manufacturing enterprise. Its purposes are simply to manage and control two varieties of inventories: (1) the *materials inventory* necessary to the production process; and (2) the finished *merchandise inventory*, which is stored for eventual customer orders.

By logical extension, then, effective inventory management calls for thorough attention to such activities as the acquisition of materials required for plant production (which involves both the purchasing and receiving functions); the handling, internal movement, and storage of materials (the stockkeeping function); and the physical distribution of materials and manufactured goods (the shipping function).

Sales objectives are first translated into the types and quantities of products to be manufactured. Based on production needs (as defined by the various bills of materials), the purchasing department

---

* Reprinted from "What Does 'Product Quality' Really Mean?" by David A. Garvin, *Sloan Management Review* 26 (Fall 1984), 29–30, by permission of the publisher. Copyright © 1984 by The Sloan Management Review Association. All rights reserved.

will seek to order the required materials so that they arrive in time and in sufficient quantities to enable production to keep up with its schedules. After they are brought into the receiving section and checked off, the materials are then assigned to the appropriate departments and sections.

Stockkeeping is charged with the handling, internal movement, and storage of materials, as well as with the finished goods inventory. The shipping department handles the distribution of the plant's product, along with the attendant recordkeeping.

A firm's inventories represent a substantial financial investment, not only because of the initial costs of purchasing the materials required for production but also for the many additional processing costs (labor, machines, electricity, and overhead expenses) and storage. Consequently, this phase of the business requires nearly continuous and responsible planning: working up projections, determining desirable inventory levels, ascertaining lead times for timely ordering, setting into position effective inventory methods and control systems, and other details. Here, the twin objectives seem to be (1) to meet the needs of plant and customers alike and simultaneously (2) to hold down inventory levels to their minimums, commensurate with those needs.

Among the more important requisites for effective control are

- Setting up a good perpetual inventory system (which may be maintained manually, mechanically, or electronically)
- Taking occasional physical inventory counts
- Establishing minimum/maximum levels for all items inventoried
- Strategically using buffer or reserve stocks
- Knowing the details of all pertinent costs

Recordkeeping is extensive in this area, and a great deal of direction for management can be derived from all this paperwork. Management can study, item by item, the *movement* or sales figures for all merchandise carried by the firm. Indeed, the need for small business owners to plan and evaluate their inventory investments cannot be overemphasized.

MATERIALS MANAGEMENT

Basically, the materials management function sees to it that the right raw materials, semifinished products, and components are brought into the plant at the right times and in sufficient quantities to meet all production requirements. Although manufacturers generally purchase the materials they require from suppliers, management may occasionally decide to fabricate some of these goods (or parts) within the plant itself. The pros and cons of each "make-or-buy" situation are weighed, and appropriate decisions are made.

MATERIALS REQUIREMENT PLANNING

One of the most difficult—and continual—tasks that confronts plant management is that of estimating the types and quantities of materials required for their production needs. Happily, the price of a microcomputer now lies well within the reach of most small firms. For this reason, more and more small business owners seem to be resorting to *Materials Requirements Planning* (or *MRP*). Among the benefits that this system offers are a reduction in inventory levels, speedier purchasing, and improved scheduling of production runs.*

MRP has been described as:

> . . . an integrated computer-based information system designed for the ordering and scheduling of dependent demand items such as raw materials, components, subassemblies, and parts. The requirements for the finished products (end items) generate the requirements for the respective components by using lead time information to determine the amount and timing of such orders. The planning horizon is broken into time brackets (e.g., weeks, months, etc.), so that scheduling for the end items and their components can be fulfilled in a timely fashion.**

FOR FURTHER INFORMATION

Dear, Anthony. *Inventory Management Demystified.* New York: Chapman and Hall, 1990.

Fogarty, Donald W., Thomas R. Hoffmann, and Peter W. Stonebraker. *Production and Operations Management.* Cincinnati: South-Western, 1989.

Gunn, Thomas G. *21st Century Manufacturing: Creating Winning Business Performance.* Essex Junction, Vt.: Oliver Wight, 1993.

Lipman, Burton E. *How to Control and Reduce Inventory.* East Brunswick, N.J.: Bell Publishing, 1988.

---

* Charles H. Davis, Feraidoon (Fred) Raafat, and M. Hossein Safizadeh, "Production and Inventory Information Processing: Material Requirements Planning," *Journal of Small Business Management* 21 (July 1983), 26.

** Ibid., 26–27.

Lunn, Terry, and Susan A. Neff. *MRP: Integrating Materials Requirement Planning and Modern Business.* Burr Ridge, Ill.: Irwin, 1992.

Narasimhan, Seetherama L. et al. *Production Planning and Inventory Control.* 2d ed. Englewood Cliffs, N.J.: Prentice-Hall, 1994.

Schonberger, Richard J. *Operations Management: Productivity and Quality.* 2d ed. Plano, Tex.: Business Publications, 1985.

Tersine, Richard J. *Principles of Inventory and Materials Management.* 4th ed. Englewood Cliffs, N.J.: Prentice-Hall, 1993.

Waters, C. D. *Inventory Control and Management.* New York: Wiley, 1992.

V

MARKETING BASICS

10

MARKETING AND PRODUCT/SERVICE MANAGEMENT

REGARDLESS OF THE nature of your new enterprise, the managing of the marketing function will demand more creativity and more astute judgment than any other single phase of the business. Your warehouses may be jammed to the rafters with inventory; your new machines may be churning out thousands of merchandise units each day; your store's shelves may be crammed with goods; yet all can come to naught if sales are not consummated. The end purpose of all this activity and preparation is the accomplishment of those exchange transactions called "sales," in which your firm receives customer dollars in exchange for its products.

THE MARKETING CONCEPT

In contrast to the old-fashioned accent on production that characterized American business only a few decades ago, today's healthy small firm is one that is, first and foremost, oriented toward the customer. This contemporary "marketing concept" approach is simple to learn:

1. Identify your intended customer groups.
2. Find out all you can about their needs and wants.
3. Try to satisfy them with the right products and/or services, supported by the right promotion and available at the right time and location.

Under this modern marketing concept, an alert entrepreneur designs the firm's organizational structure so as to give the marketing component its deserved prominence. The marketing function is fully integrated with other traditional divisions of the business, such as finance and production, and placed in a position to coordinate them. The company's marketing strategies and tactics are purposeful, well organized, and projected years into the future. Moreover, within a marketing-oriented firm, planning responds to sociocultural and even natural environmental changes and displays abundant flexibility.

In directing your company's marketing efforts, bear in mind that there is little you can do about certain elements of the environment. Two examples are the legal framework within which your firm must operate and the general business conditions of the economy. Only four factors are truly within your control, and you must learn to manipulate them skillfully to compete successfully in the marketplace. These controllable elements are *products, pricing, promotion,* and *distribution.* Together, they are commonly referred to as the *marketing mix.*

Each of these major factors in marketing decision making is sufficiently important to be treated in a separate chapter. This chapter deals with products—the first of the four elements. The next three chapters are devoted to in-depth presentation of the other elements.

PRODUCT MANAGEMENT

Of the four constituent elements in the marketing mix, products probably present the major challenge facing your company. The other three ingredients are usually only support activities which, when carefully planned, will facilitate the movement of your goods into the hands of your customers. Products are the items that you *produce* (if you are a manufacturer) or *select and buy* (in wholesaling and retailing) to fulfill the needs and wants of your customers.

To manufacturers and intermediaries alike, effective management of the product sphere is crucial. Product-line management involves many things: finding and selecting the proper items to carry; determining how wide or narrow a line to offer; deciding when to discard or retain an item, and when to add new products to the line.

WHAT IS A PRODUCT?

To the layperson, the word *product* generally signifies the actual, physical object offered for sale. Modern marketing, however, approaches the product as much more than a simple, three-dimensional object. It's as though this "thing" designed to satisfy customer needs were surrounded by an intangible, invisible aura (or *frame of refer-*

ence). Contained within this aura are other attributes not so easily discerned: the reputation of the producer or seller, the style of the packaging, past messages conveyed by advertisements of the product, other people's impressions and opinions about the item, and so on.

A product, then, is much more than an object. It's an intricate mental concept, rich in connotations. It reflects an image that literally comprises a *total package of satisfactions* for the intended user.

Products do not exist by themselves, frameless and within a vacuum. A pair of Florsheim shoes, an electric toaster emblazoned with the Proctor-Silex or General Electric label, a Gucci handbag, a tube of Mentadent toothpaste, or a Mercury Grand Marquis—each of these articles is positioned within a frame of reference that differentiates it from competitive products.

CLASSIFYING PRODUCTS

You may find it useful to learn how marketing practitioners assign products to categories, since these classifications provide an orderly basis for product management. The following are common approaches to product classification:

- Industrial and consumer goods
- Necessities and luxuries
- Durables and nondurables
- Convenience, shopping, and specialty goods
- Staples and fashion items

These labels by no means exhaust the possibilities. They are, however, sufficient to provide a basic grasp of product classification. Each category is discussed briefly in exhibit 10–1.

EXHIBIT 10–1. UNDERSTANDING PRODUCT CLASSIFICATIONS

Industrial and Consumer Goods This classification scheme is based on the user for whom the products are intended. Goods used by industry, commerce, government, and intermediaries of all types in the ordinary conduct of their operations are referred to as *industrial goods*. Partially finished as well as completely finished products may be included in this category along with lumber, industrial chemicals, tools, machines, and supplies. *Consumer goods* are the finished products intended for use by the final consumer. Clothing, household furnishings, automobiles, fishing tackle, and groceries are some examples.

EXHIBIT 10–1. (continued)

Necessities and Luxuries This grouping classifies products according to the urgency or lack of urgency people show in their buying habits. This type of consumer behavior is tied to the concept of *discretionary purchasing power.* Obviously, categorization in this manner is sometimes misleading in that one person's luxury might be another's necessity. A personal computer purchased by a salesclerk, junior-high-school student, or automobile mechanic is most likely considered a *luxury good,* yet the identical machine is probably a *necessity* to a writer of fiction, a college professor, or a business executive.

Durables and Nondurables The word *durable* means "of a lasting quality." Products that last a long time (and are consequently purchased less often), such as pocket calculators, clothing, television sets, and pots and pans are called *durable goods.* The contrasting term, *nondurable goods,* refers to items that provide temporary satisfaction: Foodstuffs and many services come under this category.

Convenience, Shopping, and Specialty Goods Here again, products are looked at from the standpoint of the consumer, taking into consideration the time and effort expended in shopping for the items. People generally spend almost no time shopping for items like chewing gum, sugar, and butter, so these are designated *convenience goods.* Such merchandise is readily available at many locations; there's little *product* difference but often substantial differentiation between one *brand* and the next.

Furniture, jewelry, fashionable clothing, carpeting, and the like are called *shopping goods* because they require more time and effort by the shopper. Here, the consumer usually wishes to compare the item with other similar offerings with regard to product attributes like price, quality, and style before making a choice.

Prospective buyers expend even greater effort before purchasing *specialty goods* such as custom-made products, special brands, and better-quality clothes. Of course, there could be some overlapping here, depending on individual consumer motivation and "search behavior." A convenience item for one person may be a shopping good or even a specialty item for the next.

Staples and Fashion Items *Staple goods* are those that enjoy a widespread and generally continuous demand over time. Examples include men's socks, razor blades, fresh eggs, and butter. When demand is erratic and subject to wide fluctuations as with nonstaple merchandise (men's shirts, women's shoes and sportswear, and the like), the products are referred to as *fashion goods.*

MANAGING THE PRODUCT LINE

The first requirement in product management is to reach a consensus on specific product objectives, which are then followed as guidelines. Among those commonly encountered in business are increasing sales, enlarging the company's market share, fully utilizing manufacturing capacity, matching new or improved products of competitors, and changing methods of distribution. Before deciding on such objectives, management should do some diligent soul-searching and ask questions like these:

- What kind of business are we in?
- Which segments of the general market are we catering to?
- Which new segments can we service in the future?
- How well do our current products meet the needs of our customers?
- Are there other items we ought to be carrying?
- Are there items in our line we should drop?
- What new products can we add to replace those we discard?
- Is each of our items compatible with the other products in our line?

THE PRODUCT LIFE-CYCLE CONCEPT AND ITS IMPLICATIONS

The *Product Life Cycle* (PLC) concept is of special importance in the first steps of market strategy development and has been well publicized over the years in the marketing literature. (See figure 10–1.) The concept attempts to describe the performance of any successful new product from the point at which it is first introduced into the marketplace through its final demise. Except for fashion merchandise and fads, most products appear to pass through four stages before reaching obsolescence. These are the *introductory, growth, maturity,* and *decline* stages of the PLC.

INTRODUCTORY STAGE

When a new product is introduced into the marketplace, it is unknown to most of its targeted purchasers. Obviously, some groundwork has to be prepared for the "launching." During the introductory stage of the PLC, the innovating firm must invest substantial funds in promotional activities of the "pioneering" type in order to carry the

FIGURE 10–1. THE LIFE CYCLE OF A TYPICAL NEW PRODUCT

"product story" to prospective buyers. Once it has provided the product information, the company must ensure that people will be able to purchase the item at convenient locations. So, manufacturers need to consider what distribution channels to employ in order to reach those prospects.

For the innovating company, this first stage is a costly one. The producer must absorb the initial costs involved in designing the product, in gearing up the machinery and internal systems for its manufacture, in promoting the item, and in securing enough initial distribution points to generate product viability in the marketplace.

Often, the manufacturer seeks to recover much of this investment by placing a higher-than-ordinary price tag on the item. Or, the company might seek mass distribution instead, by pricing the product somewhat "below-the-market" in order to secure a strong foothold. In either case, little or no profit is usually accrued during this introductory stage. Frequently, the manufacturer encounters losses, sometimes severe.

Both wholesalers and retailers are cautious about adding to their regular lines an article of merchandise that is obviously in its introductory phase. They realize that most of their regular customers are likely to be unfamiliar with the product and that it may therefore be difficult for them to sell. Consequently, these distributors may ask the supplier for such extras as free point-of-purchase signs and other materials, cooperative advertising dollars, and full return privileges. The large-scale retail firm may even request exclusive distribution in its trading area.

GROWTH STAGE

Provided these initial efforts result in gradual customer acceptance, more and more people will learn of the new product, try it, and (if satisfied) continue purchasing and using the item. During the growth stage of the PLC, greater effort is exerted in distribution so that merchandise becomes increasingly available at more locations. Sales volume starts to climb. After the start-up costs are substantially absorbed by sales, the additional revenues resulting from more market penetration lead to a sharp rise in company profit. For the manufacturer, this stage generally bears the highest profit margin. During this stage, too, manufacturing methods are generally refined as production gears up to meet demand. This, in turn, results in even lower per-unit costs.

Advertising is increased to support product growth, but now a broader sales base exists, which supports advertising expenditures. For the new small company, it might be advantageous at this juncture to expand the number of purchase points, simply to keep costs within a reasonable range.

Wholesalers and retailers who handle the new product begin to enjoy the fruits of expanding demand. They order more heavily as they experience a higher stockturn rate. The manufacturer may launch additional product variations—new sizes, new colors, or new materials. It should be noted that, even at this comparatively early point in the product life cycle, when profits peak, competition begins to enter the picture, seeking to emulate the evident success of the pioneering manufacturer.

MATURITY STAGE

Eventually, the ascending growth curve begins to level off (although this might not occur for years). By the time the successful product has entered the maturity stage of the PLC, it has found widespread consumer acceptance, and a number of competitors offering similar products have appeared on the scene. For the originating firm, the environment is then a highly competitive one and competitors' prices are sometimes much lower. The producer is frequently compelled to step up promotional efforts in an attempt to differentiate the product from those of competitors, thus protecting the initial advantage and market share so assiduously cultivated. Naturally, such tactics tend to force costs upward. In turn, profits begin to shrink. At best, efforts like these constitute a delaying action, although they can occasionally extend this particular stage for a long period of time. (The majority of products now in the marketplace are most likely in the maturity stage of their respective life cycles.)

Both retail and wholesale distributors take advantage of the competition for their business among suppliers of the same types of goods. These merchants ask their sources of supply for better terms, more extended warranties (where available), more frequent deliveries, money for cooperative advertising, and so on. They also seek to drop and replace those suppliers with whom they have not been happy.

DECLINE STAGE

In the face of declining sales and profits, manufacturers sometimes make last-ditch efforts to resuscitate the item. These include approaches like new packaging, special promotions, new versions, and price changes. Although it is often difficult to discard a product, sooner or later, as sales continue to decline, the decision has to be faced. In this final decline stage, appropriate steps include planning to phase out the item, tapering down gradually on inventory, working out equitable arrangements with intermediaries so they do not suffer losses along the way, and disposing of excess inventory.

With products that are clearly in their decline stage, distributors will begin to reduce the number of variants they carry, cut back on reorders, and gradually start phasing out the merchandise. They may even mark down their goods in order to close them out.

THE "EIGHTY-TWENTY PRINCIPLE"

A practical rule of thumb you can apply in a variety of ways to your marketing planning is the *eighty-twenty principle*. For example, if a manufacturing company lists all of its accounts according to their annual purchases, chances are the firm will discover that as much as 80 percent of its total annual sales comes from about 20 percent of its customers.

Similarly, a firm maintaining a sales force of around fifty salespeople can analyze each employee's sales productivity according to this same principle. More likely than not, management will learn that the major portion of sales has been brought in by as few as nine or ten star performers.

The eighty-twenty principle can also be applied to product-line management. One company, a wholesaler of janitorial chemicals and supplies, maintained a huge inventory of more than 8,000 items in order to service hundreds of regular customers. Sales results for a two-year period were analyzed by computer, on an item-by-item movement basis. Management was surprised to learn that 1,700 items accounted for more than 75 percent of their annual sales volume. Needless to say, the product line was drastically reduced by more than 50 percent over the next few months. This resulted in a savings of $250,000 in capital formerly tied up in inventory. Although sales initially dropped by 4 percent, fewer salespeople could thereafter devote more time to fewer products (and the firm's mail-order catalog accented the more popular merchandise), resulting in an overall sales increase of more than 15 percent by the end of the year.

NEW-PRODUCT DEVELOPMENT

From time to time, the progressive small company introduces one or more new products into its line. Many factors can spur such a move: a desire to enhance the firm's reputation as an innovator in its industry; the need to stimulate sales, replace products in a decline, or outperform a serious competitor; or simply a desire to take advantage of occasional special deals.

THE NEW-PRODUCT DEVELOPMENT PROCESS

For the manufacturing company, the new-product development process involves a logical sequence:

1. The emergence of the "raw" idea
2. A "screening" procedure whereby the idea is evaluated, along with others, against previously established criteria
3. The tedious research and development period during which the idea is gradually refined, a prototype of the item is made, cost analyses are worked up, production methods are devised, marketing factors such as price and packaging are considered, and estimates are made of demand and expected profits
4. The testing stage wherein the product's performance in one or several areas is carefully watched
5. Full-scale introduction into the market

The criteria mentioned in stage two above may include the following: the size of market for the item, the product's potential contribution to company profits, the uniqueness of the item and its effect on other products in the line, and the ease with which it can be integrated into the total production load.

Generally, the expenditures required to develop a single new product are substantial, to say the least. This fact, coupled with the recognition that most new products fail, is a serious warning to the recently established small business to think twice (or more) before embarking on this path. Until the firm is well established, management would be wiser to consider a different strategy in its product-line management: waiting until a competitor has had a substantial degree of success with an item and then producing its own improved version (thus "riding on the bandwagon").

Perhaps there is more sanity and less risk in striving to be second than in being first!

WHERE TO FIND NEW PRODUCTS

Ideas for new products come from a variety of sources: the company's suppliers and their sales representatives, customers and prospective customers, company personnel, trade journals and general publications, and competitors.

Of course, the bulk of ideas for new products or services can and should be generated internally, especially if the organization has a product development section or committee. In an "open" organization, where all employees are encouraged to come up with helpful ideas, there should be no lack of new product ideas. Certainly, a simple suggestion-box system, reinforced by efficient follow-through procedures, will be of considerable value. For the retailer, a "want-slip" system can serve the same purpose.

CREATIVE THINKING APPROACHES

The employee or internal team in charge of generating new product ideas can be quickly indoctrinated in some of the more popular "creative thinking" techniques. These include brainstorming, attribute listing, "running the alphabet," and checklists. Each of these approaches is described below in brief detail.

Brainstorming Although commonly encountered as a group procedure, brainstorming can be used by individuals as well. Generally enjoyed by participants, it provides group members with the benefits of a highly motivating atmosphere. The group, usually small, meets for the purpose of coming up with ideas in quantity within a short time span—perhaps ten or fifteen minutes. There are no holds barred; participants are encouraged to let their imaginations run wild while, at the same time, all criticism or judgment is withheld. Ideas flow so fast at times that the use of a tape recorder is recommended. Over the following two or three days, ideas generated from the "brainstorm" can be typed up for thoughtful analysis. A set of previously established criteria is then applied, and the more promising alternatives are selected.

Attribute Listing As its name suggests, this technique involves preparing a list of the significant characteristics of a product that, combined, will differentiate it from other products. Let's say your company is in the business of manufacturing ordinary pencils, and you are hunting for new, unique products to add to your line. You begin by describing the basic pencil itself: its color(s), its size and shape, its substances and constituent materials, and its function(s)— to write, and perhaps to erase. Each of these characteristics then becomes a logical candidate for change or variation.

For example, the color *yellow* could be changed to dozens of other colors or to *striped, polka-dotted,* or *transparent.* Other attributes, such as size, shape, material, function, texture, odor, and taste, can be used to originate hundreds of variations. Changing the function of a pencil, for example, from *to write* to something else, like *to play with, to eat,* or *to use as a weapon* (or myriad other possible functions) might lead to pencil-shaped objects that are toys or made of chocolate or designed for self-defense.

The manufacturer of luggage, giftware, or small appliances can employ the same approach to develop new product ideas.

Running the Alphabet Also known as the *ABC method,* this approach borrows liberally from the word association techniques of psychologists. Essentially, it consists of preparing in advance a list of words beginning with the letter *A,* then *B* words, and so on through the alphabet until forty or fifty words have been listed. From a practical point of view, it's desirable to work mostly with nouns. The words selected are then used to "mine" for ideas. (Of course, once you have gained practice with the technique, there's little need to follow the ABCs studiously. There is no reason why you can't begin anywhere in the alphabet, say, with words starting with *G, L, P,* or *S.*)

Exhibit 10–2 offers a hypothetical example of the method in action.

EXHIBIT 10–2. USING THE "RUNNING THE ALPHABET" TECHNIQUE

A toy manufacturer wanted ideas for new products in order to increase the company's market share. A sampling of the list derived from applying the creative "running the alphabet" approach follows:

abalone	badge	cabana
Africa	bakery	camera
alligator	ball	carousel
Amazon	banquet	cent
anchor	bellboy	circus
apple	blossom	closet
apricot	bridge	cot
Aquarius	brook	cougar
aspirin	bubble	crystal
asteroid	button	cup

The manufacturer considered the words one by one, and came up with many ideas, including: mechanical alligators, bubble-blowing machines, musical carousels, toy telescopes, clowns, and miniature animals in cages.

Of course, many of the ideas may not be all that original or new. More likely than not, some competitive firm may already have succeeded in linking several of the more promising concepts to new toy possibilities. Indeed, the competitor may be on the verge of launching one or more of the new products in the marketplace.

It's in the "mental manipulation" of the obviously less applicable words on this list—for example, *Aquarius, aspirin, blossom,* or *bridge* that the true worth of this technique emerges. It's easy to see how ideas generated via these unorthodox associations can result in truly innovative suggestions.

Consider, for instance, the word *Aquarius.* One immediately conceives of a toy designed specifically for consumers born under this sign and, by logical extension, a minimum of another eleven items in a new line of "astrological toys." Toying around, for example, with the "bridge" concept may spark ideas for miniature replicas of the Brooklyn Bridge and other well-known spans, train sets (complete with railroad bridges and tunnels), playing cards (along with a child-size card table and chairs), many types of toy construction equipment, model cars (with or without remote control), wagons and bicycles (or tricycles), and so on.

Of course, this technique (like brainstorming and attribute listing) can be applied to a variety of business problems, ranging from artwork and advertising copy to choosing a packaging style, planning major promotions, and producing names for new products. For example, in hunting for ways to motivate your salespeople, you might come across the *B* words *badge* and *ball*. These stimuli could trigger ideas like issuing merit badges (or, by extension, certificates) to outstanding performers of the month or quarter, instituting an annual ball for employees who surpass their quotas (or an outing at a ball park), and so on.

Checklists and Other "Pump-Primers" Checklists are used daily in business for purposes of measurement and/or control and sometimes to insure thoroughness in planning. A checklist is also a valuable device for triggering the imagination, although it's seldom used in this creative capacity.

Consider, for example, the familiar "Five Ws" of the journalist: *Who? What? Where? When? Why?* (A sixth question—*How?*—is usually added to this mini-checklist.) The "Five Ws" can be of extraordinary value in investigating and analyzing many types of business problems, such as declining sales, loss of market share, or the proper deployment of company resources. They are also useful in planning for promotion campaigns, expansion, and so on.

In addition to checklists, other "pump-primers" exist that can prod our imaginations. The classified telephone directory, for instance, can be used as a source of leads (new prospects for a salesperson to pursue). The daily newspapers and business publications are also excellent sources of ideas for your day-to-day business activities.

PACKAGING AND BRANDING

Along with the development of a new item, the manufacturer must think about *packaging:* enclosing the product in some type of package or container for purposes of protection. Of course, the item must be packaged so that it can be easily handled, placed in cartons, shipped, stored, and eventually placed on shelves or on display, all with an eye to avoiding damage to the contents. Furthermore, the modern package helps to sell the merchandise it contains through a combination of factors that include design, color, and materials used. Moreover, the package usually identifies the originating company.

Some retailers and wholesalers, of course, will package goods themselves. In this respect, the selection and subsequent popularization of a brand name, trademark, or other identifying device can be of substantial importance to the company seeking to differentiate its merchandise from competitors'. Over time, the *brand name* will establish a vital "sales personality" for the product. Hence, care should be exercised at the outset in the selection of a name. A simple name is preferable; it should be easy for the consumer or industrial buyer to spell and to pronounce. It also should be easy to recall.

Often, the name chosen is simply the firm's name, like General Electric, Heinz, Timex, Miller, Black & Decker, Atari, or Remington. At times, brand names reflect the benefits promised to users of the product or imply its important qualities. Consider the following, for example: Pepsi Free, Beautyrest, Ivory soap, and One-A-Day vitamins.

As a general rule, unless the new company has based its entire marketing effort on a single innovative product (which is rarely the case), the choice of brand name is relatively unimportant. In the long run, the popularization of a company name is more significant. In time, the firm's name can be successfully used to "brand" its products.

THE MARKETING OF SERVICES

Marketing practitioners who work for companies that offer services for sale often proceed in much the same manner as do their counterparts in organizations that market products. Yet there are sharp differences between the kinds of approaches that are needed to market services and traditional product marketing methods. Such distinctive features of services as their intangibility and their inseparability from the service provider make them more difficult to market than products.

As an illustration, let's consider the quality of *intangibility*. Products are real, not abstract. Because they are concrete objects, prospective buyers can see, touch, feel, and examine them before arriving at a purchase/no purchase decision. For example, the consumer (or organizational buyer) who is shopping for a suitcase is able to look over and compare a number of different styles and brands; determine the quality of the materials of which it is made, the hinges, and the closures; make an estimate of its durability; and so forth. On the other hand, the person who is interested in a service—for example, a complete medical examination, a Caribbean cruise, or a pair of tickets to the World Series—remains at a comparative disadvantage because he or she is unable to examine the service beforehand or compare it to a similar service offered by a competitive firm.

More information about the marketing of services is offered in chapter 25 (Improving Results in Your Service Business).

FOR FURTHER INFORMATION

Cannon, Tom. *Basic Marketing: Principles and Practice.* 4th ed. New York: Cassell, 1995.

Connor, Dick, and Jeffrey P. Davidson. *Marketing Your Consulting and Professional Services*. 3rd ed. New York: Wiley, 1994.

Cry, Donald G., and Douglas A. Gray. *Marketing Your Business: A Planning Guide for Small Business*. 2d ed. Bellingham, Wash.: Self-Counsel Press, 1994.

Diamond, Jay, and Gerald Pintel. *Principles of Marketing*. 4th ed. Englewood Cliffs, N.J.: Prentice-Hall, 1990.

Haas, Robert W. *Business Marketing: A Managerial Approach*. 6th ed. Cincinnati: South-Western, 1995.

Hiam, Alexander, and Charles Schewe. *The Portable MBA in Marketing*. New York: Wiley, 1995.

Kotler, Philip. *Marketing Management: Analysis, Planning, Implementation, and Control*. 7th ed. Englewood Cliffs, N.J.: Prentice-Hall, 1991.

——, and Paul N. Bloom. *Marketing Professional Services*. Englewood Cliffs, N.J.: Prentice-Hall, 1984.

Lamb, Charles W., Jr., Joseph F. Hair, Jr., and Carl McDaniel. *Principles of Marketing*. 2d ed. Cincinnati: South-Western, 1994.

Lehmann, Donald R., and Russel S. Winer. *Product Management*. Burr Ridge, Ill.: Irwin, 1994.

Lovelock, Christopher H. *Services Marketing*. 2d ed. Englewood Cliffs, N.J.: Prentice-Hall, 1990.

McCarthy, E. Jerome, Jr., and William D. Perreault, Jr. *Essentials of Marketing*. 6th ed. Burr Ridge, Ill.: Irwin, 1994.

Morgan, Neil. *Professional Services Marketing*. Newton, Mass.: Butterworth-Heinemann, 1991.

Stanton, William J. et al. *Fundamentals of Marketing*. 10th ed. New York: McGraw-Hill, 1993.

Thomas, Robert J. *New Product Development: Managing and Forecasting for Strategic Success*. New York: Wiley, 1993.

Trivers, Jon. *Do-It-Yourself Marketing: What Every Small Business Owner Needs to Know*. New York: Wiley, 1996.

Webster, Frederick E., Jr. *Industrial Marketing Strategy*. 4th ed. New York: Wiley, 1994.

Zikmund, William, and Michael D'Amico. *Marketing*. 3rd ed. New York: Wiley, 1989.

11

THE MANAGEMENT OF PRICES

THE PRICING AREA is of no less, and possibly greater, weight than the other ingredients of the marketing mix. It requires consummate managerial skill on your part. How a firm handles its pricing frequently spells the difference between marketing success and failure. Business survival and growth depend upon proper pricing practices.

THE MEANING OF PRICE

Clearly, the price concept is closely associated with products (and product management). Indeed, these two *P*s are often handled in tandem, although this shouldn't be the case. Price, you see, has many facets:

- Price facilitates the buying and selling process.
- Price is affected by the interplay of supply and demand.
- Price is a useful tool in promotion.
- Price can help—or hinder—sales.
- Price ties into methods of distribution.
- Price can affect your bottom-line figure for better or for worse.
- Price is related to costs and profits.
- Price can be a valuable tool when used as a competitive weapon.
- Price can be manipulated strategically from one stage of the product life cycle to the next.

To the consumer, the price of a product (or service) represents nothing more than the seller's interpretation, expressed in monetary terms, of the product's utility value: its ability to satisfy a buyer's wants or needs. Consequently, shoppers regard the price of an item as "fair" (congruent with their own perceptions of its worth in dollars and cents) or pegged higher or lower than fair. If they consider the price too high, consumers resist purchasing the item. If the price is considered low, then it becomes a "bargain" (although a low price can cause shoppers to doubt the quality of the product).

So for most products there appears to be an acceptable *price range* instead of a specific and exact *price point*. Bear this in mind when pricing your goods.

To manufacturers, price is a more complex affair. Indeed, most producers regard their *manufacturer's price* as a composite designed to cover, at the very minimum, all of the following: the cost of the raw materials that went into the product, the cost of labor required for manufacture, part of the production overhead and the administrative and selling expenses, plus a margin of profit to make it all worthwhile.

Wholesalers and retailers approach pricing in much the same way, except that the *cost of goods purchased* is substituted for materials and other manufacturing expenses.

Most small businesses use this *cost-plus* approach to pricing. Nevertheless, prices shouldn't be formulated solely in this manner. The perceptive small businessperson sees a built-in inconsistency here: the method pays no attention whatever to the *demand* for the product. When the demand for an item is heavy and people are clamoring for it, the majority of consumers will tolerate an increase in the regular (list) price. While some people will refuse to purchase the item, most will buy it anyway, and the resulting sales will generate a good deal more profit overall. Further, when demand is light, maintaining the usual price of an article may lead to a decrease in sales volume.

You should also take into consideration other pertinent factors:

- Competitors' prices
- Desired return on your investment
- Economic conditions
- Level of demand
- Location of your business
- Market factors
- Product factors
- Seasonal factors
- The *price/quality relationship* (and other psychological factors)

SETTING PRICES FOR GOODS AND SERVICES

Business organizations often find it quite difficult to arrive at the right selling prices for their goods and/or services. In actual practice, companies may approach the price-setting problem from several distinctly different vantage points. Three of the pricing bases most commonly found in industry are those of *demand, competition,* and *cost.*

Theoretically, an item's price tends to fluctuate in direct proportion to customer demand for that item. As demand intensifies, the price is apt to rise; as demand falls, we may expect the price to begin to fall. In following a *demand-oriented pricing* approach, management will strive to determine both the current demand level and the price that customers appear willing to pay for the item. The firm may proceed to work up estimates of the different levels of demand that might be expected at various selling prices—in order to determine the one price that should yield the highest sales volume and/or profit.

In *competition-based pricing,* little or no attention is paid to actual demand. Instead, the firm reviews the prices set by its major competitors before making its own pricing decisions. The company may then decide to *(a)* maintain parity with its competitors, *(b)* set its prices above those of its competition (usually to project an above-the-average image), or *(c)* undersell its competition.

By far the most popular approach of all, though, is that of *cost-oriented pricing.* It's logical to assume that any selling price should cover all pertinent costs and also produce some profit for the business enterprise.

The next section offers more details about cost-based pricing.

THE "COST-PLUS" APPROACH

Business costs are traditionally broken down into *fixed* and *variable* expenses (although some firms go further in their accounting procedures and use terms like *semivariable* costs). The term *fixed costs* encompasses all costs that remain approximately the same whether, for example, ten pieces or ten thousand pieces of Item X are produced each day in the plant. In other words, these expenses do not vary along with the ebb and flow in the production rate. The fixed-costs category includes such expenses as rent, heat, insurance, depreciation, executive salaries, interest on loans, and property taxes.

Expenses that do vary along with output are labeled *variable costs*. These include the cost of raw materials (or semiprocessed materials and components if used), wages earned by the production workers (direct labor), warehousing and shipping costs, and sales costs (commissions).

When setting prices by means of a cost-plus approach, management typically takes into consideration total variable expenses per unit as well as a per-unit share of the firm's fixed costs. Also built into the price structure is the amount of profit desired (per unit, of course). By far the most common cost-plus approach, this method is known as *full-cost pricing*.

PRICING POLICIES

Work out in advance, and to your own satisfaction, a number of specific pricing policies for every aspect of your company's marketing activity. For example, mull over the best pricing strategy to employ with relation to your competition.

In addition to the three basic pricing strategies discussed above, other marketing areas for establishing a pricing policy include:

- The marketing channels employed (setting manufacturer's, wholesaler's, retailer's, and consumer's prices)
- The stage of the product life cycle (for example, in the introductory stage, a company has the choice of adopting a *skimming* policy whereby the price is set high in an attempt to "skim the cream" of the market; or a *penetration* policy whereby the price is set low in order to establish a strong foothold within short order in the marketplace)
- The promotion mix area (the use of such devices as specials, cents- or dollars-off sales, leader items, and the like)
- Discounting, arranging terms of payment, and so on

MARKUPS (OR MARKONS)

When you set the selling price of any item you should not only cover all relevant per-unit costs but also tack on an appropriate amount so that you end up with some profit for your firm.

Take the situation where the owner of a small gift shop purchases two dozen decorative candy dishes from a jobber at $48.00 a dozen. Individually, the candy dishes have cost $4.00. The retailer decides to put them on display at $7.50, thus asking $3.50 more than the original cost. Is this amount all profit? Not really, if you're thinking in terms of *net* profit, because a store proprietor must also consider operating expenses: rent, electricity, insurance, labor, and advertising costs. So the $3.50 is really a *contribution* toward overhead. Hopefully, that figure also contains some profit as well.

The $3.50 represents the retailer's *markup*. Markup is the difference between the cost of an item and its selling price—the amount of *gross* profit earned on the article of merchandise when it is sold. Markup is usually expressed as a percentage—either of the selling price (usual in retail businesses) or of the cost (usual in manufacturing and wholesaling). *Markon* is another term used fairly interchangeably with *markup,* because the gross profit margin is *marked on* to the cost to arrive at the selling price.

Although this difference in terms could be regarded as hairsplitting, we ought to relegate markons to the manufacturing and perhaps wholesaling spheres and leave markups to the retailers. The manufacturer generally approaches the pricing of products by totaling each item's direct costs and then *marking on* a fixed percentage of the costs as a contribution to overhead and profit. The knowledgeable retailer, on the other hand, thinks first in terms of the overall percentage of sales needed to cover operating expenses and to yield the planned (net) profit margin, and then adds on this percentage to the costs of the hundreds of items brought in at different costs.

Let's attempt to work this through by way of an example. Assume that an item costs the manufacturer $2.00 to produce. This cost figure is arrived at by combining the cost of materials per unit ($.80) with the direct labor cost ($1.20). Seeking $1.00 as a contribution toward other expenses and toward profits, the producer decides to offer the item at $3.00 per unit to wholesalers. This represents a desired *markup on cost* of 50 percent ($1.00 divided by $2.00).

After buying the article at $3.00, the wholesaler prices it for sale to retailers at $3.90, apparently looking for a markup (again, on cost) of 30 percent. This percentage covers expenses and profit for performing wholesaling services as the goods travel along the marketing channel toward the final consumer. (See the section on "Marketing Channels in the Economy" in chapter 16.)

MARKUPS IN RETAILING

The majority of small retailers approach the pricing problem in the same way. Many jewelry stores, for instance, traditionally use a *keystone* markup in pricing merchandise: They simply double their costs. If a gold wedding band costs a jeweler $160, the item is usually offered to the consumer at the selling price of $320. This earns the retailer a 100 percent markup (or markon) on the cost.

A better approach is to follow the pricing procedures of department stores and large chain-store organizations. Well in advance of each season, these retail companies set their merchandise plans. Along with sales projections, they plan their inventory requirements, expenses, profits, and so forth. Their planned sales figures form the basis for their calculations; all other areas are then tied in—expressed as some percentage of the sales volume.

Of course, while a department store carries literally thousands of different items, the small retail shop might offer only a hundred or two. It's difficult for the small-store owner to keep abreast of all the separate costs, especially since the cost of a single item may vary throughout the year and from one supplier to the next. However, by maintaining all paperwork (inventory records, accounting statements) on a *retail-*, rather than a cost-valuation basis, the small-store proprietor can use this information for decision making as skillfully as department store management. For example, by using the net sales figure atop the past year's income statement, a retailer can readily calculate the firm's total operating expenses as a percentage of sales. Then, when making plans for the following year, the merchant can build both expected operating expenses and a planned profit target into the pricing of store merchandise.

To demonstrate this point, let's return to the earlier illustration of the item that costs $2.00 to manufacture and ends up being offered to the retailer (by the wholesaler) at a cost per unit of $3.90. Suppose you are the store merchant in this case, and you have calculated that your operating expenses total 36 percent of sales. You would like to shoot for an 8 percent profit goal for the year before taxes. Putting the two percentages together, you now have a 44 percent-of-sales figure that must be "covered" over and above the original cost of your merchandise. Since you need an overall markup of 44 percent of sales on goods sold during the year, you try to price most items you buy for resale with that figure in mind. The item that costs you $3.90, then, should sell at about $6.96. (*Note:* To obtain the proper selling price, divide the cost price by the *complement of the markup*. This is what you have left after you subtract the markup, whatever it may be, from 100 percent. In this case, we have 100 percent − 44 percent = 56 percent. If you divide $3.90 by .56, you'll come up with that $6.96 figure).

Of course, this figure may not seem quite right for a retail selling price—so the merchant will probably peg the price at $6.95, $6.99, or $7.00 (whichever seems, psychologically, like a better figure).

Also, the selling prices for individual items may vary somewhat from the prices derived from that 44 percent markup. Some merchandise can be sold for more money because of its appeal while other articles may have to be placed on sale for less. What's important here is that the retailer attains the targeted 44 percent (at least) on an overall, *maintained markup* basis.

BREAK-EVEN ANALYSIS

The *break-even point* is a vital concept that you should understand completely before your business even gets off the ground. It's the point at which the sales you are able to generate cover all costs. If sales do not reach that level, your firm will find itself "in the red." However, once that point has been passed, your profits will start to mount.

If you own a small factory that manufactures a single product, you may also want to know just how many units of that item must be sold before you can reach your break-even point. Here's the way to find out:

1. Bear in mind that at the break-even point, there is neither profit nor loss; costs are exactly equaled. This indicates that whatever approach we use to arrive at a break-even figure, all costs must be taken into account. Hence, we can use the following formula:

$$\text{Break-even Point (in units)} = \frac{\text{Total Fixed Costs}}{\text{Per-unit Contribution Toward Fixed Costs}}$$

2. Let's assume you have estimated that your total fixed expenses for the year will be $330,000. You have pegged your variable costs on a per-unit basis at $2.64 and your unit price to wholesalers will be $8.10. This means that every unit you sell will make its tiny contribution of $5.46 ($8.10 − $2.64) toward your fixed expenses.

3. Substituting those amounts for the terms in the formula above, we have:

$$\text{Break-even Point (in units)} = \frac{\$330,000}{\$5.46} = 60,440 \text{ (approx.)}$$

In short, you'll need to produce approximately 60,440 units before you reach your break-even point. After that, profits should start coming in.

4. To determine the sales volume you must reach in order to attain your break-even point, simply multiply the number of units required to be sold by the selling price. In this particular situation, the needed sales volume is $489,564 (60,440 × $8.10).

The manufacturer will often experiment with break-even analysis by considering what the various break-even points would be at different selling prices. This analysis aids in determining how to price products. (See exhibit 11–1 for another way of calculating the break-even point.)

EXHIBIT 11–1. ANOTHER APPROACH TO CALCULATING BREAK-EVEN POINTS

Assume you're thinking about launching a retail business. You can figure your break-even right from the *pro forma* income statement you prepared for your first year of operation. Simply follow the procedure below:

1. Add up all your expected operating expenses, both fixed and variable, for the year. (Let's say this totals $57,000.)
2. Decide on the average retail markup you expect to maintain during the year, expressed as a percentage of the sales. (For example, if you assume a 46 percent markup, then what you're really saying is that forty-six cents out of every dollar taken in will be gross profit, and that the balance of that dollar will be paid out for the merchandise you purchase for resale.)
3. Divide the total expenses (number one above) by the *per-dollar gross profit* figure (number two above) to find your break-even point. (In this case, it amounts to $57,000 divided by $.46—which is $123,913.)
4. You might want to go further and find out what your store must produce in sales in order to break even on a *monthly* basis. One way is to simply divide the yearly figure by twelve. Of course, you need to bear in mind that some months (like December) are busier than others, so you can only discuss the "average" month in this situation.
5. If you want to calculate your *daily* break-even figure, count up the number of days your store will be open during each month and divide each month's figure (number four above) by the number of days.

Source: Compiled by the author.

PROMOTIONAL PRICING

When establishing prices for their goods and/or services, companies can resort to a variety of promotional pricing strategies in order to boost sales, increase shopper traffic, or otherwise facilitate the selling process. This is especially true of wholesalers and retail firms.

Most of the popular promotional pricing techniques are briefly described in exhibit 11–2.

EXHIBIT 11–2. PROMOTIONAL PRICING TECHNIQUES

Bait Pricing   An illegal promotional practice whereby a retailer prices an item at a bargain price (with no intention of selling the item) and then advertises the offer in order to bring people into the store.

Bait-and-Switch Pricing   The "follow through" on the bait-pricing technique mentioned above. Once the seeker of the advertised "bargain" is in the store, the merchant attempts to switch the shopper to another, higher-priced brand or type.

Leader Pricing   A favorite technique of retailers, this involves lowering the customary selling price of one or more popular articles in order to attract consumers to the store. Although the firm will earn a lower-than-ordinary markup on the merchandise it sells in this manner, it will still enjoy some gross margin dollars.

Loss Leader Pricing   A variant of leader pricing, whereby the selling price of an item is reduced even more drastically, to the point at which the retailer offers it at below original cost. The technique, illegal in many states where unfair sales-practice laws are in effect, may be employed occasionally for a dual purpose: to clear out stock while simultaneously increasing in-store traffic.

Multiple Pricing   A promotional pricing technique designed to induce the shopper to purchase two or more units of a product at one time by affording some savings, such as "three for $2.50."

Odd-and-Even Price Endings   A pricing concept with psychological ramifications. Despite the fact that research in this area has been inconclusive, many retailers prefer to use prices that end in odd figures, such as $1.89, $6.49, or $19.95. On the other hand, there are some who prefer even-figure price endings or even-dollar amounts and price their merchandise accordingly.

Prestige Pricing   A technique whereby a company deliberately sets higher-than-customary prices for its offerings in order to differentiate its image from those of its competitors. This has the psychological effect of inducing people to regard the merchandise (and the firm) as better in quality.

Price Lining   A technique that seeks to make it easier for shoppers to select

EXHIBIT 11-2. (continued)

merchandise and, at the same time, simplifies stock planning for the retailer. Here, the number of choices made available to the consumer is reduced by grouping similar items within a few, rather than many, price lines. For example, a menswear store might group its neckties at $9.95, $16.95, and $22.95, depending on the quality and appearance of the goods.

Psychological Pricing A term applied to any of several pricing tactics employed by companies to create buyer interest in the product or service by appealing to certain beliefs that people hold; for example, prestige pricing or the use of odd-price endings.

Source: Compiled by the author.

In addition to the promotional pricing techniques described above, many other pricing terms are in common use in the business world. A few of these are explained in exhibit 11-3.

EXHIBIT 11-3. SOME PRICING TERMS

Advertising Allowance A contribution made by a manufacturer or distributor toward the costs incurred by another channel member to induce the latter firm to advertise the former's products.

Bid Pricing Estimating, then setting the price for, an individual job to be performed (as in construction work) in order to bid against competitors for the work.

Brokerage Allowance The fee or commission earned by a broker for the role played in bringing buyer and seller together.

Geographical Pricing Any of several distribution-oriented approaches to price determination designed to encompass solutions to the freight problem. Among them are zone, FOB-factory, and uniform delivered pricing.

Guarantee Against Price Decline A tactical management decision designed to contribute to good channel relationships. For example, a manufacturing company will try to protect its distributors against falling prices in industries (or commodities) when prices fluctuate excessively during the year.

List Price The price customarily quoted for a particular article. Also known as the *basic list price*.

Penetration Pricing A marketing tactic most often used at the introductory stage of a low-price product's life cycle. Here, management deliberately sets a low price to assure ready acceptance and to gain extensive distribution.

Uniform Delivered Pricing A form of geographical pricing whereby all cus-

EXHIBIT 11–3. (continued)

tomers are charged the same price even though they may be located in different geographical areas. Here, the company has calculated in advance the effects of differing freight charges and "built them in" to the price through some overall adjustment for freight.

Zone Pricing   A form of geographical pricing whereby, for example, a firm sells a product at one price to all purchasers east of the Mississippi and at another price to those located west of the Mississippi. (An excellent example of zone pricing is that engaged in by the U.S. Postal Service in its handling of parcel post.)

Source: Compiled by the author.

DISCOUNTS

One of the most important aspects of pricing is the area of discounts. A discount is a reduction from the regular selling price (or list price) of a product or service, usually expressed in terms of a percentage of the selling price. For example, many retail firms offer their personnel an employee discount as part of the total compensation package. This discount may run from 10 or 15 percent "off" the retail price of merchandise bought in the store to as much as 25 or 30 percent and more.

Here are some other important types of discounts:

Cash Discount   A reduction in price granted to encourage early payment of an invoice.

Introductory Discount   A reduction in the regular price to induce intermediary institutions (wholesalers, retailers) or final consumers to buy a particular (usually new) product.

Quantity Discount   A reduction in the normal selling price of an item to induce purchasers to buy in quantity.

Seasonal Discount   A reduction in selling price offered to encourage customers to purchase products in advance of a forthcoming season.

Trade Discount   Any reduction from the regular list price of goods that is offered to intermediary firms as compensation for the functions they perform along the channel structure. Usually expressed as some percentage off the quoted price as, for example, $144 per dozen, less 45 percent.

FOR FURTHER INFORMATION

Hanna, Nessim, and H. Robert Dodge. *Pricing Policies and Procedures.* New York: NYU Press, 1995.

Harvard Business School Press Staff. *How to Price Your Products and Services.* New York: McGraw-Hill, 1991.

Monroe, Kent B. *Pricing: Making Profitable Decisions.* New York: McGraw-Hill, 1990.

Montgomery, Stephen L. *Profitable Pricing Strategies.* New York: McGraw-Hill, 1988.

Morris, Michael H. *Market Oriented Pricing: Strategies for Management.* Lincolnwood, Ill.: NTC Publishing, 1992.

Nagle, Thomas T. *Strategy and Tactics of Pricing: A Guide to Profitable Decision Making.* 2d ed. Englewood Cliffs, N.J.: Prentice-Hall, 1994.

Winkler, John. *Pricing for Results.* Newton, Mass.: Butterworth-Heinemann, 1989.

12

PROMOTION MANAGEMENT

AN APT SYNONYM for *promotion* is "persuasive communication." It is through well-planned and coordinated promotional activities that prospective buyers are attracted to your products or informed about your services, persuaded to try them, and ultimately become your regular customers.

PROMOTIONAL OBJECTIVES

While promotional activities may be varied and subject to change, they do have to be congruent with the firm's long-range objectives. They must also be flexible enough to admit occasional tactical maneuvering and, less frequently, allow broad changes in strategy as your company copes with competitors' moves and environmental dynamics. Some common promotional objectives are shown in exhibit 12–1.

THE PROMOTION MIX

Promotion's first objective is to initiate demand for the company's products and services. Here, the small-business owner should think in terms of planning the blend or mixture of several basic ingredients, much like mixing a cocktail. This deliberate *promotion mix* always encompasses three major ingredients (although the proportions vary depending on the nature of the job): personal selling, advertising, and sales promotion—with a dash of public relations/publicity.

Each of the major components is treated in some depth in the next three chapters of this book.

As can be seen in figure 12–1, the promotion-mix "blends" will differ from one type of company to another.

EXHIBIT 12–1. PROMOTIONAL OBJECTIVES

- Attract new customers
- Cultivate brand or store loyalty
- Establish brand differentiation
- Encourage repeat business
- Enhance the firm's image
- Increase store traffic
- Introduce new products
- Obtain additional distributors
- Open up new territories
- Provide information
- Sell products or services
- Support the company's salespeople
- Sustain brand loyalty

THE BUDGET FOR PROMOTION

Typically, setting the annual expenditure for promotion represents a complex challenge. There's no one pat approach here; management is generally unable to assess the consequences of allocating X dollars to next year's promotional activity. Most budget decisions in this area are quite subjective. Often, they're preceded by an investigation (generally unscientific), which raises questions like:

- How much can we afford to allocate to promotion?
- Can we learn from our competitors? How much do they spend annually, on the average?
- What was the total dollar amount we spent last year, and how did it help our sales?
- Would we be better off putting some of our promotion dollars into new equipment or machinery? Office help? Additional salespeople?
- Are there particular promotion areas that need to be beefed up?

In planning the overall promotion budget, companies follow diverse strategies, perhaps gravitating from one to another every two or three years. The more popular approaches are indicated below:

FIGURE 12–1. COMMON PROMOTION-MIX BLENDS FOR VARIOUS TYPES OF SMALL COMPANIES

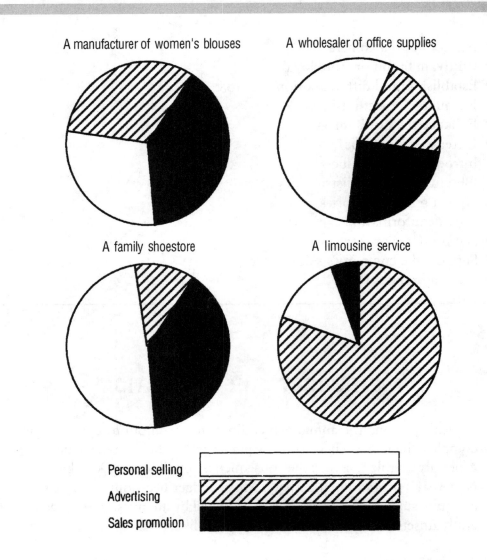

Percentage-of-Sales Allocating a percentage of the firm's sales volume, usually matching the trend within the particular industry

Meet the Competition Matching the estimated promotional expenditure of a leading competitor

Objective-and-Task Defining the job that needs to be done and then estimating how much is required to accomplish the job

Status-Quo Holding down next year's budget to the amount that will be spent during the current year (or, perhaps, making a minuscule adjustment in the percentage, upward or downward)

Multi-Budget Preparing several alternative budgets (low, medium, high), then forecasting the expected return on investment for each, and selecting the most promising one

After the size of the overall promotion budget has been determined, individual budgets need to be prepared for advertising, personal selling, sales promotion, and public relations.

A WORD OR TWO ABOUT PUBLIC RELATIONS

The phrase *public relations* is a catchall sort of term. Narrowly interpreted, it can mean little more than a stream of news releases, emitted by a company over time, that manage to find their way into print or onto radio or television. Such an interpretation leads many business executives to consider "PR" as tantamount to free, unpaid advertising. Actually, news releases of this type are more in the realm of *publicity* than of public relations.

Properly defined, public relations (PR) comprises a wide range of activities expressive of the firm's attitudes toward others. In the main, it consists of meaningful two-way communication between the company and its various publics: internal (employees, stockholders) as well as external (customers and prospective buyers, suppliers, competitors, and government agencies at all levels).

Every company has public relations; the PR may be good, fair, or poor. Well-planned PR programs start with the firm's owner(s) and are reflected throughout the organization, in good employee relations as well as in good company relationships with the outside world (see figure 12–2). Good PR involves observing guarantees on products, acting in an aboveboard fashion in conducting business, showing courtesy in the treatment of all, answering complaints promptly, and encouraging feedback from the several publics.

THE PUBLICITY RELEASE

To maintain effective public relations, a company must make sure that its several publics know what it stands for and what is going on at all times. The mainstay of a well-planned PR program is the *news* or *publicity release.*

News releases should be typed on an 8½ × 11–inch sheet of white paper. Ample margins should surround the double-spaced text. The organization's name and address usually appear at the top of the sheet. Also shown are the name, title, address, and telephone number

FIGURE 12–2. A COMPANY'S PUBLICS

of the *contact person*—the individual who can be called for more details.

Type the words *For Immediate Release* above the copy. If, however, the story is to be held over for a later date, a phrase such as *Hold for Release on . . . (time, day, date)* should be substituted.

When preparing news releases, the writer should follow the principles of good journalism. Be sure to answer the "five Ws." Use active words; avoid the passive tense. Make every word count; each release should only run as long as is necessary to tell the complete story. If it runs to several pages in length, number them and place the word *more* at the bottom of each page except the last. To signify the end of the release, type in *30* or "# # #" below the last line of text.

FOR FURTHER INFORMATION

Bagehot, Richard. *Sales Promotion, Advertising, and PR.* New York: Macmillan, 1991.

Baker, Kim, and Sunny Baker. *How to Promote, Publicize, and Advertise Your Growing Business.* New York: Wiley, 1991.

Bly, Robert W. *Targeted Public Relations.* New York: Henry Holt and Company, 1993.

Brezen, Tamara, and William Robinson. *Sales Promotion Handbook.* 8th ed. Chicago: Dartnell Corp., 1994.

Budd, John F., Jr. *Street Smart Public Relations.* Lakeville, Conn.: Turtle Publications, 1992.

Burnett, John J. *Promotion Management.* Boston, Mass.: Houghton Mifflin, 1992.

Dommermuth, William P. *Promotion: Analysis, Creativity, and Strategy.* 2d ed. Cincinnati: South-Western, 1989.

Doty, Dorothy I. *Publicity and Public Relations.* Hauppauge, N.Y.: Barrons, 1990.

Engel, James F., Martin R. Warshaw, and Thomas C. Kinnear. *Promotional Strategy: Managing the Marketing Communications Process.* 8th ed. Burr Ridge, Ill.: Irwin, 1994.

Fletcher, Tana, and Julia Rockler. *Getting Publicity.* Bellingham, Wash.: Self-Counsel Press, 1990.

Hausman, Earl, and Philip Benoit. *Positive Public Relations.* 2d ed. Blue Ridge Summit, Pa.: TAB Books, 1989.

McIntyre, Catherine V. *Writing Effective News Releases.* Colorado Springs, Colo.: Piccadilly Books, 1992.

Schultz, Don E. *Sales Promotion Essentials.* 2d ed. Lincolnwood, Ill.: NTC Publishing Group, 1994.

Smith, Jeanette. *The New Publicity Kit.* New York: Wiley, 1995.

Sutlip, Scott M. *Effective Public Relations.* 7th ed. Englewood Cliffs, N.J.: Prentice-Hall, 1994.

Ulanoff, Stanley. *Handbook of Sales Promotion.* New York: McGraw-Hill, 1985.

Yudkin, Marcia. *6 Steps to Free Publicity.* New York: Penguin Books, 1994.

ADVERTISING

ADVERTISING IS PAID, impersonal communication via advertising media and is designed to influence prospects and customers en masse. By way of contrast, personal selling involves face-to-face contact between seller(s) and buyer(s).

Effective management of the advertising function in your business requires careful attention to specifics like selecting and then researching market segments; setting objectives; conceptualizing plans; designing advertising campaigns; constructing messages and advertisements; selecting the media for reaching your targets; and measuring the effectiveness of your advertising (see figure 13–1).

TYPES OF ADVERTISING

Depending upon how you look at it, advertising may be classified in a number of ways:

- According to the company's position along the channel of distribution, either *manufacturer, wholesaler,* or *retailer advertising.* (Where the cost of advertising is shared by two channel members, this is referred to as *cooperative advertising.*)
- According to the planned geographical coverage, that is, *national, regional,* or *local advertising*
- By what is being advertised, that is, *product, brand,* or *institutional* (company, industry) *advertising*
- By the media employed, either *television, radio, print* (newspaper, magazine), *outdoor* (billboard), *car card* (subway, bus), *direct mail,* or *mail-order advertising*

FIGURE 13–1. ADVERTISING MANAGEMENT

THE ADVERTISING MEDIA

Companies depend on the advertising media (newspapers, magazines, radio, and television) to carry their promotional messages to prospective and actual customers.

Proper media selection is a difficult task for the entrepreneur. For optimum yield, specialized knowledge is a must. If you envision a moderate-sized advertising budget for your new business, I strongly urge you to enlist the services of a small advertising agency willing to take on your account and grow along with you.

Where should you advertise? One basic principle to follow here is to try to reach as much of your "preselected" audience as you can at as low a cost as possible. This may be accomplished through a variety of media: newspapers, magazines, radio, TV, direct mail, billboards, subway and bus posters, and circulars. Of course, it's difficult (if not impossible) to assess the effectiveness of your firm's advertising. Mail order and direct-mail advertising are exceptions: Responses to your advertisements can be keyed or couponed and some evaluation made of results.

Some factors to take into consideration in making media choices are the appropriateness and size of each medium's audience or readership, comparative media costs, production costs, and the relative rapidity of results you can expect. Each medium has its own particular attributes, negative as well as positive.

Where speedy action is wanted, the broadcast media (radio and television) and the daily newspaper lead all other media. Reaction to advertising in these three is almost immediate: 70 to 80 percent (if not more) of the results will be in within the first week.

Newspapers   In small towns, the local newspaper is a valuable medium for most retail operations. In a metropolitan area, however, much of the newspaper's circulation is "waste" simply because a substantial number of readers live or work miles away from the location in question. Unless the "pulling power" of the advertisement is exceptional, it's doubtful that many of those consumers would visit the premises. On the other hand, weekly area newspapers—or small-space classified advertisements used on a regular basis—can be of value to most types of enterprises.

You should know that newspapers can assist you in preparing copy as well as layout for your purposes. Often they're able to furnish standard illustrations or cuts for a more effective presentation.

Magazines   Magazines and trade journals can be effective media when used for expanding your distribution, securing additional dealers for your products or services, recruiting salespeople in different territories, or selling goods by mail order. Advertisers may expect to "pull" results for a long time, simply because these publications may lie around the office or home for many months. For this reason, too, the advertiser can count on multiple readership. Photographs reproduce well in magazines, and full-color reproduction is usually available when needed.

There are, of course, a few drawbacks to this medium. For one thing, considerable "lead time" is required: Copy and art for your ad must be submitted months in advance of the publication date to ensure getting into the particular issue. For another, the cost of space can be rather high.

Radio and Television   Both of the broadcast media are characterized by fast results, short lead time, and flexibility. Because it reaches large audiences and appeals to two senses, rather than one, television has both tremendous impact and extensive reach. Nevertheless, it is used only occasionally by the smaller firm. Air time is expensive, and the cost of preparing even a thirty-second commercial can be high.

Local radio is generally more feasible for the small company and is of value in reaching specific segments of the market or for offering special "deals" or promotions. Of course, radio copy can be written for you by your local station representative.

One disadvantage of the air media is that messages conveyed by either are short-lived. Moreover, radio announcements are limited in that they depend on sound alone, rather than sight and sound. Another problem is that in any one area of the country—and at any one time—a number of radio stations are likely to be broadcasting. Thus, listeners are, in reality, "fragmented" into a number of separate audiences, each listening to a different station. This means that your announcement being aired over one station will not reach any of the other groups.

Direct Mail   Direct mail is an exciting medium and one that has been growing in popularity by leaps and bounds over the past three decades. These days, American business spends more each year on direct mail than for either radio or magazine advertising. The medium ranks third highest in annual advertising expenditures, after newspapers and television (in that order).

An extremely versatile medium, direct mail is capable of reaching nearly every conceivable target group: plumbers or restaurant owners, mathematics teachers or physicians, hardware manufacturers or golf club members, stamp collectors or radio operators, ceramic tile wholesalers or government officials, and so forth. It's also a powerful and persuasive medium; like personal selling, it conveys a sales message directly from the seller to the potential buyer. Moreover, complete information can be presented—something that is often not possible when using other media because of the high cost of additional space or air time.

Two disadvantages of the direct-mail medium, though, are the high cost per thousand readers as compared to newspaper and magazine ad costs and the "junk-mail" problem (that is, that many recipients just toss direct mailings into the wastebasket without reading the material).

Table 13–1 summarizes some of the advantages and disadvantages of the major advertising media.

Other Media Often, a company will utilize one or more additional vehicles to carry its promotional messages to its target prospects or customers. Among these are the *position media* (outdoor and transit advertising), the ever-popular Yellow Pages, and handbills. For retailers especially, the handbill (or flier) is a relatively inexpensive, yet often effective, medium. For maximum effect, be sure to avoid distributing simplistic printed announcements. Instead, offer well-conceived and imaginative messages aimed at motivating shoppers to visit the location.

ADVERTISING MESSAGES

Any advertising you use for your company should be designed primarily to inform people about your products and/or services and to persuade them to buy. Hence, whatever the medium you select, each "message" should:

- Be clear and couched in the targeted customers' vocabulary
- Provoke interest
- Appeal to people's wants and needs
- Stress desirable features of the product or service
- Sound believable
- Motivate people to buy
- Tell them where they can buy

TABLE 13–1. MAJOR ADVERTISING MEDIA: SOME ADVANTAGES AND DISADVANTAGES

Medium	Advantages	Disadvantages
Print Media		
Newspapers	Short lead time	Competition from other ads, news stories
	Low cost per 1,000 readers	Waste circulation
	Flexibility	
	Extensive coverage of market	
Magazines	Long life of ad	Long lead time
	Multiple readership	Lack of flexibility
	Market selectivity	Waste circulation
	Good reproduction of photographs	Higher cost per 1,000 readers than newspapers
	Availability of color	
Direct Mail	Most persuasive medium	High cost per 1,000 readers
	Can reach specific target groups	"Junk-mail" problem
Broadcast (Air) Media		
Radio	Fast results	Short message life
	Short lead time	Limited to one sense
	Flexibility	Fragmentation of audience (many stations compete for listeners)
	Market selectivity	
	Relatively inexpensive	
	Substantial audience loyalty	
Television	Fast results	High cost of air time
	Impact	High cost of producing commercials
	Extensive reach	Short life of message
	Scheduling flexibility	

Source: Compiled by the author.

In addition to the message copy, artwork and layout are also essential elements in preparing newspaper advertisements. Artwork and layout complement and reinforce the copy and at the same time attract the attention of more readers. For this reason, large black type (or unusual typefaces), borders around the advertisement, illustrations, and halftones (photographs) will not only contribute to the total message but also result in expanded readership. Yes, a picture may be worth a thousand words (or more!).

As a general rule, doubling the size of an advertisement does not by any means trigger an automatic 100 percent increase in the number of readers. Often, only an additional 10 or 15 percent readership can be expected. Given the erratic, though perfectly normal, behavior of the fallible human memory, there's far more value in designing and using an *advertising campaign* than in scheduling a single, one-shot advertisement, no matter how large, in the newspaper. Preferably, one ought to think in psychological terms: the reinforcement of learning that takes place in the regular reader's mind as a result of *frequency of exposure*.

FOR FURTHER INFORMATION

Arens, William F., and Courtland L. Bovee. *Contemporary Advertising.* 5th ed. Burr Ridge, Ill.: Irwin, 1994.

Bacon, Mark S. *Do-It-Yourself Direct Marketing: Secrets for Small Business.* New York: Wiley, 1991.

Baker, Kim, and Sunny Baker. *How to Promote, Publicize, and Advertise Your Growing Business.* New York: Wiley, 1991.

Bly, Robert W. *The Perfect Sales Piece: A Complete Do-It-Yourself Guide to Creating Brochures, Catalogues, Fliers, and Pamphlets.* New York: Wiley, 1994.

Burstiner, Irving. *Mail Order Selling: How to Market Almost Anything by Mail.* 3rd ed. New York: Wiley, 1995.

Caples, John, and Fred E. Hahn. *Tested Advertising Methods.* 5th ed. Englewood Cliffs, N.J.: Prentice-Hall, 1996.

Davidson, Jeff. *Marketing On a Shoestring: Low-Cost Tips for Marketing Your Products or Services.* 2d ed. New York: Wiley, 1994.

Dennison, Dell, and Linda Tobey. *The Advertising Handbook.* Bellingham, Wash.: Self-Counsel Press, 1991.

Eicoff, Alvin. *Direct Marketing through Broadcast Media.* Lincolnwood, Ill.: NTC Business Books, 1995.

Hahn, Fred. *Do-It-Yourself Advertising: How to Produce Great Ads, Catalogs, Direct Mail, and Much More.* New York: Wiley, 1993.

Holtz, Herman. *Great Promo Pieces: Create Your Own Brochures, Broadsides, Ads, Flyers, and Newsletters That Get Results.* New York: Wiley, 1988.

Jugenheimer, Donald W., and Gordon E. White. *Basic Advertising.* Cincinnati: South-Western, 1991.

Klein, Erica Levy. *Write Great Ads: A Step-by-Step Approach.* New York: Wiley, 1990.

Norris, James. *Advertising.* 4th ed. Englewood Cliffs, N.J.: Prentice-Hall, 1990.

Nylen, David W. *Advertising: Planning, Implementation, and Control.* Cincinnati: South-Western, 1993.

Stone, Bob. *Successful Direct Marketing Methods.* 5th ed. Lincolnwood, Ill.: NTC, 1993.

14

PERSONAL SELLING

FOR MOST SMALL manufacturers or wholesalers, there's no doubt that energetic *personal selling* efforts constitute the most critical aspect of promotion. This is also true for most retail firms, though to a lesser degree. Retail selling differs radically from the traditional form of personal selling in that there's little need to "prospect" for customers in the usual sense, much less call on them to promote your wares. Good selling practices are brought into play once the shopper enters the store. This section, then, addresses the manufacturer rather rather than the retailer.*

Partnerships are frequently formed in which one partner has experience in plant operation and the other in sales. In such cases, the sales-oriented partner makes the necessary contacts and visits. More commonly, however, the young manufacturing company contracts with a *selling agent* to sell its particular product or product line. This agent works closely with the company, under contract, and is charged with selling the plant's entire output.

Manufacturers' agents (or *reps*) are intermediaries in the channels of distribution. They offer the manufacturer quick entry into a territory by providing an experienced sales staff and ready-made customers. These sales representatives can bring in orders for your company shortly after you sign up with them.**

Generally, a sales rep is compensated on a commission basis, earning a small percentage of the total billings facilitated through his or her efforts. The approach enables you to calculate your sales costs with comparative ease.

---

* See the section entitled "The Retail Selling Process Analyzed" in chapter 24.

** For help in locating suitable agents, contact your trade association or the Manufacturers' Agents National Association (MANA) at 23016 Mill Creek Road, P.O. Box 3467, Laguna Hills, CA 92654.

Engaging a sales rep to promote your product offers obvious advantages in cost and time. However, there are several drawbacks as well. Your representative also assists other clients, making it impossible to work 100 percent of the time on your behalf. In addition, if you fail to renew your agreement when it expires, your rep may take along some of your customers to your competitor. Moreover, you might find your selling expenses running rather high if your sales volume increases substantially.

However, as sales volume continues to expand, you may eventually decide to take a giant step forward and initiate a sales force of your own.

SELLING BASICS

Good selling is often tied to the well-known *AIDA Principle*. In this case, the name of an opera is employed as a mnemonic to help you remember the following key words:

Attention   Your first task is to secure the attention of your prospect.

Interest   Next, you seek to arouse his or her interest in knowing more about what you're selling.

Desire   You then begin to build desire on the prospect's part to have what you're selling.

Action   Finally, you get action by securing the order.

To a large extent, good selling is also based on the so-called *needs-satisfaction approach*. Simply put, this means that you must (1) ascertain the prospect's wants and needs, (2) match the proper choice of merchandise/service(s) to meet those wants and needs, (3) show the prospect what those products can do for him, her, or the organization, and (4) convince the person to buy.

THE SELLING PROCESS

The job of personal selling can be more easily understood if it is broken down into a series of steps. Then, by applying both analytical and creative thinking to each of these steps in succession, a new salesperson can develop a professionalism and skill that will improve his or her sales results.

Prospecting   The salesperson knows how to look for potential buyers and knows where to hunt for them.

Qualifying   Also called the *preapproach*. During this step the salesperson tries to find out as much as he or she can about the prospect, so that the presentation can be tailored to the prospect's needs.

The Approach   This is the first contact with the prospect, normally conceived of as the first minute or so after meeting the prospect. Among the better-known approaches (and rather easy to comprehend, just from the titles) are the introductory, referral, and product approaches.

The Presentation   This is the main exposition regarding the product or service being offered. The salesperson shows the prospect what the product or service can do for him or her, brings out all of its selling points, involves the prospect in the presentation (touching and feeling the materials, trying out the item, and so on), and tries to answer all the questions raised during the sales interview.

Handling Objections   Almost always, the prospective buyer will raise several objections during the presentation. A crucial factor in the selling process is the proper handling of such objections: How you handle them can make or break the sale. The majority of objections fall into one or another of the following classifications: objections to price, objections to the quality or workmanship of the product, objections about the firm the salesperson represents, and, perhaps, objections to the salesperson him- or herself. A large percentage of intermediate or advanced training time is devoted to teaching sales personnel how to counter the more common objections.

The Close   This is the culmination of the presentation, the point at which the order is written. There are any number of "closes" to use in different situations; any good book on selling will familiarize you with at least half a dozen.

The Follow-Up   Writing up the order doesn't end the selling process. Before leaving, the experienced salesperson thanks the buyer for the order and promises to call the customer shortly after the order has been delivered to check that everything is satisfactory. In the final analysis, the key to sales success is *repeat business* over the long term.

SALES-FORCE MANAGEMENT

Once the decision is reached to start its own sales force, company management will need to resolve a number of critical issues. These range from the kind and number of salespeople required, through developing training programs and plans for compensating salespeople to methods of deployment and supervision (see figure 14–1).

There are literally hundreds of kinds of selling positions. Some require little in the way of ingenuity or sales ability, like that of the route salesperson who, while making rounds, routinely notes orders for milk, pretzels, potato chips, and other items onto a preprinted order form. Other selling jobs are more demanding, requiring a high level of skill and creativity. Examples include the selling of life insurance, group pension plans, swimming pools, and retirement condominiums.

The productivity of the small company's sales force is of paramount importance in its attempt to secure a foothold in the marketplace. The salespeople are its battle troops directly on the firing line; in fact, they're the very lifeline of the business.

It is essential for outside salespeople to be backed up by: an efficient inside sales office, a fail-safe order-processing and delivery system, diligent credit supervision, competent management, and good two-way communication.

PERSONNEL ASPECTS

Evidently, good selling is more of an art than a science. The expert practitioner needs to possess not only good communication skills but also a thorough understanding of the psychological processes underlying human interactions. Salespeople are not born with these capabilities; such skills are developed and enhanced through practice and training.

FIGURE 14–1. MANAGEMENT OF A SALES FORCE

Recruiting Salespeople → Structuring the Sales Organization → Setting Up Compensation Plans → Training the Salespeople → Supervising the Salespeople → Motivating the Salespeople → Evaluating Sales Performance

Few star sales performers are out of work. Consequently, it's difficult for the small company to locate unemployed top salespeople, much less hire them. It generally makes more sense for the young firm to hire "green troops"—potential sales representatives—and then develop that potential through training. The company should search for individuals who display characteristics commonly found in successful salespeople: good communicative ability, empathy, drive, good appearance and posture, emotional balance, and so forth.

Before initiating a brand-new sales force to promote the product line, a company ought to make a careful appraisal of the characteristics and needs of its targeted prospect groups. In so doing, the firm will gain insights into the type and caliber of salespersons needed to do the job well. (For details on the recruitment, training, compensation, and supervision of employees, see chapter 8.)

ORGANIZATIONAL STRUCTURE

Sales forces are usually structured according to geographical requirements, along product lines, by customer type, or some combination thereof. Of course, the right kind of internal organization is affected by a number of important variables: the product line, the amount of capital, the desired scope of sales activity, and the nature of the customers. In the earlier stages, the salespeople should be directed by the owner(s) of the business; later on, management may consider adding a sales manager to the organization for better results.

WHAT TO DO ABOUT TRAVEL EXPENSES

Outside salespeople incur expenses while traveling from one account to the next. Included are the costs involved in traveling by rail, air, or automobile; meals on the road; overnight lodging; and telephone calls. In the majority of instances, such expenses are reimbursed by the company. Automobiles may be purchased or leased by the firm for their salespeople's use. Some companies require their sales personnel to use their own vehicles. Either approach has its benefits and drawbacks. Your accountant, who knows your business, can give you advice in this area.

In establishing an expense-reimbursement plan, you should have your salespeople report their expenses to you on a regular basis, preferably weekly. Check these expense reports carefully to ensure that they seem reasonably accurate. Your position ought to be that your people will neither gain nor lose.

As a general rule, salespeople on the road should not expect to stay overnight at exclusive luxury hotels (with certain exceptions:

specific industries, higher-level sales representatives, and so on). Neither should they be expected to stay at rundown rooming houses. Indeed, the same type of accommodations are called for as if the salesperson were traveling for personal reasons. Likewise, reasonableness should be the keynote for dining out. These days, a daily "cap" of $40.00 to $45.00 for meals is ample. (Of course, this does not refer to taking prospects to dinner. That is *entertainment!*)

DEPLOYING YOUR TROOPS

If you have the usual type of sales organization, you should consider assigning your salespeople to "manageable" territories. This approach permits you to pare travel costs substantially and to cover each area more intensively, thereby ensuring better service to your firm's accounts. The arrangement also lends itself quite well to the fixing of responsibility; you'll find it easier to hold your people accountable for both sales production and sales expenses.

In the selling game, a lot of time is frittered away on traveling to, from, and between accounts; waiting in outer reception areas until purchasing agents can be seen; and doing paperwork and keeping records. Proper attention to the scheduling and routing of your salespeople can reduce much of these wasted efforts.

TRAINING YOUR SALESPEOPLE

In a healthy sales organization, training is a continuous function, with initial training when the employee first joins the company and follow-up or refresher training later on. The content of beginning training programs should encompass topics like the history of the firm, the product line, pricing, the demographics and other characteristics of the company's clientele, internal systems, and sales instruction. More advanced training is often oriented toward improving sales performance: methods of prospecting, how to make more effective presentations, ways of handling objections, how to close a sale, and the like. Available training methods run the gamut from formal classroom lectures to programmed instruction and self-study. Included here are small-group discussions, role playing, demonstrations by top sales performers, films and other audiovisual material and equipment, and classes in selling at local universities.

ASSESSING SALES PERFORMANCE

Evaluations of sales personnel have at least two primary purposes: (1) to provide management with information for decision making in this particular promotion area, and (2) to improve the performance of salespeople over time. While continuous training for people in the selling operation is admittedly essential—not only for improving sales skills but also for teaching self-management—the gathering of comparative data does enable supervisory management to pinpoint deficiencies and correct below-par performance.

Both subjective and objective approaches should be used to assess selling performance. Subjective criteria include: the salesperson's extent of company knowledge and product knowledge, familiarity with competitive organizations and their offerings, the ability to communicate effectively, good personal appearance and proper attire, steady work habits, and the like. Objective evaluation mainly consists of comparing the "input-output" statistics of the entire salesforce. Among the more useful ratios and indexes in this connection are: the number of orders secured each month related to the number of calls made, the average sales volume per order, the number of new accounts landed per the number of visits made, and so on.

See exhibit 14–1 for some useful suggestions for improving salesperson performance.

EXHIBIT 14–1. IMPROVING SALESPERSON PERFORMANCE

One goal of measuring a salesperson's performance is to help him or her improve. The three steps in bringing about improvement, when and if it is needed, are: planning, measuring, and correcting.

PLANNING

1. Get the salesperson's agreement about what he or she is to obtain or exceed for the next year:

   - Total profit contribution in dollars
   - Profit contribution in dollars for:
     Each major product line
     Each major market (by industry or geographical area)
     Each of ten to twenty target accounts (for significant new and additional business)

2. Get the salesperson's agreement about expenses within which he or she is to stay for the next year:

   - His or her total sales expense budget in dollars
   - His or her budget in dollars for travel: customer entertainment, telephone, and other expenses

3. Have the salesperson plan the number of calls he or she will make to accounts and prospects during the next year.

EXHIBIT 14–1. (continued)

MEASURING

Review at least monthly the salesperson's record for:

- Year-to-date progress toward his or her twelve-month profit contribution goals
- Year-to-date budget compliance

CORRECTING

Meet with the salesperson if records show that he or she is 10 percent or more off target. Review with the salesperson the number of calls made on each significant account, plus what he or she feels are his or her accomplishments and problems. In addition, you may need to do some of the following to help the salesperson improve his or her performance.

- Give the salesperson more day-to-day help and direction.
- Accompany the salesperson on calls to provide coaching.
- Conduct regular sales meetings on subjects that the salesperson wants covered.
- Increase sales promotion activities.
- Transfer accounts to other salespeople if there is insignificant effort or progress.
- Establish tighter control over price variances allowed.

Source: Adapted from "Measuring the Performance of Salesmen," *Management Aid No. 190* (Washington, D.C.: U.S. Small Business Administration, 1975), 7.

FOR FURTHER INFORMATION

Alexander, Roy. *Secrets of Closing Sales.* Englewood Cliffs, N.J.: Prentice-Hall, 1989.

Churchill, Gilbert A., Neil M. Ford, and Orville C. Walker. *Sales Management.* 4th ed. Burr Ridge, Ill.: Irwin, 1993.

Coppert, John J., and William A. Staples. *Professional Selling: A Relationship Management Process.* 2d ed. Cincinnati: South-Western, 1994.

Cummings, Richard. *Contemporary Selling.* San Diego, Calif.: Harcourt Brace Jovanovich, 1987.

Dalrymple, Douglas J. *Sales Management: Concepts and Cases.* 4th ed. New York: Wiley, 1992.

Futrell, Charles M. *ABC's of Selling.* 4th ed. Burr Ridge, Ill.: Irwin, 1994.

Garofalo, Gene. *Sales Manager's Desk Book.* 2d ed. Englewood Cliffs, N.J.: Prentice-Hall, 1996.

Hair, Joseph F., Francis L. Notturno, and Frederick A. Russ. *Effective Selling.* 8th ed. Cincinnati: South-Western, 1991.

Ingram, Thomas N., and Raymond W. LaForge. *Sales Management: Analysis and Decision Making.* 2d ed. Fort Worth, Tex.: Dryden, 1992.

Johnston, Karen, and Jean Withers. *Selling Strategies for Service Businesses.* Bellingham, Wash.: Self-Counsel Press, 1988.

Mahfood, Phillip E. *Teleselling: High Performance Business-to-Business Phone Selling Techniques.* Chicago: Probus, 1993.

McHatton, Robert J. *Total Telemarketing.* New York: Wiley, 1988.

Porterfield, James D. *Teleselling: A Self-Teaching Guide.* 2d ed. New York: Wiley, 1996.

Richardson, Linda. *Selling by Phone: How to Reach and Sell Customers in the Nineties.* New York: McGraw-Hill, 1992.

Stanton, William J., Richard H. Buskirk, and Rosann L. Spiro. *Management of a Sales Force.* 8th ed. Homewood, Ill.: Irwin, 1991.

Stone, Bob, and John Wyman. *Successful Telemarketing.* 2d ed. Lincolnwood, Ill.: NTC, 1991.

15

SALES PROMOTION

SALES PROMOTION IS a composite of activities that round out the personal selling and advertising components of a company's promotion mix. The primary aims of sales promotion are to stimulate sales at the point of purchase (when selling consumer goods and services through retail stores and service shops) and to assist channel intermediaries (wholesalers and retailers) as they move these products toward the targeted purchasers. In addition, sales promotion aids both the manufacturer and the distributor handling industrial goods and services.

THE TOOLS OF SALES PROMOTION

Among the sales promotion aids often employed by firms are catalogs, reprints of advertisements, special displays and display fixtures, banners and signs, exhibits and trade shows, and premiums. Their major contribution is in the areas of training, supporting, and otherwise helping along the efforts of the salespeople involved.

Brief descriptions of the more popular sales promotion tools wielded by modern marketers appear in exhibit 15–1.

PROMOTION AT THE POINT OF PURCHASE

Of the promo tools listed in exhibit 15–1, *displays* are the single most significant category for the retail store. The majority of retail firms rely on window displays to attract attention of passersby, to hook their interest, and to induce them to enter the store. Once inside, shoppers can be persuaded to make purchases through effective selling on the part of the salesclerks, aided by additional (interior) displays.

EXHIBIT 15–1. SOME POPULAR SALES PROMOTION TOOLS

- *Advertising specialties* are inexpensive promotional items given out free to consumers and/or organizations. Generally, they bear the issuing company's name (and, perhaps, its address) as well as a brief message.
- *Audiovisuals* constitute a category that embraces films, filmstrips, tapes, videocassettes, projectors, TV monitors, recorders, and other kinds of equipment used to publicize products and/or services or for demonstration and instructional purposes.
- *Consumer information/instructions* are printed materials or informative talks tailored to a wide range of purposes ranging from assembling knocked-down furniture or installing electronic equipment to useful facts on a wide range of topics.
- *Contests and games* are promotional tools designed to whet the interest of— and generate excitement among—customers and prospective buyers, usually about a company, new product, product line, or service.
- *Coupons* are small printed certificates, distributed through newspapers, magazines, advertising flyers, or direct mail, generally designed to increase sales or promote store traffic. (*Note:* Most popular of all coupons are the cents-off type.)
- *Demonstrations* involve the presentation of products or services in action, showing viewers how they work and how to use them.
- *Displays* are creative treatments of merchandise so attractively arranged as to win the attention and spark the interest of viewers.
- *Exhibits* are attention-getting displays, generally rather static in nature, of interesting articles or collections of articles.
- *Premiums* are articles of merchandise given out free of charge ("giveaways") or sold to customers at nominal cost ("self-liquidators") along with the purchase of one or more items. (*Note:* This category includes both single-offer and continuity-offer types.)
- *PMs ("Push Money")* are modest sums of money paid to salespeople as incentives to encourage greater selling effort.
- *Rainchecks* are forms issued to shoppers in the event that a store has run out of an advertised sale item. A raincheck entitles the holder to purchase that item at the sale price whenever new stock comes in.
- *Rebates* are a promotional pricing tactic; they offer customers partial refunds of the money they spend for specific items they purchase.
- *Sampling* is a form of promotion that involves giving out free samples of merchandise to encourage shoppers to buy that merchandise.
- *Shows* are generally entertaining events that differ substantially from exhibits, which are static, in that movement is involved. Two examples are fashion shows and puppet shows.
- *Special promotional events* encompass an extensive variety of sales promotions (including, among others, anniversary, grand-opening, preseason, early-bird, back-to-school, midnight madness, and buyers' sales) as well as

EXHIBIT 15–1. (continued)

public relations/publicity affairs (such as block parties and other neighbor-hood celebrations).

- *Tie-in promotions* are promotional programs jointly planned, paid for, and conducted by two (or more) companies.
- *Trade-in promotions* are offers extended to potential buyers whereby a customer is granted a cash allowance for an old article of merchandise when purchasing a new one of the same type.
- *Trade shows* offer manufacturers and distributors opportunities to display their wares to retail and wholesale buyers.
- *Trading stamps* are gummed stamps, printed in various denominations (usually, $.10, $.25, $.50, and $1.00). They are given out to customers in amounts that correspond to 10 percent of the purchase price. The customers accumulate them, pasting them into booklets or on sheets, and later turn them in for merchandise at a redemption center.

While a detailed treatment of this important area is beyond the scope of this chapter, exhibit 15–2 offers some basic pointers to provide general directions for window displays.

EXHIBIT 15–2. SOME THOUGHTS FOR WINDOW DISPLAYS

- Shoppers will regard your storefront and show window as the "face" of your retail business. Therefore, the window treatments should always convey the impressions of quality, style, and distinctiveness that you would like to project.
- Displays should be kept clean and neat in appearance at all times. A crowded display contributes nothing but clutter; instead, use air (or "breathing") space between merchandise groupings.
- Whether you engage the services of a professional window trimmer or do the displays yourself, your windows should be changed frequently. At least ten to fifteen changes each year are recommended. (Hint: You might be able to hire someone with display training from a local high school's distributive education program.)
- Window displays are generally more effective when built around a single, unifying theme (Valentine's Day, Back-to-School, Mother's Day, Christmas, Springtime, Vacation Fun, Fall Festival, Travel, and so forth).
- Merchandise, materials, display stands, mannequins (if required), and signs or posters should be carefully selected and prepared ahead of time so that the

EXHIBIT 15–2. (continued)

window can be completely trimmed without incident within a few hours' time.

- In selecting appropriate merchandise to put into the window, pay careful attention to the seasonality factor, to product sales appeal, and to individual gross markups.
- Color is an essential ingredient of display. The color combinations used in the window should be attractive and harmonious.
- Window bases (platforms) are usually covered with appropriate materials, which contribute to the overall effect of the display—satins, netting, burlap, paper, artificial grass mats, and so forth. The retailer should build up a stock of such materials, over time.
- All point-of-purchase materials, such as sign tickets, posters, and banners, should look professional and be kept perfectly clean.
- Special effects, such as motion, lighting, and sound, can be used profitably in connection with your display to draw attention to your window. As a simple example, motion can be imparted to a section of your display through the use of a small electric (or battery-operated) turntable or ceiling turner.

Source: Compiled by the author.

FOR FURTHER INFORMATION

Bagehot, Richard. *Sales Promotion, Advertising, and P.R.* New York: Macmillan, 1991.

Baker, Kim, and Sunny Baker. *How to Promote, Publicize, and Advertise Your Growing Business.* New York: Wiley, 1991.

Brezin, Tamara, and William Robinson. *Sales Promotion Handbook.* 8th ed. Chicago: Dartnell, 1994.

Burnett, John J. *Promotion Management.* Boston: Houghton Mifflin, 1992.

Connor, Richard A., and Jeffrey P. Davidson. *Marketing Your Consulting and Professional Services.* 2d ed. New York: Wiley, 1990.

Dommermuth, William P. *Promotion: Analysis, Creativity, and Strategy.* 2d ed. Cincinnati: South-Western, 1989.

Foster, Eric, and Trudy Ralston. *How to Display It: A Basic Guide to Window and Interior Displays.* 2d ed. New York: Art Direction, 1990.

Mills, Kenneth H., and Judith E. Paul. *Applied Visual Merchandising.* 2d ed. Englewood Cliffs, N.J.: Prentice-Hall, 1988.

Ramsey, Linda M. *Successful Window Dressing and Interior Design.* Oceanside, Calif.: Touch Design, 1995.

Schultz, Don E. *Sales Promotion Essentials.* 2d ed. Lincolnwood, Ill.: NTC Publishing, 1994.

Shimp, Terence A., and M. Wayne Delozier. *Promotion Management and Marketing Communications*. 3rd ed. Orlando, Fla.: Dryden, 1993.

Stanley, Richard E. *Promotion: Advertising, Publicity, Personal Selling, Sales Promotion*. 2d ed. Englewood Cliffs, N.J.: Prentice-Hall, 1982.

Ulanoff, Stanley. *Handbook of Sales Promotion*. New York: McGraw-Hill, 1985.

White, Ken, and Frank White. *Display and Visual Merchandising*. Westwood, N.J.: St. Frances Press, 1994.

Yudkin, Marcia. *Six Steps to Free Publicity*. New York: Penguin, 1994.

16

DISTRIBUTION MANAGEMENT

THE AREA OF *distribution* is still another major constituent of the marketing mix. Involved here are the logistics necessary to deliver the company's products and/or services to the right places at the right time in the right quantities, and at the lowest cost. For the most part, distribution management encompasses the concept of *marketing channels* through which the merchandise moves, both the storage and transportation aspects of marketing, and the allocation of inventories.

Visualize a small factory that produces inexpensive women's slippers: The slipper manufacturer brings in raw materials and perhaps semifinished goods, slipper components, packaging materials, and other supplies and then manufactures the finished products on the plant's machines, packages them, cartons the packages, and ships the lot off "to market." Unless the producing firm wishes to assume the burden of selling the slippers by the pair in a door-to-door canvassing operation, the services of one or more intermediaries are required. The merchandise is funneled into a kind of "pipeline" through which it is propelled to the customers. In actuality, this "pipeline" is a set of component companies, linked together to form a *marketing channel*.

MARKETING CHANNELS IN THE ECONOMY

Without a sales force of its own, the small manufacturing firm will probably resort to consigning its output to an agent for the purposes of securing distribution. The agent, in turn, might call on various local wholesalers—or operate on a more expanded scale if the output is large—to interest them in taking on the new line of products. As alternatives, the manufacturer may decide to deal directly with one large distributor that maintains a sizable sales force or opt instead to sell directly to a number of large retail outlets in the area.

Evidently, the "more cooks who stir the broth," the less control the producer can exercise over the product line. Of course, adding intermediaries necessitates building a cost structure to compensate each of the channel members for the part it plays in the total distribution process. The small business and its management must carefully assess the benefits and drawbacks of the various alternatives, each of which may yield a different payoff for the manufacturing company. Figure 16–1 contains a diagram of the more customary channel choices for consumer goods.

FIGURE 16–1. CHANNELS FOR CONSUMER GOODS

SOME NOTES ON CHANNEL MEMBERS

Intermediaries are those individuals or firms that play a role within the channels of distribution between the producing company and the ultimate consumer. Most people are familiar with the role of the retailer within the economy, so it isn't discussed in this section. Most of us, however, haven't had much contact with wholesaling institutions.

AGENTS AND BROKERS

These intermediaries, found in many lines of business, are mostly specialized individuals and small enterprises. Essentially, their business activity consists of buying and selling on behalf of others (*principals*), thereby earning commissions or fees. Apart from well-known types such as real estate and life insurance agents, there are two major classifications the businessperson should be familiar with: the *manu-*

facturer's agent and the *selling agent*. The label depends on the scope of activities the agent performs on behalf of the principal.

Manufacturers who seek distribution in specific geographical areas and who do not have their own sales forces contract with a manufacturer's agent to represent them in the selected area; hence, the oft-employed synonym *manufacturer's representative*, or simply *rep*. The rep is usually assigned an exclusive territory in which to operate. He or she handles only a portion of the total output from the manufacturer and may also represent other producers (usually with complementary lines) in the same area. Reps are asked to sell an entire "package" handed over to them by the manufacturing company; there's little or no discussion over details like prices, terms, and quantities.

On the other hand, the manufacturer gives the *selling agent* extensive authority over the details of prices, terms, and customer selection. The agent is charged with selling the plant's entire production. Sometimes called a *commission agent,* this intermediary often maintains a sizable and effective sales force. The relationship between the selling agent and the principal is a close one. Indeed, it may even call for the agent to extend financial aid to the manufacturer when necessary.

Finally, the *broker* functions as an intermediary between buyers and sellers, bringing together the two parties while representing either side.

WHOLESALERS

Within the wholesaling sphere, several distinct categories of firms are found:

- Merchant wholesalers (*distributor* and *jobber* are alternate terms for *wholesaler*)
- Agents and brokers
- Manufacturers' sales branches/sales offices
- Petroleum bulk plants and terminals

Probably only the first two types are of interest to the majority of people reading this book, so the other categories are only briefly discussed here. *Manufacturers' sales branches and offices* are producer-owned and -maintained premises where potential buyers can examine the company's product line and place orders. *Petroleum bulk plants and terminals* are highly specialized facilities used to distribute petroleum products to both oil and gasoline retailers as well as to industry.

The majority of wholesaling firms fall into the "regular" or *merchant wholesaler* category. These merchant wholesalers are companies that purchase goods in large quantities, warehouse them, and then break these quantities down into smaller shipments for distribution to their customers. Many sell merchandise to retail firms for resale to consumers. Some sell to industry, commerce, and government markets.

Most regular wholesalers are termed *full-service* or *full-function* because they perform all the necessary functions of wholesalers in the marketing channel: buying, selling, storage, distribution, extending credit, and providing sales information and assistance. Some, on the other hand, are known as *limited-service* wholesalers because they don't perform all of the services that are expected. For instance, some do not extend credit to their customers but require cash on delivery. Others will not store the merchandise.

Full-Service Wholesale Firms
There are three types of full-service distributors:

General Merchandise Wholesaler Much like a general store that carries a variety of different lines of goods, this type of firm provides "general merchandise" to larger and departmentalized retailers.

Single-Line Wholesaler This is a firm equipped to supply its retail clients with a complete, in-depth stock in one particular line of goods, such as groceries, hardware, and the like.

Specialty Wholesaler These companies typically handle a small number of products within a particular merchandise line.

Limited-Function Wholesalers
Intermediaries in this category are far fewer in number than full-service distributors. The more common types include:

Cash-and-Carry Wholesaler Often a chain operation, this distributor sets up outlets at convenient locations where local retailers may come in, purchase needed merchandise with cash, and take the goods out with them. Common examples are those selling bottled/canned beverages and grocery items.

Drop-Shipper Found most frequently in the coal, lumber, and metals industries, this type of wholesale firm usually purveys raw materials or bulky products of a low-unit price to industrial users, though it's not limited to such products or markets. This type of intermediary doesn't take physical possession of the merchandise at any point or put it in a warehouse, but rather arranges for the producer to ship the goods directly to the customer. The company (sometimes a one-person operation, commonly called a *desk jobber*) is billed directly by the producer and, in turn, sends an invoice to the customer for payment. The customer must be billed at a price high enough to incorporate a margin of profit for the wholesaler.

Mail-Order Wholesaler This type of company offers retailers merchandise for resale, characteristically through the medium of printed catalogs issued periodically.

Rack Jobber This is the name given to the wholesale business involved in distributing a specialized line—soft-cover books and magazines, toys, health and beauty aids, novelties, household items, and the like—through supermarkets and other high-traffic outlets. The goods are merchandised with the aid of many types of display racks frequently placed on consignment within a store. It's the jobber's responsibility to keep the racks well stocked and fresh-looking.

Truck Jobber Commonly encountered in the grocery trade, this type of distributor services retail outlets directly from a truck with fast-moving products and perishable goods. In addition to fresh fruits and vegetables, truck jobbers handle dairy products, cookies, frozen foods, and similar items.

TRANSPORTATION

Transportation is an area that involves many important decisions on behalf of both manufacturer and wholesaler. Transportation costs can range from a mere fraction of an item's selling price (as is the case with grain, coal, gravel, and other bulky commodities) to as much as 40 percent or more. Consequently, transportation (or *traffic*) management must focus on two major objectives: (1) minimizing costs and, at the same time, (2) ensuring speedy, reliable delivery of the merchandise.

Goods are moved about by land, water, or air through a variety of transportation modes employed singly or in combination and with the assistance of several supporting agencies.

MAJOR TRANSPORT MODES

Materials and products move overland by means of trucks, trains, and pipelines. Goods are also shipped by air (airmail, air freight) and by water (inland waterways, ocean transport). A brief overview of these five major modes of transportation follows:

Truck Transport   The shipping method most favored by small business (and often by large enterprises as well) is trucking. Trucks offer faster and more frequent delivery to more destinations in the country than any other mode. They're particularly useful for short-distance shipments.

Trains   The railroads offer regular service to distant areas and are especially valuable in transporting machinery, heavy equipment, cattle and livestock, commodities, and so forth. Over their history of service to the nation, the railroads have developed a number of customer benefits that are peculiar to this mode. An example is diversion-in-transit, a service that permits shipments already en route to be redirected to another destination.

Pipelines   This method is generally confined to the movement of petroleum products.

Air   A more costly method of transporting merchandise, shipping by air is customarily of value for the rapid movement of highly perishable goods (exotic plants, seafood, and the like) and items of a high unit value, such as diamonds, jewelry, expensive drugs, and rare paintings.

Water   Moving material by barge along the nation's inland waterways is a low-cost method of transportation. Ocean transport, of course, is significant to the import and export trades.

AUXILIARY SERVICES

Some important transport services assist in the movement of goods. Among these are freight forwarders, shippers' associations, and the United Parcel Service. In addition, the U.S. Postal Service forwards small shipments through their parcel post service.

WAREHOUSING

Moving goods or materials from one stop to the next along the marketing channel is one major facet of distribution. Another important aspect is the temporary storage, or warehousing, of merchandise. Many labor-saving approaches to materials handling, warehousing methods, and inventory procedures exist, all of which merit managerial attention.

Companies that require warehousing facilities must decide to either *(a)* maintain their own strategically located depot(s) or *(b)* resort to holding their goods in public warehouses. In contrast to the older, multistory structures that dot metropolitan areas around the country, today's modern warehouse is commonly a long, low, one-story building located outside a city (with access to a major highway), where land costs are substantially less. With this type of construction there's no need to install and maintain freight (and passenger) elevators or build staircases and stairwells, and no concern (or added expense) is necessary for floor load limits. Furthermore, the internal flow of stock can run a straight course instead of proceeding up and down a number of levels. Goods come in at one end of the rectangular structure, are stored in the center, and then depart through the other end. Because of the excellent layout and operation of the typical modern warehouse—including wide aisles and skids (or pallets) on which cases of merchandise are stacked—heavy machinery such as forklifts can easily move the goods.

RECEIVING AND SHIPPING

Ideally, then, goods are brought in through truck bays onto receiving platforms where they are accepted by the receiving department. Here, each incoming delivery is recorded in the *receiving log,* a register where information such as date and time of shipment, name of supplier, name of transporting agency, invoice number, and number of cases or cartons received are recorded. The delivery is unloaded and checked against the accompanying bill of lading for quantities, contents, and possible damage. The goods received are then consigned to specific locations within the warehouse proper, as reserve stock for future shipment.

When the shipping department receives orders from the sales division, order pickers in the warehouse select the merchandise specified, assembling it in a staging area where it is shipped out. Of course, shipping times and routing are worked out in advance with an eye to transportation capability and costs.

INVENTORY CONTROL

A vital phase of warehouse operation is the inventory procedure established to keep track of the merchandise. You can keep a running *book inventory* of all receipts and withdrawals, either by hand or by mechanical or electronic means. However, no method is as accurate as the taking of physical inventory on a periodic basis (weekly, monthly, quarterly, or otherwise). This involves counting directly all cases, cartons, and individual pieces of stock throughout the building, including both the receiving and shipping departments. Physical inventory is usually accomplished by a team: One individual checks out every nook and cranny of the premises, calling out the count to a second person, who enters the quantities onto a preprinted inventory sheet. Totals and extensions (translating the totals into dollar figures) are done later on in the bookkeeping section.

FOR FURTHER INFORMATION

Allegri, Theodore H., Sr. *Managing Warehouse and Distribution Operations.* Englewood Cliffs, N.J.: Prentice-Hall, 1993.

Blanchard, B. *Logistics Engineering and Management.* 3rd ed. Englewood Cliffs, N.J.: Prentice-Hall, 1986.

Gopal, Christopher, and Harold Cypress. *Integrated Distribution Management: Competing on Customer Service, Time, and Cost.* Burr Ridge, Ill.: Irwin, 1993.

Harmon, Roy L. *Reinventing the Warehouse: World Class Distribution Logistics.* New York: Free Press, 1993.

Johnson, James C., and Donald F. Wood. *Contemporary Logistics.* New York: Macmillan, 1993.

Lambert, Douglas M., and James R. Stock. *Strategic Logistics Management.* 3rd ed. Homewood, Ill.: Irwin, 1992.

Mulcahy, David E. *Warehouse Distribution and Operations Handbook.* New York: McGraw-Hill, 1993.

Rice, Don A. *The Wholesale Distributor: Purpose and Function.* Bryan, Tex.: Darco Press, 1990.

17

MARKETING RESEARCH

MARKETING SUCCESS IS largely realized through

- Carefully and continually appraising the total environment, internal as well as external
- Setting realistic marketing objectives based on sound judgments
- Providing structures for reaching those objectives
- Assessing the results of marketing efforts so that further improvements can be made

The first step in the process implies *knowing* before *doing,* and knowing is therefore basic to marketing management. Far too often, small business is conducted by intuition, probably because the majority of problems repeat and, once solved, provide direction for decisions in the next similar situation. Nevertheless, it makes good sense to investigate new and more complex problems carefully before making decisions, and certainly before coming up with marketing plans.

Here's an illustration: Do you recall the last time you were in the market for a new automobile? Most likely, you visited a showroom where you were promptly greeted by a salesperson. Think back to that meeting; try to recall the conversation between the two of you. Isn't it true that what the sales representative talked about and did in those first few minutes with you were more attuned to "reading" you as a prospective customer than to anything else? This was important, simply because the sales presentation could then be tailored directly to you and your needs, thereby increasing the salesperson's chances of making the sale and earning a commission.

In that transaction, you witnessed the "exchange process" in action: You exchanged your money for the ownership of the car. Bear in mind, too, that communication was involved, on a one-to-one basis (the most persuasive way to communicate).

It's no different with any company that seeks to sell its products or services. Remember: The primary purpose behind a firm's promotional activities is to make sales. Again, this is done through communication, whether on a one-to-one basis as in personal selling, or indirectly through advertising and/or sales promotion. The key concept here is the following: The more a company knows about its intended prospects, the better it can tailor its messages to reach those prospects and induce them to become customers.

At any event, it should now be clear to you that attempts to "read" or "research" prospective customers can be of help to you in your own business.

THE NATURE OF MARKETING RESEARCH

Marketing research is a collective term; it embraces all the activities that assist management in reaching marketing decisions. In reality, it's nothing more or less than a logical, orderly approach to fact finding. Marketing research reduces unknowns to knowns, thereby reducing risks, and enables management to make more rational choices among alternatives.

It should be understood from the outset that no planning is 100 percent infallible. No one can predict the future with certainty. To put it differently, all that research can do (if done properly) is increase your chances of coming up with better decisions. Don't think of it as a substitute for business acumen but simply as an additional managerial tool for you to use.

To the small business owner, marketing research appears to be a "frill"—something that only the larger corporations can afford to pursue. Rarely do entrepreneurs get involved in this form of activity. What holds most of them back, apparently, are (1) a lack of familiarity not only with the methods and techniques of research but even with its purposes; (2) the realization that outside research services are costly; and (3) an inability to evaluate the costs in concrete terms, such as return on investment.

When you get right down to it, all business executives conduct research on occasion, usually without realizing that is what they're doing. Comparing yesterday's sales figures with those of the same day or date last year and drawing conclusions (which may be correct or erroneous) falls into the research category. Some additional examples of simple business research are telephoning a sampling of your customers to ask their opinions about a new product or service you're offering; carefully checking through the rate schedules and readership data of various magazines in order to determine the best place for your one-column advertisement; and studying the "production" ratios of your six sales representatives (number of calls made per day, number of sales per 100 calls, and so on) for the purpose of discovering which ones may need more training or assistance.

Like any other form of activity, research can be performed in a careless, slipshod manner or in a more disciplined fashion. Of course, the way you conduct it influences the extent to which you will find the results useful.

Of course, the large-scale, formal types of study cannot be undertaken on a regular basis in the small company; there just isn't enough room in the operating budget. However, both the brand-new and the established small business need to carry on simple research from time to time in such vital areas as sales, market analysis, and company growth.

TYPES OF MARKETING RESEARCH

Here's a convenient classification of the more common types of studies used in business to help managers make better decisions:

Market Research Ascertaining the needs and wants of prospective customers, assessing the potential of specific market segments, studying competitors, and trading-area measurement

Product Research Research into new-product development, testing the prices of products to determine whether they're too high or too low, brand comparisons, and other investigative activities

Promotion Research Checking the effectiveness of displays or advertising copy, comparing different newspapers and magazines as to costs involved and numbers of readers reached, measuring advertising recall, and similar studies

Sales Research Evaluating the performance of salespeople, studying sales expenses and sales, and analyzing territories

Company Research Checking business trends for the industry and the firm, investigating the firm's "image," and studying employee morale or facility locations

A SIMPLE APPROACH TO FOLLOW

If you've had any military training in your past, you're more than familiar with the "by-the-numbers" learning technique. It is a simple approach to use when you need to gather information to help you solve a business problem:

1. Try to clarify the problem in your mind by attempting to put down on paper a clear-cut statement of it, preferably in the form of a question. Some examples of common problems might be: "What method can I use to control my inventory?" "How can we increase sales by 10 percent in Illinois?" "Through what channels should we distribute our products?" "How can we motivate our sales employees?"

2. Next, do some investigating: Examine past records of your company that may pertain to the problem at hand, speak with knowledgeable people who might be able to shed some light on the subject, and try to find out if any information has been published in the particular area you're investigating. During this "searching" stage you may encounter several possible solutions to your problem. If one or more of these seem applicable, you need go no further.

3. Should you decide you need more details, and if it's worth the time, effort, and the expense involved, then you can proceed to a more sophisticated level. You may want to design a simple questionnaire, to be mailed out to your customers, your suppliers, or to specific groups in the general population, depending upon the nature of your problems. For faster results, you can query some of these people over the telephone. (Both of these approaches are treated at greater length in a later section of this chapter.)

4. Finally, for an occasional problem that resists your best efforts at solving, you might consider hiring a research firm to handle the project, provided it's worth the expense involved. Turn things over to specialists who are thoroughly familiar with suitable research designs, selection of sample populations, data collection, and statistical analysis of the findings.

Later on in this chapter is a section entitled "A Simple, Inexpensive Research Tool for the Small Business." You can use this model to tap the opinions, attitudes, likes, and dislikes of customers about your company, your products and prices, your promotional efforts, and so forth. In brief, it can produce effective "customer-oriented" facts for making decisions in business. It also has a good many other applications.

HOW TO GATHER INFORMATION

In the process of collecting information for decision making, it's helpful to think in terms of two general categories of information, or data: *primary* and *secondary.* Primary data are those facts that are not readily available and that therefore require considerable initiative and effort on the part of the investigator. The term *secondary data* encompasses facts that are normally available, although they may necessitate some searching around. The trick with secondary data is to know the sources you can tap—how and where to locate the information desired.

Chances are that most of the "fact finding" you'll be doing in your small business will involve secondary data; hence, this category is discussed first.

SECONDARY DATA

When acquiring secondary data, bear in mind the following:

- The reliability of the source
- The possibility of bias on the part of the collecting agent
- The fact that the information is dated
- The applicability of the information to your specific problems (since the facts may have been gathered originally for a completely different purpose)

Among the many sources of secondary information are internal company records of all kinds, government compilations of statistics, trade associations, public and university libraries, research organizations, business and scholarly journals, and reference works such as encyclopedias. In the majority of cases, the two most fruitful sources for solving your business problems will be the internal records of your company and government statistics.

Company Records   In the established firm, abundant records of every type are available. These include historical sales data on a daily, weekly, and monthly basis; records of inventory levels and flow; financial statements; purchasing records; and personnel files. Often, what's involved here is rearranging or reordering the facts to make sense out of them, and then applying the findings to the problem at hand.

Let's assume, for example, that you own a menswear store and that it reflects a departmentalized layout: sport jackets in one section, slacks in another, shirts and ties in a third, and so forth. Assume further that you would like to investigate the sales of these various merchandise classifications, perhaps so you could organize a more effective store layout. "After all," you reason, "if I do 20 percent of my business in sport jackets, perhaps I should devote about that percentage of my store's selling area to that particular classification."

Obviously, you need to ascertain the sales volume enjoyed by each class. You must "attack" your in-house records by merchandise classification. Further, you might want to analyze these categories not only by total dollar sales volume but also by the number of units sold. This study of company records will provide further insights to help you in thinking through your decision.

Government Statistics   The government is a formidable supplier of information of every type and description for the business world. The Department of Commerce is probably the most important government source at the federal level. This department compiles statistical data obtained periodically through its Bureau of the Census (Census of Population, Census of Manufacturers, Census of Business, Census of Agriculture, and so on). In addition, the department issues an annual summary of the economy in its *Statistical Abstract of the United States.* This can be found in most public libraries. On a monthly basis, it publishes the *Survey of Current Business,* which offers data on both sales and inventories as well as statistics on commerce and industry.

Other departments, such as the Department of Labor (with its *Monthly Labor Review*) and the Department of Agriculture, issue reports periodically.

Other Sources   A good many other sources of information exist for the alert business manager. These include newsletters and occasional reports issued through a number of organizations including the Federal Reserve Banks, the Federal Communications and Federal Trade Commissions, and various state and county agencies. Familiarize yourself with the indexes usually available in the public library, such as the *Business Periodicals Index,* the *Wall Street Journal Index,* and the *New York Times Index.* Other indexes are available in fields such as personnel administration, psychology, chemistry, and sociology.

Then there are the trade directories and other reference works that are valuable to business enterprises, including those issued by Dun & Bradstreet, the *Thomas' Register of Manufacturers,* and other trade books. Such periodicals as *Dun's, Forbes, Fortune, Business Horizons,* the *Harvard Business Review,* and various academic journals (the *Journal of Marketing,* the *Journal of Retailing,* and the *Journal of Business*) make for additional worthwhile reading.

The collecting of primary information in marketing research usually involves one of three approaches: (1) asking people (the *survey method*), (2) watching people (the *observation method*), or (3) setting up an experimental situation (the *experimental method*).

Survey Method Because surveys are relatively inexpensive and are adaptable to a wide range of problems, they seem to be by far the most popular device for gathering primary information. The survey method essentially seeks answers to specific questions through personal interviews, telephone interviews, or mail questionnaires. In one form or another, the technique can be of value in gathering information for any of the five types of research listed earlier in this chapter.

The preparation of a useful interview guide or questionnaire is difficult. It requires good thinking and planning. Consideration should be given to the wording and sequencing of questions, how easily the results can be tabulated, the validity of the questions themselves, and so forth. Mail and telephone surveys are generally less expensive than personal interviews. Of the three types, the telephone survey will produce the most immediate response. Of course, there's no substitute for the personal interview (when conducted by a competent interviewer) to extract the maximum amount of information from the person interviewed and to probe specific areas in depth.

Observation Method As the name suggests, this method involves watching people's behavior, such as their facial expressions or movements in reaction to something presented to them; for example, observing or filming customers in the act of making a purchase. In this kind of study, mechanical equipment such as cameras (often hidden from view) and tape recorders are used to gather information needed to solve the problem at hand. The major flaw with these techniques is that we can only observe *behavior*. We cannot ascertain what goes on within people's minds.

Experimental Method The experimental approach involves the deliberate setting up of an experiment under well-controlled circumstances. As an illustration, a chain-store retailer might wish to try out a new gift item at several different selling prices before deciding on the price that would yield the best possible combination of unit volume and gross profit. The merchant might then try to locate among his or her retail outlets three stores that are roughly equivalent in terms of store size, clientele, type of neighborhood, and monthly sales volume. The retailer is attempting here to "control" some of the other factors that might affect the outcome of the experiment; in other words, he or she is trying to keep all other things equal. Identical displays of the new item are set up in each store and put on sale on the same day in all three locations. There's one difference from store to store, however: At Store A, the price tag reads $8.50; at Store B, $9.95; and at Store C, $11.00. At the end of two or three weeks, a comparison of the sales data on the item from store to store should prove illuminating!

Of course, there are many other ways to set up experiments, or *experimental designs* as they are called. Further discussion of such designs, however, is beyond the scope of this book. (For more information, refer to the books on marketing research listed at the end of this chapter.)

A SIMPLE, INEXPENSIVE RESEARCH TOOL FOR THE SMALL BUSINESS

One variation of the survey method that appears to be very useful for the small firm is known as the *semantic differential*. It's an easy-to-use research tool that can be employed to tap people's impressions of, opinions about, or attitudes toward objects, concepts, or things.

Basically, the semantic differential consists of a number of pairs of adjectives and/or short phrases printed on a sheet of paper. These pairs, called *polar* words or phrases, are opposite to each other in meaning. Examples include *good/bad, high-priced/low-priced,* and *cold and businesslike/warm and neighborly.* The two opposites that form a pair are set off from each other by a number of dashes. The entire line thus formed is referred to as a *semantic differential scale.*

To ascertain a person's opinion about a particular object, you ask the individual to check off the one position on each of the several scales that most nearly coincides with the way the person feels about the object.

A sample of a semantic differential containing eight separate scales of this type is shown in exhibit 17–1. The form asks for people's impressions about a particular company. The individual who feels that the ABC Company is an *extremely progressive* firm would place a check mark over the dash in column 1. On the other hand, a person who believes that the same firm is *very backward* would check column 6. The fourth column represents a neutral position.

Once shown how to enter opinions onto the form, the average person should need no more than two or three minutes to complete a sheet that contains up to fifteen scales.

To illustrate the use of this technique, let's take as an example a wholesaler of giftware who wishes to gather information regarding the attitudes customers (retailers) hold toward the company. The distributor can use the semantic differential presented in exhibit 17–1, substituting the correct firm name for the ABC Company. The distributor then prepares a mailing to all customers, which includes the semantic differential sheet, a letter of explanation, and a stamped (or metered) return envelope. To ensure that the customers will indicate their true feelings toward the company, they're advised in the letter to return the sheet anonymously.

In the event that this wholesaler has a lengthy customer list, the cost of the research can be reduced by limiting the mailing to 10, 20, or 30 percent of the customers. This is often done when conducting a survey. In such cases, it's wise to try to select the sample on a random basis so that every firm on the list has an equal chance of being selected. An easy approach is to choose every third, fifth, tenth, etc. name from the entire list and mail to those selected names only.

Tallying up the responses for any number of people is relatively simple. Each scale (the two opposite words or phrases plus the spaces in between) is treated separately. You add up the total number of individuals who have checked off Column 1, Column 2, and so on. Then, you multiply the number of individuals per column by the

EXHIBIT 17–1. A SAMPLE SEMANTIC DIFFERENTIAL INSTRUMENT

QUESTION: *What are your impressions of the ABC Company?*

	(1) Extremely	(2) Very	(3) Somewhat	(4) DON'T KNOW	(5) Somewhat	(6) Very	(7) Extremely	
Progressive	—	—	—	—	—	—	—	Backward
Cold and businesslike	—	—	—	—	—	—	—	Warm and neighborly
Reliable	—	—	—	—	—	—	—	Unreliable
High-priced merchandise	—	—	—	—	—	—	—	Low-priced merchandise
Poor credit policies	—	—	—	—	—	—	—	Good credit policies
Wide variety	—	—	—	—	—	—	—	Little variety
Poor customer relations	—	—	—	—	—	—	—	Good customer relations
Little-known company	—	—	—	—	—	—	—	Well-known company

number at the top of the column to obtain a total score. This total score is then divided by the total number of people who have responded in order to obtain an average score for the entire group.

This may sound somewhat complicated, so let's use a concrete example: the 100 returns received by the giftware distributor mentioned above. The following distribution of check marks was observed on the first scale, *progressive/backward*:

Number of Column	Number of People Checking Column
1	2
2	3
3	12
4	9
5	31
6	26
7	17

The first step in analyzing the results is to obtain a total score by multiplying the number of individuals who have checked off each column by the number of the column. In brief, we must multiply 2 by 1, which yields 2; then 3 by 2, yielding 6; next, 12 by 3, to obtain 36; and so on to the last entry. Then, total all the sums. In the distribution above, the total score amounts to 510. Then, divide this total by the number of people who responded to the scale. In this case, it was one hundred. Dividing 510 by 100, we come up with an average rating of 5.1 for the entire group. This would indicate that, as a whole, the one hundred respondents regarded the giftware firm as being *somewhat backward*.

It's just as easy to translate these average (or *mean*) scores into pictorial form so that management can readily grasp their significance. Take a blank sheet containing the semantic differential and mark off for each scale the approximate position where the group's mean score falls. Then, connect all of the marks with straight lines. What then emerges is a *profile* or *image* of the group's collective response to the various scales of the semantic differential.

By way of illustration, exhibit 17–2 shows the profile of customer reactions to the salesclerks of a medium-size store.

Not only is this procedure valuable for obtaining insights into people's attitudes toward your business but it can also be useful in ascertaining their opinions about your competition. All you need do is repeat the process, asking others to rate your major competitor. (Of course, the proper way to conduct this kind of survey is to make

EXHIBIT 17–2. A PROFILE OF CUSTOMER REACTIONS

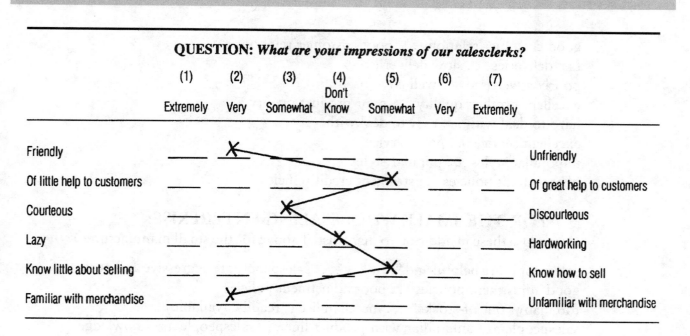

certain that the people you survey do not know who is behind the survey. This way, you're more likely to receive unbiased opinions!)

By placing the two profiles side by side on a single page, you will be able to view rather graphically your company's strengths and weaknesses vis-à-vis those of your competitor. This can lead to your taking steps to bolster your weak points and to publicize your strong ones to greater avail.

There is one problem with the semantic differential: the difficulty of selecting the right adjectives or phrases to fit your particular needs. To help you, three lists of suggested scales are offered in exhibit 17–3 for use by small manufacturers, wholesalers, and retailers. These are not meant to be all-inclusive. However, they should provide enough material to yield some useful information for your business.

EXHIBIT 17–3. SCALE SUGGESTIONS FOR VARIOUS TYPES OF ENTERPRISES

FOR THE SMALL MANUFACTURING COMPANY:

progressive . . . backward
cold and businesslike . . . warm and neighborly
wide variety of products . . . little variety of products
unreliable firm . . . reliable firm
low prices . . . high prices

EXHIBIT 17–3. (continued)

good customer relations . . . poor customer relations
fast deliveries . . . slow deliveries
poorly advertised . . . well advertised
excellent product quality . . . poor product quality
hard to deal with . . . easy to deal with
excellent service . . . poor service
unpopular styles . . . popular styles
liberal credit policies . . . stringent credit policies

FOR THE SMALL WHOLESALING ENTERPRISE:
(*Note:* Use these in addition to many listed above for the small manufacturer.)

salespeople are helpful and "low key" . . . salespeople are aggressive and pushy
good adjustment policies . . . poor adjustment policies
too many "out-of-stocks" . . . merchandise is readily available
salespeople are unfamiliar with product line . . . salespeople are knowledgeable about products
provides excellent help with advertising . . . does not provide advertising help

FOR THE SMALL RETAILING FIRM:
(*Note:* Use these in addition to many listed in the above category.)

attractive displays . . . unattractive displays
quite a shabby place . . . store is spotlessly clean
poor store layout . . . excellent store layout
convenient store hours . . . store hours are inconvenient
a comfortable place to shop . . . an uncomfortable place to shop
sensitive to customer needs . . . insensitive to customer needs
slow checkout . . . speedy checkout
easy return privileges . . . strict return privileges

FOR THE SMALL SERVICE BUSINESS:
(*Note:* Use these in addition to many listed in the above category.)

a dependable company . . . company is not dependable
offers top-quality service . . . offers poor-quality service
competent personnel . . . incompetent personnel
service carries a superior guarantee . . . service is not guaranteed

Source: Compiled by the author.

FOR FURTHER INFORMATION

Aaker, David A. et al. *Marketing Research*. 5th ed. New York: Wiley, 1995.

Blankinship, A. B. *State-of-the-Art Marketing Research*. Lincolnwood, Ill.: NTC Publishing, 1994.

Churchill, Gilbert A., Jr. *Basic Marketing Research*. 2d ed. Orlando, Fla.: Dryden Press, 1992.

Davis, Duane, and Robert M. Cosenza. *Business Research for Decision Making*. 3rd ed. Cincinnati: South-Western, 1993.

Dillon, William R., Thomas J. Madden, and Neil H. Firtle. *Essentials of Marketing Research*. Burr Ridge, Ill.: Irwin, 1993.

Gorton, Keith, and Isobel Doole. *Low-Cost Marketing Research: A Guide for Small Business*. 2d ed. New York: Wiley, 1989.

McDaniel, Carl, Jr., and Roger H. Gates. *Contemporary Marketing Research*. 2d ed. St. Paul, Minn.: West Publishing, 1993.

Parasuraman, R. A. *Marketing Research*. 2d ed. Reading, Mass.: Addison-Wesley, 1990.

Pope, Jeffrey L. *Practical Marketing Research*. New York: AMACOM, 1993.

Weiers, Ronald M. *Marketing Research*. 2d ed. Englewood Cliffs, N.J.: Prentice-Hall, 1988.

Zikmund, William G. *Exploring Marketing Research*. 5th ed. Orlando, Fla.: Dryden Press, 1993.

18

COMPUTERIZING YOUR BUSINESS OPERATION

DURING THE 1960s, a veritable technological revolution rocked the industrial sector as manufacturers recognized the value of installing electronic data processing (EDP) equipment to manage such labor-intensive activities as bookkeeping, inventory control, cost analyses, and sales forecasting. Generally, EDP was much faster and more accurate than clerical processing.

Some large-scale retailers soon followed their lead. Over time, the proliferation of EDP installations led to further refinements and such innovations (now taken for granted) as the bar coding of products and electronic checkout systems.

In those days, though, most companies found the costs of such equipment prohibitive. To process data needed for decision making, thousands of managements either signed contracts with computer service bureaus or resorted to time-sharing. Both of these earlier choices are now largely outmoded; they have been replaced by a desktop microcomputer. Moreover, over the past decade, millions of consumers have embraced the revolution, using personal computers to pay bills, send E-mail, engage in at-home shopping, play games, access databases, cruise along the information superhighway, and perform other electronic feats.

TODAY'S MICROCOMPUTERS

Tremendous strides have been made in EDP equipment over the past several decades. Once room-sized and even larger, computers have evolved drastically to mini- and micromodels—including user-friendly desk-top and even lap-held types. An entire spectrum of these useful machines is now available; costs can range from more than

$1 million (for a giant installation) down to as little as a few hundred dollars. Yes, the smaller machines have come down in price to the point that even the smallest business operation can afford one. Nowadays, for less than $3,000, you can purchase a good PC (personal computer) that can handle just about all of the tasks that need to be managed in your business. For this price, you can acquire the necessary hardware, software, and even some of the supplies you will need.

As of this writing, there are many moderately priced PCs being offered for sale at the computer superstores. For example, for around $1,600 or so you'll find a Packard Bell PC with a 150 megahertz Pentium® chip, a 1.6-gigabyte hard drive, lots of useful software, an eight-speed CD-ROM drive, 32 megabytes of memory, a fax/modem, a telephone answering system, a speakerphone, and a color monitor. Also available is an ACER 150 megahertz Pentium® multimedia computer that offers a 1.6-gigabyte hard drive (with built-in software), 16 megabytes of memory, an eight-speed CD-ROM drive, fax, modem, telephone, monitor, and color inkjet printer.

If you're willing to spend a bit more, say around $2,000 or $2,200, you can buy even faster equipment such as the Compaq personal computer that boasts a 166-megahertz Pentium® microprocessor, a 3.8-gigabyte hard drive, 16 megabytes of random access memory, an 8X CD-ROM drive, and a speakerphone—along with considerable built-in software—and a monitor.

There's also Packard Bell's multimedia system, with a 200 megahertz Pentium® microprocessor, 3.2-gigabyte hard drive (and lots of useful software), 48 megabytes of RAM, a 33.6 fax/modem, a 16X CD-ROM drive, telephone answering device, and color monitor.

Little training or skill is needed to run these and other microcomputers. More and more, PCs are being profitably used by doctors, dentists, accountants, attorneys, and other professionals. Owners of home-based businesses find them of exceptional value. Indeed, the cost is so low that many small business managers have one PC at their place of business and a second at home.

YOUR PC WILL HELP YOU MANAGE YOUR BUSINESS BETTER!

Listed below are the many functional areas of your business where the use of a PC can really make a difference; under each function, you'll find suggestions for helpful PC applications.

HUMAN RESOURCES

- Maintain and continually update personnel files
- Conduct studies of employee turnover
- Tabulate job analyses data, prepare job descriptions, and issue job specifications
- Project human resources needs for the future
- Evaluate results of training programs
- Manage the company's profit-sharing plan
- Plan and construct work schedules

PRODUCTION

- Plan production requirements
- Maintain quality control
- Analyze labor costs
- Furnish bills of materials
- Systematize routing and scheduling
- Maintain inventories and manage stockkeeping
- Conduct variance analyses
- Construct network charts (CPM, PERT)
- Keep maintenance records

THE FINANCIAL END

- Maintain all journals and ledgers
- Do payrolls; print and issue paychecks
- Conduct cash-flow analyses
- Construct pro forma as well as actual balance sheets and income statements
- Prepare tax forms; maintain all tax-related records
- Prepare invoices and bill customers
- Work up all budgets (production, sales, expense, advertising promotion, and so on)
- Make comparisons of actual amounts with budgeted figures
- Analyze and evaluate capital-budgeting opportunities
- Perform credit checks
- Maintain insurance files (expenditures, losses sustained, and amounts recovered)
- Do banking and fund transfers
- Set up a series of collection letters for past-due accounts

MARKETING AND PRODUCT/SERVICE MANAGEMENT

- Prepare sales forecasts
- Product-line management
- Merchandise planning and control
- Print up purchase orders and place orders with suppliers
- Maintain and analyze product movement records (by product, product line, gross margin, and territory)
- Compute and analyze inventory turnover rates
- Conduct ABC analyses
- Maintain continuous inventory records
- Install an automatic replenishment ordering system for staple goods
- Keep track of OTB ("open-to-buy") dollars

PRICING

- Monitor all expenses: fixed, semivariable, and variable
- Conduct break-even analyses
- Calculate various kinds of markups as needed (for example: initial, maintained, cumulative, and average markups)
- Set selling prices
- Assess the results of special price promotions
- Explore the price elasticity of products

PROMOTION

- Prepare all promotion budgets: advertising, public relations/ publicity, sales, and sales promotion
- Identify and mark for investigation deviations from budget
- Compute and compare milline (a measure of ad costs, computed by multiplying the newspaper's line rate by 1 million, then dividing by the newspaper's circulation) rates and cost per thousand to help in media-selection decisions
- Evaluate advertising campaigns
- Track the results of direct mailings
- Maintain and continually update mailing lists
- Address sales letters and envelopes; print mailing labels
- Maintain all sales office files
- Track and compare salesperson performance records
- Tabulate survey results
- Set up a telemarketing program
- Construct a customer database

- Access other databases by modem
- Promote the company and its products/services via the information superhighway

DISTRIBUTION

- Monitor warehouse security
- Evaluate performance of distribution channels
- Schedule shipments and transportation modes
- Prepare shipping documents

FOR FURTHER INFORMATION

Dologite, Dorothy G., and R. J. Mockler. *Using Computers*. 3rd ed. Englewood Cliffs, N.J.: Prentice-Hall, 1991.

Elwood, Brian C. *Introduction to Personal Computers*. 2d ed. Palmyra, Nebr.: BCS, 1993.

Kraynak, Joe. *The Complete Idiot's Guide to PCs*. Carmel, Ind.: Alpha Books, 1993.

LeDoux, John C. *The Computer Tutor: A Manager's Guide to Using Personal Computers*. Amherst, Mass.: Human Resources Development, 1991.

Lewis, Colin. *Essence of Personal Computing*. Englewood Cliffs, N.J.: Prentice-Hall, 1991.

Magid, Lawrence J. *The Little PC Book*. Berkeley, Calif.: Peachpit Press, 1993.

Ryan, Ken. *Computer Anxiety? Instant Relief!* 2d ed. Anchorage, Alaska: Castle Mountain Press, 1992.

The Software Encyclopedia, 1993. New Providence, N.J.: R. R. Bowker, 1993.

Traynor, David. *Understanding Computers—In a Weekend*. 3rd rev. ed. Friday Harbor, Wash.: DOT Publishing, 1995.

Valenti, Vince. *Computer Basics*. Las Vegas, Nev.: JV Enterprises, 1990.

Zimmerman, Steven M., and Leo M. Conrad. *Understanding and Using Microcomputers*. St. Paul, Minn.: West Publishing, 1988.

FINANCIAL MANAGEMENT OF THE SMALL FIRM

MANAGING THE COMPANY'S FINANCES

IN OUR FRONTIER days, trappers and Indians brought furs and animal skins to the local trading post where they bartered them for foodstuffs and other products proferred by the settlers. Finished goods imported from Europe also found their way into these earliest retail outlets.

But bartering as a way of American life has, for the most part, long since vanished—except to reveal itself on occasion in "trading" situations where, for example, a person might exchange a ten-year-old electronic typewriter for someone else's used (and rusted!) bicycle. In the business world, we may still find an occasional firm that will exchange, or barter, some of its products or services for those of another company—merchandise or services of equivalent value, of course. There are also some companies that carry on such exchanges through the medium of a barter club. (*Note:* According to the U.S. Internal Revenue Service, a company must include in its income the fair market value of any and all property or services received in bartering.)

Today, all business organizations, even the nonprofit type, run on money. Indeed, money is the fuel that fires up the business engine.

The inability to interpret and control the financial factor effectively is one of the prime causes of business failure. Efficiency in production, dynamic sales delivery, top-notch human resources management, and adroit handling of other phases of the business—all of these activities take a distant second place to the consummate skill needed for managing a company's finances.

This brings us to the whys and wherefores of *accounting*.

SOME ACCOUNTING FUNDAMENTALS FOR THE SMALL-BUSINESS OWNER

Every company needs a systematic approach to money management: an accounting system that helps the owner(s) keep track of all business transactions and other financial information. Inputs must be fed into the system and outputs registered so that a state of equilibrium can be maintained. Further, it's obvious that all the entries in and out of the system must be classified in a sensible, useful fashion so they can be "worked"—that is, added up, subtracted, and compared. Accounting isn't bookkeeping; bookkeeping is simply a necessary part of a firm's accounting system.

Here are some of the things an accounting system enables us to do:

- Interpret past performance
- Measure present progress
- Anticipate and plan for the future
- Control operations
- Uncover significant trends
- Compare results with similar firms and within the particular industry
- Make decisions
- Comply with government regulations

Your firm's accounting system is based on a simple, balanced equation:

Assets = Liabilities + Net Worth

A second important concept with which you need to become familiar is the *profit equation*. It's important to every profit-oriented business:

Profit = Sales − Costs

You've already run across these two basic equations—in different form—in chapter 5. For the sake of convenience, we reproduce here the two major accounting statements presented in that chapter. (See exhibits 19–1 and 19–2.)

Check the balance sheet for the ADG-Tenafly Manufacturing Company (exhibit 19–1). Note how it's divided into two major sections: (1) assets, and (2) liabilities + capital (net worth). Both sections total up to $374,870. Notice that the sections conform to each other.

Now, refer to the income statement in exhibit 19–2 for The Two Sisters' Dress Shoppe. This is, in fact, a detailed expansion of the profit equation.

RATIO ANALYSIS

The two major accounting statements—the balance sheet and the income statement—contain a great deal of information about the results of company operations and the current state of the firm's finances. Company management can manipulate this information in ways that yield meaningful insights for decision making. One of these ways is *ratio analysis*. Using this technique, you juxtapose one item of information against another, thereby forming a ratio. (A ratio is a proportion that expresses or implies some kind of relationship between two numbers.) For example, consider this statement: "Your chances of losing in this game are about one out of three." The ratio implied in that statement can be expressed as 1 in 3, ⅓, or simply 1:3.

A ratio is like a fraction—a numerator placed over a denominator. It's often and easily converted to a percentage by first dividing out the fraction and then multiplying the result by 100 percent.

As an example, assume your company earned $800,000 in sales last year, that your total labor costs were $200,000, and that the rental for your premises came to $48,000. Two helpful ratios can easily be constructed here—namely, a *labor-to-sales* ratio and a *rent-to-sales* ratio:

$$\text{Labor/Sales} \; = \; \frac{\$200,000}{\$800,000} \; = \; \frac{1}{4} \; = \; 25\%$$

$$\text{Rent/Sales} \; = \; \frac{\$48,000}{\$800,000} \; = \; \frac{6}{100} \; = \; 6\%$$

You can now determine (from putting the figures together in a meaningful way) that last year you paid out one dollar in labor for every four you took in (¼, or 25 percent of sales); and six out of every hundred dollars in sales (⁶⁄₁₀₀, or 6 percent) went for rent. You can literally track your progress, or lack of it, from one year to the next by comparing these ratios and others. Of course, businesspeople often find it more helpful to compare percentages over time, since they're easier to work with.

Now we can get on to the business of learning about more of the useful ratios that you can obtain from your basic accounting statements.

LIQUIDITY RATIOS

Here we're interested in finding out just how "liquid" our company appears to be. Comparing *liquidity ratios* over a period of years is helpful in determining whether things are improving or deteriorating.

EXHIBIT 19–1. A SAMPLE BALANCE SHEET

ADG-Tenafly Manufacturing Company
Balance Sheet
December 31, 1996

Assets

CURRENT ASSETS

Cash on hand	$500	
Cash in bank	28,850	
Accounts receivable, less		
allowance for bad debts	47,730	
Merchandise inventory	52,600	
Total current assets		**$129,680**

FIXED ASSETS

Land	$21,440	
Building, less depreciation	143,310	
Equipment, less depreciation	58,640	
Furniture and fixtures, less		
depreciation	21,800	
Total fixed assets		**$245,190**
Total Assets		**$374,870**

A firm is said to be liquid when it has enough in assets to pay all its debts and still has some funds left over.

The Current Ratio Current assets divided by current liabilities gives you the *current ratio*.

Check the balance sheet of the ADG-Tenafly Manufacturing Company once more. The firm's current assets are listed as $129,680 and its current liabilities as $27,060:

$$\text{Current Ratio} = \frac{\$129,680}{\$27,060} = 4.8\text{:}1$$

As a general rule of thumb, a current ratio of at least 2:1 (twice as much in current assets as in current liabilities) is desirable. This reflects a fairly sound financial situation for most firms. However, the safe current ratio will vary by industry, and it might be wiser to compare the current ratio with that of other companies similar to yours. Also, if your current ratio decreases over time, you may have a developing problem that you should look into.

The Quick Ratio Also called the *acid-test ratio*, the *quick ratio* is a more significant indicator than the current ratio of a firm's ability

EXHIBIT 19–1.   (continued)

ADG-Tenafly Manufacturing Company
Balance Sheet
December 31, 1996

		Liabilities
CURRENT LIABILITIES		
Accounts payable	$16,800	
Notes payable within one year	6,000	
Accrued payroll taxes	4,260	
Total current liabilities		**$27,060**
Long-Term Liabilities		
Note payable, due 1998	$12,000	
Note payable, due 1999	18,000	
Note payable, due 2000	18,000	
Total long-term liabilities		48,000
Capital (Net Worth)		
Capital, December 31, 1996		$299,810
Total Liabilities and Capital		**$374,870**

Source: Compiled by the author.

to liquidate its debts. It's similar to the current ratio, except that the valuation of the merchandise inventory is omitted:

$$\text{Quick Ratio} = \frac{\text{Cash} + \text{Negotiable Securities} + \text{Accounts Receivable}}{\text{Current Liabilities}}$$

Here's the quick ratio for the ADG-Tenafly Manufacturing Co.:

$$\text{Quick Ratio} = \frac{\$77,080}{\$27,060} = 2.85:1$$

As with the current ratio, the higher this ratio the better. The quick ratio should be at least 1:1. If it's less than this, the company may be headed for financially troubled waters. Again, it would be fruitful not only to compare your quick ratios for several years to watch for trends in direction but also to compare your ratios to those of other firms in your industry.

EXHIBIT 19–2. A SAMPLE P&L

The Two Sisters' Dress Shoppe
Profit-and-Loss Statement
October 1996

Gross Sales for October	$35,450	
Less returns and allowances	980	
Net sales		$34,470
Cost of Goods		
Merchandise inventory, October 1	16,415	
Purchases during month	9,080	
Freight charges	165	
Total merchandise handled	**25,660**	
Less inventory, October 31	8,470	
Cost of goods sold		17,190
Gross profit (margin)		$17,280
Operating Expenses		
Salaries	6,825	
Utilities	680	
Rent	2,300	
Stationery and printing	225	
Insurance	390	
Advertising and promotion	865	
Telephone	270	
Travel and entertainment	255	
Dues and subscriptions	110	
Bad debts	290	
Depreciation	1,835	
Total operating expenses		**$14,045**
Operating profit		3,235
Other Income		
Dividends	120	
Interest on bank account	70	
Total other income		190
Total income before taxes		3,425
Less provision for income taxes		1,370
Net Income (or Loss)		$2,055

Source: Compiled by the author.

PROFITABILITY RATIOS

Profitability ratios let you know how profitable (or unprofitable) your company's operations are. Of course, profits may be lined up and measured against a variety of data, such as sales, net worth, assets, and so forth. Generally, profitability ratios are expressed as percentages rather than proportions or fractions.

The Profit-to-Sales Ratio   If you examine the data furnished on the P&L statement of The Two Sisters' Dress Shoppe, you can see that for the month of October the store earned a net profit after taxes of $2,055 on a net sales volume of $34,470. Here's how you calculate the *profit-to-sales ratio* for this store:

$$\text{Profit/Sales} = \frac{\text{Net Profit (after taxes)}}{\text{Net Sales}} \times 100\%$$
$$= \frac{\$2,055}{\$34,470} \times \%$$
$$= 6.0\%$$

This means that for every dollar of sales during October of 1996, the retailer earned 6.0 cents. You must remember that this particular ratio varies from one month to the next, because retail businesses will not enjoy the same dollar sales nor the same expenses each month. December sales, for instance, may increase dramatically while the store's outlay for labor, advertising, and other expenses may constitute a less-than-usual percentage of sales. Generally, the true picture is reflected more accurately by semiannual or yearly computations of this and other profitability ratios. The month-to-month fluctuations wash out over time.

Incidentally, for the majority of small retail firms, the annual profit-to-sales ratio runs about 2 to 5 percent (higher or lower in individual cases).

Other Indications of Profitability   Additional ratios may be computed similarly. Here are two others frequently used by businesspeople:

$$\text{Profit/Net Worth} = \frac{\text{Net Profit (after taxes)}}{\text{Net Worth}} \times 100\%$$

$$\text{Return on Assets} = \frac{\text{Net Profit (after taxes)}}{\text{Assets}} \times 100\%$$

Other informative ratios that can indicate profitability and are especially useful to retail companies include sales/square foot of selling space, average sale/customer, and sales-to-inventory.

Inventory turnover—or *stockturn*—is not a direct profitability ratio, but business owners make good use of it to ascertain how fast (or slow) their inventory is moving and to help them in ordering goods. Three different stockturn ratios are used:

$$\text{Stockturn (in Units)} = \frac{\text{Number of Units Sold}}{\text{Average Inventory in Units}}$$

$$\text{Stockturn (at Cost)} = \frac{\text{Cost of Goods Sold}}{\text{Average Inventory at Cost}}$$

$$\text{Stockturn (at Retail)} = \frac{\text{Retail Sales}}{\text{Average Inventory at Retail}}$$

In all three instances, we derive the figure for *average inventory* by averaging the inventory listings by dollar valuation or by unit count. For example, if a physical inventory is taken on January 1 and then again on December 31 (or on January 1 of the following year), there would be two listings. In this case, the value of both (or their total number of units) would be added together and then divided by two to obtain the average inventory. Where management regularly takes inventory at the end of each month, thirteen listings would be used to calculate the average inventory.

YOU CAN AVOID CASH-FLOW PROBLEMS

At one time or another during the year, an acute shortage of cash seems to plague many firms. At times the business is extremely "tight" for operating capital; it may temporarily lack the funds to purchase raw materials or merchandise, to buy supplies, or to pay various bills.

To maintain good financial control of your business, managing the cash flow is imperative. The "ebb and flow" of ready cash within the year can actually be plotted out in advance with a simplified *funds-flow* form, such as the one in exhibit 19–3. Details are, of course, filled in from the monthly profit-and-loss statements you have developed.

EXHIBIT 19–3. A FUNDS-FLOW STATEMENT

ESTIMATED CASH FORECAST

	JAN.	FEB.	MAR.	APR.	MAY	JUN.	JUL.	AUG.	SEP.	OCT.	NOV.	DEC.
(1) Cash in Bank (Start of Month)												
(2) Petty Cash (Start of Month)												
(3) Total Cash—Add (1) and (2)												
(4) Expected Cash Sales												
(5) Expected Collections												
(6) Other Money Expected												
(7) Total Receipts—Add (4), (5) and (6)												
(8) Total Cash and Receipts—Add (3) and (7)												
(9) All Disbursements (for Month)												
(10) Cash Balance at End of Month. In Bank Account and Petty Cash— Subtract (9) from (8)*												

*This balance is your starting cash balance for the next month.

Source: "Business Plan for Retailers," *Small Marketers Aid No. 150* (Washington, D.C.: Small Business Administration, 1970), 17.

BUDGETING FOR PLANNING AND CONTROL

Budgets are detailed plans that represent set objectives against which to measure results. They're valuable management tools: In effect, they are blueprints that enable you to anticipate what will be, establish specific objectives, and chart the right course to help you attain those objectives.

Additionally, by monitoring what happens as your firm passes through the budget period, you'll be in a position to make the necessary adjustments that will keep your plan on target. While budgets may be reviewed semiannually or quarterly, a monthly budget review should be much more productive.

Despite their value as both planning and control devices, though, budgets are not found all that often in small-scale enterprises. This is especially true for small retail organizations. Conjecturing as to the possible reasons behind the lack of "budget orientation," I can only surmise that *(a)* budgeting is an activity that runs contrary to the entrepreneurial personality; *(b)* the small business owner is not conversant with budgeting techniques; and/or *(c)* the preparation of budgets for various phases of a business consumes an inordinate amount of time (a commodity that the entrepreneur feels must be dispensed frugally).

Although budgets can be prepared for any time period, a good way to initiate the budgeting process for your firm is to devise an *overall*, or *master* budget for the coming year. Once you have worked your way through your first annual budget, you might then consider the preparation of overall budgets for each quarter of the year.

You'll need to start construction of your master budget with a realistic estimate of the sales volume you expect to realize. This projection of future sales will enable you to construct not only your sales budget but also budgets for every other area of your business: your production, labor, selling expenses, and overhead expenses. You'll even be able to prepare budgeted operating statements and balance sheets.

At this point, let's take a look at a basic sales budget. Assume that you manufacture and sell three different products and that your sales representatives cover four states. Your sales budget might then look like table 19–1.

Starting with your sales budget, you can then begin to work up other useful budgets: for the amount of units to produce, materials to be purchased, selling expenses, administrative expenses, and so on. When you have established budgets for all segments of the business, you can use this information to prepare your two basic accounting statements.

TABLE 19–1. A BASIC SALES BUDGET

Projected Sales for Next Year, by Units

State	Product A	Product B	Product C	Total Units
Ohio	17,000	12,500	8,600	38,100
Michigan	14,800	9,700	13,400	37,900
Illinois	25,600	14,300	12,600	52,500
Indiana	5,200	15,000	6,100	26,300
Totals:	62,600	51,500	40,700	154,800

Projected Sales for Next Year, by Dollars

State	Product A	Product B	Product C	Total
Ohio	$ 76,500	$ 75,000	$ 28,380	$179,950
Michigan	66,600	58,200	44,220	169,020
Illinois	115,200	85,800	41,580	242,580
Indiana	23,400	90,000	19,830	133,230
Totals:	$281,700	$309,000	$134,010	$724,710

Source: Compiled by the author.

As an example, table 19–2 is the proposed production budget for Product A for the small manufacturing business discussed above, based on a quarterly approach. Note that individual budgets need to be prepared for each of the three products made.

TABLE 19–2. A PROPOSED PRODUCTION BUDGET

Production Budget (in Units)—Product A

Needed for	First Quarter	Second Quarter	Third Quarter	Fourth Quarter
Planned Sales	12,200	14,400	20,000	16,000
End-of-Quarter Inventory	3,600	4,400	5,000	3,900
Total Needs for Period	15,800	18,800	25,000	19,900
Less Beginning of Quarter Inventory	2,500	4,700	6,000	2,900
Need to Manufacture	13,300	14,100	19,000	17,000

Source: Compiled by the author.

CAPITAL BUDGETING

Budgeting today, of course, is a way of business life. In a healthy firm, budgets are strategically employed in every phase of the enterprise, for both planning and control purposes.

Capital budgeting involves setting aside moneys each year for large investments that might need to be made. Throughout the lifetime of your business, you will occasionally be confronted with major decisions involving your company's finances. A few common examples are purchasing costly equipment or machines, instituting a complete internal reorganization, developing and launching a new product. Consequently, you need a logical method to follow in planning and evaluating budgetary alternatives.

In this context, there are some important "money concepts" to keep in mind:

- A firm's capital is always limited.
- Money borrowed for capital expenditures will cost more money.
- Today's dollar is worth one dollar-plus, in the sense that it can be held in a bank account and draw interest.
- Tomorrow's dollar will probably be worth one dollar-minus.
- Money assigned to capital expenses may sometimes be put to different, more productive uses.

CAPITAL SPENDING DECISIONS

Capital investments are made for two basic reasons: (1) to lower operating costs, or (2) to increase sales. Any major commitment of your firm's funds warrants due caution and consideration on your part. Indeed, a common mistake of many small enterprises is to put too many dollars into capital assets, thereby precipitating a cash crisis that can immobilize operations and even cause bankruptcy.

Of course, such investments can be made directly from the company bank account through borrowed or equity capital and long-term leasing. Whatever the approach (or combination thereof), you will find the following procedure of value in making decisions of this nature:

1. List all of the alternatives on a sheet of paper. Remember also to list the one alternative that's always present in such situations: *Do nothing.*

2. Work up all the costs involved for each of the choices. Be sure to include estimates of details like the cost of borrowing additional sums of money if you don't have enough and the value of leaving your firm's current dollars untouched and earning interest in a savings account.

3. Estimate the most likely results (outcomes), in dollars and cents, of each of the alternatives.

4. Select the best alternative—for example, the one with the greatest payoff (after subtracting the total costs from the most likely results).

CAPITAL BUDGETING IS A SERIOUS PROCESS

Needless to say, any financial commitment that will involve a substantial portion of your capital must be regarded as a major move. Because the resources of most small businesses are quite limited, their owners need to devote serious thought to the capital budgeting process.

When faced with the need to consider such moves, you should begin by preparing several alternative budgets to help you make the buy/don't buy decision. These budgets must, of course, take two significant aspects into consideration: (1) the total cost of the purchase (or "outlay"); and (2) how much time it will take for you to repay your bank account through the "inflow" of net income attributed to the capital item.

The two most popular approaches to resolving such problems are the *payback period method* and the *net present value method*. When using the first method, you work out the length of time it will take to recover the cost of the purchase from earned net income (after taxes, of course). As an example, let's suppose you're thinking of replacing an old machine with a newer model. Your total cost for the new machine, installed in your plant, will amount to $28,000. You're convinced, though, that it should help you turn out about 30 percent more units per week than the old machine. After working up all the necessary figures, you reach the conclusion that the additional production should bring you—annually, after taxes—about $9,200 in additional profit. By dividing the cost ($28,000) by the annual earnings ($9,200), you can assume that the original outlay will be repaid in a little over three years. Chances are, then, that you would decide to purchase the new machine. On the other hand, had you calculated that your annual earnings would be only $3,000, you might well pass up the opportunity to buy the machine. Rather than wait nine years or longer to recoup your investment, you would be better off placing that money in, say, a long-term savings account at a good rate of interest.

The net present value method is preferable to the payback period method because it recognizes that, over time, the value of money depreciates (in the face of inflation). It calls for adjusting the expected inflow of income according to value tables that show the discounting of one dollar at different specified rates over the expected number of "payback years."

EXPENSE MANAGEMENT

Three areas of internal activity can be found within any company involved in the manufacturing or distribution of goods and/or services: (1) production, or buying for resale; (2) selling; and (3) the financial aspects of operating the business. By tackling one area at a time and applying sound business judgment, you should be able to increase your net profits over time.

Essentially, there are only two ways to make more money in business. Either you increase sales while holding down costs, or you lower costs while holding up sales. Expense management deals with the second approach: lowering costs in every segment of your business.

TYPES OF BUSINESS EXPENSES

Most small firms use what is called a *natural classification of expenses,* assigning each cost incurred in operating the enterprise to a particular debit account. Below is a categorization of business expenses that is suitable for the average small company:

Advertising	Office expenses
Bad debts	Pension and profit-sharing plans
Car and truck expense	Rent
Commissions	Repairs and maintenance
Depreciation	Salaries and wages
Dues and contributions	Taxes
Insurance	Travel, meals, and entertainment
Interest	Utilities
Legal and professional services	

If you scan the above list, you'll quickly see that many of the expenses lie within your control, that some of them are *fixed* (that is, they continue whether your sales volume increases or decreases), and that most of them seem to be *variable* in nature and fluctuate along with sales.

To hold down costs, your challenge is to work out a delicate balance between sales and expenses all along the way, and in all areas of variable costs. Consequently, it's wise to bear in mind at all times the basic accounting equations mentioned earlier in the book:

$$\text{Assets} = \text{Liabilities} + \text{Net Worth}$$

and

$$\text{Profits} = \text{Sales} - \text{Costs}$$

Many management tools are available to assist you in your endeavors, among them ratio analysis, operational techniques (such as time and methods study, work simplification, value analysis, and critical path method), and budgeting. All of these approaches are quite useful in making comparative analyses of information, so arranged that you can compare the present period with past periods—that is, make projections (based on trend extrapolation) into the future.

CREDIT MANAGEMENT

There are two basic types of credit: *trade credit* and *consumer* credit. In either case, a firm that offers credit is engaged in more than a simple service; credit is a deliberate marketing strategy designed to stimulate business and give a firm a competitive edge.

Companies extend trade credit to give their customers some leeway in operating. A retailer who purchases goods for resale from a wholesaler might simultaneously owe substantial amounts of money to other wholesalers and to other creditors, such as the telephone and electric companies, the insurance company, and the landlord. This retailer simply does not have enough cash on hand to pay all of the business's bills upon receipt of goods or services and is extended credit by the wholesale supplier.

This is not too different from the shopper to whom consumer credit has been extended: He or she must wait until the next paycheck before being able to pay various bills.

EXTENDING CREDIT

Each company, of course, must determine its own credit policy. While credit is a must for both manufacturer and wholesaler, other types of firms need to weigh the advantages and disadvantages of credit extension. Obviously, there are risks attached to the strategic deployment of credit as a sales-generating tool. Credit is an area of business operations that cannot be taken lightly. Indeed, it merits a well-thought-out approach, careful and continual monitoring, and occasional reappraisal.

Generally, a firm's credit approach involves:

1. Setting policies, including standards for measuring each applicant
2. Devising a credit application form to be completed by the firm or person applying for credit
3. Checking on the data provided on the application form
4. Evaluating, then approving, the application
5. Setting a credit limit for the applicant
6. Monitoring credit usage carefully
7. Establishing a collection policy for delinquent accounts

THE THREE Cs OF CREDIT

A decision to extend credit to any specific client is generally based on what is called the *three Cs of credit*. These are the following:

Character   Since an individual's character—in the sense of personality or behavior patterns—is extremely difficult to appraise, much less define, *character* is usually translated to mean the applicant's willingness to pay bills when they are due. Hence, records must be studied to determine what kind of behavior was evidenced by the applicant in the past with respect to debts.

Capacity   This criterion refers to a person's (or firm's) ability to pay debts out of current income.

Capital   Another indication of the credit applicant's ability to pay is, of course, his or her financial resources (or net worth, in the case of a business firm).

The information provided in the application form is then checked carefully by mail or telephone, and/or with a credit bureau or mercantile agency, such as Dun & Bradstreet.

CONSUMER CREDIT

Often, a retail enterprise tries to avoid unnecessary risk by signing up with one or more of the major credit card entities, such as VISA, MasterCard, American Express, or Diner's Club. While it is true that a credit card arrangement requires the business firm to yield a small percentage of sales volume to the agency (a fee often between 3 and 6 percent), offering such a service to customers generally results in an overall sales increase that more than compensates for the agency fee.

When retailers extend credit to consumers, it usually takes one of several basic forms described as follows:

Open Credit   Also referred to as *open account, open book,* or *regular* credit, this form extends short-term credit to customers without requiring any down payment and without adding either interest or carrying charges to the bill. It is usually extended for a thirty-day period.

Installment Credit   Here, a customer is required to place a down payment on merchandise and then pay up the balance in full over a period of time in regular installments. Most often, the buyer signs a conditional sales contract and is charged for the service (for example, 1½ percent per month on the unpaid balance).

Option-Terms Credit   This type of credit permits a customer to charge up to a limit and pay (if he or she so desires) within thirty days of the billing date without penalty. A firm can assign a carrying charge for any amount not paid within that time period and release additional credit (up to the limit) as payments are made. Thus, the features of both open credit and *revolving charge* credit are combined in one plan. (The latter refers to the continual releasing of credit to the credit ceiling as payments are made.)

COLLECTIONS

No matter how tightly supervised your credit activities may be, there will still be some customers who pay their bills late and others who won't pay them at all. The structuring of a good collection procedure helps to reduce "delinquency" to an appreciable degree. A working policy might include the following steps:

1. Institute some kind of "red flag" bookkeeping technique to alert you when an account is tardy in payments.
2. Mail a duplicate invoice—stamped *past due, second notice,* or some similar phrase—to the customer shortly after discovering an amount overdue.
3. After several weeks elapse without your receiving a response, send out the first in a series of form letters. (Prepare these long in advance.) The first letter should be pleasant in tone and

suggest that the customer may have accidentally overlooked payment of such-and-such an amount. (You might consider placing a telephone call in between the first and second letters to find out what has been happening.)

4. If you hear nothing further, send out the other letters, each of which becomes progressively stronger. These should be spaced so that they reach the addressee about every ten days or two weeks. Your last letter in the series should emphasize the fact that you're about to turn the delinquent account over to your attorney.

5. Turn the matter over to your attorney.

RECORD KEEPING FOR YOUR COMPANY

Keeping books properly is essential to your firm's accounting system. Before you start your operation it's generally advisable to have an accountant set up your books according to the specific needs of your company. Thereafter, you can maintain your own books until the business can afford to pay for a full-time or even part-time bookkeeper. Another approach is to use the services of a firm in the "bookkeeping systems" business. For a fee, they will maintain your books for you. Note, though, that the Small Business Administration advises that you will need to maintain (at the very minimum) four basic types of records, regardless of whether you or someone else keeps your books.* These are

- Sales records
- Cash receipts
- Cash disbursements
- Accounts receivable

If you decide on a "do-it-yourself" approach, there are simplified, one-book systems available at most business stationery stores. However, I'd still recommend that you seek the assistance of a qualified accountant. This person can set you up with a tailor-made approach designed not only to meet your accounting needs but also to provide information over time to help you make decisions.

As an overall guide, every transaction should be entered in a journal on a daily basis. If this is done—if you keep copies of all bills,

---

* John Cotton, "Keeping Records in Small Business," *Small Marketers Aids No. 155* (Washington, D.C.: U.S. Small Business Administration, 1974), 2.

receipts, canceled checks, checkbook stubs, and so on—your book-keeper will be able to make sense of it all.

How Long to Keep Records It's customary to keep business tax records for at least six years and your basic journals of original entry for about the same length of time. General ledgers, corporate minutes, leases, contracts, copyrights and patents, and other important documents should be kept indefinitely. It's also advisable to keep employee payroll records for at least five years (sometimes longer, depending on the requirements of the state in which your company is located).

Receiving documents, purchase orders, sales records, and other internal records are typically kept for three years or so. You can usually discard job tickets upon completion of the job; production orders, though, should be held for a few months.

FOR FURTHER INFORMATION

DeThomas, Art. *Financing Your Small Business: Techniques for Planning, Acquiring, and Managing Debt.* Grant's Pass, Ore.: Oasis Press, 1992.

Fleury, Robert E. *The Small Business Survival Guide: How to Manage Your Cash, Profits, and Taxes.* Naperville, Ill.: Sourcebooks, 1992.

Glau, Gregory R. *The Small Business Financial Planner.* New York: Wiley, 1989.

O'Hara, Patrick D. *SBA Loans: A Step-by-Step Guide.* 2d ed. New York: Wiley, 1994.

Plewa, Franklin, and George T. Friedlob. *Understanding Cash Flow.* New York: Wiley, 1995.

Scott, Gina Graham. *Positive Cash Flow: Complete Credit and Collections for the Small Business.* Holbrook, Mass.: Bob Evans, 1990.

Shim, Jae K., Joel G. Siegel, and Abraham J. Simon. *The Vest-Pocket MBA.* Englewood Cliffs, N.J.: Prentice-Hall, 1996.

Simini, Joseph P. *Budgeting Basics for Nonfinancial Managers.* New York: Wiley, 1989.

Tabet, Joseph, and Jeffrey Slater. *Financial Essentials for Small Business Success.* Dover, N.H.: Upstart, 1994.

20

HOW TO PROTECT YOUR BUSINESS

Every new business venture represents a gamble, for it is difficult to predict the future. Even with a well-conceived business plan, adequate financing, and managerial experience in the same field, you'll still find the chances for success hovering around the fifty-fifty mark at best. The odds are no different from those you face in flipping a dime and calling "Heads!" or "Tails!" The risk present in this situation is two-directional: either you win or you lose.

Many of us willingly embrace *speculative risk* where, although we might lose, it is also possible to win—at times a substantial sum. Indeed, the psychological excitement of gambling is a well-known phenomenon. Witness the thousands who place bets at the race track, buy lottery tickets, or play poker. Small-business owners, too, are quite familiar with this type of risk; it characterizes the new-product development process, the selection of a second or third location, or the installation of a major piece of machinery.

In some situations, the risk might run in only one direction, that of loss. Should a fire, for example, suddenly envelop your home or apartment, the expected outcome can only involve loss, not gain. This kind of risk is called *pure risk*. Insurance exists primarily to protect individuals and organizations against loss caused by damage to property, life, or limb in such situations.

Yes, accidents can happen. Disaster can strike without warning. Furthermore, there's no way any business, much less any individual, can be exempted from such calamities. A serious fire can put you out of business overnight—or in an hour. A lesser blaze could cause considerable property damage, forcing you to close down your operation for weeks. A lawsuit seeking to hold you accountable for negligence that resulted in injury can threaten not only your business but also your personal assets (if your business isn't incorporated).

To protect your business, it's imperative that you not only accept the existence of pure risk but also learn how to live with it and manage it.

HOW TO APPROACH THE RISK-MANAGEMENT PROBLEM

Managements adopt a variety of positions on the problem of handling risk. These range from doing nothing at all, thereby consigning their chances to fate, to attempting to cover just about every possible calamity with some kind of insurance policy.

If you don't want to join the thoroughly illogical "do-nothing" school, here are some common ways to approach risk management:

- *Set up risk-reduction programs* to reduce the possibility of property damage or loss and accidental injuries within your place of business.*
- *Transfer your risk to insurance companies,* especially the major perils such as fire and casualty.
- *Assign risk to third parties,* where possible, as in the case of the retailer who requests product liability coverage from the manufacturer in order to be protected from possible litigation.
- *Set aside as large a contingency fund* as you can manage, to cover potential losses, thus adopting a self-insurance posture.

Also, be sure to review the basic pointers outlined in exhibit 20–1.

EXHIBIT 20–1. BASIC POINTERS

Here are a few helpful suggestions for protecting your company from risk:

1. *Think in terms of a well-planned program* that you need to set up initially and then maintain throughout the life of your business. Risk management consists of more than a set of insurance policies, even though such coverage will play a substantial role in the program.
2. *Seek professional help at the outset.* You are certainly not an expert in this field. Your most valuable asset here is a knowledgeable and capable insurance representative. This agent or broker can tailor a program to your precise needs, place your insurance with responsible companies, help you in negotiating claims, and advise you when in doubt.

   List your risk priorities: Write down the various perils that could affect your business, consult with the professional, and then arrange them in

---

* See the list under "Protection Means More Than Insurance" later in this chapter.

EXHIBIT 20–1. (continued)

order from most to least serious in their potential for damaging your business. Obviously, insurance protection against a catastrophe should find itself toward the top of your list. Included in this category are property, casualty, and workers' compensation insurance. At the bottom of the list should be less significant risks that would involve the loss of smaller amounts of money. These risks you may elect to transfer or not; examples include plate glass insurance, credit insurance, and rent insurance.

3. *Hold down excessive costs* in several ways: Set up internal risk-reduction programs; talk frankly with your representative about policy terms and conditions; compare insurance coverages and companies where premiums might be exorbitant or where the loss value incurred would be small; and use deductibles. Finally, it's a wise move to investigate the advantages of package policies.

4. *Keep accurate records* not only of your various coverages but also of all insured property. For example, in the event of a claim for property destroyed by fire, the insurance company will require a complete listing, down to description, age, cost or replacement value, and so forth. Photographs are extremely useful. In this respect, "a picture is worth a thousand words!" Nowadays, many business owners prefer to record their property on videocassettes. Put these, along with your detailed descriptions, in your vault or give them to your insurance agent. Update your records each year.

5. *Adapt your insurance policies to changing conditions.* Keep your eye on both internal (within the firm) and external conditions. Be sure you have sufficient coverage at all times. It's wise to review your risk-management program annually and make necessary changes to ensure the vitality of your business.

Source: Compiled by the author.

PROTECTING YOUR PROPERTY: FIRE INSURANCE

No business should be initiated without insuring against fire. Although chances are good that your plant or store will never burn down, the fact that it *could* happen—that your machinery, equipment, fixtures, or inventory could be damaged, if not destroyed, by fire—should convey the urgency of such coverage.

A fire insurance policy will put you back where you were prior to the loss. It's also important for credit reasons. Unless your place is insured against fire, you'll find it just about impossible to obtain a mortgage on it.

While a basic fire policy insures only against damage from fire or lightning, most business owners extend the scope of coverage to include additional perils, such as smoke, windstorm, hail, explosion, and riot. Protection against possible damage from vandalism and malicious mischief can also be included in your fire policy. The cost of adding these various coverages to the fire premium itself is relatively small.

A fire policy will *exclude* coverage for other types of items, such as cash, stock certificates, bonds, and property deeds. To cover these, additional *floater* policies might be required.

The premium you pay will be based on several factors, including the location of your business (the town it's in, the neighborhood, the surrounding buildings, and so forth), the condition and maintenance of your premises, and the structure and type of your building.

When you first apply for this type of coverage, it's wise to set the overall amount based on what's referred to as the *actual cash value*. This is the replacement cost of the property at current market prices less depreciation. The alternative is to use the purchase cost. Bear in mind, however, that when your insured amount has been based on initial cost, an allowance for depreciation over several years could bring down the covered sum considerably. A piece of equipment that originally cost you $6,000 might now be valued at less than $4,000.

COINSURANCE

The concept of *coinsurance,* often misunderstood by the small-business owner, merits some explanation. It's designed to spread the cost of fire insurance more equitably among users. In effect, it grants lower premium rates to those who insure their property more fully. The insured firm agrees to maintain coverage on its property at a stipulated percentage of its current value; the most commonly used percentage is 80 percent. Should this agreed-upon figure not be continued and a loss occurs, then the firm suffers a penalty in proportion to the deficiency.

For example, companies X and Y have each taken out a policy on their respective properties, valued in each case at $200,000. Firm X has arranged for 80 percent coinsurance; its policy carries a face amount (for total loss) of $160,000. It pays about $3,000 annually in premiums. Firm Y's management feels that the chances of a total loss due to fire are rather remote and wants to "save" on its premium payments. Firm Y thus secures a policy in the amount of $100,000 and finds that its annual cost is about $1,900—or $1,100 less than the cost to firm X. Assume, now, that both companies have fires, and the damage in both instances totals $20,000. Firm X can then expect to receive the full $20,000 that it claims. However, firm Y is penalized because it was "underinsured." Because it had been insured for only half of the actual value ($100,000, instead of $200,000), only half of the claim value is paid—$10,000.

LIABILITY INSURANCE AND OTHER COVERAGES

There is always the possibility that you may become embroiled in legal actions brought by individuals who suffer injuries and then seek to attribute them to negligence on your part. This is an ever-present threat, one that can have serious (even fatal) consequences to a small business. Unfortunately, courts and juries in recent years have more often favored the claimant than the defendant in such cases. Moreover, the amounts of judgments awarded in these lawsuits have skyrocketed. These actions not only cover medical, surgical, disability, and funeral expenses but are also designed to include compensation for "loss of future earnings" to dependents and the costs of defending the action.

In this context, you may be sued by anyone: customers or passersby, messengers and delivery people, employees, and even, peculiarly enough, trespassers. Court action can follow such common situations as these: someone breaking a capped tooth on a piece of shell in a bowl of soup or on a chocolate-covered filbert; a person tripping over a broken tile or slipping on a highly waxed floor; or an individual being knocked down by another while entering through the doorway of your store or plant.

Moreover, the accident doesn't have to take place on your business premises. One of your employees, on the way to the bank to make a deposit, may accidentally injure another person, who may promptly initiate a suit against your employee and you. According to both common and statutory law, you can be held accountable for negligence that causes personal injury. Consequently, you need liability insurance for protection in this area. These policies generally cover such things as the costs of defending lawsuits, the medical and surgical expenses incurred, and judgments awarded. They also contain specified limits.

It's important to realize that the amount of liability coverage can usually be increased substantially with a small increase in premium. On the basis of the actual, unfortunate experiences of a good many small companies, it is prudent to seek greater, rather than lesser, coverage in this area.

AUTOMOBILE INSURANCE

Generally, a business firm insures its automobiles, trucks, and other vehicles against the possibility of physical damage and theft, as well as against bodily injury to others. To this end, they purchase commercial vehicle insurance, including collision insurance. Rates vary considerably from one locale to another. The rates depend not only on the particular area involved but also on the type and age of the vehicles, the distances traveled, the ages of the drivers, and so forth.

SOME OTHER TYPES OF INSURANCE TO THINK ABOUT

A good many other kinds of business situations that involve pure risk can be covered by insurance. Some of the more common risks are listed in exhibit 20–2. Of course, not every one is necessarily applicable to your business, nor would they all be advisable to have. You should discuss your particular needs in depth with your insurance agent or broker.

EXHIBIT 20–2. OTHER TYPES OF INSURANCE COVERAGES

- *Boiler and Machinery Insurance*   Some small-business owners find this type of insurance of considerable interest. It's also called *power-plant insurance*. It protects a firm against loss due to the explosion of boilers, furnaces, engines, and similar equipment.
- *Business Interruption Insurance*   In the event that your premises suffer a serious fire, the insurance policy you carry covers your direct losses in merchandise, equipment, and the plant itself. However, you may sustain other, indirect losses. You might not be able to get back into operation for weeks or months after extensive fire damage. This setback would mean that little or no income would be forthcoming for some time. Yet you might want to continue paying salaries to your key people in the interim. At the same time, you might have to pay your monthly utility bills, meet payments on loans, send in insurance premiums that fall due, and so on.
  Business interruption insurance will compensate you for the fixed expenses that ordinarily have to be paid out while your business is interrupted.

EXHIBIT 20–2. (continued)

- *Crime Insurance*   The small-business owner seldom links the possibility of loss through robbery, burglary, or theft to the concept of insurance coverage. Yet, it has been estimated that the total amount of business property damaged each year by fire might, in fact, be *less* than losses due to criminal acts.

   Robbery insurance covers you against property loss by force or by threat of violence; burglary insurance covers property stolen by someone who leaves visible signs of forced entry. The *Storekeeper's Burglary and Robbery Policy* is a special form of insurance available to retailers.

   Comprehensive crime policies will cover both of these perils as well as other types of property theft, disappearance, or destruction. Crime insurance may not be readily available in high-risk areas. In such cases, the entrepreneur can seek coverage under the Federal Crime Program. (Your agent or broker can provide you with details.)

- *Fidelity and Surety Bonds*   Fidelity bonds are obtained from insurance or bonding companies. They are designed to protect a business against loss due to dishonesty on the part of its employees. Such bonds are available on an individual or group basis. They're especially useful where employees have access to large sums of money or inventory. Surety bonds are of a similar nature, except that they are generally issued to guarantee performance by contractors.

- *Glass Insurance*   Through a comprehensive glass policy, your business can be insured against damage to glass panes, doors, showcases, counter tops, signs, and the like.

- *Group Health Insurance*   This popular type of insurance policy covers you and your employees for sickness, injury, or accidental death. Three classes of coverage are usually offered: a basic medical plan, including hospitalization and surgery; a major medical plan that provides for the high cost of physician and nurse expense both in and out of the hospital; and a disability income plan that compensates for lost earnings due to accidental injury or an illness.

- *Water-Damage Insurance*   Property may be insured against accidental damage caused by water in various forms: escaping steam, overflows from refrigeration and air conditioning equipment, and melting snow that leaks through roofs or basement walls.

Source: Compiled by the author.

WORKERS' COMPENSATION INSURANCE

Under common law you must, to the best of your ability, provide for your employees an environment free from the possibility of accidental injury (or occupational and radiation diseases). Responsibilities include safe working conditions; adequate servicing and maintenance of machinery, tools, and equipment; and work procedures that prevent accidents on the job. You're even required to exercise care in hiring, selecting, and assigning workers in your business.

One of the most important features of workers' compensation laws is that employees are made eligible for benefits regardless of whether you, as an employer, are guilty of negligence or not. Compliance with state law is usually accomplished by acquiring a workers' compensation insurance policy. This insurance provides benefits to injured employees in the form of medical expense reimbursement and replacement of lost wages.

Your premium is based on the size of your payroll and on the kinds of jobs within your organization. The extent of the hazards faced in your type of business is also a factor. Your premium could range from as little as 1 percent of your payroll to as much as 20 percent or more. You can lower your premium, over time, through internal safety measures that reduce the accident rate in your place of business below the average for that particular type of business.

LIFE INSURANCE

WHY PURCHASE BUSINESS LIFE INSURANCE?

Few mature individuals need to be convinced of the benefits offered by personal life insurance. As responsible people, they're prone to seek protection from life's uncertainties by purchasing one or more life insurance policies in addition to their homeowners' and automobile policies. Yet many business owners are reluctant to think in terms of *business* life insurance, feeling this is a luxury they cannot afford.

This is a shortsighted attitude. Indeed, business life coverage may be something you cannot afford to be without! Think of the long-range possibilities. When you die, or if you become disabled, what will happen to that successful business you have built? How will your family manage? If the business must be liquidated, who will take care of this? Or, if yours is a partnership and a partner passes away, how can you protect your share of ownership?

With the help of your insurance representative (and your attorney and accountant), you can tailor your business life insurance to your specific needs. Business life policies can be written to protect owners and their families against financial loss due to death or serious injury. Prearrangements can be made to assure the business continues in this event. With life insurance to provide necessary cash and a properly prepared "buy-and-sell" agreement, the deceased's share of ownership may be returned quickly and fully to the heirs, and the surviving owners will be able to carry on the business without interruption.

Key-person insurance provides a similar kind of protection. The untimely death of a valuable employee (for example, a top salesperson, the production manager, or a chief designer) can seriously affect the performance of a firm. The insurance proceeds from key-person coverage can be used by your business to offset a loss in profits or to pay for the cost of hiring and training a replacement.

Incidentally, an important benefit of business life insurance lies in the fact that the cash accumulation in the permanent-type policy is available as a reserve fund for contingencies, or even for retirement.

The basic types of life insurance are described in exhibit 20–3.

EXHIBIT 20–3. TYPES OF LIFE INSURANCE

Whole Life   This is also known as *ordinary* or *straight* life. You are covered for the face amount of the policy throughout your lifetime. The premium, too, is calculated to be paid over the course of your lifetime. This type of policy carries a limited cash surrender value as well as loan privileges and other nonforfeiture values.

Limited Payment Life   A variation of whole life insurance, the limited policy requires the payment of premiums for a set number of years (fifteen, twenty, or more). At the end of this period, no more premiums are paid; the policy is then fully paid up. Thereafter, the insured remains covered for the rest of his or her life. Since the premiums are higher than those paid for a whole life policy, this type has a substantial cash surrender and loan value.

Endowment Life   This form of insurance has many provisions similar to the limited payment life policy in that the policy owner continues to pay premiums for a designated number of years until the policy is fully paid up. At this point, the accumulated cash value equals the face amount and is paid out in a lump sum (*endowment*) to the policy owner. Other provisions for payment are also available.

Term Life   Generally, this requires the lowest dollar outlay for life insurance because the premiums paid are completely used up for the sole purpose of insurance protection. Because of this, the policy does not accumulate a cash reserve for the insured and, consequently, has no cash surrender value or loan possibilities.

Source: Compiled by the author.

PROTECTION MEANS MORE THAN INSURANCE

Even though insurance coverage is available to protect your business against nearly every kind of threat, relying on insurance alone is foolhardy. You can take many steps to help reduce risk. Consider carefully the various kinds of risk and how to guard against them, and you will keep your losses down.

SOME WAYS TO AVOID PROPERTY AND CASUALTY LOSSES

You can also take many preventive measures to safeguard your business against fire or accidental injury. Here are a few examples:

- Place approved fire extinguishers in selected spots around the facility. Check them on a regular basis. See to it that your employees know of their locations.
- Hold fire drills periodically until everyone in your place knows exactly what to do and where to go in case of fire.
- Store flammable materials in proper, closed containers and keep those containers in a cool area.
- Install a sprinkler system. Use smoke alarms in storage rooms.
- Make sure that fire doors and exits are clearly marked.
- Keep aisles, passageways, and stairwells free from all encumbrances.
- Maintain all equipment and machines in good condition. Place guardrails and other protective devices around machinery with moving parts. Train employees thoroughly in the proper handling of all equipment.
- Practice good housekeeping. Do not permit trash to accumulate on the premises.

REDUCING THEFT

Every business is vulnerable to loss through criminal activity. Theft is a blanket term: It includes shoplifting, embezzlement, and employee pilferage as well as the more "professional" crimes of burglary and robbery.

Shoplifting Retail stores are particularly susceptible to larceny by shoplifters, amateurs as well as professionals. Unfortunately, assaults upon the retail merchant's profit picture are so prevalent these days that department stores, discount houses, and other large retailers maintain their own private security forces, in addition to employing every imaginable type of security device. Generally, small-scale retailers can't afford this kind of expense.

Employee Theft   Employees can steal small, inexpensive articles (pens, typewriter ribbons, staplers) and they can take home larger merchandise, too. Occasionally, an employee who is in a position of substantial trust steals money from the cash drawer or juggles the books to conceal theft.

Ways to Reduce Losses from Theft   The business owner can take many steps to hold down losses from criminal acts. (See exhibit 20–4 for some useful suggestions along these lines.)

EXHIBIT 20–4.   SUGGESTIONS FOR REDUCING LOSSES FROM THEFT

YOUR EMPLOYEES CAN HELP

- In hiring new people, make certain your selection and screening procedures are good. Make it known from the beginning that you expect honesty in all your employees and set a personal example with your own behavior at all times.
- Train your personnel to be calm and cooperative in the event of a holdup. A life is a precious thing that no amount of money can replace.
- If possible, always schedule at least two individuals to open up in the morning and close at night, and to make bank deposits.
- Train your employees to be alert: to watch people who enter your store with coats over their arms or carrying shopping bags or bulky packages; to keep an eye on those who look or act suspicious; to wait promptly on customers.
- Try to maintain adequate floor coverage by adding extra salespeople during busy hours.

TIGHTEN UP ON PROCEDURES AND POLICIES

- Keep good records in accordance with good accounting procedures.
- If possible, sign all checks yourself. Never sign blank checks to leave behind when traveling or on vacation.
- Make certain all cash disbursements have your personal approval.
- Try to reconcile all bank statements throughout the year. Review all canceled checks and their endorsements.
- Keep close watch over the shipping and receiving functions. This includes setting up tight recordkeeping systems within both departments, supervising the loading and unloading of trucks, and even fencing off the two areas from other departments.

EXHIBIT 20–4. (CONTINUED)

- Always remove excess cash from the cash register and place it in the safe. Bank frequently and at different times from day to day. Leave the cash drawer empty and open at night (to avoid possible forced entry that might damage the equipment).
- Keep all keys locked up when not in use and issue as few as you have to, in order to avoid unnecessary duplication.
- Prosecute any shoplifter who is apprehended and any employee caught stealing. (If there's any doubt whatsoever in a particular incident, it might be wiser to avoid prosecution because of the possibility of a lawsuit for false arrest.)
- To prevent salesclerks from pocketing change or bills from the register, insist on issuing register receipts to all customers. An even better arrangement is to make out sales slips for each and every sale.

What to Do with the Premises

- Install a good alarm system, preferably a central system, on the premises. In high-risk areas, consider additional safeguards, such as gratings and a private patrol service.
- Protect all doors and entrances with properly installed, pin-tumbler-type cylinder locks and deadbolts.
- Safes should be of high quality, fire resistant, and fastened to the building itself.
- Your business premises should be adequately illuminated at night. This applies to the area around the building or store (front/sides/back) as well as inside.
- In a retail store, place small, expensive items in locked showcases. Tie down merchandise on display wherever practical.
- Use antishoplifting signs around the premises to discourage petty larceny.
- Locate your check-out stand or cash register near the store's exit. If you can afford to, station a guard at the exit as well.
- Equip your store with convex wall mirrors, two-way mirrors, and closed-circuit television cameras that move to encompass a view of a wide area (even if these are only dummies!).

Source: Compiled by the author.

For Further Information

Bintliff, Russell. *Crimeproofing Your Business.* New York: McGraw-Hill, 1994.

Curtis, Bob. *Retail Security: Controlling Loss for Profit.* Stoneham, Mass.: Butterworth, 1983.

Dorfman, Mark S. *Introduction to Risk Management and Insurance.* 5th ed. Englewood Cliffs, N.J.: Prentice-Hall, 1993.

Farrell, Kathleen L., and John A. Ferrara. *Shoplifting: The Antishoplifting Guidebook.* New York: Praeger, 1985.

Green, Mark et al. *Risk and Insurance.* 8th ed. Cincinnati: South-Western, 1991.

Mehr, Robert I. *Fundamentals of Insurance.* 2d ed. Homewood, Ill.: Irwin, 1986.

Nelson, James, and Terry Davis. *Protect Your Business.* Naperville, Ill.: Sourcebooks, 1993.

Rejda, George E. *Principles of Risk Management and Insurance.* 5th ed. New York: HarperCollins, 1994.

Trieschmann, James S., and Sandra G. Gustavson. *Risk Management and Insurance.* 9th ed. Cincinnati: South-Western, 1995.

Vaugh, Emmett J. *Fundamentals of Risk and Insurance.* 6th ed. New York: Wiley, 1992.

Williams, C. Arthur et al. *Risk Management and Insurance.* 7th ed. New York: McGraw-Hill, 1995.

21

ASPECTS OF LAW AND TAXATION FOR THE SMALL FIRM

LIKE SOCIETIES EVERYWHERE, our own society is governed by myriad laws. Out of necessity for our common good, we live and function within a vast and extremely complex framework of rules, regulations, customs, practices, and ordinances. These exist at every level of government: federal, state, and local. They are enforced through our court system. If we are to avoid unnecessary risk or penalty, we need to see to it that our behavior conforms to the law.

LEGAL ASPECTS

While we are, of course, familiar with much of our legal environment, certain aspects are of particular interest to the business world. Instances of business law in operation include the choice of legal form under which to operate an enterprise (discussed in chapter 4); the dissolution of partnerships and the formation of corporations; agency law; contract law; the law of torts; and "commercial law" (embracing sales and the transfer of title, warranties, commercial paper, and the like).

Some of the more significant aspects for the business owner are briefly addressed in this chapter. Of course, a detailed discussion of the legal environment lies well beyond the scope of this book. However, table 21–1 presents a summary of the major federal legislative acts that may affect your business enterprise. For additional, in-depth information regarding this entire area, you may wish to refer to the books on business law listed in the bibliography at the end of the chapter.

COMMON LAW AND STATUTORY LAW

Basically, our American legal system rests on two distinct bodies of law: *common law* and *statutory law*.

Common Law   The existing body of common law that underlies our legal system is also called *customary* or *unwritten* law. We can trace its origins back to colonial times and, beyond that, to England. Our early colonists were quick to adopt for their own use the extensive system of laws and constraints by which the English people were then being governed. Of course, that impressive legal environment that defined individuals' duties, responsibilities, and ways of behaving was itself the end result of an evolutionary process that took place over centuries. Rooted for the most part in custom, the British legal system was continually being modified and refined by decisions made in their nation's courts.

TABLE 21–1.   FEDERAL LAWS OF SIGNIFICANCE TO THE SMALL-BUSINESS OWNER

Year	Legislation	Major Thrust of Law
1890	Sherman Antitrust Act	Prohibited combinations, trusts, and conspiracies that restrain trade.
1906	Pure Food and Drug Act	Banned the adulteration or misbranding of foods and drugs sold in interstate commerce. Created the Food and Drug Administration (FDA).
1914	Clayton Act	Further strengthened the Sherman Act. Barred tying contracts and price discrimination that tends to reduce competition.
1914	Federal Trade Commission Act	Prohibited unfair methods of competition. Created the Federal Trade Commission (FTC).
1935	National Labor Relations Act (Wagner Act)	Gave workers the right to organize and engage in collective bargaining. Created the National Labor Relations Board (NLRB).
1936	Robinson-Patman Act	Barred sellers from offering buyers goods of like grade and quality at different prices in order to lessen or injure competition. Declared that promotional allowances offered must be made available on proportionately equal terms to all buyers.

TABLE 21–1. (continued)

Year	Legislation	Major Thrust of Law
1938	Food, Drug, and Cosmetic Act	Broadened the authority of the FDA, adding cosmetics and therapeutic devices to foods and drugs.
1938	Fair Labor Standards Act (Federal Wages and Hours Law)	Established wage and hour regulations, minimum hourly wage, and conditions for minors who work.
1938	Wheeler-Lea Act	Banned deceptive packaging; expanded FTC authority to include false or misleading advertising.
1939	Wool Products Labeling Act	Required specific information to be placed on labels attached to products made of wool.
1951	Fur Products Labeling Act	Established label requirements for fur products, including type of fur and country of origin.
1953	Flammable Fabrics Act	Prohibited interstate shipment of apparel that contains flammable goods. Later amended to include fabrics, materials, and home furnishings.
1960	Hazardous Substances Labeling Act	Mandated that warning notices be affixed to household products that contain poisonous, corrosive, or otherwise dangerous substances.
1963	Equal Pay Act	Required employers to give men and women equal pay for the same work.
1964	Civil Rights Act	Outlawed discrimination in employment practices because of race, religion, sex, color, or national origin. Created the Equal Employment Opportunity Commission (EEOC).
1966	Fair Packaging and Labeling Act	Required that the ingredients be disclosed on many packaged products or on labels attached to them.
1967	Age Discrimination in Employment Act	Prohibited employment practices aimed at discriminating against persons between the ages of forty and sixty-five. (Subsequently amended to age seventy.)
1968	Consumer Credit Protection Act (Truth in Lending Act)	Mandated that terms and interest charges be fully disclosed to persons who buy on credit.
1969	Child Protection and Toy Safety Act	Banned harmful or dangerous toys from the marketplace.

TABLE 21–1. (continued)

Year	Legislation	Major Thrust of Law
1970	Fair Credit Reporting Act	Required that credit reporting agencies keep accurate records and provide interested consumers with access to their records.
1970	Occupational Safety and Health Act	Required employers to provide their workers with a safe work environment. Established the Occupational Safety and Health Administration (OSHA).
1972	Equal Employment Opportunity Act	Widened the scope and authority of the EEOC.
1972	Consumer Products Safety Act	Prohibited the sale of harmful products. Created the Consumer Product Safety Commission (CPSC), empowered to set product safety standards.
1974	Employee Retirement Income Security Act	Designed to protect and regulate employee pensions.
1975	Equal Credit Opportunity Act	Barred discrimination against credit applicants because of sex or marital status. (Later amended to prohibit discrimination on the basis of age, religion, race, or national origin.)
1975	Fair Credit Billing Act	Aimed at shielding consumers from unfair credit billing practices.
1975	Magnuson-Moss Warranty Act	Required full disclosure of warranty terms in clear language.
1977	Fair Debt Collection Practices Act	Banned the use of deception, harassment, and other unreasonable tactics in attempts to collect past-due accounts.
1984	Toy Safety Act	Gave the federal government the right to recall harmful toys.

Source: Compiled by the author.

STATUTORY LAW

A statute is a law that has been passed by a legislature. *Statutory law,* then, is the term we apply to laws that governments—again, at all levels—have enacted. Thus, we are subject to federal, state, county, municipal, and town statutes. As you might suspect, the collective body of statutory law in the United States is far greater than the common law.

THE LAW OF AGENCY

Of critical importance to the business world is the *law of agency*. The term *agency* can be defined as "a contractual relationship involving an agent and a principal, in which the agent is given the authority to represent the principal in dealings with third parties.*

Agency situations call for a mutual agreement to be reached by two parties (persons, organizations), the principal and the agent. Typically, the principal authorizes the agent to act on his or her behalf. Thus, the agent is an authorized representative of the principal. The agreement may be in the form of a written contract, or it may be simply an oral agreement.

THE LAW OF CONTRACTS

The *law of contracts* has been called "the basic foundation of business law."** Each of the following instances calls for the signing of a contract:

- A homeowner selects carpeting to be installed in her six-room house.
- A consumer puts a down payment on a new Chevrolet sedan and then arranges to repay the balance over a period of three years.
- A manufacturer arranges with a salesperson to "represent" the company in three southern states.
- A construction firm offers to build a second warehouse for a large wholesaler.
- The comptroller of a large consumer service company enlists the aid of an office machine repair firm to service the company's equipment.
- A chain-store retailer hires a maintenance firm to polish the brass on its storefronts on a monthly basis.

For a contract to be legal and enforceable in a court of law, it must meet the following requirements:

---

* John Jude Moran, *Practical Business Law* (Englewood Cliffs, N.J.: Prentice-Hall, 1985), 332.

** Ibid., 48.

- An offer or a proposal must have been made by one party to another.
- The purpose of the offer/proposal must be legal.
- The offer/proposal must be accepted by both parties.
- Acceptance must be voluntary; intimidation, coercion, or threat cannot be used.
- "Consideration" must be present—that is, each party must give the other something of value.
- Parties to the contract must be competent—that is, of legal age and mentally sound.

THE LAW OF TORTS

The *law of torts* deals with private, or civil, wrongs—as contrasted with public wrongs such as criminal acts. A tort is a wrongful act committed by one person or organization against another or against that other's property or reputation. If a tort has been committed, the wronged party can seek redress in court.

Two types of torts can be distinguished: intentional and unintentional torts. "Intentional torts include assault, battery, conversion, defamation, fraud, false imprisonment, invasion of privacy, interference with business relations, malicious prosecution, nuisance, strict liability, and trespass. Unintentional torts include negligence, products liability, and misrepresentation."*

THE LAW OF PROPERTY

The *law of property* deals with all those materials, goods, and other things of value that people or organizations own. This body of law obtains in an extensive variety of situations that range from real estate transactions and tenant-landlord relationships to mortgages, wills, bankruptcy, and so forth. It applies to real property as well as to personal property. Real property consists of land, homes, and other buildings that are permanently affixed to land.

---

* Moran, *Practical Business Law*, 32.

PROTECTING PATENTS AND COPYRIGHTS

Patents are granted by the federal government to those who have designed innovative products and submitted the required paperwork. If granted a patent, you have the exclusive right to manufacture and market your invention for a period of seventeen years. All other individuals and organizations are barred from producing or selling the item.

If you have invented something and wish to obtain a patent for your own protection, be sure to enlist the services of a patent attorney. This specialist will conduct a patent search to determine if the item is patentable—that is, whether or not a similar invention has already been registered. The cost of this procedure may run to a few hundred dollars. You then need to prepare an application, submit the required filing fee, and register the product with the Commissioner of Patents and Trademarks, Washington, DC 20231.

TRADEMARKS

A *trademark* is a letter, word, mark, symbol, sound, or device—or some combination of these—that is used by a manufacturer or seller to identify a product or service. Companies develop trademarks, brand names, and logos (logotypes) in order to differentiate their organizations, products, and services from those of competitors. As they are publicized over time, these distinguishing marks can grow to be of considerable marketing importance.

COPYRIGHTS

A *copyright* is the legal right to reproduce and sell an original work or composition, such as a poem or essay, an article or short story, a book, a musical composition, a painting or illustration, or a photograph.

Any original work that is written, typed, recorded, taped, photographed, illustrated, or otherwise fixed in a tangible form of expression belongs to its creator. Under the Copyright Act of 1976, the author or creator owns the work for the length of his or her lifetime plus fifty years. The law applies to unpublished works as well as those that are published.

To forestall any infringement of the copyright by persons who may attempt to use the work without permission, be sure to register your ownership. The procedure entails the completion and filing of an application form, along with a small fee and two copies of the work, with The Register of Copyrights, Library of Congress, Washington, DC 20559. (For "nondramatic" literary works, ask for Form TX.)

TAXATION AND YOUR BUSINESS

It has been said that nothing is as certain as death and taxes. This is unfortunately a truism, and your new business is no exception to the rule.

Your enterprise is subject to taxes at all three levels of government: federal, state, and local. This alone ought to convince you that you're in dire need of as much professionalism in the tax management area as in all segments of your business—production, sales, and personnel. Because of the complexities of tax law, frequent new rulings, changing regulations, and difficulties of interpretation, it's nearly impossible to adopt a do-it-yourself stance in this field.

What taxes do you face? Let's first consider those imposed by the federal government.

FEDERAL TAXES

The major tax bite taken by Uncle Sam is in the form of income and social security taxes. Incidentally, new responsibilities accompany your transition from worker to business owner. Not only are you taxed on your earnings but you're also automatically conscripted into service as a deputy tax collector.

FEDERAL INCOME TAXES

The legal form of the business you have selected has a major impact on the way tax regulations apply to your new enterprise.

Sole Proprietorship You'll recall that, for legal purposes (which of course include taxation), the individual owner and the business activity are inseparable. Consequently, if you have chosen this form, you're required to file your annual federal tax return on the familiar Form 1040 (Individual Income Tax Return). This is the same form you completed as an employee.

In addition, you need to complete and submit, attached to your Form 1040, a separate Schedule C (Profit or Loss from Business—Sole Proprietorship). A sample of the schedule is shown in exhibit B–1, Appendix B.

On this schedule, you must furnish details about your business activity for the year just ended: your sales, the cost of goods sold (and how you arrived at the figures), the resulting gross profit, your business expenses and other deductions, explanations of such items as depreciation, and your net profit. This last figure is added to other income you earned during the year and entered on your Form 1040.

As sole proprietor, you're also required to calculate what your expected income tax will be for the coming year. Submit Form 1040ES (Declaration of Estimated Tax for Individuals). The IRS provides you with instructions, a worksheet on which you can work out your estimated tax, and four declaration vouchers. Each of these vouchers must be mailed, in turn, before the fifteenth of April, June, September, and January. Part payment of your estimated tax must accompany each voucher.

Partnership As with the sole proprietorship, tax liability is assessed only for the earned income of the individual partners involved and not against the business directly. Each partner files a tax return on Form 1040, where his or her distributive share of the business profits is noted. In addition, you're required to submit a report of your business operation on Form 1065 (U.S. Partnership Return of Income). This is only an information report; no tax payment accompanies its submission. A sample of Form 1065 is included in exhibit B–2. You must also file Schedule K–1 (Partner's Share of Income, Credits, Deductions, etc.); an example is shown in exhibit B–3. And, as with the sole proprietor, each partner also files an estimated tax.

Corporation If you elected this form of ownership, your tax reporting problems are more complicated. As an employee of the firm, you report your earnings (and other income) during the taxable year—as well as dividends from the corporation—on Form 1040. As a separate entity, the corporation must file its own return as well; for this purpose, use Form 1120 (U.S. Corporation Income Tax Return).* If the firm operates on the calendar-year basis, the return is due on or before March 15. Many corporations, however, prefer the fiscal-year basis; in such cases, the corporation tax is due by the fifteenth of the third month following the close of its fiscal year. A sample Form 1120 is shown in exhibit B–4.

Estimated tax payments must be made by every corporation whose tax liability is expected to be $500 or more. Payments are

---

* You may file Form 1120–A (U.S. Corporation Short-Form Income Tax Return) instead, providing the firm's gross receipts, total income, and total assets are all under $500,000 and you meet several other requirements.

made to an authorized financial institution or to a Federal Reserve Bank.

At present, corporations are required to pay federal income tax on profits for the year according to the following tax-rate schedule:*

If Taxable Income Is Over	But Not Over	The Tax Is	Of the Amount Over
$0	$50,000	15%	$0
50,000	75,000	$7,500 + 25%	50,000
75,000	100,000	13,750 + 34%	75,000
100,000	335,000	22,250 + 39%	100,000
335,000	10,000,000	113,900 + 34%	335,000
10,000,000	15,000,000	3,400,000 + 35%	10,000,000
15,000,000	18,333,333	5,150,000 + 38%	15,000,000
18,333,333	-----	35%	0

S Corporation You may elect to be taxed as an *S corporation* (a small-business entity) and thereby avoid being taxed as the usual type of corporation. In this case, you report your income and taxable dividends in much the same fashion as do the partners of a partnership. Certain restrictions obtain in this situation: Yours must be a domestic corporation with only one classification of stock issued; this stock must be held by no more than thirty-five shareholders; all shareholders must give their consent; and the shareholders may not be nonresident aliens.**

To gain status as an S Corporation, you need to file Form 2553 (Election by a Small Business Corporation.) Tax returns are filed on Form 1120S (U.S. Income Tax Return for an S Corporation.)

SOCIAL SECURITY TAXES

According to the provisions of the Federal Insurance Contributions Act (FICA), your employees are covered by old age, survivors, disability, and hospital insurance. To pay for such coverage, Social Security and Medicare taxes are levied on both employee and employer. The employer is responsible for collecting this tax from employees by withholding it in the same way the employees' income tax is withheld.

Currently (1997), the deduction for Social Security tax amounts to 6.2 percent of each employee's annual earnings, up to the first $65,400 of wages. The rate for the Medicare tax is 1.45 percent; there

---

* Internal Revenue Service, "1995 Tax Guide for Small Business," *Publication 334* (Washington, D.C.: Internal Revenue Service, rev. November 1995), 142.

** "1995 Tax Guide," 145.

is no wage-base limit for this tax. In addition, the firm is required to match the total amount collected from its employees, at the same rates (6.2 percent plus 1.45 percent).

FICA and withheld income taxes are reported and paid together. Within one month after the end of each calendar quarter, you need to report these taxes on Form 941 (Employer's Quarterly Federal Tax Return.) Bear in mind, too, that you'll need to make deposits periodically to a Federal Reserve bank or an authorized financial institution.

UNEMPLOYMENT TAX

The employer is also subject to federal unemployment tax (FUTA) if he or she has paid wages of $1,500 or more during any quarter of the calendar year, or if one or more employees were working at least once each week (not necessarily for a full day) during each of twenty calendar days. Currently, the rate of taxation is 6.2 percent on the first $7,000 of wages paid to each employee during the year. Credit of up to 5.4 percent is granted, however, for contributions made to state unemployment taxes.

Deposits are required if the firm's tax liability exceeds $100 for any calendar quarter. Such deposits are made to a Federal Reserve bank or to an authorized financial institution. The employer must also file an annual return on Form 940 (Employer's Annual Federal Unemployment Tax Return [FUTA]) on or before January 31.

EXCISE TAXES

Excise taxes are levied on the sale of certain articles, on certain types of transactions and occupations, and on the use of certain products. Such taxes are not to be included in the selling price of such items but are to be charged separately by the manufacturer or the retailer.

Among the more common excise taxes are those imposed on gasoline, diesel fuel, and fuels used in noncommercial aviation; manufacturers' excise taxes on tires, coal, and sport fishing equipment; and taxes on certain transportation and communications services. Businesses liable for excise taxes must file Form 720 (Quarterly Federal Excise Tax Return). For more information about these taxes, secure a copy of Publication 510 (Excise Taxes for 1997).

STATE AND LOCAL TAXES

Tax rates and other specifics vary considerably from locale to locale across the country. Prominent among such forms of taxation are the state (and sometimes the city) tax on income, real estate taxes, and sales taxes. State and local income taxes are tied in most ways to the details you provide on your federal income tax return. Real estate taxes furnish most of the revenue required for the operation of local governments and the services they provide. Sales taxes are levied by most states, many cities, and some counties on the retail prices of products (and sometimes services). Retailers are required to collect these sales taxes from their customers, keep records of what they collect, and then turn over these moneys to the appropriate taxing authorities.

Business owners may also be responsible for other, lesser taxes including unemployment and disability taxes, the corporation (or the unincorporated business) tax, and taxes on licenses and permits, among others.

HOW TO HANDLE WITHHOLDING

The federal government insists that business managers withhold from the regular paychecks of all employees a percentage of their earnings for income and Social Security taxes. Further, they are required to turn over such moneys to the government on a regular basis. (For instructions, refer to the section above on Social Security Taxes.)

Consequently, you should ask each new employee to complete a W–4 form (Employee's Withholding Allowance Certificate) by his or her first day of work. Based on the information contained therein, you withhold the required percentage of each employee's gross earnings according to tables available from the Internal Revenue Service in their Publication 15: Employer's Tax Guide (Circular E). The tables cover different payroll periods: weekly, semimonthly, and monthly.

Thereafter, each succeeding year (before December 1) you should check all employees for changes in status. If there has been a change, ask the employee to complete a new W–4 form.

Finally, before the end of each January, you must also provide each of your employees with a completed W–2 form (Wage and Tax Statement) for the year just ended.

DEPRECIATION

Business property with a useful life of more than one year is subject to *depreciation*. This involves deducting, each year, some portion of that property's cost—a figure that can play an important role in determining the amount of business earnings on which you'll need to pay income tax.

Property can be tangible or intangible. Buildings, machinery, equipment, furniture, and automobiles and delivery trucks are considered tangible property; they can be seen, touched, and felt. Copyrights and franchises are examples of intangible property. Land, though, is property that can never be depreciated.

To be depreciable, business property must meet three basic requirements. It must

1. Be used in business (or held for the production of income)
2. Have a determinable useful life of more than one year
3. Be something that wears out, decays, gets used up, becomes obsolete, or loses value from natural causes

The modified accelerated cost recovery system (MACRS) applies to all tangible property placed in service after 1986. A more detailed description of MACRS as well as information about the "Section 179 deduction" are beyond the scope of this discussion. For further information, you may wish to refer to the following IRS publications:

Publication 334   Tax Guide for Small Business

Publication 534   Depreciating Property Placed in Circulation Before 1987

Publication 946   How to Depreciate Property

Publication 463   Travel, Entertainment, Gift, and Car Expenses

FOR FURTHER INFORMATION

Adams, Paul. *155 Legal Do's and Don'ts for Small Business*. New York: Wiley, 1996.

Ashcroft, John D., and Janet E. Ashcroft. *Law for Business*. 11th ed. Cincinnati: South-Western, 1992.

Christianson, Stephen G. *Business Law Made Simple*. New York: Doubleday, 1995.

Cihon, Patrick J., and James O. Castagnera. *Labor and Employment Law*. 2d ed. Cincinnati: South-Western, 1993.

Du Boff, Leonard D. *The Law (in Plain English) for Small Businesses*. 2d ed. New York: Wiley, 1991.

Ernst & Young. *The Ernst & Young Tax Guide, 1995*. New York: Wiley, 1995.

Foster, Frank H., and Robert L. Shook. *Everything You Need to Know about Patents, Copyrights, and Trademarks*. New York: Wiley, 1989.

Goldstein, Arnold S., and Robert L. Davidson III. *Starting Your Subchapter "S" Corporation*. 2d ed. New York: Wiley, 1992.

Hancock, William A. *The Small Business Legal Advisor*. 2d ed. New York: McGraw-Hill, 1992.

Lane, Marc J. *Legal Handbook for Small Business*. rev. ed. New York: AMACOM, 1989.

Moran, John Jude. *Practical Business Law*. 2d ed. Englewood Cliffs, N.J.: Prentice-Hall, 1989.

Roberson, Cliff. *The Businessperson's Legal Advisor*. 2d ed. Blue Ridge Mountain, Pa.: TAB Books, 1990.

Twomey, David P. *Equal Employment Opportunity Law*. 3rd ed. Cincinnati: South-Western, 1994.

IMPROVING THE NEW BUSINESS OPERATION

IMPROVING RESULTS IN YOUR MANUFACTURING PLANT

As A CONSERVATIVE estimate, at least eight out of ten small factories operate well below their optimum capability.

Why this dire situation? For one thing, so long as a plant is producing and the operation is profitable, the factory manager is usually quite content. Handicapped by the lack of a more sophisticated level of knowledge of plant operations, this executive doesn't realize things could be better. Other factors that contribute to manufacturing inefficiency often include improper costing practices, machine operators who aren't well trained, inadequately maintained or obsolete equipment, lack of familiarity with the use of variance analysis techniques, sloppy purchasing practices, and a host of other possibilities.

These days, in the face of spiraling costs and intensified competition, the name of the manufacturing game is no longer production but *productivity*.

To improve plant productivity, no magical "open sesame" need be invoked; the pathway to improvement in manufacturing is as simple as counting 1-2-3:

1. Buy better.
2. Produce better.
3. Sell better.

Actually, entries one and three are ancillary problem areas; the central problem in manufacturing is that number two: *How to produce better.*

As you have already seen, effective business administration involves skillfully planning, organizing, directing, and controlling all of the elements that combine to comprise the business. In short, it calls for more efficient deployment and use of all company resources: capital, machinery, human resources, materials, and methods. Moreover, efficiency in manipulating these assets is inextricably tied to costs. Producing better (or, for that matter, buying or selling better) implies that output will be increased while cost factors representing the input will be held steady (if not reduced).

STANDARDS: THE BASES FOR IMPROVEMENT

To increase productivity, you must understand fully how your plant is operating at present, decide in a logical manner on goals that are higher than today's outputs, and then figure out ways to attain those goals. In short, *measurements* need to be taken—today, tomorrow, and beyond tomorrow. Only by recording and comparing those measurements over time can you determine whether or not plant productivity is increasing.

Such measurements are called *standards;* these are based on averages obtained through observing and recording what transpires in the factory. Of course, standards are established for control purposes and, more important, as points of departure for improvement. They can be set up in every division of your manufacturing enterprise, not only within the production process itself but also in purchasing, sales, and even office administration. They provide answers to dozens of questions, such as:

- How much of material A goes into each unit of product B?
- How long does it take an operator to perform task C?
- How many widgets roll off machine D each hour, each week?
- What is the yield in pounds of compound Z when fifty pounds of material X are mixed with twenty-five pounds of material Y?
- If this piece of equipment is in operation eight hours each day on a five-day-week basis, how much electricity will be used?

In the area of production, the following standards should be established:

- Direct labor cost/product unit
- Number of labor-hours needed/unit of work
- Number of machine-hours needed/operation
- Setup time/operation
- Amount of materials used/product
- Power usage/machine
- Number of products produced/day

Standards that might prove useful in the sales area include the number of new accounts opened per salesperson, the average monthly sales per salesperson, the cost of sales per sales dollar, and the gross margin contribution per territory.

SETTING STANDARDS

In efficient plant management, standards such as those mentioned above are developed and monitored regularly, perhaps with the aid of industrial engineers or consultants. These standards, of course, represent averages that are *real*. By definition, then, they are not *ideal* averages. So your next move is to work out ideal standards; in other words, strive to project the company's output if it were operating at maximum efficiency. Then, somewhere between the ideal and the real, you must find a spot where you can pinpoint an attainable level of performance that is higher than the one your plant now evidences.

Time and motion studies are techniques available to help you maximize efficiency. Time studies record the time it takes to perform each task in a factory, in order to set up time standards for every job. Motion studies analyze all movements made in accomplishing each task and arrive at the most effective sequence of motions for each.

As a final comment on standards, remember that the ratios derived from analyzing the basic accounting statements (balance sheet, income statements) serve as standards for comparison, control, and further improvement. (See the section on "Ratio Analysis" in chapter 19.)

VARIANCE ANALYSIS

Variances are differences or deviations from the norm or average. After you have worked up your initial standards, the averages you have calculated from daily plant operations will appear to fluctuate. In manufacturing, you can expect all sorts of variances: labor variances, materials variances, overhead variances, and so on. As an illustration, those standards you have developed for materials used in production can vary because of poor handling and storage, changes in the purchase price, inadequately serviced equipment, fluctuations in quality, and the like.

For each of the major cost areas (labor often being the most significant), you'll have to decide just how much tolerance, or deviation from the standard, you can permit. When variances are analyzed—compared to the standards you have decided are acceptable—those that exceed tolerable limits should be investigated thoroughly and corrective action taken at once. Often, better production planning and flow control, improved maintenance, and more training for factory personnel can be helpful here. Then, too, *network techniques* such as Critical Path Method (CPM) and Program Evaluation and Review Techniques (PERT) may occasionally prove useful.

Helpful steps for improving plant productivity include upgrading the quality of the labor component (through further training, better hiring practices, more skilled supervision); moving in the direction of semiautomation through the purchase of additional machinery and equipment (and introducing computers); and making sizable capital expenditures for plant expansion or improvement, additional personnel, and so forth.

SOME THOUGHTS ON UPGRADING PLANT PRODUCTIVITY

PRODUCTION

In a healthy factory operation, production planning is accomplished well in advance. Better planning means increasing the accuracy of your sales forecasting. Devote lots of good thinking to this thorny problem; involve your best people in the process. It is worth your while to learn about the more popular methods companies depend on for developing their sales forecasts.

Forecasting Techniques   Both qualitative and quantitative techniques are available. Among the qualitative approaches—which, incidentally, are frequently referred to as *judgmental* or *naive* methods—are:

- *The Jury of Executive Opinion* a technique that involves asking your company's executives for their opinions
- *The Delphi Method* a variation of the above whereby executive judgments are reconsidered and refined by the executives over two or more resubmissions of the information
- *The Salesforce Composite* a technique whereby you ask your salespeople for estimates of the amounts each individual will produce, and then tally these estimates to produce an overall forecast
- *The Survey of Customer Intentions* which is precisely what it sounds like

Of course, you'll need to narrow down and reconcile discrepancies in the data you collect.

Quantitative approaches make use of historical information and statistics. In addition to such quantitative techniques as trend extension and time series extrapolation, there are the correlation methods. The latter seek to tie company sales to specific variables in the economy, such as the level of consumer spending, the prime rate, and the Gross National Product. Thus we have *leading, coincident,* and *lagging* indicators, depending on whether they seem to rise or fall before, during, or after fluctuations in sales.

Prepare your production budget just as carefully as you prepare every other component of the master budget. Consider your budgets for labor, for materials, for manufacturing overhead, and for maintenance.

Plot your production with great care every step of the way. Set up a foolproof production reporting system. Involve your senior people in planning, preparing work orders, routing, scheduling, expediting, and other activities.

Set specific objectives: Your quickest route to process improvement is *production-by-objectives.* Indeed, fuller utilization of all production resources leads to a higher return on investment.

Work on moving away from intermittent production and toward longer, uninterrupted machine runs. Gang orders where possible during slack periods. If your products are branded, investigate the benefits of running private-label merchandise. Build up your finished goods inventories in advance of selling seasons.

If inventory levels exceed sales or if you can foresee the need for more cash in the near future, offer "early-bird" discounts that will induce your customers to place orders earlier than usual.

In the production process, two or more pieces of equipment are often used in sequence. The machines usually operate at different speeds; this raises the strong possibility that bottlenecks will form. Bottlenecks can be avoided by balancing the flow lines; use flow process charts and flow diagrams to work out the ideal flow of materials. Additional machinery, proper scheduling, and the application of queuing theory can all be of assistance in this problem area.

Apply cost-accounting techniques to all manufacturing operations; watch variances from all standards; take action whenever indicated; and use ratio analysis to improve efficiency.

LAYOUT

Many small manufacturing establishments use the *process* type of layout whereby the machinery and equipment needed for each distinct type of production processing (cutting, stamping, grinding, polishing, and the like) are grouped together. This enables plants to manufacture different products on the same equipment, thus ensuring flexibility. However, there are some drawbacks: excessive materials handling costs, inefficient utilization of both machinery and labor, unnecessary delays, and so forth. By combining or anticipating orders (and by writing more business!) you may be able to introduce some line production, or *product layout,* into your manufacturing. In this kind of layout, both machinery and equipment are set up to follow a specific sequence of operations that culminate in the production of one kind of product. This will give you the best of both types of processes—namely, lower-cost production-line output and the flexibility you need to handle job lots.

Plan all layout changes yourself with the aid of a qualified consultant. Always consider your future requirements (three to five years hence); think in terms of additional facilities, offices, new electrical wiring, plumbing, and waste lines. Use drawings, plans, and renderings. Machinery can be represented by templates of cardboard or other materials, and dimensions indicated on these. Scale models are also useful.

Many smaller plants have a U-shaped layout where both the shipping and receiving departments are at the same end of the factory. This way, the same loading area and single bay can be used for both purposes. These setups are often supervised by one person.

MACHINERY AND EQUIPMENT

Survey all machinery: Check performance records, purchase dates, and warrantees. Replace antiquated equipment or machines of below-par performance with newer models of higher capacity. Remember that used equipment is often costlier in the long term.

When considering new machinery, strive for trouble-free operation, good-quality work and materials, reliable performance, and a good service contract with the manufacturer. Where possible, deal directly with the manufacturer and not with the distributor.

If not already in existence, a strict preventive maintenance program should be instituted. This should include regular inspections, prompt repairs, and spare parts on hand for important equipment. Work out procedures and even backup equipment for floods, power failures, fires, and other major events that could affect production.

Leasing arrangements are at times (when cash is "tight" or interest charges are low) more beneficial than outright purchases of equipment, especially those that provide options to buy.

All maintenance supplies and tools should be controlled with a careful recordkeeping system. Maintenance personnel should represent a range of skills and should include electricians, carpenters, machinists, and mechanics (depending upon the particular needs of your plant).

MATERIALS HANDLING

Where possible, contract for six months' or a year's supply of materials that you use in large quantities. Make sure that the price you pay is guaranteed for the life of the contract and that quantity discounts apply. Have deliveries made to your plant as they are needed.

Materials are forever being moved about within a factory. All types of power equipment and conveyors are available for this purpose. Suppliers will submit various proposals to you over the year; evaluate all of them with an eye to economizing on movement and thereby increasing plant efficiency.

Follow two principles commonly used by experienced warehouse people: The *straight-line principle* teaches you to minimize the distances materials must travel within a plant (not adhering slavishly to straight lines but avoiding sideways or backward movements). The *unit load principle* holds that the greater the quantity of merchandise moved at the same time, the less it costs to move each individual item in the load (usually palletized).

Many kinds of materials used in manufacturing require special care: handling precautions, proper storage containers, temperature-controlled and/or moisture-free atmosphere, ventilation (or lack of it), specially built tanks or drums, and so forth. Proper attention to these needs prevents deterioration, spoilage, and other "wastage" of materials.

In this connection, plastic and fiber containers can frequently be used to replace more expensive and heavier items such as steel drums.

PERSONNEL

Productivity improvement in a manufacturing plant should begin with your employees. Having the right people, with the right skills and the proper training, in the right positions within your organization, lays a strong foundation for eventual improvement.

If your company does not already have them on hand, written and detailed job specifications should be prepared for all positions. New hires should be matched against those specifications. If at all possible, try to hire people who are proficient in two or more skill areas. This way, you can build valuable flexibility into the personnel component.

Set up an operations manual as a guide for your people. Seek a professional personnel specialist to help you produce this guide.

At all times, train your employees in good work habits. Then, insist on careful adherence to rules and instructions. Don't tolerate sloppy performance.

Strive for good management-worker relations and safe and comfortable working conditions. Encourage worker input and suggestions.

If yours is a one-shift operation that runs for five days each week, this means that your machines are lying idle for sixteen hours a day on weekdays and twenty-four hours per day over the weekend. Aim at building up business to the point at which two shifts are needed (perhaps 8 A.M. to 4 P.M. and 4 P.M. to 12 midnight). This will bring your per-item overhead costs down sharply.

QUALITY CONTROL

The quality-control function in manufacturing is an essential one. Ordinarily, its foremost application is to the product or products being made. It's used to detect inferior or defective work early enough so that adjustments can be made quickly in production. Indeed, quality control should embrace all purchased raw, semifinished, or finished materials used in the plant and equipment, machinery, and supplies as well.

In a small plant, there's often no quality-control department per se, simply one or several technicians who perform necessary tests and report the results to the production head.

It's not unusual for a small manufacturer to request that suppliers conduct quality-control tests on their materials before shipping them. This is a helpful type of arrangement that will save you time and money. (It's wise to verify the results from time to time yourself.)

IMPROVING YOUR SALES EFFORTS

In the beginning, the new manufacturer may rely on his or her own efforts (or those of partners) to obtain the company's first regular customers. Later on, the firm will most likely select one or more manufacturer's representatives to take charge of the selling end of the business, thus leaving the owner(s) more time to concentrate on production.

Eventually, a sales force may be initiated. (For more on managing a sales force and helpful insights into the personal selling area, refer to chapter 14.)

MANAGING THE SALES OFFICE

An essential element in the marketing of goods by the manufacturing (or, for that matter, the wholesaling) organization is the company's inside sales office. This is where orders from field sales representatives arrive each day. They may come by mail, over the telephone, or by salespeople or messengers. Typically, the orders are "logged," or registered, and then routed through the firm's customary order-handling procedure—perhaps being forwarded first to the credit section for approval, then to the shipping department to be filled, and thereafter to bookkeeping where packing slips and invoices are made out.

To ensure a healthy operation, the sales office must be run efficiently. Incoming orders should be processed quickly and accurately. The office staff needs to keep current with just about every phase of operations: orders, prices, terms, special promotions in effect and those planned for the future, the salespeople in the field, and so forth. These inside people need to keep in close touch with customers as well; they must be able to respond intelligently to questions and to make suggestions, when necessary.

As is the case with offices of any type, of course, improvements can be effected in the sales office, too. Little more is required than a detailed study of the existing situation, reference to one or two good books on office management (or the hiring of a consultant on a temporary basis), and the development of a list of worthwhile suggestions for upgrading office productivity.

You may find the recommendations below of some value when you get ready to undertake this task:

EXHIBIT 22–1. A PROCEDURE FOR INCREASING OFFICE PRODUCTIVITY

1. Start by keeping close track of your own work activities for a week or ten days. Record everything you do, hour by hour and day by day.
2. Next, pore over the detailed schedule you have kept. At this point, your main objective should be to begin working toward a sensible reorganization of your workload. You also need to think in terms of prioritizing the many tasks you need to perform. Even though this may prove difficult for you to do, you should learn to order these tasks—from most essential to least essential.
3. Bear in mind that your time—like everyone else's time—is limited. You must learn how to manage your time ably, how to make maximum use of it.

EXHIBIT 22–1. (continued)

4. In this context, delegation can be a tremendous asset to you. It's also a vital tool in helping to reduce your workload.

   If you do not already know how to do so, learn how to give work out—at least most of the work that others can perform and that need not (and ought not) be performed by you.

5. Learn how to make decisions. Don't procrastinate; never put off till tomorrow any decision you can arrive at today.

6. Be sure to teach your managers how to make their own decisions and how to delegate in turn to their assistants.

7. Finally, review your office equipment and furnishings, your internal systems, the stationery and office forms you use, and so forth with an inquisitive eye toward raising productivity.

Source: Compiled by the author.

For Further Information

Dilworth, James B. *Production and Operations Management.* 5th ed. New York: McGraw-Hill, 1993.

Fogarty, Donald W., Thomas R. Hoffmann, and Peter W. Stonebraker. *Production and Operations Management.* Cincinnati: South-Western, 1989.

Gunn, Thomas G. *21st Century Manufacturing: Creating Winning Business Performance.* Essex Junction, Vt.: Oliver Wight, 1993.

Haas, Robert W. *Business Marketing: A Managerial Approach.* 6th ed. Cincinnati: South-Western, 1995.

Harmon, Roy L., and Leroy D. Peterson. *Reinventing the Factory: Productivity Breakthroughs in Manufacturing Today.* New York: Wiley, 1993.

Lehman, Ronald R., and Russel S. Winter. *Product Management.* Homewood, Ill.: Irwin, 1993.

Lunn, Terry, and Susan A. Neff. *MRP: Integrating Materials Requirement Planning and Modern Business.* Burr Ridge, Ill.: Irwin, 1992.

Mather, Hal. *Competitive Manufacturing.* Englewood Cliffs, N.J.: Prentice-Hall, 1988.

McClain, John, and L. Joseph Thomas. *Operations Management: Production of Goods and Services.* 2d ed. Englewood Cliffs, N.J.: Prentice-Hall, 1985.

Meredith, Jack R. *The Management of Operations.* 4th ed. New York: Wiley, 1992.

Moffats, Donald W. *Plant Monitoring and Inspecting Handbook.* Englewood Cliffs, N.J.: Prentice-Hall, 1996.

Narasimhan, Seetherama L. et al. *Production Planning and Inventory Control.* 2d ed. Englewood Cliffs, N.J.: Prentice-Hall, 1994.

Rohrs, W., and R. Colton. *Industrial Purchasing and Effective Materials Management.* Englewood Cliffs, N.J.: Prentice-Hall, 1985.

Shonberger, Richard J. *Operations Management: Productivity and Quality.* 2d ed. Plano, Tex.: Business Publications, 1985.

Webster, Frederick E., Jr. *Industrial Marketing Strategy.* 4th ed. New York: Wiley, 1994.

Young, Allan. *Complete Plant Operations Handbook: A Guide to Cost Reduction, Quality Control and On-Time Delivery.* Englewood Cliffs, N.J.: Prentice-Hall, 1990.

23

IMPROVING RESULTS IN YOUR WHOLESALE BUSINESS

AS YOU WILL recall from the discussion of marketing channels in chapter 16, a large majority of wholesaling establishments in the country are classified as *merchant wholesalers*. The remainder include manufacturers' sales branches and offices, petroleum bulk terminals, agents and brokers, and assemblers. Since these latter types make up fewer than one-third of all wholesale distributors, the improvements suggested in this chapter are oriented toward the more prevalent type—the merchant wholesaler. Nevertheless, much of the information presented here can be of value to the other kinds of wholesalers as well.

Let's begin with a typical organizational chart for a small merchant wholesaler operation. Figure 23–1 is fairly representative of this type of distributor in the grocery, automotive equipment, hardware, or electrical supplies business. By studying this chart, we can arrive at a simple conclusion: To improve the firm's operating results, we should seek improvement within all four major areas of activity: purchasing, warehouse operations, sales, and office management.

In order to end up with a better operating statement, you'll need to:

- Buy better
- Sell better
- Improve internal operations

Since the sales area has been dealt with extensively in chapter 14 and a section devoted to buying will be upcoming in the very next chapter, nothing more is added here on these two subjects. (However, be sure to reread the appropriate sections of the two chapters on techniques for improving the purchasing and sales aspects of your

FIGURE 23–1. SMALL MERCHANT WHOLESALER ORGANIZATION CHART

business.) The concentration here is on improving internal operations, for this is the one area where able management, better procedures and systems, and improved controls can really work wonders.

INTERNAL OPERATIONS REVOLVE AROUND ORDERS

To maximize productivity and minimize costs, most internal operations should be designed for the sole purpose of facilitating the delivery of goods to the wholesaler's accounts. There are, then, two primary components to be coordinated: (1) the entire order flow system and (2) those auxiliary structures—such as departments and the warehouse itself—that enable the order flow system to operate.

THE ORDER FLOW SYSTEM

Except for assemblers of farm products, most wholesale companies buy goods in large quantities and then break down their inventory into smaller lots for resale to other enterprises. Since these latter types (retailers, service businesses) require frequent, repeat deliveries, the typical wholesale distributor can count on receiving hundreds of orders every month—if not every week—of the year.

This is all the more reason why the successful merchant whole-saler gives prompt attention and quick, dependable service to incoming orders. Ideally, every incoming order should be filled and the merchandise sent on its way to its destination within forty-eight hours. However, delays and bottlenecks are characteristically encountered. This is especially true when orders come into the house in heavy quantities as happens before a holiday season or specific holidays, or when there isn't enough labor available to fill them, or when the customary transportation facilities are overburdened.

Another fairly common problem among wholesaling firms is occasionally losing track of orders as they are processed through the internal system. When customers phone in to inquire about the current status of their orders or to add or subtract merchandise, the result is confusion and upsetting delay for both customer and supplier.

These and other problems can be avoided 95 percent of the time if you give the situation some time, diligent study, and careful thought. To help you streamline your order flow system, consider the following breakdown of its various stages and apply some thought to each one:

1. *The Order Form* A lot of time can be saved and careless omissions or errors avoided when the order form itself is carefully tailored to the needs of your organization. Preferably, it should be prepared (or revised) with the assistance of a specialist in business forms. Preprinted snap-out carbon sets will effect substantial savings for you.

2. *Order Writing* All sales representatives must be thoroughly trained to complete the order form properly. This applies not only to the field sales force but also to any inside salespeople. Terms, discounts, names and addresses, delivery information, and all special instructions must be written legibly. Poorly written-out order forms, or forms with mistakes, should be acted on immediately. Salespeople should be called in such instances and reproved. You must constantly keep on top of this kind of carelessness if you want to stop it.

3. *Forwarding Orders* It's essential that orders gathered by the field sales force are transmitted as quickly as possible to the home office. A delay of even a day or two can result in customer dissatisfaction. If the sales representative's territory is within an hour's drive of the office, a good procedure is to have that salesperson deliver the day's orders in person, either immediately after completing rounds or early the next morning before starting out again.

Of course, if the sales force operates at substantial distances from the home office, this cannot be done. Indeed, many organizations prefer to keep their salespeople constantly in the field to maximize selling time. With this method, orders must be mailed in each evening. An even better procedure is to assign specific "call-in times" to individual salespeople during the evening hours; they can then telephone their orders to a night clerk or, preferably, a recording machine. The actual order forms are then mailed in the next morning.

4. *Receiving Orders* Regardless of the method employed in getting the orders to the office (in-person, mail, or telephone), there should be a central clerk to receive all orders. It is this person's responsibility to check all orders for accuracy, clarity, and conformance with company policy. Those that contain mistakes or omissions should be put aside for rechecking later. This clerk must be instructed to record every order on a *daily order sheet* (which can be mimeographed or printed). Each day's sheets should have columns for writing in the order number, the time received, the customer's name, and perhaps the salesperson's initials. Additional columns should be used to indicate the routing of the order (including the time sent) to its next stop along the system.

5. *Processing Orders* If additional copies of the order are needed (other than the set forwarded by the sales representative), avoid transcribing the information. A good office copier will speed up your operation; this fact, plus the convenience of the machine for copying other documents, more than offsets the purchase cost. Usually, all copies go first to the internal sales department where prices are checked, then to the credit desk for an okay. After approval, they're sent on to the warehouse for filling.

6. *Filling Orders* On receiving the order, the warehouse supervisor should register it in a log book and then check over its details. At this point, priorities and routing considerations tend to be taken into account. With respect to routing, transportation "runs" to different areas are usually scheduled for different days of the week or month. Orders destined for those areas can accumulate in different boxes or trays.

Orders are distributed as the order pickers become available. These pickers then select the merchandise called for in the order. Various types of handling equipment—dollies, carts of different kinds, conveyors, even moving belts—can facilitate movement of the merchandise from the warehouse proper to the staging area. (Therefore, good warehouse lay-out and proper utilization of space can be of value in increasing the pickers' speed in filling orders.)

Work tables, corrugated cartons, tape, and other materials must be conveniently available when special packing arrangements are called for.

All outgoing orders, of course, should be carefully double-checked before loading.

ENABLING ACTIVITIES

Chapter 9 described such facets of operations as receiving, stockkeeping, shipping, and maintenance (albeit in connection with the manufacturing plant), while chapter 20 offered useful information about how to protect company premises. Here are just a few additional pointers on transportation and warehouse security.

TRANSPORTATION

It's well worth your while to conduct a review of the entire area of transportation with the assistance of a physical distribution specialist. Investigate the pros and cons of using your own trucks versus common carriers or leased equipment. Are transportation costs adequately reflected in your current prices? Are your terms F.O.B. (Free on Board) warehouse or destination? You may consider geographical zoning in setting up your prices or arrange a flat charge per shipment (based either on total weight or a percentage of the total invoice cost).

WAREHOUSE SECURITY

You can always brush up on security arrangements for your premises, especially with regard to doors, locks, key control, and lighting. Review the information in chapter 20 on techniques for maintaining tight security.

Unhappily, employee stealing (*pilferage* is much too weak a term in this case!) is all too common in wholesale operations. Often, this type of theft involves collusion on the part of two or more persons. Sometimes one of them is a supervisor. Tight controls must be instituted in order to contain this type of problem. No merchandise should be moved—from the warehouse proper to the ready stocks area to the shipping department—without attendant paperwork. Moreover, those records should be carefully scrutinized on a daily basis by office personnel. If stealing is suspected, you might consider planting an undercover detective in the warehouse to work alongside the others, perhaps as an order picker.

Instruct all warehouse employees to enter and leave the premises through the same doorway. Station a security guard at that location at all times; this will help curtail the amount of merchandise that "walks out" with the help. Needless to say, security checks should be run on all workers before they are hired; this, too, will help hold down your rate of shrinkage.

Other preventive measures include fencing off the receiving and shipping areas, keeping unauthorized people out of those departments, making certain that truck bays are well illuminated both inside and outside of the building, and spot-checking incoming shipments and outgoing deliveries at different times (both day and night) and on different days of the week.

INVENTORY CONTROL

The order flow system can be adequately fueled and kept in continuous motion only if inventory levels are skillfully controlled. This means you must at all times maintain as complete an inventory as is needed to meet your customers' requirements. As you know, this is no simple feat.

Especially in the wholesale trades, inventory represents a major financial commitment. An overloaded inventory poses a serious threat to your cash position; hence, the continued need to buy merchandise at the most economical prices and under the most favorable terms. Yet, it isn't only the actual purchase costs that tie up your capital but also expenses like insurance, storage, handling, damage or spoilage, and taxes, as well as the very cost of maintaining good inventory records. For these reasons, you should decide right now to weed out and liquidate all slow-selling items so that you will end up about six months from now with a lean yet sturdy stock of fast-moving merchandise.

This kind of product-line review ought to be conducted every year; the end result will surely be appreciably faster turnover and more profit. It's true that a wholesaler is often reluctant to drop certain items from the line that it has supplied for years only out of courtesy, for fear of losing some customers' business altogether. While this attitude is understandable, it doesn't stand up very well in the face of logical business acumen.

Referring to the now-familiar eighty-twenty principle (chapter 10), if you carry as many as 2,000 different items in your warehouse, it's likely that fewer than 400 of them account for as much as 80 percent of your yearly sales. Logically extended, this means that you now maintain an inventory of around 1,600 products just to produce one fifth of your current sales.

Seems wasteful, doesn't it?

Your inventory control system should be organized to provide you with all the information you need to make sensible decisions about your product line.

ABC ANALYSIS

A helpful suggestion might be to use ABC analysis, a procedure you initiate by classifying all your products both by merchandise type (for example: staple items, seasonal products, perishable goods) and by dollar value. You then examine your turnover records for the past year and divide each of these three merchandise categories into three groups, according to sales movement: the *A* group for fast-moving merchandise, the *B* group for moderate sellers, and the *C* group for slow-moving goods. You want to keep close tabs on the first group (*A*) in each classification by maintaining a perpetual inventory of them. There's little practical value in doing the same for the *B* group of products, and none whatsoever for the *C* merchandise. Indeed, these last two are best handled by occasional inventory checks.

SALES ANALYSES AND EXPENSE CONTROL

Regular, frequent sales analyses ought to be part of your modus operandi. These are vital for effective stock planning and control, for generating recommendations for increasing sales volume, and for holding down expenses.

In the area of merchandising, we have already touched on the merits of analyzing inventory movement item by item, both by unit and by total dollar contribution to sales. The sales area is the place where a perceptive and aggressive management can make the most headway.

A number of different tactics can be taken here. Sales and expenses may be investigated from a variety of vantage points: Those of the customer, the salespeople, company finances, and geography are among the most common.

Typically, the customer list may be broken down by type of firm, size (in assets value), annual volume of purchases placed with the wholesaler, location, and other characteristics. The results of such analyses are useful in the decision-making process, in establishing objectives, and in setting plans for business growth. (This also holds true for other types of sales analyses.) You can take steps to measure the relative performances of all salespeople (individually as well as collectively) in the number of accounts opened each month, average size of orders taken, total contribution to gross profit or sales, expenses incurred, dollar value of orders returned, and the like. Or you can analyze the *territorial yield,* that is, obtain the same data indicated above but examine the results from the various sales territories instead of from the individual salespeople.

PUSHING UP SALES

In chapter 12, you were introduced to the complex area of promotion management. In chapters 13 through 15, we explored in considerable depth those vital ingredients of the promotion mix: advertising (along with publicity and public relations), personal selling (and sales management), and sales promotion. Despite this rather extensive treatment of the entire promotion area, there are still additional steps to be taken, which are singularly appropriate for the wholesaling company.

At the very core of these approaches lies the raison d'être of your operation: *to render services to your customers.* Indeed, you ought to adopt this simple concept as your motto. Internalize the thought; make it part and parcel of every action you take; accept it as your prime directive. If you can convince your customers—and new prospects as well—that you can be of more value to them than your competitors, you'll have little difficulty boosting that sales curve of yours!

This is within your grasp if you broaden the list of services you now offer, either by adding to that list or by improving on the quality of those services. You should preferably aim at doing both.

Exhibit 23–1 contains a representative list of services that a merchant wholesaler may offer. Match them against your current offerings, one by one.

BETTER OFFICE MANAGEMENT

As concerned citizens, we chafe against the sluggishness of bureaucracy. We rant about the red tape that ties its operations into knots. We applaud ongoing efforts to extricate government agencies from the mountainous paper blitz that practically immobilizes their activity, wishing ever so strongly that those agencies could be run more like private enterprise.

EXHIBIT 23–1.   REPRESENTATIVE SERVICES OF A MERCHANT WHOLESALER

- Introduce your customers to modern methods of stock control.
- Provide them with instructional materials on all aspects of managing their operations.
- Once or twice each year, run problem-solving clinics where your customers can talk over mutual business problems.
- If you make use of EDP equipment, offer assistance in stockplanning and inventory counts.
- Furnish stands, display racks, signs, and other point-of-purchase materials at nominal cost or (if possible) free of charge.
- Keep your customers abreast of newer methods and techniques that they can apply in their own businesses, through your salespeople and perhaps through a monthly newsletter.
- Offer more favorable payment terms and (without going overboard) higher credit limits than your competitors.
- As a service, offer free newspaper mats (or templates) of professionally prepared advertisements, making sure to leave space for the individual retailer's name and address. (The same treatment, incidentally, can be accorded to brochures, flyers, and catalogs.)
- Give extended terms and small loans to financially troubled businesses; this kind of service can help cement long-term relationships.
- Organize occasional contest promotions; they can create both retailer and consumer excitement and boost sales. "Demonstrators" (people sent to stores to demonstrate one or more products to shoppers) and "PMs" ("Push Money," a promotional technique whereby retail salespeople earn small sums of money for "pushing" a particular product) are also helpful.
- Customers outside your territorial coverage can be serviced by mail through your wholesale catalog and order form. It's sometimes worthwhile to open a "cash-and-carry" branch in a distant city where there is sufficient demand for your products to warrant such an outlet.

As a final thought, don't overlook the public relations value of maintaining close contact with your customers. You can build rapport with them via newsletter, but it's far better to get out of your office as often as you can to visit them in person.

Source: Compiled by the author.

Sometimes it seems that the merchant wholesaler is the private sector's counterpart to a government agency. For there are mounds of paperwork in a wholesale operation. Some of it is necessary; other paperwork can and should be discarded. Not only are there customary accounts to keep track of (like payables, and the larger number of receivables) but the whole, intricate affair of controlling both merchandise and order flow is also in and of itself a tremendous task. In addition, the operation requires bounteous correspondence and collection letters ad infinitum for delinquent accounts.

Other than the obvious techniques of good human resources administration, the answers to better office management lie in the study, systematization, elimination of paperwork, and the introduction of specialized office equipment to save time and labor. (Review the information on computerization in chapter 18.)

PAPERWORK

Errors in paperwork can be costly. Here we are referring not only to typographical errors but also to errors in manual writing, beginning with the initial order written by the salesperson, through the transcription and processing of the order, to all the internal forms used for conducting business. Delays, too, can be costly. So can an office with too many typists, stenographers, and other clerical help for the quantity of work present. You need a capable office manager well versed in organizational methods to set objectives (together, of course, with the employees), to uphold performance standards, and to monitor output. If necessary, an outside consultant might be brought in to help in the process.

The following factors, among others, can affect the output of your office staff:

The Working Environment   poor ventilation, heating, or lighting; uncomfortable chairs, desks; poor sanitary conditions; too much noise or activity

The Management Itself   unclear company goals, little or no supervision, faulty management attitudes and poor personnel relations, incapable management, poor personnel recruitment and selection policies

The Employees Themselves   lack of experience, poor training, ineptitude at mathematics or poor writing skills, personal and emotional problems

The System   improperly worked-out methods, badly designed forms, poorly functioning office equipment, a predominance of "rush jobs," and so on

FOR FURTHER INFORMATION

Allegri, Theodore H., Sr. *Managing Warehouse and Distribution Operations*. Englewood Cliffs, N.J.: Prentice-Hall, 1993.

Ballou, Ronald H. *Business Logistics Management: Planning and Control*. 2d ed. Englewood Cliffs, N.J.: Prentice-Hall, 1985.

Brezen, Tamara, and William Robinson. *Sales Promotion Handbook*. 8th ed. Chicago: Dartnell Corp., 1994.

Burnett, John J. *Promotion Management*. Boston, Mass.: Houghton Mifflin, 1992.

DeVries, Mary A. *The Complete Office Handbook*. Avenal, N.J.: Random House Value, 1993.

Green, Harry. *Office Management Made Simple*. New York: Doubleday, 1992.

Haas, Robert W. *Business Marketing: A Managerial Approach*. 6th ed. Cincinnati: South-Western, 1995.

Haddock, Patricia, and Marilyn Manning. *Office Management: A Guide to Productivity*. Menlo Park, Calif.: Crisp Publications, 1990.

Lambert, Douglas M., and James R. Stock. *Strategic Logistics Management*. 3rd ed. Homewood, Ill.: Irwin, 1992.

Mulcahy, David E. *Wholesale Distribution and Operations Handbook*. New York: McGraw-Hill, 1993.

Rice, Don A. *The Wholesale Distributor: Purpose and Function*. Bryan, Tex.: Darco Press, 1990.

Rosenbloom, Bert. *Wholesale Distribution Channels: New Insights and Perspectives*. Binghamton, N.Y.: Haworth Press, 1994.

Scott, Gini Graham, and John J. Harrison. *Collection Techniques for the Small Business*. Grants Pass, Ore.: Oasis Press, 1994.

Webster, Frederick E., Jr. *Industrial Marketing Strategy*. 4th ed. New York: Wiley, 1994.

24

IMPROVING RESULTS IN YOUR RETAIL STORE

THE AVERAGE SMALL store is shaped much like a shoe box with a top, bottom, and sides. At one end are the entrance and show window; at the other, a partition and back room. Its inner surfaces are lined with ceiling, flooring, and wall coverings. The store also contains fixtures, merchandise, displays, store personnel, and, hopefully, shoppers.

This description is accurate wherever the store is located: on a busy thoroughfare in downtown Los Angeles or midtown Manhattan, on a neighborhood shopping street, in a strip or regional shopping center, or in an off-street location.

In brief, your store and all its sundry parts combine to form a selling system. As with any other system (or machine), if you improve one or more of its parts, chances are excellent that the system's entire output will increase. To help you maintain a clear, conceptual overview of your business, study the chart in figure 24–1.

If you're serious about improving your retail operation—and netting more profit by the end of the year—then a good approach is to tackle each of the seven major areas indicated on the chart, preferably one at a time. There are two "prime directives" that you'll need to bear in mind at all times: (1) increase your sales and (2) lower your costs. Only from these two directions can any real improvement come. A combination of the two produces the best results. As you know, however, the second direction is by far the least important of the two. Certain expenses, such as rent, cannot be reduced; among the "reducible" ones, you'll only be able to go so far and no further. Of course, you should always try to hold down your controllable expenses.

FIGURE 24–1. RETAIL STORE MANAGEMENT

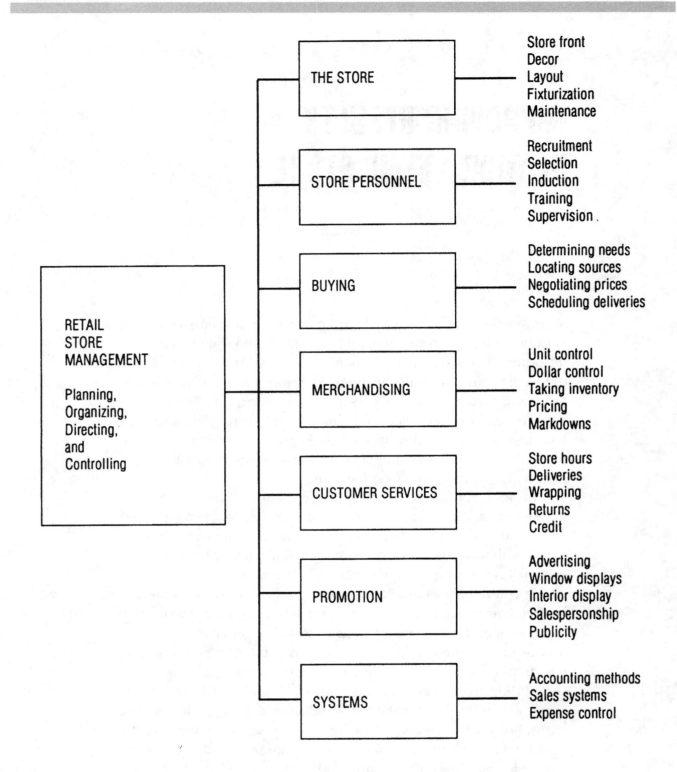

Reducing costs will indeed increase net profit, assuming your sales volume remains intact. Yet, what about next year—and the year after that? If you want your business to grow, then you obviously must increase your sales over time.

When it comes down to reality, there are only two ways to take in more sales dollars. Either you sell to more customers than you now have or you sell more to your present customers. (For the sake of simplicity, let's set aside the strategic use of pricing as a device for increasing sales volume.)

Although all aspects of store operations touch on this business of boosting sales, three areas are more critical than the others in this connection. Selling more is primarily the outcome of improvements made in (1) buying, (2) merchandising, and (3) promotion and personal selling.

These, then, are the major topics for discussion in the balance of this chapter.

BETTER BUYING FOR HIGHER PROFITS

Owners of small retail enterprises have to plan, organize, direct, and evaluate all buying activity properly. They need to decide *what* to buy, *when* to buy, *where* to buy, and *how much* to buy. Some of the attendant activities include

- Ascertaining customer needs
- Forecasting sales
- Selecting merchandise
- Deciding on the breadth and depth of the merchandise variety
- Receiving and marking
- Pricing

Usually it is you, the owner, who must do the buying, for the business has not yet grown to the point that you can afford a specialist. Yet you're a busy person. You're probably tied to your store and find you cannot spare much time away from it in search of new sources of supply. Moreover, if you're not located in New York, Chicago, or Los Angeles, you can't afford many long-distance trips to visit showrooms there. Instead, you must rely for the most part on wholesalers' sales representatives who drop in to see you or, in some cases, on catalogs from wholesale supply houses.

One alternative that exists in many retail lines is the *independent buying office*. There are hundreds of such firms in business to assist retailers, large and small. Most are located in New York City and a few other major metropolitan centers.

For more information about buying offices and services, see exhibit 24–1.

EXHIBIT 24–1. Buying Offices and Merchandise Brokers

THE INDEPENDENT BUYING OFFICE

The independent buying office operates as your market representative. Among other things, this firm will:

- Send their buyers out to scout the marketplace
- Provide a steady stream of advice on new items, new sources, and special promotions
- Place orders for you
- Keep you abreast of changing consumer preferences, fashions, and so forth
- Provide you with desk space and telephone when you do come into town
- Notify suppliers of your impending arrival

The customary charge for their services runs about ½ of 1 percent of your store's annual sales, most often payable in monthly installments. However, if your sales are too low, they may request a minimum fee and payment each month. Usually, they'll require a signed agreement for the term of one year, cancelable by either party.

THE MERCHANDISE BROKER

A second type of buying service that may be available to you is the *merchandise broker*. These firms are far fewer in number than the independent offices. They'll place orders on your behalf and, to that end, keep you informed of the latest market information. There's no charge whatsoever to the retailer. The merchandise broker earns commissions from the manufacturers who receive the orders. (Commissions run generally from 2 to 5 percent.)

Some retailers are attracted to the merchandise broker because the services are free. This might be a shortsighted view for two reasons: (1) the services provided are far fewer than those offered by independent buying offices, and (2) the broker's primary responsibility is to sell goods for the companies that he or she represents.

EXHIBIT 24–1. (continued)

After all, wouldn't it be worth ½ of 1 percent of your sales to have competent, experienced buyers—and a whole supporting staff behind them—working on your behalf?

To locate a buying office suited to your needs, check with your trade association, local Small Business Administration office, or the National Retail Federation in Manhattan. You might also consult the Yellow Pages in the telephone directories of such major metropolitan areas as New York City, Chicago, Dallas, and San Francisco.

Source: Compiled by the author.

THE ART OF NEGOTIATING

While you may not be able to do too much about the prices of merchandise offered to you for resale (simply because yours is a small operation and you buy in limited quantities), there are ways to lower your cost of goods. Other than the price itself, you can frequently do better in areas such as discounts, special allowances, terms, job lots, and so forth.

Buy directly from the manufacturer, if this is at all possible. This will save you money. More likely than not, however, most of your purchases will come from wholesalers. Bear in mind that the wholesaler has a vital stake in keeping your business alive, hale, and hearty, in order to retain you as a good customer. Some distributors offer valuable services and terms that others do not. Among the many possibilities are advanced dating of invoices, special allowances, providing information about market conditions, special point-of-purchase materials, preticketing of merchandise, and free delivery.

Rating Your Suppliers One worthwhile approach in your buying endeavors is to work up a simplified supplier rating plan. You can use this to compare sources of similar merchandise not only on the quality of goods offered but also on the variety carried, dependability of service, prices, production capacity, and special services offered. Use simple ratings, such as:

1 = Poor
2 = Fair
3 = Good
4 = Very good
5 = Excellent

Of course, you may wish to "weight" some of the criteria you employ more heavily than others.

During Negotiations Before you even begin the bargaining process, you should have a clear idea as to the overall average markup you need to cover all store expenses and to provide at least a modest profit by the year's end. If you have done your planning and kept good inventory turnover records, you'll know whether or not you have been maintaining the necessary markup. If you need to "pull it up" somewhat, then you should look for a higher-than-usual gross margin on your new purchases.

In considering merchandise offered to you, you must first decide whether or not it's merchandise that you can comfortably integrate with your present stock, that your customers would want to buy, and that is within the price range your customers are willing to pay. Only if you can answer these questions affirmatively should you begin weighing the markup needed against the price asked by the supplier. If there's a considerable discrepancy between the price asked and the price you can pay, the need for bargaining becomes apparent. In the bargaining process itself, be open and honest with the sales representative. Say the price is too high and that you can't sell the particular item to your customers because you won't be earning enough gross margin dollars.

The salesperson may attempt to convince you that your judgment is faulty and assure you that you'll be able to sell the merchandise readily at prices higher than you believe you can get. Be careful. Don't be swayed by clever, persuasive sales talk. You might even suggest that the rep's company let you try out the merchandise on a small scale—placing it in your store on consignment. Sometimes this works.

After you've settled on the price, you then have an opportunity to garner available extras. These will help you not only to reduce your overall costs but also to increase your store's sales. Explore with the salesperson the terms you'll obtain. Will the goods be shipped directly to your store at supplier's cost or will you have to pay for transportation, F.O.B. warehouse? How much time will you have before you must pay the bill—thirty days from invoice date, forty-five days, sixty days? If you pay your bill early, how many points can you count on earning as a cash discount? What about repeat orders—will the same prices and terms still be valid? What about quantity discounts, either noncumulative or cumulative? That is, if you buy a certain quantity within a six-month period, can you get a discount in the form of a rebate?

Also find out whether the supplier offers any advertising aids, such as mats for reproducing newspaper ads, copy for radio commercials, signs or posters you can display in your store, special contests or promotions you can tie into, and cooperative advertising moneys.

JOB LOTS AND CLOSEOUTS

From time to time, you'll receive offers of *closeout* or *job lot* merchandise. Generally, this represents stock that the vendors have been unable to sell or that has been left over toward the end of a season. The articles are offered at attractively reduced prices; consequently, the temptation is great to seize this opportunity to increase your store's average gross margin.

Exercise caution. Often, this kind of merchandise doesn't reflect the proper balance you need in selection appeal. There may be too many of the less common sizes and not enough of the popular ones. The mixture of colors may not be in proportion to your customers' needs. The styles may be currently in vogue or in a downtrend. This doesn't mean that you should ignore these offers. In considering the purchase of such goods, try to separate them into three groups: (1) merchandise you'll have no trouble selling in your regular price lines, (2) articles you might be able to sell at higher prices, and (3) items you know will have to be sold off at marked-down prices. If you then tally up the total amount of sales you believe you can easily derive from the entire lot, you'll be in a good position to know whether or not you should "make the buy."

The best time for you to buy such merchandise is probably right after the peak of each season. However, you need to be careful in your judgment of anticipated sales; obviously, you won't want to carry any goods over for a full year.

Occasionally you'll come across merchandise that is not entirely perfect; these goods are referred to as *irregulars* or *seconds*. (Never bother with "thirds"!) Some retailers prefer to avoid such products at all costs, believing that to carry seconds would cheapen their store image. Other merchants do put them on display and find they enjoy brisk sales on these items. The latter approach certainly wouldn't damage store image at all if (1) such merchandise is clearly identified as seconds or irregulars; (2) the total supply of these items represents only a small percentage of the store's inventory; and (3) these goods are offered only occasionally during the year.

MERCHANDISE MANAGEMENT

Initial success and steady growth in your retail enterprise are contingent on having the right merchandise at the right time in the right quantities at the right prices. The control of the ebb and flow of the goods you offer for sale isn't a simple matter. Indeed, improper merchandise management practices are commonplace in small-scale retailing.

Many small independent retailers keep track of store inventory by means of the "eyeball control" method. For the most part, they depend on a practiced eye to ascertain whether or not they have enough on hand of any particular item, if more should be ordered, or if they are overstocked. Over time, this elementary form of stock supervision usually leads to an inventory much heavier than what's needed and the carryover of outmoded, shopworn, or otherwise unsalable merchandise.

Furthermore, unless you maintain a sensible inventory control system and good stock-movement records, you'll have little factual knowledge of the sales enjoyed by each classification of goods relative to your overall sales volume.

Data processing, whether through a service bureau or your own home or desktop microcomputer, can be of considerable value in controlling your inventory.

THE IMPORTANCE OF TAKING INVENTORY REGULARLY

One essential ingredient of good stock control is the taking of physical inventory, preferably on a regular monthly basis. To accomplish this properly, you need to prepare an inventory sheet on which you list all items carried in your store, grouped according to merchandise classifications. For example, a menswear shop might find it convenient to use such categories as shirts, sweaters, slacks, underwear, and neckties. A grocery might use classifications such as cereals, dairy products, canned fruits and vegetables, cookies, and salad dressings.

Descriptions (including names, brands, sizes, and other variants) and prices of the individual items should be spelled out in detail underneath each of the major headings. Ample space must be provided for writing in the various amounts of each product found in the bins, on the shelves, and in the back room. A column for totals should be provided, and another for indicating how many (if any) should be ordered.

By reviewing your monthly inventory sheets and your delivery records, after a while you'll be able to determine approximately how much you sold of every item in stock and its average rate of movement per week, month, or season.

YOUR BASIC STOCK LIST

In managing your inventory, it's helpful to think in terms of a *basic stock list*—a list of goods to be carried at all times. Break it down into kinds, types, and quantities. In most retail lines, the majority of items handled by the typical store unit are considered *staple goods*. These are products that consumers ask for repeatedly; demand for such products is typically of a continual nature. Examples in the grocery field include sugar, salt, flour, eggs, butter, bacon, ham, baby foods, and canned vegetables.

Even within these common categories there are some products not properly classified as staple goods but rather as *selection types* or *nonstaple* merchandise. In the grocery business, for instance, items such as a new kind of breakfast cereal, an imported French cheese, a new brand of pancake syrup, and the like are nonstaples. In the apparel and related fields, selection-type items are referred to as *fashion goods*. The demand for such merchandise is not continual; indeed, it is often characterized by wide fluctuations due to any number of reasons.

AUTOMATIC REORDERING

You can easily control items for which there is regular, repeat business by setting up a basic stock list and establishing a simple *automatic replenishment system* (see exhibit 24–2). A retailer who takes inventory monthly can accumulate enough information within a few months to figure out the average weekly rate of sale for all such items. Regular reorders are tied to the inventory (except, perhaps, for fast-moving merchandise, for which a telephone order may have to be placed with the supplier).

EXHIBIT 24–2.   AUTOMATIC SYSTEM FOR STOCK REPLENISHMENT

To maintain an in-stock position, you can use the following formula:

$$O = (a + b)R - I$$

Where:

O = the quantity of the item to be ordered
a = the amount of time between inventory counts (expressed in weeks)

EXHIBIT 24–2. (continued)

b = the amount of time that will elapse between order placement and the actual delivery of the merchandise into the selling stock (also expressed in weeks)

R = the item's average weekly rate of sale

I = how many are in stock (and are expected in) at inventory time

To illustrate, let's assume you take inventory on a monthly basis (every four weeks or so), and you've determined the following facts:

You have eighteen pieces of Item X on hand.
Another dozen are due to arrive within a day or two.
Delivery from the particular supplier usually takes two weeks.
You sell about thirty-six pieces each week.

Now, we apply the formula:

$$
\begin{aligned}
\text{(Step 1)} \quad 0 &= (a + b)R - I \\
\text{(Step 2)} \quad &= (4 + 2)36 - 30 \\
\text{(Step 3)} \quad &= (6 \times 36) - 30 \\
\text{(Step 4)} \quad &= 216 - 30 \\
\text{(Step 5)} \quad &= 186
\end{aligned}
$$

Obviously, you'll need to order 186 pieces of Item X to make sure you'll have enough. Just as obviously, you won't need to have all 186 pieces on hand at one time, since these will be sold over a period of four weeks. If you lay in one month's stock for every item you carry, this could unnecessarily tie up a sizable chunk of your operating capital. It's more prudent to phase in your deliveries, preferably over a number of weeks, if this can be done.

Perhaps a simpler approach (once you have the hang of things) might be to determine both a minimum and a maximum stock figure for every staple item in your line and order only when the inventoried amounts approach minimum levels.

Adding "Safety Stock" After some months of experience with the automatic replenishment system, you can take care of chance fluctuations in demand by building a reserve factor into the formula.

As an example, consider this dilemma faced by the proprietor of a menswear store:

Ordinarily, the proprietor maintains in stock at all times six pieces of each commonly asked for size of a particular brand and style shirt, in each of four basic colors: white, blue, tan, and gray. He has found that these quantities are usually sufficient to take care of consumer demand for at least one month. One afternoon, a shopper drops by, likes the particular shirt, and decides to purchase six, all of the same dimensions (16″ neck, 33″ sleeves). He selects three blue and three white, thereby depleting the store's month's supply of the two colors by 50 percent.

Chances are good that, unless the merchant can arrange for speedy replacement delivery of the inventory, the store will be out of stock on the two varieties long before the end of the month.

To reduce drastically the number of "stockouts" in your store, you'll need to make a slight adjustment in the basic formula, as indicated below:

$$O = (a + b)R - I + r$$

The small r that has been added represents the amount of *reserve,* or *safety stock,* needed. The additional merchandise should take care of about 99 percent of all extraordinary fluctuations in demand due to chance factors.

To calculate r, use the following formula:

$$r = 2.3 \sqrt{(a + b) R}$$

In the earlier example involving Item X, r is worked out in this manner:

(Step 1)	$r = 2.3 \sqrt{(a + b)R}$
(Step 2)	$= 2.3 \sqrt{(4 + 2)36}$
(Step 3)	$= 2.3 \sqrt{216}$
(Step 4)	$= (2.3)(14.7)$
(Step 5)	$= 33.8$

To build in the reserve factor, the proprietor should add 34 pieces to the order, which would then total 220 pieces of Item X.

Source: Compiled by the author.

CONTROLLING NONSTAPLES

The regular, automatic fill-in approach used for staple goods is not applicable to the control of nonstaple or fashion merchandise. Here it's better to think in terms of setting up seasonal *model stocks.* They may be set up on a twice-yearly basis (spring-summer; fall-winter) or, ideally, on a quarterly basis. You plan your stock in advance, using merchandise classifications and breaking down each class according to selection factors (brand, style, color, size, material, and so on).

For the sake of illustration, assume that one component of your model stock is the *sweaters* classification. Before preparing your projections for the coming fall-winter season, you should (*a*) study the records of last year's performance in this category and (*b*) take into account any trends you may have perceived (in your store, in the trade literature, and from knowledgeable suppliers). Of course, you initially need to make an estimate of the total dollar volume you expect to reach in this classification during the season, then break this down into two more manageable three-month periods.

Dollars are then easily translated into units by dividing the total dollars for each basic sweater style by the price points you've set. Total dollars for those styles are derived by approximating how much of the total sweater business is enjoyed by each style (percentage-wise).

Now, let's assume you've worked through your dollar projections for the three-month period September through November, and you estimate that you'll need about 300 sweaters of all types for that period. You stock four basic styles: V-necks, cardigans, turtlenecks, and pullovers. (For simplicity's sake, we're not at this point concerned with either brands or materials.) Your planning indicates that the four different styles will enjoy the percentages of total sweater sales shown in table 24–1 along with those percentages translated into units. Of course, you haven't finished with your homework as yet. The *number needed* for each of the four types of sweaters must be analyzed further: by sizes (small, medium, large, extra-large) and colors. When it's finally worked out, your resulting plan for the *sweaters* classification might look something like the chart in exhibit 24–3.

TABLE 24–1. DETERMINING UNITS NEEDED WITHIN A CLASSIFICATION

Type of Sweater	Percent of Total	Number Needed
V-necks	30%	90
Cardigans	25%	75
Turtlenecks	10%	30
Pullovers	35%	105
Totals	**100%**	**300**

Source: Compiled by the author.

EXHIBIT 24–3. SAMPLE STOCK-PLANNING CHART

Period __Sept.–Nov., 1996__ CLASSIFICATION __Sweaters__ Total Needed __300__

Types Carried	SIZES			COLORS			
	Size	%	No.	Blue 25%	Gray 25%	Tan 20%	White 30%
1. _V-Necks_ % _30%_ No. _90_	S	10%	9	2	2	2	3
	M	30%	27	7	7	5	8
	L	40%	36	9	9	7	11
	XL	20%	18	4	5	4	5
TOTALS:		100%	90	22	25	18	27
2. _Cardigans_ % _25%_ No. _75_	S	10%	7	2	2	1	2
	M	30%	23	5	6	5	7
	L	40%	30	8	7	6	9
	XL	20%	15	3	4	3	5
TOTALS:		100%	75	18	19	15	23
3. _Turtlenecks_ % _10%_ No. _30_	S	10%	3	1	1	0	1
	M	30%	9	2	2	2	3
	L	40%	12	3	3	3	3
	XL	20%	6	2	1	1	2
TOTALS:		100%	30	8	7	6	9
4. _Pullovers_ % _35%_ No. _105_	S	10%	10	2	3	2	3
	M	30%	32	8	8	6	10
	L	40%	42	11	10	8	13
	XL	20%	21	5	5	5	6
TOTALS:		100%	105	26	26	21	32

Adapted with permission of Prentice Hall, Inc., from _Mathematics of Merchandising_, 3d ed., by A. P. Kneider. Copyright 1986 by Prentice Hall, Inc.

HOW TO IMPROVE RETAIL SELLING

YOU *CAN* COMPETE WITH THE LARGER STORES!

Having a capable, well-trained sales staff is one decided advantage the small store can enjoy over today's chain, discount, and even department stores. Over the past few decades, a high proportion of the larger retail companies have curtailed personal selling activity in favor of self-service and self-selection approaches. This long-term trend reflects the retailers' efforts to control operating expenses where the single biggest cost factor, other than the cost of goods itself, has been (and still is) the payroll expense.

As a rule, the larger stores rely more often on stacked shelves, massed displays, and an overall "impersonal" approach to sales. Thus, the singular potential of the small retail firm lies in the caliber of its personal selling efforts.

TYPES OF SHOPPERS

An interesting tidbit from a classic study may prove illuminating in this context.* In his investigation, the researcher queried women shoppers on their attitudes toward store shopping. An analysis of their responses enabled him to group the women into four major categories: economic shoppers (33 percent of the total), personalizing shoppers (28 percent), ethical shoppers (18 percent), and apathetic shoppers (17 percent). (There were about 4 percent who couldn't be assigned to any of the four listed categories.)

The key features of the four groups follow:

Economic shoppers are more interested in prices, values, merchandise quality, and other "economic" considerations than in other store aspects (including sales personnel).

Personalizing shoppers seem to enjoy personal relationships with salespeople. They prefer to shop where they are recognized and feel welcome.

Ethical shoppers avoid large stores and the chains because they feel that such firms are cold and impersonal. They prefer doing business with independent retailers since they believe that these merchants also need to earn a living.

* Gregory P. Stone, "City Shoppers and Urban Identification: Observations on the Social Psychology of City Life," *American Journal of Sociology* 60 (July, 1954), 36–45.

Apathetic shoppers dislike shopping and only shop because they must. For them, the most important store attribute is convenience of location.

Here's food for thought. Set aside for the moment the one-third of "economic shoppers" who may be attracted elsewhere by better prices/quality/values than you offer. (We'll return to these consumers later on.)

Wouldn't you agree that those 18 percent known as "ethical shoppers" would almost automatically favor your store, given the right degree of "warmth" emanating from your salespeople? Moreover, with good treatment, prompt and courteous attention, and excellent interpersonal relations, there should be no doubt that the 28 percent in the "personalizing" category would respond quite well, too!

So, you can already count on nearly one-half of all the shoppers in your area as potential customers. You should have little difficulty "stealing" them away from your competition.

You can even expect to acquire some of the "apathetic shoppers" in your neighborhood. After all, your location must be more convenient to some percentage of them than the location of your next nearest competitor!

As a final point, let's return to that one-third that we discounted at the very beginning of this discussion—the "economic shoppers." It's completely up to you to garner some of those people by monitoring your prices, quality of goods, and assortment mix. No reason why you can't do some competitive merchandising!

Are you convinced by now that you ought to take a good hard look at your current sales staff and your selling approaches?

RETAIL SELLING

No matter how fortunate you've been in selecting and training your salespeople, and no matter how good a job you've done in this area, your people probably haven't yet reached their peak efficiency. (No one ever does!) Consequently, there's still room for improvement.

The basic way to improve your staff's selling performance is through a planned, continual program. The keys to mastery here are:

- Training
- Training
- Training
- More training

An integral portion of your success in training employees resides in your attitude toward them. Salespeople are not simply "bodies" or "hands and feet" to help you make sales. So many retailers wrongly think of their selling personnel only in terms of "store coverage"— that is, how many salespeople ought to be on the floor at which hours of the day or night to take proper care of the shopper traffic. These are people, not robots, who process orders for you. They can make or break your business.

Among the more desirable personal attributes your salespeople should possess are:

- A good appearance (including good posture and cleanliness)
- A pleasant personality
- Courtesy and tact
- An enjoyment of selling
- An understanding of psychology (practical, not theoretical)

Typically, small-business owners are quick to teach their salespeople about all of the following topics:

- The merchandise carried in the store
- Where to find the merchandise
- The prices of the goods
- How to ring the register and make change
- Store policies
- Bagging and wrapping merchandise
- How to keep things neat

Rarely does the typical independent retailer spend much time teaching employees *how* to sell (other than, of course, advising the new salesperson to greet the incoming shopper with a prompt "May I help you?" and to thank the customer after ringing up the sale).

THE RETAIL-SELLING PROCESS ANALYZED

Selling in the retail store follows much the same lines as the personal-selling process described in chapter 14, except that the retail salesperson doesn't need to do any prospecting. Show windows, interior displays, advertising, and sales promotion take care of this. Happily, prospects are drawn to and into the store.

It might be advantageous to take apart this personal selling process, step by step, with an eye to study and improvement. If you, the owner, spend some time mulling over each step, you'll doubtless come up with at least two or three usable ideas in each case. Only a few comments are made below; they are designed to set you thinking:

The Approach   Salespeople often confuse this first step with the salutation or greeting; for example, "Good morning, sir!" or "Can I help you?" All the greeting does is initiate a conversation; this has little or nothing to do with selling. Actually, the approach ought to be the beginning of the sales presentation, for what goes on in that first minute or so of contact should facilitate the presentation.

Give customers time to "get into" the store. Neither lurch at nor pounce on them. If they know what they want, they'll most likely walk directly to you (or a salesperson). If they're not sure what they want, they might enter hesitatingly, look around at the displays, or glance perplexedly toward the salesperson. The salesperson who is approached directly should smile, greet the shopper cordially (preferably by name), and ask, "How may I help you?" This, of course, implies that you have trained your employees to recall customers' names; this technique could be especially valuable if yours is a specialty goods store. (A "guest register" in which your customers can record their names and addresses would be helpful here. It can also come in handy when you run occasional special promotions for "favored customers.")

When shoppers seem to be "just looking" or appear otherwise not ready for service, the salesclerk should at least comment on the fact that he or she is available if the customer needs assistance (after greeting the customer, naturally).

When a shopper is evidently interested in an item on display, your employee should approach the person and point out some interesting feature of the product or, better still, some benefit that the item can bring to the customer.

When there are several shoppers (and not enough sales help), the experienced salesperson will assure those who are waiting that they will be served shortly.

The Presentation   Having learned of the shopper's needs during the approach, perhaps with several well-chosen questions, the salesperson then makes a smooth transition into the presentation itself. Here, the object is to arouse the interest of the prospect, build desire on the consumer's part to purchase the item, and then "close" the sale. In reality, people buy benefits, not products per se. Therefore, concentrate on what the merchandise can or will do for the consumer. Try to involve the prospect in touching the material, holding the item, putting it on if it's a garment, and so on.

To make an effective presentation, the salesperson must

- Know the selling points of the merchandise
- Be familiar with its qualities and characteristics
- Know how to care for it and, if it's a mechanical item, how it is operated

339

The effective salesperson is also familiar with your competitors' merchandise and with how your products compare.

Meeting Objections   As in any type of personal selling, shoppers may raise all sorts of issues during the presentation. Objections are to be expected. These obstacles to making the sale challenge the imagination of the good salesperson. Some comments may be no more than excuses that people present so that they don't seem like easy targets for sales pitches. Others are real objections: to price; to style, quality, or other features; to the store's service policies; and so forth. Sometimes, objections are not spoken aloud. In such cases, it's up to the salesperson to determine why the shopper is reluctant, perhaps by asking a few probing (though tactful) questions, perhaps by observation alone.

A variety of techniques can be used effectively in meeting shopper objections. Sometimes, these can be "turned around" so that what has been proposed as a negative by the consumer can be made into a positive selling point. Another method, called the "Yes, but . . ." technique, enables the salesperson to appear to agree gracefully with what the consumer has been saying while, at the same time, giving him or her the opportunity to point out one or more additional, positive facts that may help to clear up the problem.

There are other methods, too. The bibliography at the end of this chapter, as well as that in chapter 14, can assist you in your selling efforts.

The Close   The *close* or *closing* represents the culmination of the sales effort. At this point, the salesperson takes down the customer's order (if you use the sales-slip method), rings up the register (if you don't), and delivers the merchandise to the customer (or arranges for its delivery). However, knowing *when* and *how* to close a sale is perhaps a more difficult feat for the sales employee. Again, a good book on retail selling methods should help tremendously.

Suggestive Selling   While suggestive selling may be used during the sales presentation itself, it is most commonly used after the close. All too often, the salesperson will ask, "Will there be anything else?" before proceeding with the bagging or wrapping of the merchandise selected. How superfluous can a question be? The phrase *anything else* marks the lazy, inefficient salesperson. Unless the customer intends to buy something additional—in which case it would already have been mentioned—a negative response is certain.

On the other hand, statements such as the following may elicit a completely different sort of response:

At a confectionery shop: "Did you know that our salted cashews are on sale for this week only, at one dollar less than the regular price?"

At a gift shop: "We're now taking orders for delivery on Mother's Day. May I show you a display of unusual gifts for your mother?"

At a men's store: "I believe we have just the right necktie for the shirt you've selected. May I show it to you?"

At a hardware store: "That's a fine pair of pliers you've picked out. Would you be interested in a good hammer?"

At a bakery: "Here's a sample of our chocolate-chip cookies. I'd like you to taste one to see how delicious it is."

Concrete suggestions do pay off. When you suggest an additional item, you plant an idea in the customer's mind, thus confronting the shopper with the necessity of making a decision. While the response may still be "No, thank you" in many cases, there's a good chance of an occasional affirmative answer. Remember that old adage, "Nothing ventured, nothing gained."

Closing suggestions are aided by a display of the suggested item near the register so that the salesperson can point to the merchandise while talking about it. These kinds of suggestions are particularly effective with inexpensive items of the "pick-up" variety or with products that are timely, on sale, or related to the merchandise the customer has already selected.

Many experienced salespeople claim they can sell additional merchandise to at least three out of every ten customers.

USING PROMOTIONAL CREATIVITY

You'll recall that there are essentially three facets to the promotion mix: personal selling, advertising, and sales promotion. We have just discussed the first area in this chapter; the remaining two facets were treated in some depth in chapters 13 and 15. It's true that the typical small retail firm does little media advertising throughout the year. When it does advertise, it generally does so in the busy season or around holiday times. In view of this fact, little more need be said on this subject other than:

- Refer to the material presented in chapter 13.
- Strive for more creativity in your ads.
- Try to make your advertising dollars go further.

In this connection, some additional "hints" are given in exhibit 24–4.

EXHIBIT 24–4. SOME HELPFUL SUGGESTIONS ABOUT YOUR ADVERTISING

1. Doubling the size of your ad will not double the number of people who read it.
2. Do not overwrite. Layout and copy should be simple, clear, and understandable.
3. Use active, not passive, words and phrases.
4. Feature the right merchandise in your advertising.
5. Stress the benefits—the major selling points. Build in the right appeals.
6. A photo or illustration is much more compelling than copy alone.
7. Your store name, address, and telephone number should be readily discernible.
8. A series of advertisements will have a more powerful effect on your targeted public than an occasional, one-shot ad. (Continuity!)
9. Exercise care in your media selection.
10. An advertiser can often obtain free publicity from a local or area newspaper, radio station, or television station.

Source: Compiled by the author.

FOR FURTHER INFORMATION

Berman, Barry, and Joel R. Evans. *Retail Management: A Strategic Approach.* 4th ed. New York: Macmillan, 1989.

Burstiner, Irving. *Basic Retailing.* 2d ed. Homewood, Ill.: Irwin, 1991.

———. *How to Start and Run Your Own Retail Business.* New York: Carol Publishing, 1992.

Dunne, Patrick, Robert Lusch, and Myron Gable. *Retailing.* 2d ed. Cincinnati: South-Western, 1995.

Levy, Michael, and Barton A. Weitz. *Retailing Management.* Homewood, Ill.: Irwin, 1992.

Lewison, Dale M., and M. Wayne DeLozier. *Retailing.* 3rd ed. Columbus, Ohio: Merrill Publishing, 1989.

Lusch, Robert F., Patrick Dunne, and Randall Gebhardt. *Retail Marketing.* 2d ed. Cincinnati: South-Western, 1994.

Mason, J. Barry, Morris L. Mayer, and Hazel F. Ezell. *Retailing.* 5th ed. Burr Ridge, Ill.: Irwin, 1994.

Minichiello, Robert. *Retail Merchandising and Control.* Homewood, Ill.: Irwin, 1990.

Shuch, Milton L. *Retail Buying and Merchandising.* Englewood Cliffs, N.J.: Prentice-Hall, 1988.

25

IMPROVING RESULTS IN YOUR SERVICE BUSINESS

THE SERVICE SECTOR of our economy includes so many varied business types that it's difficult to generalize about improving the service operation—other than by suggesting ways to reduce expenses, increase sales and profits, or specify approaches other than the customary ones. Service firms range the entire spectrum: from tiny, one-person enterprises to large corporations such as advertising agencies, universities, and other multiemployee institutions.

Nevertheless, in addition to good overall management and plain common sense, there are other guidelines for improving results in your service business that merit your attention. Some of the more important ones are listed in exhibit 25–1. Frankly, they're just as applicable to the small service undertaking (tutoring, typing service, crafts or music school, dry-cleaning service, and so on) as to the large corporations mentioned above. They are, in fact, useful keys to successful business growth, aids that will help you build a loyal clientele.

EXHIBIT 25–1. TEN KEYS TO REPEAT SALES IN A SERVICE BUSINESS

1. *Make a fetish of honesty.* Customer confidence and loyalty are logical outcomes of fair, ethical treatment. Do not try to fool other people. Never embroider the truth. Never oversell yourself, your capabilities, or your service.
2. *Practice good human relations.* Treat others as you would want to be treated yourself. Be responsive to community problems; join in local activities. Never, never lose control of your emotions.
3. *Become the epitome of dependability.* Never make promises you cannot

EXHIBIT 25–1. (continued)

fulfill. Have things ready for the dates promised. Keep your word; become known by others as someone on whom they can rely.

4. *Take pride in your work.* Demonstrate a professional, proprietary attitude in whatever you do. Proficiency and technical skill should characterize your service operation.

5. *Do not stint on materials.* Always use the best-quality parts, materials, and equipment. Do not be penny-wise and pound-foolish; be willing to spend more on better materials than your competition does.

6. *Give freely of your time.* The service business is unique in that customers often ask endless questions (as in the tool or equipment rental service) and present a variety of complaints. Be patient. Spend time explaining and giving advice. This kind of personal attention and helpful service can only enhance your firm's reputation.

7. *Know your trade.* More than in any other type of business, the service enterprise demands mastery of the area of specialization. Learn all you can about your craft through reading, attending seminars and conventions, and from your trade association.

8. *Train your personnel well.* Customers will come to judge your business by the way they are treated at the hands of your employees. Courtesy and tact are always expected; no doubt, you have already inculcated these two traits in your employees. However, it is equally important to the service business to make certain your employees are knowledgeable, continually informed, and technically proficient. Training should be a continuous process.

9. *Offer better guarantees than your competitors.* Find out the details of your competition's guarantees/warranties. Then, set your own standards, going well beyond theirs. Where others offer a six-months' guarantee, for instance, offer yours for a full year.

10. *Improve all internal systems.* Work-in-process, materials and supplies, and schedules must all flow smoothly in your operation. Accompanying paperwork and records should be detailed and exact to assist this flow. Cut down on excess reports; simplify the forms you use; substitute office equipment for manual clerical operations.

Source: Compiled by the author.

THE MARKETING OF SERVICES

The marketing of services must, of necessity, differ substantially from product marketing. Whether the services are destined for organizational use (*industrial* services) or for use by the final consumer (*con-*

sumer services), most reflect three characteristics that clearly distinguish them from products:

- *They are intangible.* Potential buyers cannot touch or handle them. This makes it difficult for people to compare and evaluate similar offerings as they can so easily do with products (and brands) that are on the market.

  Unlike products, too, services cannot be "produced" (performed) at one place and then delivered to another. This means, of course, that to sell the service to many customers, the producing firm needs to offer it at a number of different locations. To "mass market" the service successfully, then, substantial promotional effort is indicated.
- *They are perishable.* They cannot be stored or warehoused. As a simple example, a failure to sell all available admission tickets to a stadium for a particular football game results in the stadium's loss of some income for the day.
- *They cannot be separated from those who perform them or who personally contact the customer.* Because of this fact alone, standardization of services becomes nearly impossible. Then, too, it makes it difficult for potential buyers to "shop around," since the quality of a service so greatly depends on the people involved. Thus, the need for capable and well-trained "contact personnel" is quite evident.

It would appear, then, that marketing services may be more difficult than marketing products. However, one useful tactic the service company might take in pursuit of the mass marketing ideal would be to try to expand distribution and increase its sales revenues "by routinizing operations and systems and through mechanization."*

The importance of other aspects of the operation, such as the service personnel and the physical plant itself, also cannot be underestimated. As one business writer pointed out:

> Services marketing planning and execution should focus attention on seven Ps: the traditional 4 Ps plus three additional marketing mix elements that are crucial to service success—personnel, physical assets, and process management.**

---

* Irving Burstiner, *Basic Retailing,* 2d ed. (Homewood, Ill.: Irwin, 1991), 28.

** A. J. Magrath, "When Marketing Services, 4 Ps Are Not Enough," *Business Horizons* 29 (May–June 1986), 50.

THOUGHTS ABOUT SERVICE QUALITY

As we have already noted, most service offerings resist attempts at standardization. One of the more crucial aspects of service marketing, then, is that of the *quality* of the service. To a substantial degree, of course, this is dependent on the caliber of those who deliver the service. A management intent on improving business results will work toward upgrading, over time, its people, systems, procedures, and all other facets of the enterprise.

The following quotation from an article in *Business Horizons* underscores the importance of this aspect:

> The service quality challenge is to meet—or better yet, exceed—customer expectations. For most firms, this is a complex undertaking. Most service businesses are labor intensive and the service is subject to variability. Customers are frequently present when the service is performed, in effect witnessing its production. Even if customer contact personnel have the talent, training, and motivation to deliver high-quality service, they may nonetheless be dependent on "good service" from the operations part of the firm to be fully effective. . . .*

The same article summarized the findings of an exploratory study of some retail services (banking, securities brokerage, product repair, and so on). The researchers interviewed business executives and made use of consumer focus groups as well. They stressed the following "ten determinants of service quality":

1. Reliability ("consistency of performance," "dependability")
2. Responsiveness ("willingness," "readiness")
3. Competence ("knowledge," "skill")
4. Access ("approachability," "ease of contact")
5. Courtesy
6. Communication ("keeping customers informed," "listening to customers")
7. Credibility ("believability," "honesty")
8. Security ("physical safety," "financial security")
9. Understanding the customer
10. Tangibles ("physical evidence of the service")**

---

* Leonard L. Berry, Valarie A. Zeithaml, and A. Parasuraman, "Quality Counts in Services, Too," Reprinted from *Business Horizons* 28 no. 3 (May–June 1985). Copyright 1985 by the Foundation for the School of Business at Indiana University. Used with permission.

** Adapted from Ibid., 45–46.

MAKE THE MOST OF YOUR FACILITIES

Your premises may be just right for your current needs. On the other hand, they might be inadequate, or even more than adequate. If you're like most owners of service enterprises, you feel that your premises are too "tight" and that if you had larger quarters you would be able to enjoy more business. Yet you may feel a sense of helplessness about all of this because you are tied into your present location with a lease that still has a few years to go.

What to do?

The answer may lie in making a thorough appraisal of your present layout. Hire a consulting firm with experience in your line of business. Often by rearranging your stock and work areas and by updating your equipment, you can gain extra space. Reserve inventory, for example, can be relegated to a basement, office, the second floor of a taxpayer (a small building, usually two stories, with a retail store on the street level), or other nearby site.

The ideal layout depends on the kind of business you're in. Some types require a great deal of space for *customer contact* (beauty salons and dance studios come readily to mind). In other kinds of businesses, *working space* is at a premium—for example, pet-care establishments, auto repair shops, upholsterers, and laundries.

In all these firms, some space is needed for meeting and serving the customer. Whatever your business, the surroundings for "customer contact space" should be attractive. They don't have to be in high-fashion design; neither should the furnishings or decor be cheap or shabby. It's not always necessary or desirable to convey too expensive-looking an image. New, attractive wall covering or even a good paint job can work wonders for your place of business. The interior can easily be enhanced by better lighting or a new floor or ceiling. These relatively minor changes can have a positive effect on upgrading the public's image of your firm.

You should also check both entrances and exits to make certain they're clear and inviting, so that traffic won't be impeded in any way. Make sure doors are easy to open and close and that company identification (signs, lettering) is completely legible.

Incidentally, the terms of your present lease should not preclude you from planning seriously for an eventual move to larger quarters. Such preparation should be started well beforehand so that you can, together with experienced advisers, project not only your long-term space requirements but also the optimum layout and even the exact equipment you'll need.

REFINE OPERATIONS

Just as with any other type of business, a service enterprise can benefit by your probing into various fundamental aspects of its operation. With some thought and application, you can refine your approaches and techniques to all of the following areas:

- The purchasing of materials, supplies, and equipment
- Inventory methods and inventory control
- Advertising, sales promotion, publicity, and public relations
- Personal selling methods
- Budgets and other financial controls
- Personnel administration
- The internal work flow and other systems

All of these have been amply discussed in earlier chapters; you can locate detailed information on these areas by checking the index at the back of this book. However, the general promotion area that embraces advertising, personal selling, sales promotion, publicity, and public relations merits more extended treatment here, in the following section.

INCREASING YOUR SALES VOLUME THROUGH PROMOTION

Word-of-mouth advertising is the cheapest of all forms of promotion. It costs nothing, yet it is the most effective. The keys to repeat sales mentioned earlier in this chapter, if followed, will generate plenty of this kind of advertising. You can precipitate even more of it by being more active: visit offices, retail stores, and factories in the vicinity to introduce yourself, to talk about your business, and to outline the services you offer. Carry along business cards and leave one with everyone you speak to. Better still, distribute four-by-six-inch index cards printed with necessary details. The cost of a thousand such cards is minimal.

Many supermarkets make bulletin boards available for local notices; put up an eye-catching flier in your neighborhood market. A special offer on the flier will bring results and so will delivering the same flier to all residents in the area.

Refer to exhibit 25–2 for additional ideas for promoting your service enterprise.

EXHIBIT 25–2. SUGGESTIONS FOR PROMOTING YOUR SERVICE BUSINESS

- A listing in the Yellow Pages of the telephone directory is essential for a service firm. Paying for a bold-type listing and a small advertisement would be even better. The costs for these are quite reasonable.
- Ask your customers to register in the "Guest Register" book when they come in. The book should have columns for names, addresses, and telephone numbers. This will help you build and maintain an up-to-date customer file, a valuable list that you can periodically "milk."
- Display a framed copy of your industry's code of ethics in your shop.
- Keep your clientele posted on upcoming specials either by mail or by telephone. In fact, there are a number of ways you can profitably use the telephone: to call people when their repaired items are ready, to discuss with them any problems that come up, to give them advice, and so forth.
- Ask your customers for recommendations; work out an inexpensive giveaway promotion to encourage them.
- If you have a storefront and some selling space, do a little merchandise retailing to help pay the rent. Put in a display of fast-selling items that will appeal to your customers. (Beauty salons have long profited from this technique.)
- Look over your list of services. Are you able to make deliveries in the neighborhood free of charge or for a nominal amount? How about credit? Can you make a "promotion tool" out of extending credit by publicizing it? Can you furnish an appropriate substitute for your customers' use while their appliances, tools, and the like are in the shop for repairs? Can you afford to finance large purchases?
- Finally, apply creative thinking approaches to the problem of how you can successfully differentiate your service business from those of your competitors.

FOR FURTHER INFORMATION

Burstiner, Irving. *Start and Run Your Own Profitable Service Business.* Englewood Cliffs, N.J.: Prentice-Hall, 1993.

Butterfield, Ronald W. *Quality Service: Pure and Simple.* Milwaukee, Wisc.: ASQC Quality Press, 1990.

Chant, Ben, and Melissa Morgan. *How to Start a Service Business.* New York: Avon, 1994.

Cohen, William A. *Model Business Plans for Service Businesses.* New York: Wiley, 1995.

Connor, Dick, and Jeffrey P. Davidson. *Marketing Your Consulting and Professional Services.* 3rd ed. New York: Wiley, 1994.

Crane, F. G. *Professional Services Marketing: Strategy and Tactics.* Binghamton, N.Y.: Haworth Press, 1993.

Lovelock, Christopher H. *Services Marketing.* 2d ed. Englewood Cliffs, N.J.: Prentice-Hall, 1991.

McKay, Robert. *Opportunities in Your Own Service Business.* Lincolnwood, Ill.: NTC Publishing, 1994.

Palmer, Adrian, and Catherine Cole. *Services Marketing.* Englewood Cliffs, N.J.: Prentice-Hall, 1995.

Putman, Anthony O. *Marketing Your Services: A Step-by-Step Guide for Small Businesses and Professionals.* New York: Wiley, 1990.

THE FUTURE
OF YOUR
BUSINESS

GROWTH AND CONTINUITY

DO YOU RECALL, back in chapter 10, the discussion of the *product life cycle* concept? Businesses—like products and people—evidence several different stages during their life spans (see figure 26–1).

THE BUSINESS LIFE CYCLE

The newly launched small business, if successful, begins to grow. It passes through a perhaps turbulent adolescence, attains maturity, and then, eventually, fades away. Like the life cycle of the innovative product that meets with customer acceptance, the new enterprise will most likely pass through four phases: the *introductory, growth, maturity,* and *decline* stages.

INTRODUCTORY STAGE

It's during the initial stage of the business life cycle that the entrepreneur starts up operations, hoping to carve out the beginnings of a niche in a particular industry. This introductory stage is the most perilous of the four; success or failure lies in the offing. If the enterprise is viable, well-managed, and if the owner is lucky, the end-of-year bottom-line figure will be registered in black ink instead of in red. At this point, the entrepreneur directly controls all the major business functions. Sales thereafter will continue to grow, albeit perhaps slowly. If tight reins are held on spending, the business will continue to prosper.

Several employees (part-time or full-time) may be added and profits repeatedly ploughed back into the business. This, however, is more of a holding operation or a clinging to survival than real business growth. This type of situation may prevail for a year or two, sometimes longer. Indeed, some businesses may never fully attain the next phase.

FIGURE 26–1. LIFE CYCLE OF A TYPICAL BUSINESS

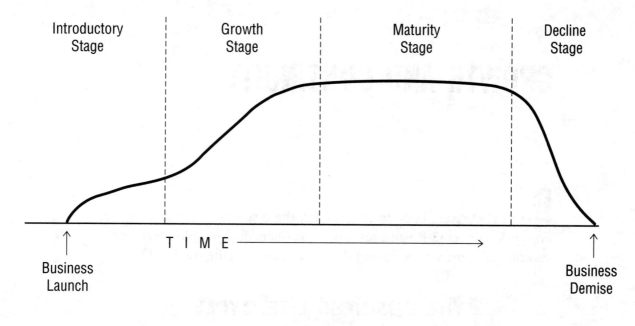

GROWTH STAGE

This next phase is characterized by more accelerated progress, the consolidation and strengthening of the enterprise's position relative to its industry, an ascending sales curve, and a growing number of employees. The entrepreneur may purchase more capital equipment, thus increasing the total value of company assets. More capital may be brought in, perhaps through the original owner's taking on one or more partners, borrowing substantial sums from a financial institution, or selling some of the corporation's stock. Supervision is gradually given over to employees; several layers of management soon evolve between owner and rank and file. During this stage, profits are excellent. Expansion begins. Indeed, some firms at this stage begin to consider such moves as acquisitions and mergers in addition to internal growth and relocation.

MATURITY STAGE

Eventually, the company appears to reach its limits in size and performance. No one knows, of course, how many years it will take for any particular firm to enter the maturity stage. By now the firm may enjoy a sizable market share. Perhaps it can no longer be called a "small" business. When growth slows down to a mere crawl, the future cannot look promising.

Any no-growth situation will inevitably lead to decay, to that fourth and last stage of the business life cycle—the decline stage. At the end of this final phase, one can only expect the demise of the company.

For any one enterprise, each stage in the life cycle may be lengthened or shortened. In the final analysis, it's management's vision (or lack of it) that is responsible for the pacing.

Growth is essential to the well-being of your business; so is continuity in management. Both of these ideas are developed further in the balance of this chapter. Before we continue, however, it might prove illuminating to read through the brief synopses of small business growth in exhibit 26–1.

CONTROLLED VERSUS EXPLOSIVE BUSINESS GROWTH

Growth means expansion. It creates additional revenues—and additional profit. It must be planned for, organized for, and then guided and nurtured. To realize company growth, top management must be highly motivated along these lines and must possess the ability to grow.

A distinction needs to be made between deliberate, planned growth and unchecked, even explosive growth. The first is cautious and carefully charted—carried along through regular planning sessions, periodic progress reviews, and program modifications. The second embraces a substantial element of peril that may actually destroy the potential of the budding company. Unprecedented initial success often leads to serious complications. In those firms that experience runaway growth patterns, we see many of the following symptoms:

- An excessive number of employees
- The proliferation of departments
- Confused lines of authority
- Runaway costs
- A lack of coordination and thus a loss of control
- Improperly trained department heads and supervisors
- A climbing employee turnover rate
- General dissatisfaction and even dissension

EXHIBIT 26–1. TYPICAL EXAMPLES OF INITIAL SMALL-BUSINESS GROWTH

Greeting-Card Stores   In a metropolitan area on the West Coast, two competitive greeting-card shops were located within three blocks of each other. Both had started in business seven or eight years earlier. The owner of one store decided to expand his operation by renting the stores on either side of his location, breaking through the walls, and thus quadrupling the size of his original establishment. He added several new merchandise lines (records, stereo equipment, high-quality chocolates) and departmentalized the premises.

The owner of the other shop took in two partners, along with their additional investment capital. They found desirable locations in several neighboring towns and built a small chain over the next several years. By then, only three of their six stores were profitable; leases for the others were not renewed.

Hardware Distributor   A hardware wholesaler expanded her operation into a contiguous state. She advertised for, interviewed, and trained three additional sales representatives for the new territory. Subsequently, a new compensation plan was prepared for the entire miniature sales force, and both a sales manager and a "trainer" were employed. Within two years, the new territory had been built up substantially and the company went on to "attack" two neighboring states.

Gift Shop   A middle-aged couple, successful operators for twenty-three years of a gift and souvenir shop in a New England resort area, sought a warm climate in which to spend their winters and their eventual retirement. They opened another outlet in southern Florida, an almost exact copy of their northern store down to layout, fixturization, and merchandise carried in stock. Unhappily, the newer store does less than half of the sales volume that the older store enjoys. They do not seem to be able to reach their break-even point. Nevertheless, the couple decides to use the profits of the first store to carry along the second one, hoping to build it up over time.

Land Developer   A small land developer placed a down payment on some wooded acreage in the mountains of Pennsylvania, bulldozed roads through the property, and then subdivided the land into homesites. The property was offered in its semideveloped state, one lot at a time, for vacation or retirement homes. Within two years after start-up, more than $10 million worth of land had been sold through television, direct mail, and telephone solicitation. Meanwhile, the company expanded to the point at which several hundred salaried employees and commission salespeople were on the books.

Soft-Drink Stand   After registering an instant, sound success with their first soft-drink-and-frankfurter stand, three partners managed to open up two additional outlets within the next six months. This way, they reasoned, each stand could be operated and tightly controlled by a partner. All three units enjoyed brisk sales. Soon thereafter, the owners decided to go the franchise route. They hired a franchise director on a commission basis, worked out all details of the franchise "package" with the director's assistance, and succeeded in blanketing the state with fourteen additional stores.

Manufacturer of Kitchen Furniture   An Arizona firm that manufactured

EXHIBIT 26–1. (continued)

kitchen dinette sets perceived the profitability of installing a similar plant in the Midwest close to several of its major, though long-distance customers. This way, not only are they better able to service these accounts and add new customers to their books but they will save considerably on transportation costs.

Source: Compiled by the author.

PLANNING FOR GROWTH

Planned growth is by far the more sensible approach. This planning, incidentally, may be even more vital to the small firm than to the large company simply because the former cannot afford to make many errors. It does not have the financial reserves to make amends for mistakes.

HOW TO DEVELOP YOUR COMPANY GROWTH PLAN

Once top management has made the commitment to pursue a growth pattern, the very next step ought to be the preparation of a "master plan" for growth. This document should embrace all of the required elements:

- The specific targets set (including objectives such as desired return on investment, the number of additional units to be opened, new plants or warehouses to be set up, and the sales levels to be attained)
- The schedule for organizing and putting into operation the successive stages of the plan
- Methods of gathering and allocating company resources (labor, management, methods, materials, and goods)
- The arranging for needed financing; the setting up of checks and balances to ensure that all activities are on track

At the very least, a plan coordinator (or even better, a two- or three-person committee) should be charged with overseeing the necessary coordination for developing the plan. Responsibility must be assigned since day-to-day activities need to continue uninterruptedly throughout.

WAYS TO GO

Planned growth may be either an internal or an external affair, or perhaps a combination of the two. By ploughing back each year's profits, acquiring one or two new partners, selling stock to friends and relatives (if a corporation), or securing a large loan, the small company can generate sufficient capital to finance an appreciable degree of internal growth. Such growth is usually accomplished through new-product development, the purchase of additional machinery, innovation, product-line expansion, automation, different methods of distribution, promotional creativity, and a variety of other approaches.

However, external growth can be made to proceed at a more rapid pace; this is sometimes more expedient for the healthy young firm. Management's attention may be directed toward going public, becoming franchisors, acquiring another company, or merging with another firm—all of which generally takes more capital than can be generated by reinvestment of profits or borrowing.

MERGERS AND ACQUISITIONS

In the typical merger, two companies of roughly equal market strength and asset value decide to combine. This "marriage" usually results in a new and stronger entity, with all of the resources of the original two at its command. In the acquisition situation, the two firms are unequal in net worth, sales volume, and so forth. The larger one buys out the smaller—lock, stock, and barrel. Payment may be made entirely in cash or in some combination of cash plus common stock, bonds, and so on.

The majority of combinations are of the so-called *horizontal* type, in which companies conducting similar business operations combine, such as two supermarket chains, two hotels, or two appliance manufacturers. Other types include the *vertical combination,* in which companies integrate backward or forward along the marketing channels as when a large wholesaler acquires a manufacturing plant or a manufacturer opens retail outlets for its own products; and the *conglomerate,* whereby a company will buy up other firms in entirely different industries in order to diversify its holdings.

For the interested firm, the names of prospective candidates for acquisition may be obtained from banks, management consultants, investment bankers, CPAs, business brokers, law firms, and other sources.

Many of the potential advantages offered by mergers and acquisitions are outlined in the paragraphs below:

MARKETING: increased turnover; more intensive use of existing markets, adding new markets, perhaps expanding from local or regional markets to national markets; access to new market-research information; adding new products or services to the product line to help existing customers and/or add new customers with associated needs; offsetting any seasonal or cyclical fluctuations related to the existing product line; acquiring brand names and any special market reputation.

PRODUCTION: new products and/or markets making greater use of existing plant and machinery, thus leading to increased economies of scale; acquiring patent rights, licenses, etc., and additional R. and D. facilities; augmenting or complementing productive capacity, additional factory buildings, plant and equipment; new manufacturing processes; vertical integration, acquiring sources of raw materials and/or customer outlets.

FINANCE: better utilization of joint resources, employing idle capital or gaining additional funds (as, for example, a progressive company acquiring a dormant company having little ambition, but ample cash or marketable securities); taking advantage of a tax loss situation; spreading the business risk; minimizing stockheld balances; increasing the market value of shares; exploiting large-scale opportunities; enhanced profits and reserves.

MANAGEMENT AND PERSONNEL: outlet for excess managerial capacity; acquiring additional management skills, key workers, trained staff, etc.; access to training facilities, management development plans, etc.*

MANAGEMENT SUCCESSION

Along with growth and expansion, there is mounting pressure on top management to devise a strong talent acquisition program. Additional specialists are needed to fill the new supervisory and executive

---

* W. F. Coventry and Irving Burstiner, *Management: A Basic Handbook* (Englewood Cliffs, N.J.: Prentice-Hall, 1977), 399.

slots as they are created in the developing organization and to replace those managers who leave or are weeded out due to incompetence. Managerial talent is difficult to locate; in this country there has been a serious shortage of executives for years.

Usually, management that is sophisticated enough to embark on an expansion program rises to the challenge by initiating needs assessment for five or more years into the future. Simultaneously, a personnel talent inventory is prepared. Promising employees, those deemed to have the potential for growth and promotion, are identified; a comprehensive training and development program is begun; and the management skills of the selected candidates are nurtured through a variety of methods, including university courses, job rotation, committee work, and project assignments.

Strangely, though, while most entrepreneurs provide for this continuity of management talent long into the future, they rarely apply this concept to themselves. In the entrepreneurial personality, an owner is not only regarded as indefatigable but as indestructible. Soul-searching questions such as "What will happen to my business if I become ill and am unable to carry on my duties?" and "Who will take over the reins later on?" are shunted off into the distant future. Yet, as the key in the entire business, the owner should realize that more than anyone, he or she needs a backup for eventual replacement. Certainly, the firm would suffer most if his or her services were to be lost.

THE FAMILY-OWNED BUSINESS

Often, one or two family members are active in the business. This leads the founder(s) to look forward to the time when sons or daughters—or perhaps sisters or brothers—will take over at the helm. Several friction-generating possibilities accrue to this type of situation:

- No one else in the family may possess the vision, requisite skills, desire, or self-direction to manage the business someday.
- Personality clashes between owner(s) and relatives—or among the latter alone—will probably occur from time to time.
- Jealousy and rivalry among family members can ruin their relationships, if not the business itself.

Frequently, it's wiser to think of hiring a capable administrator, perhaps someone with an excellent track record as president or executive vice president of another company. This is preferable to designating one of the family as your eventual successor.

In any event, that new executive should be brought into your business as early in the game as possible, despite the fact that it's an expensive move. More likely than not, several years of thorough training and hands-on application will go by before this manager will acquire mastery of your operations. You'll also want to maintain close supervision over this person and make frequent evaluations before deciding that you have sufficient confidence in his or her capabilities to turn over the major portion of your own responsibilities when it becomes necessary.

FOR FURTHER INFORMATION

Ernst & Young. *Mergers and Acquisitions.* 2d ed. New York: Wiley, 1994.

Justis, Robert T., and Richard J. Judd. *Franchising.* Cincinnati: South-Western, 1989.

Krallinger, Joseph. *How to Acquire the Perfect Business for Your Company.* New York: Wiley, 1991.

Lea, James W. *Keeping It in the Family: Successful Succession of the Family Business.* New York: Wiley, 1991.

Lewis, Mack O. *How to Franchise Your Business.* 3rd ed. New York: Pilot Books, 1990.

Mirvis, Philip H., and Mitchell L. Marks. *Managing the Merger: Making It Work.* Englewood Cliffs, N.J.: Prentice-Hall, 1991.

Reed, Stanley Foster, and Lane & Edson, P.C. *The Art of M&A: A Merger/Acquisition/Buyout Guide.* Homewood, Ill.: Business One Irwin, 1989.

Scharf, Charles A., Edward E. Shea, and George C. Beck. *Acquisitions, Mergers, Sales, Buyouts, Takeovers: A Handbooks with Forms.* Englewood Cliffs, N.J.: Prentice-Hall, 1991.

QUIZZES FOR SELF-ANALYSIS

Though tongue-in-cheek, this quiz will help you decide whether you "have what it takes" to start a business of your own. For the next few minutes, enjoy answering the questions! After you have finished, follow the scoring instructions and then read the last paragraph.

Under Each Question, Check the Answer That Says What You Feel or Comes Closest to It. Be Honest with Yourself.

Are you a self-starter?

_____I do things on my own. Nobody has to tell me to get going.

_____If someone gets me started, I keep going all right.

_____Easy does it, man. I don't put myself out until I have to.

How do you feel about other people?

_____I like people. I can get along with just about anybody.

_____I have plenty of friends—I don't need anyone else.

_____Most people bug me.

Can you lead others?

_____I can get most people to go along when I start something.

_____I can give the orders if someone tells me what we should do.

_____I let someone else get things moving. Then I go along if I feel like it.

Can you take responsibility?

_____I like to take charge of things and see them through.

_____I'll take over if I have to, but I'd rather let someone else be responsible.

_____There's always some eager beaver around wanting to show how smart he is. I say let him.

How good an organizer are you?

_____I like to have a plan before I start. I'm usually the one to get things lined up when the gang wants to do something.

_____I do all right unless things get too goofed up. Then I cop out.

_____You get all set and then something comes along and blows the whole bag. So I just take things as they come.

How good a worker are you?

_____I can keep going as long as I need to. I don't mind working hard for something I want.

_____I'll work hard for a while, but when I've had enough, that's it, man!

_____I can't see that hard work gets you anywhere.

Can you make decisions?

_____I can make up my mind in a hurry if I have to. It usually turns out OK, too.

_____I can if I have plenty of time. If I have to make up my mind fast, I think later I should have decided the other way.

_____I don't like to be the one who has to decide things. I'd probably blow it.

Can people trust what you say?

_____You bet they can. I don't say things I don't mean.

_____I try to be on the level most of the time, but sometimes I just say what's easiest.

_____What's the sweat if the other fellow doesn't know the difference?

Can you stick with it?

_____If I make up my mind to do something, I don't let *anything* stop me.

_____I usually finish what I start—if it doesn't get fouled up.

_____If it doesn't go right away, I turn off. Why beat your brains out?

How good is your health?

_____Man, I *never* run down!

_____I have enough energy for most things I want to do.

_____I run out of juice sooner than most of my friends seem to.

Now count the checks you made.

How many checks are there beside the *first* answer to each question?

How many checks are there beside the *second* answer to each question?

How many checks are there beside the *third* answer to each question?

If most of your checks are beside the first answers, you probably have what it takes to run a business. If not, you're likely to have more trouble than you can handle by yourself. Better find a partner who is strong on the points you're weak on. If many checks are beside the third answer, not even a good partner will be able to shore you up.

Source: *Small Marketers Aid No. 71* (Washington, D.C.: U.S. Small Business Administration, 1975), 4–5.

Note: I developed and copyrighted this chart some years ago and have used it in a few studies of supervisory and managerial personnel.

Essentially, the chart consists of two lists of characteristics—twenty-five "Creativity Traits" and twenty-five "Leadership Traits"—culled from literature and research in these two areas.

More likely than not, entrepreneurs who hope to succeed will register an above-average score on the total list of "leadership" characteristics. Although the need for a high score on "creativity" traits may not be as apparent, I believe that creativity is essential for success over the long term. Among other things, it enables the business owner to cope with both new and recurring challenges, the efforts of competitors, and an ever-changing business environment.

Top company executives appear to earn comparatively high scores in both dimensions of the Self-Rating Chart.

People who see themselves as "average" in all traits (a rating of "4" multiplied by 25 traits) would earn scores of 100 on each of the two parts. The majority of successful executives tested with this chart score in the "110 and above" range on the Creativity Traits—and even higher on the Leadership Traits. Total test scores above 240 are quite common among them.

How well do you know yourself?

Below is a list of nouns and short phrases. You are to consider each item carefully and then place an X in one of the boxes alongside the trait you are rating. There are seven choices available to you (Columns 1 through 7). Placing an X in Column 1 would indicate that you rate yourself "Extremely Low" in the particular trait; an X in Column 4 would signify an "Average" rating; and X in Column 7 would mean "Extremely High."

Forget your natural modesty, yet do be honest with your self-evaluation.

THE CHART AS A DIAGNOSTIC INSTRUMENT

If you are entirely honest with yourself—and perceive yourself clearly—an analysis of your responses on the chart will pinpoint your strengths and expose your weaknesses. Low ratings on any qualities (Xs in "Extremely Low" to "Average" columns) show that you do realize your deficiencies. You can improve these through study and effort.

Finally, many leadership qualities develop on the job as you work hard making your own business a success.

PART I: CREATIVITY TRAITS

Item	Extremely Low 1	Quite Low 2	Somewhat Low 3	Average 4	Somewhat High 5	Quite High 6	Extremely High 7
Ability to express oneself							
Adaptability							
Awareness							
Curiosity							
Drive							
Enthusiasm							
Facility with numbers							
Flexibility of thinking							
Independence of outlook							
Lack of compulsion to conform							
Open-mindedness							
Originality							
Positive attitude							
Powers of concentration							
Productivity							
Resourcefulness							
Self-confidence							
Self-sufficiency							
Sense of humor							
Sensitivity to problems							
"Stick-to-itiveness"							
Verbal fluency							
Wide and varied interests							
Willingness to take chances							
Zest for solving puzzles							
Creativity Traits Totals:							

PART II: LEADERSHIP TRAITS

Item	Extremely Low 1	Quite Low 2	Somewhat Low 3	Average 4	Somewhat High 5	Quite High 6	Extremely High 7
Ability to clarify ideas for others							
Ability to enlist the cooperation of others							
Ability to judge people							
Ability to see the whole picture							
Ability to set priorities							
Communication skills							
Decision-making capability							
Evaluation skills							
Giving credit when due							
Good judgment							
Interest in people (in contrast to things)							
Knack for interpersonal relations							
Planning ability							
Powers of persuasion							
Receptivity to change							
Self-control							
Sensitivity to others							
Skill at motivating others							
Skill in scheduling							
Supportive of subordinates							
Taking the initiative							
Talent for analyzing situations							
Technical knowledge of my job							
Warmth of personal relations							
Willingness to listen to subordinates							
Leadership Traits Totals:							

SCORING INSTRUCTIONS

To score the chart after rating yourself, follow these steps:

1. Part I of the Chart lists twenty-five "Creativity Traits"; Part II lists twenty-five "Leadership Traits." Mark each half of the Chart separately.
2. Put the total number of Xs in Column 1 ("Extremely Low") at the bottom of the first column.
3. Continue totaling Columns, 2, 3, 4, and so on, until you have totaled all seven columns.
4. (First, your various totals should add up to 25—the number of traits you have rated.) Now, multiply each column total by the number at the top of the column. For example, your self-report shows the following numbers of Xs: 1, 2, 4, 8, 3, 5, and 2. Here's how you work out a sample score on Part I of the chart:

Column Number		Number of Xs		Total Value
1	×	1	=	1
2	×	2	=	4
3	×	4	=	12
4	×	8	=	32
5	×	3	=	15
6	×	5	=	30
7	×	2	=	14

Total Creativity Traits Score = 108

Scoring Chart _____
Creativity Traits
_____
Leadership Traits
_____
Total Test:
_____

5. Write your Total Creativity Traits Score in the box on the Scoring Chart.
6. Repeat the entire procedure with Part II, "Leadership Traits." Write your total score in the "Leadership" box on the Scoring Chart.
7. Add up the totals in the Scoring Chart box. Write in "Total Test" score.

SAMPLE FEDERAL INCOME-TAX RETURNS

SCHEDULE C (Form 1040) Department of the Treasury Internal Revenue Service	**Profit or Loss From Business** (Sole Proprietorship) ▶ Partnerships, joint ventures, etc., must file Form 1065. ▶ Attach to Form 1040 or Form 1041. ▶ See Instructions for Schedule C (Form 1040).	OMB No. 1545-0074 19**96** Attachment Sequence No. **09**

Name of proprietor	Social security number (SSN)
Susan J. Brown	111 00 1111

A	Principal business or profession, including product or service (see page C-1) Retail, family clothing	B Enter principal business code (see page C-6) ▶ 3 9 3 9

C	Business name. If no separate business name, leave blank. Family Fashions	D Employer ID number (EIN), if any 1 0 1 2 3 4 5 6 7

E Business address (including suite or room no.) ▶ 725 Big Sur Drive
City, town or post office, state, and ZIP code Franklin, NY 18725

F Accounting method: (1) ☐ Cash   (2) ☑ Accrual   (3) ☐ Other (specify) ▶

G Did you "materially participate" in the operation of this business during 1996? If "No," see page C-2 for limit on losses.   ☑ Yes   ☐ No

H If you started or acquired this business during 1996, check here . . . . ▶ ☐

Part I Income

1	Gross receipts or sales. **Caution:** *If this income was reported to you on Form W-2 and the "Statutory employee" box on that form was checked, see page C-2 and check here* . . . . ▶ ☐	1	397,742	00
2	Returns and allowances	2	1,442	00
3	Subtract line 2 from line 1	3	396,300	00
4	Cost of goods sold (from line 42 on page 2)	4	239,349	00
5	**Gross profit.** Subtract line 4 from line 3	5	156,951	00
6	Other income, including Federal and state gasoline or fuel tax credit or refund (see page C-2) . . .	6		
7	**Gross income.** Add lines 5 and 6 . . . . ▶	7	156,951	00

Part II Expenses. Enter expenses for business use of your home **only** on line 30.

8	Advertising	8	3,500	00	19	Pension and profit-sharing plans	19		
9	Bad debts from sales or services (see page C-3) . .	9	479	00	20	Rent or lease (see page C-4):			
						a Vehicles, machinery, and equipment .	20a		
10	Car and truck expenses (see page C-3)	10	3,850	00		b Other business property . .	20b	12,000	00
11	Commissions and fees . .	11			21	Repairs and maintenance . .	21	964	00
12	Depletion	12			22	Supplies (not included in Part III) .	22	1,203	00
13	Depreciation and section 179 expense deduction (not included in Part III) (see page C-3) . .	13	4,231	00	23	Taxes and licenses	23	5,727	00
					24	Travel, meals, and entertainment:			
14	Employee benefit programs (other than on line 19) . . .	14				a Travel	24a		
						b Meals and entertainment			
15	Insurance (other than health) .	15	238	00		c Enter 50% of line 24b subject to limitations (see page C-4)			
16	Interest:								
	a Mortgage (paid to banks, etc.) .	16a				d Subtract line 24c from line 24b .	24d		
	b Other	16b	2,633	00	25	Utilities	25	3,570	00
17	Legal and professional services	17			26	Wages (less employment credits) .	26	59,050	00
18	Office expense	18	216	00	27	Other expenses (from line 48 on page 2)	27	8,078	00

28	**Total expenses** before expenses for business use of home. Add lines 8 through 27 in columns . ▶	28	105,739	00
29	Tentative profit (loss). Subtract line 28 from line 7	29	51,212	00
30	Expenses for business use of your home. Attach **Form 8829**	30		
31	**Net profit or (loss).** Subtract line 30 from line 29. • If a profit, enter on **Form 1040, line 12,** and ALSO on **Schedule SE, line 2** (statutory employees, see page C-5). Estates and trusts, enter on Form 1041, line 3. • If a loss, you MUST go on to line 32.	31	51,212	00

32 If you have a loss, check the box that describes your investment in this activity (see page C-5).

• If you checked 32a, enter the loss on **Form 1040, line 12,** and ALSO on **Schedule SE, line 2** (statutory employees, see page C-5). Estates and trusts, enter on Form 1041, line 3.

• If you checked 32b, you MUST attach **Form 6198.**

32a ☐ All investment is at risk.
32b ☐ Some investment is not at risk.

For Paperwork Reduction Act Notice, see Form 1040 instructions.   Cat. No. 11334P   Schedule C (Form 1040) 1996

Schedule C (Form 1040) 1996

Page **2**

Part III **Cost of Goods Sold (see page C-5)**

33 Method(s) used to
value closing inventory: **a** ☑ Cost **b** ☐ Lower of cost or market **c** ☐ Other (attach explanation)

34 Was there any change in determining quantities, costs, or valuations between opening and closing inventory? If
"Yes," attach explanation . . . . ☐ **Yes** ☑ **No**

35	Inventory at beginning of year. If different from last year's closing inventory, attach explanation . .	35	42,843 00
36	Purchases less cost of items withdrawn for personal use	36	240,252 00
37	Cost of labor. Do not include salary paid to yourself	37	
38	Materials and supplies	38	
39	Other costs	39	
40	Add lines 35 through 39	40	283,095 00
41	Inventory at end of year	41	43,746 00
42	**Cost of goods sold.** Subtract line 41 from line 40. Enter the result here and on page 1, line 4 . .	42	239,349 00

Part IV **Information on Your Vehicle. Complete this part ONLY if you are claiming car or truck expenses on
line 10 and are not required to file Form 4562 for this business. See the instructions for line 13 on page
C-3 to find out if you must file.**

43 When did you place your vehicle in service for business purposes? (month, day, year) ▶ . . . . / . . . . . . / . . . .

44 Of the total number of miles you drove your vehicle during 1996, enter the number of miles you used your vehicle for:

a Business . . . . **b** Commuting . . . . **c** Other . . . .

45 Do you (or your spouse) have another vehicle available for personal use? . . . . ☐ **Yes** ☐ **No**

46 Was your vehicle available for use during off-duty hours? . . . . ☐ **Yes** ☐ **No**

47a Do you have evidence to support your deduction? . . . . ☐ **Yes** ☐ **No**

b If "Yes," is the evidence written? . . . . ☐ **Yes** ☐ **No**

Part V **Other Expenses. List below business expenses not included on lines 8–26 or line 30.**

Bank service charges	180	00
Chamber of Commerce	60	00
Free Credit Card Co.	6,000	00
Trash removal	1,600	00
Window washing	238	00
48 Total other expenses. Enter here and on page 1, line 27	48	8,078 00

Source: "1996 Tax Guide for Small Business," *Publication 334* (Washington, D.C.: Internal Revenue Service,
January 1997), 40–41.

Form **1065**	U.S. Partnership Return of Income	OMB No. 1545-0099
Department of the Treasury Internal Revenue Service	For calendar year 1996, or tax year beginning ...., 1996, and ending ...., 19 .... ▶ See separate instructions.	**1996**

A Principal business activity
Retail

B Principal product or service
Books

C Business code number
5942

Use the IRS label. Otherwise, please print or type.

10-9876543   DEC96   D71
AbleBaker Book Store
334 West Main Street
Orange, MD   20904

I R S

D Employer identification number

E Date business started
10-1-79

F Total assets (see page 10 of the instructions)
$ 45,391

G Check applicable boxes: **(1)** ☐ Initial return **(2)** ☐ Final return **(3)** ☐ Change in address **(4)** ☐ Amended return

H Check accounting method: **(1)** ☐ Cash **(2)** ☑ Accrual **(3)** ☐ Other (specify) ▶ ....

I Number of Schedules K-1. Attach one for each person who was a partner at any time during the tax year ▶ 2

Caution: *Include only trade or business income and expenses on lines 1a through 22 below. See the instructions for more information.*

Income

1a Gross receipts or sales	**1a**	409,465	
b Less returns and allowances	**1b**	3,365	**1c** 406,100
2 Cost of goods sold (Schedule A, line 8)			**2** 267,641
3 Gross profit. Subtract line 2 from line 1c			**3** 138,459
4 Ordinary income (loss) from other partnerships, estates, and trusts *(attach schedule)*			**4**
5 Net farm profit (loss) *(attach Schedule F (Form 1040))*			**5**
6 Net gain (loss) from Form 4797, Part II, line 20			**6**
7 Other income (loss) *(attach schedule)*			**7** 559
8 **Total income (loss).** Combine lines 3 through 7			**8** 139,018

Deductions (see page 11 of the instructions for limitations)

9 Salaries and wages (other than to partners) (less employment credits)	**9**	29,350
10 Guaranteed payments to partners	**10**	25,000
11 Repairs and maintenance	**11**	1,125
12 Bad debts	**12**	250
13 Rent	**13**	20,000
14 Taxes and licenses	**14**	3,295
15 Interest	**15**	1,451
16a Depreciation (if required, attach Form 4562)	**16a** 1,174	
b Less depreciation reported on Schedule A and elsewhere on return	**16b** -0-	**16c** 1,174
17 Depletion **(Do not deduct oil and gas depletion.)**	**17**	
18 Retirement plans, etc.	**18**	
19 Employee benefit programs	**19**	
20 Other deductions *(attach schedule)*	**20**	8,003
21 **Total deductions.** Add the amounts shown in the far right column for lines 9 through 20	**21**	89,648
22 **Ordinary income (loss)** from trade or business activities. Subtract line 21 from line 8	**22**	49,370

Please Sign Here

Under penalties of perjury, I declare that I have examined this return, including accompanying schedules and statements, and to the best of my knowledge and belief, it is true, correct, and complete. Declaration of preparer (other than general partner or limited liability company member) is based on all information of which preparer has any knowledge.

▶ *Frank H. Able*   ▶ 3-12-97
Signature of general partner or limited liability company member   Date

Paid Preparer's Use Only

Preparer's signature ▶	Date	Check if self-employed ▶ ☐	Preparer's social security no.
Firm's name (or yours if self-employed) and address ▶		EIN ▶	
		ZIP code ▶	

For Paperwork Reduction Act Notice, see page 1 of separate instructions.   Cat. No. 11390Z   Form **1065** (1996)

Form 1065 (1996)   Page **2**

| | Schedule A | Cost of Goods Sold (see page 13 of the instructions) |

1	Inventory at beginning of year	**1** 18,125
2	Purchases less cost of items withdrawn for personal use	**2** 268,741
3	Cost of labor	**3** -0-
4	Additional section 263A costs (attach schedule)	**4** -0-
5	Other costs (attach schedule)	**5** -0-
6	**Total.** Add lines 1 through 5	**6** 286,866
7	Inventory at end of year	**7** 19,225
8	**Cost of goods sold.** Subtract line 7 from line 6. Enter here and on page 1, line 2	**8** 267,641

9a Check all methods used for valuing closing inventory:

    (i) ☐ Cost as described in Regulations section 1.471-3

    (ii) ☑ Lower of cost or market as described in Regulations section 1.471-4

    (iii) ☐ Other (specify method used and attach explanation) ▶ ....

  b Check this box if there was a writedown of "subnormal" goods as described in Regulations section 1.471-2(c) . . . ▶ ☐

  c Check this box if the LIFO inventory method was adopted this tax year for any goods (if checked, attach Form 970) . ▶ ☐

  d Do the rules of section 263A (for property produced or acquired for resale) apply to the partnership? . . ☐ Yes ☑ No

  e Was there any change in determining quantities, cost, or valuations between opening and closing inventory? ☐ Yes ☑ No

    If "Yes," attach explanation.

| | Schedule B | Other Information |

		Yes	No
1	What type of entity is filing this return? Check the applicable box:		
a	☑ General partnership **b** ☐ Limited partnership **c** ☐ Limited liability company		
d	☐ Other (see page 14 of the instructions) ▶		
2	Are any partners in this partnership also partnerships?		✓
3	Is this partnership a partner in another partnership?		✓
4	Is this partnership subject to the consolidated audit procedures of sections 6221 through 6233? If "Yes," see **Designation of Tax Matters Partner** below		✓
5	Does this partnership meet **ALL THREE** of the following requirements?		
a	The partnership's total receipts for the tax year were less than $250,000;		
b	The partnership's total assets at the end of the tax year were less than $600,000; **AND**		
c	Schedules K-1 are filed with the return and furnished to the partners on or before the due date (including extensions) for the partnership return.		
	If "Yes," the partnership is not required to complete Schedules L, M-1, and M-2; Item F on page 1 of Form 1065; or Item J on Schedule K-1		✓
6	Does this partnership have any foreign partners?		✓
7	Is this partnership a publicly traded partnership as defined in section 469(k)(2)?		✓
8	Has this partnership filed, or is it required to file, **Form 8264,** Application for Registration of a Tax Shelter?		✓
9	At any time during calendar year 1996, did the partnership have an interest in or a signature or other authority over a financial account in a foreign country (such as a bank account, securities account, or other financial account)? See page 14 of the instructions for exceptions and filing requirements for Form TD F 90-22.1. If "Yes," enter the name of the foreign country. ▶		✓
10	During the tax year, did the partnership receive a distribution from, or was it the grantor of, or transferor to, a foreign trust? If "Yes," see page 14 of the instructions for other forms the partnership may have to file		✓
11	Was there a distribution of property or a transfer (e.g., by sale or death) of a partnership interest during the tax year? If "Yes," you may elect to adjust the basis of the partnership's assets under section 754 by attaching the statement described under **Elections Made By the Partnership** on page 5 of the instructions		✓

Designation of Tax Matters Partner (see page 15 of the instructions)

Enter below the general partner designated as the tax matters partner (TMP) for the tax year of this return:

Name of
designated TMP ▶ _____   Identifying
number of TMP ▶ _____

Address of
designated TMP ▶ _____

Form 1065 (1996) Page **3**

Schedule K — Partners' Shares of Income, Credits, Deductions, etc.

	(a) Distributive share items		(b) Total amount
Income (Loss)	**1** Ordinary income (loss) from trade or business activities (page 1, line 22)	**1**	49,370
	2 Net income (loss) from rental real estate activities (attach Form 8825)	**2**	
	3a Gross income from other rental activities **3a**		
	b Expenses from other rental activities (attach schedule) **3b**		
	c Net income (loss) from other rental activities. Subtract line 3b from line 3a	**3c**	
	4 Portfolio income (loss): **a** Interest income	**4a**	
	b Dividend income	**4b**	150
	c Royalty income	**4c**	
	d Net short-term capital gain (loss) (attach Schedule D (Form 1065))	**4d**	
	e Net long-term capital gain (loss) (attach Schedule D (Form 1065))	**4e**	
	f Other portfolio income (loss) (attach schedule)	**4f**	
	5 Guaranteed payments to partners	**5**	25,000
	6 Net gain (loss) under section 1231 (other than due to casualty or theft) (attach Form 4797)	**6**	
	7 Other income (loss) (attach schedule)	**7**	
Deductions	**8** Charitable contributions (attach schedule)	**8**	650
	9 Section 179 expense deduction (attach Form 4562)	**9**	
	10 Deductions related to portfolio income (itemize)	**10**	
	11 Other deductions (attach schedule)	**11**	
Investment Interest	**12a** Interest expense on investment debts	**12a**	
	b (1) Investment income included on lines 4a, 4b, 4c, and 4f above	**12b(1)**	150
	(2) Investment expenses included on line 10 above	**12b(2)**	
Credits	**13a** Low-income housing credit:		
	(1) From partnerships to which section 42(j)(5) applies for property placed in service before 1990	**13a(1)**	
	(2) Other than on line 13a(1) for property placed in service before 1990	**13a(2)**	
	(3) From partnerships to which section 42(j)(5) applies for property placed in service after 1989	**13a(3)**	
	(4) Other than on line 13a(3) for property placed in service after 1989	**13a(4)**	
	b Qualified rehabilitation expenditures related to rental real estate activities (attach Form 3468)	**13b**	
	c Credits (other than credits shown on lines 13a and 13b) related to rental real estate activities	**13c**	
	d Credits related to other rental activities	**13d**	
	14 Other credits	**14**	
Self-Employment	**15a** Net earnings (loss) from self-employment	**15a**	74,370
	b Gross farming or fishing income	**15b**	
	c Gross nonfarm income	**15c**	
Adjustments and Tax Preference Items	**16a** Depreciation adjustment on property placed in service after 1986	**16a**	
	b Adjusted gain or loss	**16b**	
	c Depletion (other than oil and gas)	**16c**	
	d (1) Gross income from oil, gas, and geothermal properties	**16d(1)**	
	(2) Deductions allocable to oil, gas, and geothermal properties	**16d(2)**	
	e Other adjustments and tax preference items (attach schedule)	**16e**	
Foreign Taxes	**17a** Type of income ▶ .... **b** Foreign country or U.S. possession ▶		
	c Total gross income from sources outside the United States (attach schedule)	**17c**	
	d Total applicable deductions and losses (attach schedule)	**17d**	
	e Total foreign taxes (check one): ▶ ☐ Paid ☐ Accrued	**17e**	
	f Reduction in taxes available for credit (attach schedule)	**17f**	
	g Other foreign tax information (attach schedule)	**17g**	
Other	**18** Section 59(e)(2) expenditures: **a** Type ▶ .... **b** Amount ▶	**18b**	
	19 Tax-exempt interest income	**19**	50
	20 Other tax-exempt income	**20**	
	21 Nondeductible expenses	**21**	
	22 Distributions of money (cash and marketable securities)	**22**	52,880
	23 Distributions of property other than money	**23**	
	24 Other items and amounts required to be reported separately to partners (attach schedule)		
Analysis	**25a** Income (loss). Combine lines 1 through 7 in column (b). From the result, subtract the sum of lines 8 through 12a, 17e, and 18b	**25a**	73,870

b Analysis by type of partner:	(a) Corporate	(b) Individual		(c) Partnership	(d) Exempt organization	(e) Nominee/Other
		i. Active	ii. Passive			
(1) General partners		73,870				
(2) Limited partners						

Form 1065 (1996)
Page **4**

Note: *If Question 5 of Schedule B is answered "Yes," the partnership is not required to complete Schedules L, M-1, and M-2.*

Schedule L   **Balance Sheets per Books**

Assets	Beginning of tax year (a)	(b)	End of tax year (c)	(d)
1 Cash	7,150	3,455	10,990	3,350
2a Trade notes and accounts receivable		7,150		10,990
b Less allowance for bad debts				
3 Inventories		18,125		19,225
4 U.S. government obligations				
5 Tax-exempt securities		1,000		1,000
6 Other current assets (attach schedule) . . .				
7 Mortgage and real estate loans				
8 Other investments (attach schedule) . . .		1,000		1,000
9a Buildings and other depreciable assets . . .	15,000		15,000	
b Less accumulated depreciation	4,000	11,000	5,174	9,826
10a Depletable assets				
b Less accumulated depletion				
11 Land (net of any amortization)				
12a Intangible assets (amortizable only). . . .				
b Less accumulated amortization				
13 Other assets (attach schedule)				
14 Total assets		41,730		45,391
Liabilities and Capital				
15 Accounts payable		10,180		10,462
16 Mortgages, notes, bonds payable in less than 1 year .		4,000		3,600
17 Other current liabilities (attach schedule) . . .				
18 All nonrecourse loans				
19 Mortgages, notes, bonds payable in 1 year or more .				7,739
20 Other liabilities (attach schedule)				
21 Partners' capital accounts		27,550		23,590
22 Total liabilities and capital		41,730		45,391

Schedule M-1   **Reconciliation of Income (Loss) per Books With Income (Loss) per Return** (see page 23 of the instructions)

1	Net income (loss) per books	48,920	6	Income recorded on books this year not included on Schedule K, lines 1 through 7 (itemize):	
2	Income included on Schedule K, lines 1 through 4, 6, and 7, not recorded on books this year (itemize):			a Tax-exempt interest $ ...50..............	
					50
3	Guaranteed payments (other than health insurance)	25,000	7	Deductions included on Schedule K, lines 1 through 12a, 17e, and 18b, not charged against book income this year (itemize):	
4	Expenses recorded on books this year not included on Schedule K, lines 1 through 12a, 17e, and 18b (itemize):			a Depreciation $	
	a Depreciation $				
	b Travel and entertainment $		8	Add lines 6 and 7	50
			9	Income (loss) (Schedule K, line 25a). Subtract line 8 from line 5	
5	Add lines 1 through 4	73,920			73,870

Schedule M-2   **Analysis of Partners' Capital Accounts**

1	Balance at beginning of year	27,550	6	Distributions: a Cash	52,880
2	Capital contributed during year			b Property	
3	Net income (loss) per books	48,920	7	Other decreases (itemize):	
4	Other increases (itemize):			....	
			8	Add lines 6 and 7	52,880
5	Add lines 1 through 4	76,470	9	Balance at end of year. Subtract line 8 from line 5	23,590

Source: "Partnerships," Publication 541 (Washington, D.C.: Internal Revenue Service, January 1997), 20–23.

SCHEDULE K-1 (Form 1065) Department of the Treasury Internal Revenue Service	**Partner's Share of Income, Credits, Deductions, etc.** ▶ See separate instructions. For calendar year 1996 or tax year beginning _____ , 1996, and ending _____ , 19 ___	OMB No. 1545-0099 19**96**

Partner's identifying number ▶ *123-00-6789*   Partnership's identifying number ▶ *10 : 9876543*

Partner's name, address, and ZIP code	Partnership's name, address, and ZIP code
Frank W. Able *10 Green Street* *Orange, MD 20904*	*Able Baker Book Store* *334 West Main Street* *Orange, MD 20904*

A This partner is a ☑ general partner ☐ limited partner
 ☐ limited liability company member

B What type of entity is this partner? ▶ *Individual*

C Is this partner a ☑ domestic or a ☐ foreign partner?

D Enter partner's percentage of:

	(i) Before change or termination	(ii) End of year
Profit sharing	...... %	*50* %
Loss sharing	...... %	*50* %
Ownership of capital	...... %	*50* %

E IRS Center where partnership filed return: *Philadelphia*

F Partner's share of liabilities (see instructions):

Nonrecourse . . . . $ ....

Qualified nonrecourse financing . $ ....

Other . . . . $ *10,900*

G Tax shelter registration number . ▶ *N/A*

H Check here if this partnership is a publicly traded partnership as defined in section 469(k)(2) . . . . ☐

I Check applicable boxes: **(1)** ☐ Final K-1 **(2)** ☐ Amended K-1

J   Analysis of partner's capital account:

(a) Capital account at beginning of year	(b) Capital contributed during year	(c) Partner's share of lines 3, 4, and 7, Form 1065, Schedule M-2	(d) Withdrawals and distributions	(e) Capital account at end of year (combine columns (a) through (d))
14,050		*24,460*	(*26,440*)	*12,070*

		(a) Distributive share item		(b) Amount	(c) 1040 filers enter the amount in column (b) on:
Income (Loss)	1	Ordinary income (loss) from trade or business activities	1	*24,685*	See pages 5 and 6 of Partner's Instructions for Schedule K-1 (Form 1065).
	2	Net income (loss) from rental real estate activities	2		
	3	Net income (loss) from other rental activities	3		
	4	Portfolio income (loss):			
	a	Interest	4a		Sch. B, Part I, line 1
	b	Dividends	4b	*75*	Sch. B, Part II, line 5
	c	Royalties	4c		Sch. E, Part I, line 4
	d	Net short-term capital gain (loss)	4d		Sch. D, line 5, col. (f) or (g)
	e	Net long-term capital gain (loss)	4e		Sch. D, line 13, col. (f) or (g)
	f	Other portfolio income (loss) (attach schedule)	4f		Enter on applicable line of your return.
	5	Guaranteed payments to partner	5	*20,000*	See page 6 of Partner's Instructions for Schedule K-1 (Form 1065).
	6	Net gain (loss) under section 1231 (other than due to casualty or theft)	6		
	7	Other income (loss) (attach schedule)	7		Enter on applicable line of your return.
Deductions	8	Charitable contributions (see instructions) (attach schedule)	8	*325*	Sch. A, line 15 or 16
	9	Section 179 expense deduction	9		See page 7 of Partner's Instructions for Schedule K-1 (Form 1065).
	10	Deductions related to portfolio income (attach schedule)	10		
	11	Other deductions (attach schedule)	11		
Investment Interest	12a	Interest expense on investment debts	12a		Form 4952, line 1
	b	(1) Investment income included on lines 4a, 4b, 4c, and 4f above	b(1)	*75*	See page 7 of Partner's Instructions for Schedule K-1 (Form 1065).
		(2) Investment expenses included on line 10 above	b(2)		
Credits	13a	Low-income housing credit:			
		(1) From section 42(j)(5) partnerships for property placed in service before 1990	a(1)		
		(2) Other than on line 13a(1) for property placed in service before 1990	a(2)		
		(3) From section 42(j)(5) partnerships for property placed in service after 1989	a(3)		Form 8586, line 5
		(4) Other than on line 13a(3) for property placed in service after 1989	a(4)		
	b	Qualified rehabilitation expenditures related to rental real estate activities	13b		
	c	Credits (other than credits shown on lines 13a and 13b) related to rental real estate activities	13c		See page 8 of Partner's Instructions for Schedule K-1 (Form 1065).
	d	Credits related to other rental activities	13d		
	14	Other credits	14		

For Paperwork Reduction Act Notice, see Instructions for Form 1065.   Cat. No. 11394R   **Schedule K-1 (Form 1065) 1996**

EXHIBIT B–3. (continued)

	(a) Distributive share item	(b) Amount	(c) 1040 filers enter the amount in column (b) on:
Self-employment 15a	Net earnings (loss) from self-employment	15a 44,685	Sch. SE, Section A or B
b	Gross farming or fishing income.	15b	See page 8 of Partner's Instructions for Schedule K-1 (Form 1065).
c	Gross nonfarm income.	15c	
Adjustments and Tax Preference items 16a	Depreciation adjustment on property placed in service after 1986	16a	
b	Adjusted gain or loss	16b	See pages 8 and 9 of Partner's Instructions for Schedule K-1 (Form 1065) and Instructions for Form 6251.
c	Depletion (other than oil and gas)	16c	
d	(1) Gross income from oil, gas, and geothermal properties .	d(1)	
	(2) Deductions allocable to oil, gas, and geothermal properties	d(2)	
e	Other adjustments and tax preference items (attach schedule)	16e	
Foreign Taxes 17a	Type of income ▶		Form 1116, check boxes
b	Name of foreign country or U.S. possession ▶		
c	Total gross income from sources outside the United States (attach schedule)	17c	Form 1116, Part I
d	Total applicable deductions and losses (attach schedule) .	17d	
e	Total foreign taxes (check one): ▶ ☐ Paid ☐ Accrued . .	17e	Form 1116, Part II
f	Reduction in taxes available for credit (attach schedule) .	17f	Form 1116, Part III
g	Other foreign tax information (attach schedule)	17g	See Instructions for Form 1116.
Other 18	Section 59(e)(2) expenditures: a Type ▶		See page 9 of Partner's Instructions for Schedule K-1 (Form 1065).
b	Amount	18b	
19	Tax-exempt interest income	19 25	Form 1040, line 8b
20	Other tax-exempt income.	20	
21	Nondeductible expenses	21	See page 9 of Partner's Instructions for Schedule K-1 (Form 1065).
22	Distributions of money (cash and marketable securities) . . .	22 26,440	
23	Distributions of property other than money	23	
24	Recapture of low-income housing credit:		
a	From section 42(j)(5) partnerships	24a	Form 8611, line 8
b	Other than on line 24a.	24b	
Supplemental Information 25	Supplemental information required to be reported separately to each partner (attach additional schedules if more space is needed):		

Source: "Partnerships," Publication 541 (Washington, D.C.: Internal Revenue Service, January 1997), 24–25.

Form **1120**	**U.S. Corporation Income Tax Return**	OMB No. 1545-0123

Department of the Treasury
Internal Revenue Service

For calendar year 1996 or tax year beginning .... , 1996, ending .... , 19 ...
▶ Instructions are separate. See page 1 for Paperwork Reduction Act Notice.

1996

A Check if a:
1 Consolidated return (attach Form 851) ☐
2 Personal holding co. (attach Sch. PH) ☐
3 Personal service corp. (as defined in Temporary Regs. sec. 1.441-4T— see instructions) ☐

Use IRS label. Otherwise, print or type.

10-0395674   DEC96   071   3998
Tentex Toys, Inc.
36 Division Street
Anytown, IL 60930

B Employer identification number

C Date incorporated
3-1-72

D Total assets (see page 6 of instructions)
$ 879,417

E Check applicable boxes: (1) ☐ Initial return (2) ☐ Final return (3) ☐ Change of address

Income

1a	Gross receipts or sales 2,010,000 b Less returns and allowances 20,000 c Bal ▶	1c	1,990,000
2	Cost of goods sold (Schedule A, line 8)	2	1,520,000
3	Gross profit. Subtract line 2 from line 1c	3	470,000
4	Dividends (Schedule C, line 19)	4	10,000
5	Interest	5	5,500
6	Gross rents	6	
7	Gross royalties	7	
8	Capital gain net income (attach Schedule D (Form 1120))	8	
9	Net gain or (loss) from Form 4797, Part II, line 20 (attach Form 4797)	9	
10	Other income (see page 7 of instructions—attach schedule)	10	
11	**Total income.** Add lines 3 through 10 ▶	11	485,500

Deductions (See instructions for limitations on deductions.)

12	Compensation of officers (Schedule E, line 4)	12	70,000
13	Salaries and wages (less employment credits)	13	38,000
14	Repairs and maintenance	14	800
15	Bad debts	15	1,600
16	Rents	16	9,200
17	Taxes and licenses	17	15,000
18	Interest	18	27,200
19	Charitable contributions (see page 8 of instructions for 10% limitation)	19	23,150
20	Depreciation (attach Form 4562) 20 17,600		
21	Less depreciation claimed on Schedule A and elsewhere on return 21a 12,400	21b	5,200
22	Depletion	22	
23	Advertising	23	8,700
24	Pension, profit-sharing, etc., plans	24	
25	Employee benefit programs	25	
26	Other deductions (attach schedule)	26	78,300
27	**Total deductions.** Add lines 12 through 26 ▶	27	277,150
28	Taxable income before net operating loss deduction and special deductions. Subtract line 27 from line 11	28	208,350
29	**Less:** a Net operating loss deduction (see page 10 of instructions) 29a		
	b Special deductions (Schedule C, line 20) 29b 8,000	29c	8,000

Tax and Payments

30	**Taxable income.** Subtract line 29c from line 28	30	200,350
31	**Total tax** (Schedule J, line 10)	31	55,387
32	**Payments: a** 1995 overpayment credited to 1996 32a		
b	1996 estimated tax payments 32b 69,117		
c	Less 1996 refund applied for on Form 4466 32c ( ) d Bal ▶ 32d 69,117		
e	Tax deposited with Form 7004 32e		
f	Credit from regulated investment companies (attach Form 2439) 32f		
g	Credit for Federal tax on fuels (attach Form 4136). See instructions 32g	32h	69,117
33	Estimated tax penalty (see page 11 of instructions). Check if Form 2220 is attached ▶ ☐	33	
34	**Tax due.** If line 32h is smaller than the total of lines 31 and 33, enter amount owed	34	
35	**Overpayment.** If line 32h is larger than the total of lines 31 and 33, enter amount overpaid	35	13,730
36	Enter amount of line 35 you want: **Credited to 1997 estimated tax** ▶ 13,730 **Refunded** ▶	36	

Sign Here

Under penalties of perjury, I declare that I have examined this return, including accompanying schedules and statements, and to the best of my knowledge and belief, it is true, correct, and complete. Declaration of preparer (other than taxpayer) is based on all information of which preparer has any knowledge.

▶ James O. Barclay   Signature of officer |3-7-97 Date ▶ President Title

Paid Preparer's Use Only

Preparer's signature ▶	Date	Check if self-employed ☐	Preparer's social security number
Firm's name (or yours if self-employed) and address ▶		EIN ▶	
		ZIP code ▶	

Cat. No. 11450Q

Form 1120 (1996)   Page **2**

Schedule A Cost of Goods Sold (See page 11 of instructions.)

1	Inventory at beginning of year	1	126,000
2	Purchases	2	1,127,100
3	Cost of labor	3	402,000
4	Additional section 263A costs (attach schedule)	4	40,000
5	Other costs (attach schedule)	5	123,300
6	**Total.** Add lines 1 through 5	6	1,818,400
7	Inventory at end of year	7	298,400
8	**Cost of goods sold.** Subtract line 7 from line 6. Enter here and on page 1, line 2	8	1,520,000

9a Check all methods used for valuing closing inventory:

    (i) ☐ Cost as described in Regulations section 1.471-3

    (ii) ☑ Lower of cost or market as described in Regulations section 1.471-4

    (iii) ☐ Other (Specify method used and attach explanation.) ▶ ....

  b Check if there was a writedown of subnormal goods as described in Regulations section 1.471-2(c) . . . . . ▶ ☐

  c Check if the LIFO inventory method was adopted this tax year for any goods (if checked, attach Form 970) . . . . . ▶ ☐

  d If the LIFO inventory method was used for this tax year, enter percentage (or amounts) of closing inventory computed under LIFO **9d**

  e If property is produced or acquired for resale, do the rules of section 263A apply to the corporation? . . . . ☑ Yes   ☐ No

  f Was there any change in determining quantities, cost, or valuations between opening and closing inventory? If "Yes," attach explanation . . . . ☐ Yes   ☑ No

Schedule C Dividends and Special Deductions (See page 12 of instructions.)

		(a) Dividends received	(b) %	(c) Special deductions (a) × (b)
1	Dividends from less-than-20%-owned domestic corporations that are subject to the 70% deduction (other than debt-financed stock)		70	
2	Dividends from 20%-or-more-owned domestic corporations that are subject to the 80% deduction (other than debt-financed stock)	10,000	80	8,000
3	Dividends on debt-financed stock of domestic and foreign corporations (section 246A)		see instructions	
4	Dividends on certain preferred stock of less-than-20%-owned public utilities		42	
5	Dividends on certain preferred stock of 20%-or-more-owned public utilities		48	
6	Dividends from less-than-20%-owned foreign corporations and certain FSCs that are subject to the 70% deduction		70	
7	Dividends from 20%-or-more-owned foreign corporations and certain FSCs that are subject to the 80% deduction		80	
8	Dividends from wholly owned foreign subsidiaries subject to the 100% deduction (section 245(b))		100	
9	**Total.** Add lines 1 through 8. See page 12 of instructions for limitation			8,000
10	Dividends from domestic corporations received by a small business investment company operating under the Small Business Investment Act of 1958		100	
11	Dividends from certain FSCs that are subject to the 100% deduction (section 245(c)(1))		100	
12	Dividends from affiliated group members subject to the 100% deduction (section 243(a)(3))		100	
13	Other dividends from foreign corporations not included on lines 3, 6, 7, 8, or 11			
14	Income from controlled foreign corporations under subpart F (attach Form(s) 5471)			
15	Foreign dividend gross-up (section 78)			
16	IC-DISC and former DISC dividends not included on lines 1, 2, or 3 (section 246(d))			
17	Other dividends			
18	Deduction for dividends paid on certain preferred stock of public utilities			
19	**Total dividends.** Add lines 1 through 17. Enter here and on line 4, page 1 ▶	10,000		
20	**Total special deductions.** Add lines 9, 10, 11, 12, and 18. Enter here and on line 29b, page 1 ▶			8,000

Schedule E Compensation of Officers (See instructions for line 12, page 1.)

Complete Schedule E only if total receipts (line 1a plus lines 4 through 10 on page 1, Form 1120) are $500,000 or more.

(a) Name of officer	(b) Social security number	(c) Percent of time devoted to business	(d) Common	(e) Preferred	(f) Amount of compensation
1 James O. Barclay	581-00-0936	100 %	45 %	%	55,000
George M. Collins	447-00-2604	100 %	15 %	%	31,000
Samuel Adams	401-00-2611	50 %	2 %	%	14,000

2	Total compensation of officers	100,000
3	Compensation of officers claimed on Schedule A and elsewhere on return	30,000
4	Subtract line 3 from line 2. Enter the result here and on line 12, page 1	70,000

Form 1120 (1996)   Page **3**

Schedule J   Tax Computation (See page 13 of instructions.)

1 Check if the corporation is a member of a controlled group (see sections 1561 and 1563) . . . . . ▶ ☐

   Important: Members of a controlled group, see instructions on page 13.

2a If the box on line 1 is checked, enter the corporation's share of the $50,000, $25,000, and $9,925,000 taxable income brackets (in that order):

   (1) ☐ $ _____   (2) ☐ $ _____   (3) ☐ $ _____

b Enter the corporation's share of:

   (1) Additional 5% tax (not more than $11,750) ☐ $ _____

   (2) Additional 3% tax (not more than $100,000) ☐ $ _____

3 Income tax. Check this box if the corporation is a qualified personal service corporation as defined in section 448(d)(2) (see instructions on page 13). . . . . ▶ ☐ | **3** | 61,387

4a Foreign tax credit (attach Form 1118) . . . . | 4a |

b Possessions tax credit (attach Form 5735) . . . . | 4b |

c Check: ☐ Nonconventional source fuel credit ☐ QEV credit (attach Form 8834) | 4c |

d General business credit. Enter here and check which forms are attached:

   ☐ 3800 ☐ 3468 ☑ 5884 ☐ 6478 ☐ 6765 ☐ 8586 ☐ 8830

   ☐ 8826 ☐ 8835 ☐ 8844 ☐ 8845 ☐ 8846 ☐ 8820 ☐ 8847 | 4d | 6,000

e Credit for prior year minimum tax (attach Form 8827) . . . . | 4e |

5 **Total credits.** Add lines 4a through 4e . . . . | **5** | 6,000

6 Subtract line 5 from line 3 . . . . | **6** | 55,387

7 Personal holding company tax (attach Schedule PH (Form 1120)) . . . . . . | **7** |

8 Recapture taxes. Check if from: ☐ Form 4255 ☐ Form 8611 . . . . . | **8** |

9 Alternative minimum tax (attach Form 4626) . . . . | **9** |

10 **Total tax.** Add lines 6 through 9. Enter here and on line 31, page 1 . . . . | **10** | 55,387

Schedule K   Other Information (See page 15 of instructions.)

		Yes	No
1	Check method of accounting: **a** ☐ Cash **b** ☑ Accrual **c** ☐ Other (specify) ▶		
2	See page 17 of the instructions and state the principal:		
a	Business activity code no. ▶ 3998		
b	Business activity ▶ Manufacturing		
c	Product or service ▶ Toys		
3	Did the corporation at the end of the tax year own, directly or indirectly, 50% or more of the voting stock of a domestic corporation? (For rules of attribution, see section 267(c).)		✓
	If "Yes," attach a schedule showing: (a) name and identifying number, (b) percentage owned, and (c) taxable income or (loss) before NOL and special deductions of such corporation for the tax year ending with or within your tax year.		
4	Is the corporation a subsidiary in an affiliated group or a parent-subsidiary controlled group?		✓
	If "Yes," enter employer identification number and name of the parent corporation ▶		
5	Did any individual, partnership, corporation, estate or trust at the end of the tax year own, directly or indirectly, 50% or more of the corporation's voting stock? (For rules of attribution, see section 267(c).)		✓
	If "Yes," attach a schedule showing name and identifying number. (Do not include any information already entered in 4 above.) Enter percentage owned ▶		
6	During this tax year, did the corporation pay dividends (other than stock dividends and distributions in exchange for stock) in excess of the corporation's current and accumulated earnings and profits? (See secs. 301 and 316.)		✓
	If "Yes," file Form 5452. If this is a consolidated return, answer here for the parent corporation and on **Form 851,** Affiliations Schedule, for each subsidiary.		

		Yes	No
7	Was the corporation a U.S. shareholder of any controlled foreign corporation? (See sections 951 and 957.) . . .		✓
	If "Yes," attach Form 5471 for each such corporation. Enter number of Forms 5471 attached ▶		
8	At any time during the 1996 calendar year, did the corporation have an interest in or a signature or other authority over a financial account (such as a bank account, securities account, or other financial account) in a foreign country?		✓
	If "Yes," the corporation may have to file Form TD F 90-22.1. If "Yes," enter name of foreign country ▶		
9	During the tax year, did the corporation receive a distribution from, or was it the grantor of, or transferor to, a foreign trust? If "Yes," see page 16 of the instructions for other forms the corporation may have to file		✓
10	Did one foreign person at any time during the tax year own, directly or indirectly, at least 25% of: **(a)** the total voting power of all classes of stock of the corporation entitled to vote, or **(b)** the total value of all classes of stock of the corporation? If "Yes,"		✓
a	Enter percentage owned ▶		
b	Enter owner's country ▶		
c	The corporation may have to file Form 5472. Enter number of Forms 5472 attached ▶		
11	Check this box if the corporation issued publicly offered debt instruments with original issue discount . ▶ ☐		
	If so, the corporation may have to file Form 8281.		
12	Enter the amount of tax-exempt interest received or accrued during the tax year ▶ $ 5,000		
13	If there were 35 or fewer shareholders at the end of the tax year, enter the number ▶		
14	If the corporation has an NOL for the tax year and is electing to forego the carryback period, check here ▶ ☐		
15	Enter the available NOL carryover from prior tax years (Do not reduce it by any deduction on line 29a.) ▶ $		

Form 1120 (1996) Page **4**

Schedule L — Balance Sheets per Books

Assets	Beginning of tax year (a)	(b)	End of tax year (c)	(d)
1 Cash		14,700		28,331
2a Trade notes and accounts receivable	98,400		103,700	
b Less allowance for bad debts	( )	98,400	( )	103,700
3 Inventories		126,000		298,400
4 U.S. government obligations				
5 Tax-exempt securities (see instructions)		100,000		120,000
6 Other current assets (attach schedule)		26,300		17,266
7 Loans to stockholders				
8 Mortgage and real estate loans				
9 Other investments (attach schedule)		100,000		80,000
10a Buildings and other depreciable assets	272,400		296,700	
b Less accumulated depreciation	(88,300)	184,100	(104,280)	192,400
11a Depletable assets				
b Less accumulated depletion	( )		( )	
12 Land (net of any amortization)		20,000		20,000
13a Intangible assets (amortizable only)				
b Less accumulated amortization	( )		( )	
14 Other assets (attach schedule)		14,800		19,300
15 Total assets		684,300		879,417
Liabilities and Stockholders' Equity				
16 Accounts payable		28,500		34,834
17 Mortgages, notes, bonds payable in less than 1 year		4,300		4,300
18 Other current liabilities (attach schedule)		6,800		7,400
19 Loans from stockholders				
20 Mortgages, notes, bonds payable in 1 year or more		176,700		264,100
21 Other liabilities (attach schedule)				
22 Capital stock: a Preferred stock				
b Common stock	200,000	200,000	200,000	200,000
23 Paid-in or capital surplus				
24 Retained earnings—Appropriated (attach schedule)		30,000		40,000
25 Retained earnings—Unappropriated		238,000		328,783
26 Less cost of treasury stock		( )		( )
27 Total liabilities and stockholders' equity		684,300		879,417

Note: *You are not required to complete Schedules M-1 and M-2 below if the total assets on line 15, column (d) of Schedule L are less than $25,000.*

Schedule M-1 — Reconciliation of Income (Loss) per Books With Income per Return (See page 16 of instructions.)

1 Net income (loss) per books	147,783		7 Income recorded on books this year not included on this return (itemize):		
2 Federal income tax	55,387		Tax-exempt interest $ 5,000		
3 Excess of capital losses over capital gains	3,600		Insurance proceeds 9,500		14,500
4 Income subject to tax not recorded on books this year (itemize):					
			8 Deductions on this return not charged against book income this year (itemize):		
5 Expenses recorded on books this year not deducted on this return (itemize):			a Depreciation . . . $ 1,620		
a Depreciation . . . . $			b Contributions carryover $		
b Contributions carryover $ 850					
c Travel and entertainment $					1,620
See attached itemized statement (not shown) $16,850	17,700		9 Add lines 7 and 8		16,120
6 Add lines 1 through 5	224,470		10 Income (line 28, page 1)—line 6 less line 9		208,350

Schedule M-2 — Analysis of Unappropriated Retained Earnings per Books (Line 25, Schedule L)

1 Balance at beginning of year	238,000		5 Distributions: a Cash		65,000
2 Net income (loss) per books	147,783		b Stock		
3 Other increases (itemize):			c Property		
Refund of 1993 income tax due to IRS examination			6 Other decreases (itemize): Reserve for contingencies		10,000
	18,000		7 Add lines 5 and 6		75,000
4 Add lines 1, 2, and 3	403,783		8 Balance at end of year (line 4 less line 7)		328,783

Source: "Corporations," *Publication 542* (Washington, D.C.: Internal Revenue Service, January 1997), 27–30.

Form **1120-A**	**U.S. Corporation Short-Form Income Tax Return**	OMB No. 1545-0890
Department of the Treasury Internal Revenue Service	See separate instructions to make sure the corporation qualifies to file Form 1120-A. For calendar year 1996 or tax year beginning ...., 1996, ending ...., 19	19**96**

A Check this box if the corp. is a personal service corp. (as defined in Temporary Regs. section 1.441-4T—see instructions) ▶ ☐

Use IRS label. Otherwise, print or type.

10-2134567   DEC96   5995
Rose Flower Shop, Inc.
38 Superior Lane
Fair City, MD 20715

B Employer identification number

C Date incorporated 7-1-82

D Total assets (see page 6 of instructions) $ 65,987

E Check applicable boxes: **(1)** ☐ Initial return **(2)** ☐ Change of address
F Check method of accounting: **(1)** ☐ Cash **(2)** ☑ Accrual **(3)** ☐ Other (specify) . ▶

Income

1a	Gross receipts or sales 248,000 **b** Less returns and allowances 7,500 **c** Balance ▶	1c	240,500
2	Cost of goods sold (see page 11 of instructions)	2	144,000
3	Gross profit. Subtract line 2 from line 1c	3	96,500
4	Domestic corporation dividends subject to the 70% deduction	4	
5	Interest	5	942
6	Gross rents	6	
7	Gross royalties	7	
8	Capital gain net income (attach Schedule D (Form 1120))	8	
9	Net gain or (loss) from Form 4797, Part II, line 20 (attach Form 4797)	9	
10	Other income (see page 7 of instructions)	10	
11	**Total income.** Add lines 3 through 10 ▶	11	97,442

Deductions (See instructions for limitations on deductions.)

12	Compensation of officers (see page 7 of instructions)	12	23,000
13	Salaries and wages (less employment credits)	13	24,320
14	Repairs and maintenance	14	
15	Bad debts	15	
16	Rents	16	6,000
17	Taxes and licenses	17	3,320
18	Interest	18	1,340
19	Charitable contributions (see page 8 of instructions for 10% limitation)	19	1,820
20	Depreciation (attach Form 4562) 20		
21	Less depreciation claimed elsewhere on return 21a	21b	
22	Other deductions (attach schedule)	22	3,000
23	**Total deductions.** Add lines 12 through 22 ▶	23	62,800
24	Taxable income before net operating loss deduction and special deductions. Subtract line 23 from line 11	24	34,642
25	**Less: a** Net operating loss deduction (see page 10 of instructions) 25a		
	b Special deductions (see page 10 of instructions) 25b	25c	

Tax and Payments

26	**Taxable income.** Subtract line 25c from line 24	26	34,642
27	**Total tax** (from page 2, Part I, line 7)	27	5,196
28	**Payments:**		
a	1995 overpayment credited to 1996 28a		
b	1996 estimated tax payments 28b 6,000		
c	Less 1996 refund applied for on Form 4466 28c ( ) Bal ▶ 28d 6,000		
e	Tax deposited with Form 7004 28e		
f	Credit from regulated investment companies (attach Form 2439) 28f		
g	Credit for Federal tax on fuels (attach Form 4136). See instructions 28g		
h	**Total payments.** Add lines 28d through 28g	28h	6,000
29	Estimated tax penalty (see page 11 of instructions). Check if Form 2220 is attached ▶ ☐	29	
30	**Tax due.** If line 28h is smaller than the total of lines 27 and 29, enter amount owed	30	
31	**Overpayment.** If line 28h is larger than the total of lines 27 and 29, enter amount overpaid	31	804
32	Enter amount of line 31 you want: **Credited to 1997 estimated tax** ▶ 804 **Refunded** ▶	32	

Sign Here

Under penalties of perjury, I declare that I have examined this return, including accompanying schedules and statements, and to the best of my knowledge and belief, it is true, correct, and complete. Declaration of preparer (other than taxpayer) is based on all information of which preparer has any knowledge.

▶ George Rose Signature of officer | 2-15-97 Date ▶ President Title

Paid Preparer's Use Only

Preparer's signature ▶	Date	Check if self-employed ▶ ☐	Preparer's social security number
Firm's name (or yours if self-employed) and address ▶		EIN ▶	
		ZIP code ▶	

For Paperwork Reduction Act Notice, see page 1 of the instructions. Cat. No. 11456E Form **1120-A** (1996)

Form 1120-A (1996)   Page **2**

Part I   Tax Computation (See page 13 of instructions.)

1	Income tax. If the corporation is a qualified personal service corporation (see page 13), check here ▶ ☐	**1** 5,196

2a General business credit. Check if from Form(s): ☐ 3800 ☐ 3468
  ☐ 5884 ☐ 6478 ☐ 6765 ☐ 8586 ☐ 8830 ☐ 8826
  ☐ 8835 ☐ 8844 ☐ 8845 ☐ 8846 ☐ 8820 ☐ 8847 | **2a** |
  b Credit for prior year minimum tax (attach Form 8827) . . . . . . | **2b** |

3	**Total credits.** Add lines 2a and 2b	**3**
4	Subtract line 3 from line 1	**4** 5,196
5	Recapture taxes. Check if from: ☐ Form 4255 ☐ Form 8611 . .	**5**
6	Alternative minimum tax (attach Form 4626)	**6**
7	**Total tax.** Add lines 4 through 6. Enter here and on line 27, page 1 . . .	**7** 5,196

Part II   Other Information (See page 15 of instructions.)

1 See page 17 of the instructions and state the principal:
  a Business activity code no. ▶ 5995
  b Business activity ▶ Flower shop
  c Product or service ▶ Flowers
2 Did any individual, partnership, estate, or trust at the end of the tax year own, directly or indirectly, 50% or more of the corporation's voting stock? (For rules of attribution, see section 267(c).) Schedule not shown. ☑ Yes ☐ No
  If "Yes," attach a schedule showing name and identifying number.
3 Enter the amount of tax-exempt interest received or accrued during the tax year . . . . . ▶ |$ –0–|
4 Enter amount of cash distributions and the book value of property (other than cash) distributions made in this tax year . . . . ▶ |$ –0–|

5a If an amount is entered on line 2, page 1, see the worksheet on page 11 for amounts to enter below:
  (1) Purchases . . . . | 134,014 |
  (2) Additional sec. 263A costs (attach schedule) . . . . . |
  (3) Other costs (attach schedule) . | 9,466 |
  b If property is produced or acquired for resale, do the rules of section 263A apply to the corporation? . . . . ☐ Yes ☑ No
6 At any time during the 1996 calendar year, did the corporation have an interest in or a signature or other authority over a financial account (such as a bank account, securities account, or other financial account) in a foreign country? . . . . . ☐ Yes ☑ No
  If "Yes," the corporation may have to file Form TD F 90-22.1
  If "Yes," enter the name of the foreign country ▶

Part III   Balance Sheets per Books

		(a) Beginning of tax year	(b) End of tax year
1	Cash	20,540	18,498
2a	Trade notes and accounts receivable		
b	Less allowance for bad debts	( )	( )
3	Inventories	2,530	2,010
4	U.S. government obligations	13,807	45,479
5	Tax-exempt securities (see instructions) . . .		
6	Other current assets (attach schedule)		
7	Loans to stockholders		
8	Mortgage and real estate loans . . , . .		
9a	Depreciable, depletable, and intangible assets . . .		
b	Less accumulated depreciation, depletion, and amortization	( )	( )
10	Land (net of any amortization)		
11	Other assets (attach schedule)		
12	Total assets	36,877	65,987
13	Accounts payable	6,415	6,079
14	Other current liabilities (attach schedule) . . .		
15	Loans from stockholders		
16	Mortgages, notes, bonds payable		
17	Other liabilities (attach schedule)		
18	Capital stock (preferred and common stock)	20,000	20,000
19	Paid-in or capital surplus		
20	Retained earnings	10,462	39,908
21	Less cost of treasury stock	( )	( )
22	Total liabilities and stockholders' equity	36,877	65,987

Part IV   Reconciliation of Income (Loss) per Books With Income per Return (You are not required to complete Part IV if the total assets on line 12, column (b), Part III are less than $25,000.)

1 Net income (loss) per books	29,446	
2 Federal income tax	5,196	
3 Excess of capital losses over capital gains . .		
4 Income subject to tax not recorded on books this year (itemize)		
5 Expenses recorded on books this year not deducted on this return (itemize)		

6 Income recorded on books this year not included on this return (itemize)
7 Deductions on this return not charged against book income this year (itemize)
8 Income (line 24, page 1). Enter the sum of lines 1 through 5 less the sum of lines 6 and 7 . . . | 34,642 |

Source: "Corporations," *Publication 542* (Washington, D.C.: Internal Revenue Service, January 1997), 23–24.

INDEX

Index